Queer Studies and Education

Series Editors
William F. Pinar
Department of Curriculum and Pedagogy
University of British Columbia
Vancouver, British Columbia, Canada

Nelson M. Rodriguez
Department of Women's, Gender, and Sexuality Studies
The College of New Jersey
Ewing, NJ, USA

Reta Ugena Whitlock
Department of Educational Leadership
Kennesaw State University
Kennesaw, GA, USA

LGBTQ social, cultural, and political issues have become a defining feature of twenty-first century life, transforming on a global scale any number of institutions, including the institution of education. Situated within the context of these major transformations, this series is home to the most compelling, innovative, and timely scholarship emerging at the intersection of queer studies and education. Across a broad range of educational topics and locations, books in this series incorporate lesbian, gay, bisexual, transgender, and intersex categories, as well as scholarship in queer theory arising out of the postmodern turn in sexuality studies. The series is wide-ranging in terms of disciplinary/theoretical perspectives and methodological approaches, and will include and illuminate much needed intersectional scholarship. Always bold in outlook, the series also welcomes projects that challenge any number of normalizing tendencies within academic scholarship from works that move beyond established frameworks of knowledge production within LGBTQ educational research to works that expand the range of what is institutionally defined within the field of education as relevant queer studies scholarship.

More information about this series at
http://www.palgrave.com/series/14522

Elizabeth McNeil • James E. Wermers
Joshua O. Lunn
Editors

Mapping Queer Space(s) of Praxis and Pedagogy

palgrave
macmillan

Editors
Elizabeth McNeil
Languages and Cultures
College of Integrative Sciences
and Arts, Arizona State University
Phoenix, Arizona, USA

James E. Wermers
Languages and Cultures
College of Integrative Sciences
and Arts, Arizona State University
Phoenix, Arizona, USA

Joshua O. Lunn
Snowflake, Arizona, USA

Queer Studies and Education
ISBN 978-3-319-87838-6   ISBN 978-3-319-64623-7   (eBook)
DOI 10.1007/978-3-319-64623-7

Cover image © Jane Lackey, *Golden Maze, East*, tape, stickers, thread, paint on paper, 45" x 54" (photo credit: Tim Thayer)

Printed on acid-free paper

This Palgrave Macmillan imprint is published by Springer Nature
The registered company is Springer International Publishing AG
The registered company address is: Gewerbestrasse 11, 6330 Cham, Switzerland

ACKNOWLEDGMENTS

The contributors to this volume are generous, provocative thinkers, researchers, writers, artists, activists, performers, and educators. It has been an immense pleasure working with them and to see the tremendous gifts they give the world.

We are grateful for permission from Routledge India, Taylor and Francis Group, to republish segments from Chap. 2 of Rohit K. Dasgupta's *Digital Queer Cultures in India* (2017) in Chap. 10 of this volume, "Online Romeos and Gay-dia: Exploring Queer Spaces in Digital India." Excerpts from *Teaching Queer: Radical Possibilities for Writing and Knowing*, by Stacey Waite, © 2017, are reprinted herein by permission of the University of Pittsburgh Press in Chap. 12 "Intersextionality: Embodied Knowledge, Bodies of Knowledge." We appreciate permission to reprint, as Chap. 14, Kerri A. Mesner's "Innovations in Sexual-Theological Activism: Queer Theology Meets Theatre of the Oppressed," from *Theology & Sexuality: The Journal of the Institute for the Study of Christianity & Sexuality* 16 (3) (2010): 285–303.

For the visual elements in this volume, we want to thank Branden Buehler and Roxanne Samer for their network images of queer academic kinship in Chap. 2 "Queer Acknowledgments." Jane Lackey has graciously allowed us to use *Golden Maze, East*—her mixed-media depiction of a 2007 protest march in Rangoon by Burmese monks, nuns, activists, and students—both in Libby Balter Blume and Rosemary Weatherston's "Queering the Campus Gender Landscape through Visual Arts Praxis," Chap. 5, and as the cover of our book. We thank the other artists featured in this chapter, too—Molly Marie Nuzzo, Bren Ahearn,

Danielle Hermann, Libby Balter Blume, Vagner M. Whitehead, Owen Eric Wood, Alana Bartol, K. Steven Sherrill, Joyce Polance, Amanda Dillingham, and the Flatlands Dance Theatre—who gave us permission to publish their work from the juried international Women's and Gender Studies Biennial Art Exhibition, University of Detroit Mercy, which, for the last 12 years, has interrogated and deconstructed ideas of gender, sexuality, and binary models of identity in academic space.

Milana Vernikova, our editor at Palgrave, has provided invaluable help and good cheer all along the way, for which we are most grateful.

CONTENTS

LIST OF CONTRIBUTORS

Libby Balter Blume University of Detroit Mercy, Detroit, MI, USA

Branden Buehler Department of Communication and Media, SUNY Oneonta, Oneonta, NY, USA

Kimberly Cosier University of Wisconsin–Milwaukee, Milwaukee, WI, USA

Rohit K. Dasgupta Institute for Media and Creative Industries, Loughborough University, London, UK

Melanie Davenport Georgia State University, Atlanta, GA, USA

Bruce E. Drushel Miami University, Cincinnati, OH, USA

Amy Gall Brooklyn, NY, USA

Katie Goldstein Brooklyn, NY, USA

Adam J. Greteman School of the Art Institute of Chicago, Chicago, IL, USA

Joshua O. Lunn Snowflake, AZ, USA

Mark McBeth Department of English, John Jay College/CUNY, New York, NY, USA

Elizabeth McNeil Languages and Cultures, College of Integrative Sciences and Arts, Arizona State University, Phoenix, AZ, USA

Kerri A. Mesner Arcadia University School of Education, Glenside, PA, USA

Sarah Murray Covina, CA, USA

Garrett W. Nichols Department of English, Bridgewater State University, Bridgewater, MA, USA

Tara Pauliny Department of English, John Jay College/CUNY, New York, NY, USA

Aneil Rallin Soka University of America, Aliso Viejo, CA, USA

Mindi Rhoades The Ohio State University, Columbus, OH, USA

Roxanne Samer Department of Visual and Media Arts, Grand Valley State University, Allendale, MI, USA

James H. Sanders III The Ohio State University, Columbus, OH, USA

Michael Angelo Tata Coral Gables, FL, USA

Justin N. Thorpe Salt Lake Community College, Salt Lake City, UT, USA

Stacey Waite English Department, University of Nebraska–Lincoln, Lincoln, NE, USA

Rosemary Weatherston University of Detroit Mercy, Detroit, MI, USA

Courtnie Wolfgang University of South Carolina, Columbia, SC, USA

Margot Young Site for Contemporary Psychoanalysis, Church Hill, Lydbrook, UK

LIST OF FIGURES

CHAPTER 1

Introduction: Mapping Queer Space(s)

The Editors

Mapping Queer Space(s) of Praxis and Pedagogy explores the linked processes of learning and teaching to break down traditional, and often oppressive, regimes of knowing and being—reconstituting, in their place, potential and possibility. Our project is not a new one—queer pedagogues have been rethinking and reworking learning and teaching for over two decades now. Contributing to this important ongoing project, *Mapping Queer Space(s)* pushes in intriguing directions the ever-expanding genealogy of queer pedagogy, helping us to consider new avenues of investigation.

QUEER PEDAGOGY

If you are reading this book, then it is more than likely that you have a working understanding of "queer" as it is used in academic circles. As such, a thorough review of the development of queer studies during the last 20 plus years is unnecessary. Further, such a project could be counterproductive, given that each chapter in this collection articulates its own relationship to queer or queerness. However, given the complexity and polysemy of "queer"—especially in academic circles—we consider here some common foundations that inform this volume.

The Editors (✉)
Languages and Cultures, College of Integrative Sciences and Arts,
Arizona State University, Phoenix, AZ, USA

© The Author(s) 2018
E. McNeil et al. (eds.), *Mapping Queer Space(s) of Praxis and Pedagogy*, Queer Studies and Education,
DOI 10.1007/978-3-319-64623-7_1

1

Perhaps the most often-cited definition of queer, and one that is central to all the chapters herein, was put forward by Eve Sedgwick in her *Tendencies* (1993). As Sedgwick articulates, one possible meaning of queer is "the open mesh of possibilities, gaps, overlaps, dissonances and resonances, lapses and excesses of meaning when the constituent elements of anyone's gender, of anyone's sexuality aren't made (or *can't* be made) to signify monolithically" (8). For us, and for so many others, this deceptively simple definition of queerness captures the paradoxical cutting power and flexible indeterminacy that have made queer theory such a vibrant field during the last quarter century. While the authors in *Mapping Queer Space(s)* take queerness in new, challenging directions, this uniquely focused pliability remains central to everything in this collection.

If queer theory asks us to consider, as Sedgwick suggests, the "open mesh of possibilities," we still need to ask what that open mesh has to do with pedagogy. What exactly might a queer pedagogy look like? As with the term queer, a complete retelling of this history of queer pedagogy is beyond the scope of this introduction. However, it will be helpful to consider some key moments in the development of queer pedagogy that have set the stage for this text.

In many ways, the roots of *Mapping Queer Space(s) of Praxis and Pedagogy* begin with the recognition on the part of queer pedagogues that education has often been a tool of oppression instead of liberation. As William F. Pinar notes in the introduction to his germinal *Queer Theory in Education* (1998), "Homophobia (not to mention heterosexism) is especially intense in the field of education, a highly conservative and reactionary field" (2). While education, and especially formal education, is often touted as an opportunity to expand minds and horizons, such expansion has too often been curtailed within the strict, and frequently invisible, boundaries of monolithic social and cultural institutions. From the rigidity of educational architecture to the rigidity of canonicity, education has often feigned the promise of intellectual progress as a cover for the reality of the reproduction of normality. For Pinar, queer pedagogy marks the possibility of a response to the systematic and heteronormative structure of education. If the term queer can signify an "open mesh of possibilities," queer pedagogy, argues Pinar, can signify the possibility of opening education to those possibilities.

Echoing Pinar, Mary Bryson and Suzanne de Castell, in "Queer Pedagogy: Praxis Makes Im/Perfect" (1993), assert that the value of queer pedagogy is its potential to disrupt the coercive *status quo* by rethinking education in terms that run counter to the reproductive telos of dominant ideology. For Bryson and de Castell, queer pedagogy is "a radical form of educative praxis implemented deliberately to interfere with, to intervene in, the production of 'normalcy' in schooled subjects" (285). In their view, and ours, queer pedagogy can transform education, changing it from a tool in service to tacitly heteronormative reproduction—which, as Pinar notes, has underpinned so much of Western learning and teaching—to a tool for actively disrupting normalcy.

The radical potential of queer pedagogy to destabilize (hetero)normalcy, as explored by Bryson and de Castell, has been further unpacked by Susanne Luhmann, in her "Queering/Querying Pedagogy? Or, Pedagogy Is a Pretty Queer Thing" (1998). Luhmann cautions against seeing queer pedagogy as a panacea for all social ills, while suggesting that queer pedagogy—pedagogy that engages students in a "conversation about how ... positions are being taken up or refused"—can "take on the problem of how identifications are made and refused in the process of learning" (130). In other words, queer pedagogy can destabilize hegemonic conceptions of the *status quo* or the normal precisely because it can push both learners and teachers to think about the grounds on which their own identities are constructed.

More recently, Judith Halberstam, in "Reflections on Queer Studies and Queer Pedagogy" (2003), has made similar observations, noting that queer pedagogy can, by taking on the problem of how identifications are made and refused, help us to "break with the oedipal deadlock that creates and sustains intergenerational conflict..." (363). As way to examine identities, queer pedagogy not only has the potential to break down barriers that have emerged in discussions of queer theory (the central focus of Halberstam's reflections on queer pedagogy), but also pushes both teachers and learners to consider how the production of knowledge is culturally situated and thus constantly open to radical revision. As Halberstam points out, queer pedagogy demands that we entertain "flexible and innovative notions of archiving, canonicity, disciplinarity, and intellectual labor..." (364).

A clear line of development runs through the work of each of these thinkers that identifies in queer pedagogy a potential to rethink learning and teaching in ways that force us to reconsider the concepts of knowing and being, as Donald Hall has effectively articulated. Responding to challenges that queer pedagogy was focused merely on disowning knowledge, Hall argues, in "Cluelessness in the Queer Classroom" (2007), that queer pedagogy goes beyond the need to disown knowledge, and demands the willingness to interrogate the foundations on which education has been built. In doing so, Hall calls for "a project of critical inquiry" that can "link the projects of queer studies, Graffian pedagogy, and Gadamerian philosophical hermeneutics" (186). To this end, urges Hall, we "must attend to the presuppositions behind other naturalized positions and opinions" (187). Thus, the story of queer pedagogy we have tracked here is one of the transformation of pedagogy as (tacitly heteronormative) reproductive tool to an open mesh of possibilities that forces us to rethink how and why we learn.

QUEER LANDSCAPES

Featuring both established scholars and new voices, *Mapping Queer Space(s) of Praxis and Pedagogy* explores intersections of theory and practice to engage queer theory and education as it happens both in and beyond the university. Furthering work on queer pedagogy, this volume brings together educators and activists who explore how we see, write, read, experience, and, especially, teach through the fluid space of queerness. The contributors are interested in how queer-identified and queer-influenced people create ideas, works, classrooms, and other spaces (e.g., digital, activist, interspecies) that vivify relational and (eco) systems thinking, thus challenging accepted hierarchies, binaries, and hegemonies that have long dominated pedagogy and praxis.

SECTION I: *QUE(E)RYING THE ACADEMY*

The authors in Section I examine seemingly conventional spaces of pedagogy to argue that we might learn to think or to be queer in academe. Beginning this discussion, in Chap. 2, "Queer Acknowledgments," Branden Buehler and Roxanne Samer examine a model of academic kinship that supplants the traditional model rooted in the idea of genealogy, thereby suggesting that to be or think queer in academic spaces requires that we rethink the way that scholars and ideas are related in the academy. Academia, including the system of advisors, dissertation committees, peer groups, and the departments to which we belong, is often conceptualized as a family tree. However, the classic tree metaphor—borrowed from heteronormative forms of kinship structures—might not be the best model for a system that is often more circular than linear, more communal than hierarchical. Buehler and Samer explore how scholars become oriented toward the ideas of others and directed by certain lines of thought. Building on Sara Ahmed's work on queer phenomenology and Gérard Genette's theories of paratexts, Buehler and Samer take up acknowledgments sections as archives chronicling their authors' intellectual influences and look at the kinship structures traceable within, between, and across them. Their theorizing of queer academic genealogies is further informed by their deployment of social network analysis software, which they use to map the web of queer studies' thank-yous, anecdotes, and in-jokes that can be found within its acknowledgments sections. In doing so, they identify academic relationships and social bonds that normally go unseen. While they focus their study in terms of sample and critical investment, their approach could be extended to demonstrate in a broader fashion the ways in which all intellectual concerns, disciplines, and methodologies take shape over time. Buehler and Samer's analysis thus offers up a way of mapping structures and systems of knowledge, informed not by trite metaphors, but by the flexibility and dialectics of queer theory.

Garrett W. Nichols, in Chap. 3, "Queer Settlers in a One-Room Schoolhouse: A Decolonial Queerscape," makes a related argument in his call for a rethinking of the classroom as space for disrupting heteronormative discourses—discourses that Nichols links to a kind of settler colonialism—to open a space where we can hear, or sometimes re-hear, queer voices. Settler colonialism is a heteronormative project that relies on rhetorics of reproductive "inheritance" to naturalize the erasure of indigenous cultures. Pedagogies attuned to the realities of heteronormativity and settler colonialism require a pedagogical commitment to interrupting these discourses, especially in institutional structures whose existence relies on and supports settler ideologies. Queerscapes, per Gordon Brent Ingram, are spaces and planes of queer alliances formed within and overlapping with heteronormative spaces; the university classroom, with its imbricated personal histories, institutional memories, and power dynamics, is always-already a queerscape. Importantly, the classroom is also a "settlerscape," composed of the multiple subjectivities that constitute modern settler society and made meaningful through histories of indigenous displacement. Recognizing this dynamic opens a space for unheard queer voices, argues Nichols, and lets us "re-hear" how non-queer stories and perspectives are made meaningful through their unspoken proximity to queerness and colonization. Nichols proposes a decolonial queerscape pedagogy that foregrounds the marginalized and oppressed identities that populate every classroom, while also denaturalizing the supposedly "natural" and "inevitable" rhetorics of heteronormativity, white supremacy, and settler colonization that inform the American academy.

In Chap. 4, "Queering the First-Year Composition Student (and Teacher): A Democratizing Endeavor," Mark McBeth and Tara Pauliny further the arguments in the preceding chapters, demonstrating that the disruption of traditionally academic spaces through queer thinking creates a space for "democratizing sensibilities" that allow students a greater sense of investment in equality and justice. McBeth and Pauliny ask, what if we proposed to our first-year composition students that they seem out of the ordinary (even extraordinary), all working within a space of shifting identities, and all, therefore, queer? Then, what if we asked them to explore (rather than resist) this non-normative subjective position? The first year of college acts as a liminal space where students "leap forward—or linger at the door," and freshmen often confront conundrums about their place in academia, their feelings of (dis)identification with intellectual labor, and a burgeoning sense of self that often feels "out of fashion" (Sommers and Saltz 133). For students, scrutinizing this liminal queerness allows their oft-disenfranchising feelings about school to become, instead, productive moments of learning. Using the triangulated frameworks of queer theory, performance studies, and composition/rhetoric research, McBeth and Pauliny provoke their students (and readers) to consider how their own non-normative positions have shaped their intellectual abilities, how these examined experiences can evoke interconnections with other people's differences, and how these investigations can become an undertaking in identity deconstruction/reconstruction. They demonstrate how many of these discoveries occur in composition classrooms where students do not just absorb information from unilateral lectures but, instead, where they construct knowledge through self-generated, dynamic language that expands their boundaries of knowing (themselves). While incoming students often wrangle with ideas that they heretofore could not bear to know (Britzman), they can also gain a greater sense of the futurity of their own becoming (Halberstam; Muñoz). Ultimately, this study flirts with the idea that when everyone considers their "queerness" in a personal yet socially grounded context, democratizing sensibilities may emerge through writing, and a greater investment in equality and justice may occur.

The last two chapters in Section I echo and expand the world of McBeth and Pauliny by asserting that both visual arts and quantification can also be employed to expand students' understandings of queerness in ways that open up radical potential for education. In their illustrated essay, "Queering the Campus Gender Landscape through Visual Arts Praxis," Chap. 5, Libby Balter Blume and Rosemary Weatherston critically analyze the pedagogy and praxis of queering the gender landscape on an urban, Catholic university campus through 12 years of international juried fine arts exhibitions co-curated by women's and gender studies faculty. Past exhibition themes have included (re)visioning gender, embodiment, gender politics, gendered space/s, masculinities and feminism, and (trans)ition. These campus interventions have used visual arts, poetry, performance, environmental installation, interdisciplinary lectures, and course work to interrogate gender as a socially constructed, relational category and to deconstruct male/female binaries and dominant/minority discourses in academic space. Blume and Weatherston's interdisciplinary essay utilizes both social science and humanities frameworks of "queering" and queer pedagogy to examine intersections of artistic practices of "seeing differently" and activist re/productions of visual arts discourses. Finally, they address the limitations and potential of using the curatorial space of the exhibitions to engender change as well as reflection.

Like Blume and Weatherston's academic space that also draws in and helps to define—and re-define—a greater community, Adam J. Greteman and Justin N. Thorpe, in Chap. 6, "Safety in Numbers: On the Queerness of Quantification," examine how quantification constructs queerness. The landscapes surrounding American schools are littered with numbers, and numbers have become the dominant object used to portray contemporary school experiences. From scores on exams, numbers on a scale, and the quantification of violence against queer bodies, a rather strange safety in numbers has emerged. Numbers have come to illustrate what Jane Gallop calls "logical eroticism." In contemporary educational discourses, instruments and the data they produce have come to speak and judge the reality of experience in order to make political demands persuasive (see Lorraine Daston; Ian Hacking; Theodore Porter; Nikolas Rose), and quantification promises progress and an end to any given crisis (e.g., obesity, anti-gay bias, achievement gap). Utilizing queer theory and rhetorical studies, Greteman and Thorpe critique the quantification of anti-gay bias violence, looking specifically at the major reports released by the Gay Lesbian Straight Education Network (GLSEN) to explore the queerness of numbers (e.g., their fetishization) and the rhetorical-ness of quantification regarding the queer experience. Their project does not seek simply to negate the use of quantification or numbers, but, rather, critically investigates how such numbers impact and produce the subjective possibilities of queer students.

SECTION II: *Queer Out Here:*
Public Bodies and Spaces

The authors in Section II further expand the book's focus beyond the traditional space of the classroom or academy, to consider how we might learn to be queer in public spaces. In Chap. 7, "Out There: The Lesbian in Literature," Amy Gall discusses how she exited a closet (both metaphorically and physically), realizing the possibility of a complex self-education through porn, internet sci-fi fan-fiction, adult science fiction, and eventually queer/mainstream fiction. Gall reminds us that we all look to stories to reflect and inform who we are. Though never actually providing a reflection of her own self, the texts she encountered inspired her, nonetheless, to think about and craft an identity through writing. Gall explores how delimiting literary depictions of lesbians shaped her sense of who she was and what she could be: in porn collections and internet sci-fi fan fiction, lesbians were defined only by their sexuality; in adult sci-fi, specifically Samuel Delany's *Dhalgren*, lesbians were desexualized and so peripheral that they were almost nonexistent. In queer/mainstream fiction lesbians did not hide their sexuality, nor were they defined by it. All these types of lesbians helped Gall to understand that identity is complicated and incomplete, and that only through the act of writing can she fully identify herself.

Like Gall's essay, Michael Angelo Tata's "Work This Cunt Bucket: Knowledge, Love, and De-containment in Sapphire's *Push*," Chap. 8, also examines the potency of language to create identity. Through queer theory, Tata looks at the metaphysics of a key offensive term from Sapphire's socially critical urban novel, *Push* (1996), to reveal how the transmission of knowledge transforms the story's protagonist, Precious Jones. The language of *Push* is raw, rude, and offensive—brilliantly descriptive passages about sex, body, rape, ravishment, nutrition, locomotion, visage, and comestibility. Yet among all the words Sapphire uses to bring her protagonist's precious pedagogy to light, the noun "cunt bucket" is the most critical—a word too hot for Tyler Perry and Oprah, a buried compound noun that continues to throb off-camera. Tata engages the term "cunt bucket" both figuratively and metaphorically, tying it to Precious's epistemic, even Gnostic, journey. Via Julia Kristeva's theories of the feminine receptacle in *Revolution in Poetic Language*, female containment can be traced back to the cosmological Platonic chora, revealing ways in which identifying Precious as storage device have both hurt her (as in the sperm receptacle that her father makes her) and helped her (the lesbian Blu Rain's refashioning of her as a fountain of knowledge). Most importantly, Plato's original reflections on the relation between container and form, place and production in his *Timaeus,* along with his theories of intellectual midwifery and the strange transmissivity of knowledge in his *Theaetetus,* all help create a model of transformation converting Precious from cold metal pail to warm and pulsing center of ideas, concepts, and *rêverie.* Other interpretations of the chora by Judith Butler in her schema of sexual materiality (*Bodies That Matter*) and Jacques Derrida in his emphasis on the non-reciprocity of dissemination also shed light on the metaphysics—even pataphysics—of the cunt bucket.

Where Gall and Sapphire's Precious find in popular culture stereotyped images that bear little resemblance to their own thoughts and experiences, Bruce E. Drushel, in Chap. 9, "'Modern' Is as *Modern* Does: *Modern Family* and the Disruption of Gender Binaries," opens our eyes to the possibility of a growing complexity in the representation of queer characters in media by examining Mitch and Cam from the popular sitcom *Modern Family.* Even before commercial television series began regularly to feature openly gay and lesbian characters in the 1970s, writers suggested them through character behaviors that were violations of conventional gender norms. The current ABC situation comedy *Modern Family* distinguishes itself through its willingness to develop characters, most notably the gay male couple Mitch and Cam, that freely depart from these binaries. While a surface-level view of the pair suggests the continuation of at least an approximation of traditional couple gender roles—Mitch as the masculine breadwinner, complete with beard and conventional masculine appearance and background, and Cam as the feminine stay-at-home nurturer and domestic problem-solver—episodes reveal more sophisticated and multidimensional types. Drushel analyzes the gender behaviors of the Mitch and Cam characters, contrasting theirs with those of characters represented as lesbian or gay among both recent and past US television sitcoms. Among the questions Drushel addresses is whether the Mitch and Cam characters are part of a revolution in representations of gender and sexuality, a pioneering example of gender parody, or merely encouraging anomalies.

In Chap. 10, "Online Romeos and Gay-dia: Exploring Queer Spaces in Digital India," Rohit K. Dasgupta builds on the complexity of negotiating identity in public spaces that is at the heart of the preceding pieces by refocusing our attention on the subversive potential of what he identifies as digital queer spaces in new media in India. Dasgupta notes that academic discourses on queer sexuality in contemporary India have so far concentrated almost entirely on textual, cinematic, and sociological representations, with little to no scholarship on the digital landscape and the various ways in which it shapes the construct of queer male identity in India. Dasgupta examines how internet and digital technologies, the media industry, and sociohistorical contexts provide a subversive space within which queer male identity is negotiated. He offers an overview of media development in India, then discusses queer representations in mass media and digital queer spaces in India, which are a consequence of the shifting political and socioscape of urban and suburban India. Dasgupta also reviews key debates in digital culture and queer studies, situating the Indian queer digital space within the intersection of globalization and postcolonial praxis.

This section ends with Sarah Murray's reflections on the radical potential of public negotiations of identity in Chap. 11, "Femme Is a Verb: An Alternative Reading of Femininity and Feminism." On the surface, Murray's piece proposes the possibility of revisionist feminine heterosexuality as a queer femme experience, asking questions about accessing a specific femininity through queer space. However, within each piece of her textual collage, she also submits herself as subject and attempts to create a piece of queer literature that struggles with a "straight" privileged identity coming to terms with femininity. In other words, "in its most simple terms," Murray explains, "this is the story of how a straight girl tries to say 'thank you' to the queers who brought her home."

SECTION III: *ENSPIRITING, LIVING, TEACHING QUEER*

The authors in Section III further expand the boundaries of queer pedagogy by turning toward a more explicit focus on teaching itself, rethinking academic and public spaces in ways that reshape how current and future students learn. In Chap. 12, "Intersextionality: Embodied Knowledge, Bodies of Knowledge," Stacey Waite tracks her own journey from a child beginning to negotiate the complexities of identity to an adult carefully crafting a classroom that is a space of radical possibility, rather than hegemony. Waite's essay is a series of vignettes mapping out educational moments that impacted her as a child who grew up intersexed in a culture with rigid binary gender regulations. The vignettes form a narrative argument for both why she became a scholar of queer pedagogies and why queer pedagogies are so important in all levels of education, illuminating multiple ways students are shaped by normativity during our years of schooling. While a queer pedagogical perspective is essential for students who might find themselves queer, it is even more significant for students who might not see themselves as queer. With her vignettes beginning in her early childhood and moving, by the end, to scenes from her own classroom, Waite hopes this progression will lead teachers to think about the complex ways that pedagogy is always bound up in who we are, inextricably linked to our own experience as students and as bodies moving through the world.

Following Waite, the next two chapters focus on the ways in which church or theology might also be refashioned as pedagogical spaces engendering queer possibility. In Chap. 13, "Take a Left at the Valley of the Shadow of Death: Exploring the Queer Crossroads of Art, Religion, and Education through Big Gay Church," a collective of queer art educators—Mindi Rhoades, Kimberly Cosier, James H. Sanders III, Courtnie Wolfgang, and Melanie Davenport—engage the intersections of art, religion, and education as an occasion for queer thinking and performance. Within academic contexts, these educators use queer theory and critical performance pedagogies (Denzin; Garoian and Gaudelius) to research, critique, and re-present the intersections of conservative protestant religion, education, the arts, and LGBTQ identities in the US. In addition, for five years, Big Gay Church has presented as a formal session at the National Art Education Association's annual convention, serving as a playful yet substantive forum for collaboratively pursuing and performing serious academic arts-based educational research around specific issues of identity, equity, power, and social justice in education.

In Chap. 14, "Innovations in Sexual-Theological Activism: Queer Theology Meets Theatre of the Oppressed," Kerri A. Mesner combines queer theologies and Theatre of the Oppressed to bridge a gap between activist approaches and sexual-theological activism. Despite extraordinary strides in queer religious activism in recent decades, religiously motivated anti-queer violence continues to be both prevalent and inadequately addressed. Both subtle and outright homophobia, biphobia, and transphobia are among the few remaining forms of societal discrimination that still carry an air of acceptability. This discrimination appears to be further exacerbated by complacency within queer communities and by an increasing normalization and mainstreaming of queer religious activist movements. Mesner introduces a new body of work combining queer theologies and Theatre of the Oppressed to develop strategic interventions for addressing religiously motivated anti-queer violence, specifically drawing on queer theologian Marcella Althaus-Reid and Theatre of the Oppressed creator Augusto Boal. In so doing, notes Mesner, this new area of ministry aims to bridge the gap between academic and activist approaches to sexual-theological activism.

The focus on crafting queer spaces for radical pedagogies continues in the last two chapters in this section. In Chap. 15, "Queer Homes in a Non-Queer World," Katie Goldstein explores the proliferation of queer communal homes in Brooklyn, New York, as a physical manifestation of the queer landscape. New York City has been a queer home for decades (known throughout the US as LGBQ homes). In Brooklyn, the queer home trend is growing as the queer community puts down roots, solidifying the sense of community and laying the groundwork for political organizing to fuel greater queer participation in urban space. A founder and resident of a queer collective house in Brooklyn and a professional housing organizer, Goldstein draws on interviews with queer folks who live in and have helped to create queer homes. She also charts the genesis of QUORUM: Queers Organizing for Radical Unity and Mobilization as it relates to building and unifying queer community. Noting that queer homes are tools of protection for the queer community, Goldstein explores the possibilities, manifestations, and limits of queer collective houses in Brooklyn.

In Chap. 16, "Teaching Desire in Third Space: A Queer Prison Pedagogy for the Unknowing Spirit," Elizabeth McNeil and Joshua O. Lunn examine their relationship—one free and the other incarcerated—and their work as teachers of queer thought in the radical context of prison. As commonplace as incarceration is (the US has the highest rate of incarceration in the world), and as familiar as it is in our news and creative media, we do not often engage, through academic or other social discourse, what it means to be institutionalized by legal confinement, or how the incarcerated might break free of the dehumanizing constructs of imprisonment. Incarceration inculcates and violently enforces rigid racial, gender, and power binaries, provoking even deeper adherence to US hegemonic social norms that engender the cycle of recidivism funding the nation's prison industrial complex. As a place that profoundly delimits aspects of human being, prison is abnormal, ill, obsessive—by (one) definition, "queer." As such, prison can also be, however, a fractious and creative a "third space" of hybridity and synergy, of thoughtful disruption of received and perceived norms and patterns of thought and behavior (Bhabha). In his work on queer studies in education, David V. Ruffolo defines "queer" not as a state of being but as an action, a process that "is in many ways a third space outside binary categorizations" (290). Besides identifying, vis-à-vis Judith Butler's "Desire, Rhetoric, and Recognition in Hegel's *Phenomenology of Spirit*," binary strictures of prison that condemn desire and the self, Lunn and McNeil locate queer pedagogy as intellectual, relational, and social action revealing the potential for liberated thought and being.

SECTION IV: *AnimalQueer*

The authors in Section IV simultaneously look toward the past and the future by pushing us to rethink the human being that is implicitly at the center of both learning and teaching. In Chap. 17, "The Bestiary of Friends," Margot Young reveals a history of making bestial that which is not normative, and in doing so formulates a call for expanding our understanding of what it means to be human—a project with clear links to how we are educated and how we educate. For Young, queering landscapes involves subverting normalized agricultural identities, which include that of "being a human." Historically, those who could not or would not be assimilated to humanity's hetero-agro-colonial norm were bestialized, extirpated, and driven to peripheral spaces. Agro-colonialism has resurfaced the face of the earth, and humans have cemented their position of ecological separativity rather than inter-connectedness. Young argues that historical shifts in notions of what constitutes a "human" and an "animal" reveal conceptual instabilities that render the terms unsustainable as markers of difference. Proposing that the bestial can be queerly recuperated in a reversal of the presumption of human-ization as norm, Young suggests that agro-colonial demonization has lost ground as queer desires arise within humans to become not-so-human. Wolves, seen by colonialists as the most deviant of beasts, and closely associated with Native peoples and sexual predation, are once again being hunted in the US. Specters from decades and centuries of violences are being raised. Young discusses alliances of resistance to wolf-hunting in the context of affinities among the bestialized, emerging from histories of co-subjections to, and exclusions from, colonizing agriculturalism; a bestiary of friends who share mortal commonality on the borderlines of what counts as human, where who will be made to live and who to die are determined.

In the final essay in the volume, "Animalqueer/Queeranimal: Scatterings," Chap. 18, Aneil Rallin also pushes us to consider the boundaries of the human, and thereby the formation of the human through education, and to do so through "excavating" or "reframing" ideological apparatuses. Engaging work currently being undertaken in queer theory and critical animal studies, and using "experimental" form (a queer form?), Rallin makes "scattered speculations" that (a) point to collisions and disjunctures between animal studies/lives and queer theory/lives, (b) explore what political and rhetorical responsibility means in the here and now, and (c) make a case for the urgency of both excavating/reframing the ideological apparatus motivating dominant constructions of "animal," human, and nonhuman and sustaining conditions that allow for animal/queer (lives) to flourish.

* * *

Challenging our understandings of the spaces, objectives, and nature of pedagogy, the contributors to this volume add to the ongoing queer pedagogical conversation by asking us to reconsider just what counts as knowledge. In the process, *Mapping Queer Space(s) of Praxis and Pedagogy* calls for our continuing to expand our understanding of queer pedagogy, and by extension all pedagogy, to recognize the diverse ways in which the intimately intertwined processes of teaching and learning are lived in an ever-changing world.

The synthesis of theory and practice in this book works across many boundaries that have traditionally been points of contention in queer studies, pedagogy, and Western thought more generally: traditional disciplinary boundaries, the gulf between academia and community activism, the distance between teacher and student, and the chasm between humans and other life forms. In addition to illuminating physical and mental/intellectual spaces, *Mapping Queer Space(s) of Praxis and Pedagogy* concomitantly provides a unique examination of continuing and emerging queer theories and practices rooted in the experimentation inherent to processes of queering, as is seen in both the more traditionally academic analyses and the less academically located, personal, and experimental pieces herein.

This volume is intended for teachers and practitioners of queer educative thought in the university, the arts, and the greater community. In addition to faculty members working in the rapidly growing field of queer studies, this volume will appeal to advanced undergraduates and graduate students in various fields who have strong interests in queer perspectives, including education, gender studies, media studies, geography, philosophy, sociology, visual arts, English (both composition and literary studies), social work, psychology, environmental and animal studies, and so on. The interdisciplinary scope of the book, its focus on bringing together theory and praxis, the inclusion of transnationally/postcolonially focused chapters, and the accessibility of much of the work all promise broad appeal among academics and social activists in the US, UK, Europe, and other postcolonialist enclaves.

WORKS CITED

Ahmed, Sara. 2006. *Queer Phenomenology: Orientations, Objects, Others*. Durham: Duke University Press. Print.

Althaus-Reid, Marcella. 2001. The Divine Exodus of God: Involuntarily Marginalized, Taking an Option for the Margins, or Truly Marginal? In *God: Experience and Mystery*, ed. Werner Jeanrond et al., 27–33. London: SCM. Print.

———. 2002. *Indecent Theology: Theological Perversions in Sex, Gender and Politics*. New York: Routledge. Print.

———. 2003. *The Queer God*. New York: Routledge. Print.

———. 2004. Introduction: Queering Theology. In *The Sexual Theologian*, ed. Lisa Isherwood and Marcella Althaus-Reid, 1–15. London: T & T Clark. Print.

Bhabha, Homi. 1994. *The Location of Culture*. Abingdon/New York: Routledge. Print.

Boal, Augusto. 1985. *Theatre of the Oppressed*. New York: Theatre Communications Group. Print.

Britzman, Deborah. 1998. *Lost Subjects, Contested Objects*. Albany: SUNY Press. Print.

Bryson, Mary, and Suzanne de Castell. 1993. Queer Pedagogy: Praxis Makes Im/Perfect. *Canadian Journal of Education / Revue canadienne de l'éducation* 18 (3): 285–305. Print.

Butler, Judith. 1993. *Bodies that Matter: On the Discursive Limits of Sex*. New York: Routledge. Print.

———. 2004. Desire, Rhetoric, and Recognition in Hegel's Phenomenology of Spirit (1987). In *The Judith Butler Reader*, ed. Sara Salih and Judith Butler, 39–89. Malden/Oxford/Victoria: Blackwell. Print.

Daston, Lorraine. 2007. *Things that Talk: Objects Lessons from Art and Science*. Brooklyn: Zone Books. Print.

Delany, Samuel R. 1977. *Dhalgren*. Boston: Gregg. Print.

Denzin, Norman K. 2009. A Critical Performance Pedagogy that Matters. *Ethnography and Education* 4 (3): 255–270. Print.

Derrida, Jacques. 1981. *Dissemination*. Trans. Barbara Johnson. Chicago: University of Chicago Press. Print.

Edelman, Lee. 2004. *No Future: Queer Theory and the Death Drive*. Durham: Duke University Press. Print.

Gallop, Jane. 1988. *Thinking Through the Body*. New York: Columbia University Press. Print.

Garoian, Charles R., and Yvonne M. Gaudelius. 2008. *Spectacle Pedagogy: Art, Politics and Visual Culture*. Albany: SUNY Press. Print.

Genette, Gérard. 1997. *Paratexts: Thresholds of Interpretation*. Trans. Jane E. Lewin. Cambridge: Cambridge University Press. Print.

Hacking, Ian. 1990. *The Taming of Chance*. Cambridge: Cambridge University Press. Print.

Halberstam, Judith. 2003. Reflections on Queer Studies and Queer Pedagogy. In *Queer Theory and Communication: From Disciplining Queers to Queering the Discipline(s)*, ed. Gust A. Yep, Karen E. Lovaas, and John P. Elia, 361–364. Binghamton: Haworth Press. Print.

———. 2005. *In a Queer Time and Place: Transgender Bodies, Subcultural Lives*. New York: New York University Press. Print.

Hall, Donald. 2007. Cluelessness in the Queer Classroom. *Pedagogy* 7 (2): 182–191. Print.

Ingram, Gordon Brent. 1997. Marginality and the Landscapes of Erotic Alien(n)ations. In *Queers in Spaces: Communities, Public Places, Sites of Resistance*, ed. Gordon Brent Ingram, Anne-Marie Bouthillette, and Yolanda Retter, 27–52. Seattle: Bay Press. Print.

Jones, Amelia. 2012. *Seeing Differently: A History and Theory of Identification and the Visual Arts*. London: Routledge. Print.

Kristeva, Julia. 1984. *Revolution in Poetic Language*. Trans. Margaret Waller. New York: Columbia University Press. Print.

Luhmann, Susanne. 1998. Queering/Querying Pedagogy? Or, Pedagogy Is a Pretty Queer Thing. In *Queer Theory in Education*, ed. William F. Pinar, 120–132. Mahwah: Lawrence Erlbaum Associates. Print.

Modern Family. Twentieth Century Fox. Hollywood. Television.

Muñoz, José Esteban. 1999. *Disidentifications: Queers of Color and the Performance of Politics*. Minneapolis: University of Minnesota Press. Print.

Pinar, William F. 1998. Introduction. In *Queer Theory in Education*, ed. William F. Pinar, 1–39. Mahwah: Lawrence Erlbaum Associates. Print.

Pinar, William F. *Introduction*. Ed. Pinar, 1–39. Print.

Plato. 1987. *Theaetetus*. Trans. Robin H. Waterfield. New York: Penguin Classics. Print.

———. 2008. *Timaeus and Critias*. Trans. Robin Waterfield. Cambridge: Oxford University Press. Print.

Porter, Theodore M. 1986. *The Rise of Statistical Thinking: 1820–1900*. Princeton: Princeton University Press. Print.

———. 1995. *Trust in Numbers*. Princeton: Princeton University Press. Print.

Rose, Nikolas. 1991. Governing by Numbers: Figuring Out Democracy. *Accounting, Organizations and Society* 16 (7): 673–692. Print.

Ruffolo, David V. 2012. Educating-Bodies: Dialogism, Speech Genres, and Utterances as the Body. In *Queer Masculinities: A Critical Reader in Education*, ed. John Landreau and Nelson Rodriguez, 289–306. Dordrecht/Heidelberg/London/New York: Springer Science+Business Media B.V. Print.

Sapphire. 1996. *Push*. New York: Vintage. Print.

Sedgwick, Eve Kosofsky. 1993. *Tendencies*. Durham: Duke University Press. Print.

Sommers, Nancy, and Laura Saltz. 2004. The Novice as Expert: Writing the Freshman Year. *CCC* 56 (1): 124–149. Print.

Que(e)rying the Academy

CHAPTER 2

Queer Acknowledgments

Branden Buehler and Roxanne Samer

In January 2005, a group of neuroscientists created *Neurotree*, a user-edited web database that would "document training relationships within the field of neuroscience and display them in an intuitive 'family tree' format." Since then, the site has expanded to include the genealogies of many other academic disciplines, and the multidisciplinary *Academic Family Tree* now encompasses a "large, overlapping canopy of trees" with a database growing at approximately 150 people each week. Moreover, the website allows visitors to visualize these institutional and disciplinary relationships, explicitly mapping out the connections between academics. Along with other similar websites like *PhDTree* and *The Mathematics Genealogy Project*, *The Academic Family Tree* captures how many scholars, especially young scholars, tend to think of their doctoral training as a form of kinship. As graduate students, it is not uncommon to conceive of advisors as our—often strict, but occasionally consoling—parents and the members of our cohort as the siblings with whom we come up and learn

B. Buehler (✉)
Department of Communication and Media, SUNY Oneonta,
Oneonta, NY, USA

R. Samer
Department of Visual and Media Arts, Grand Valley State University,
Allendale, MI, USA

© The Author(s) 2018
E. McNeil et al. (eds.), *Mapping Queer Space(s) of Praxis and Pedagogy*, Queer Studies and Education,
DOI 10.1007/978-3-319-64623-7_2

21

this thing called academe. If asked to map out such relationships, like those who founded the sites above, we would likely produce something akin to a family tree as well. As the site indicates, such trees are intuitive. More than an innocuous metaphor, though, the common sense behind these family trees carries serious implications about the significance we place on where we receive our graduate training and under whom, as it suggests that such family structures determine who we are as scholars, as well as who we will, as we mature, go on in turn to reproduce. But is this how academia actually functions? Do our advisors make us who we are? Can academia be neatly mapped into distinct—if overlapping—disciplines, as *The Academic Family Tree*'s "canopy of trees" suggests? One place we might turn to for a more expansive and divergent sense of academic influence is book acknowledgments, in which readers are offered a greater sense of the communities from which scholarship emerges and the interpersonal relationships therein. In this chapter, we use these acknowledgment sections to theorize an alternative model for academic kinship that encompasses the many diverse influences surrounding any given scholar or her work.

"Queer acknowledgments" suggests two tracks in our pursuit of this endeavor. For one, it refers to our selection of the acknowledgments sections of queer scholarship written over four years as our data. By entering the names of those acknowledged in 28 queer studies books, published by five presses between 2009 and 2012, into a database and running it through social network analysis software, we map out the connections within to produce a model of intellectual influence that reveals hundreds of relationships unaccounted for by the academic family tree. More significantly, however, it signals our own queer approach to this mapping, as we theorize the results of this software analysis in a manner informed by queer theory's own work on kinship and genealogy. In particular, we turn to Sara Ahmed's *Queer Phenomenology* to think about how family trees serve to orient graduate students as they feel their way through this strange space of academia, such that other important relations, necessary to our scholarship, appear less legitimate. Acknowledgments sections, though overlooked and neglected by many, in fact expand or "queer" traditional conceptions of academic kinship, as their mapping out through network analysis illustrates the many ways in which scholarship gets researched and written. While this method comes with its own limitations, obfuscating certain material and temporal realities affecting such scholarship, queer acknowledgments as an approach to academic kinship offers scholars invaluable new possibilities not just for conceiving of academia, at large, but for grappling with what it means to work as an individual within academia's sprawling networks of influence.

Acknowledgments as Networked Paratexts

In *Paratexts: Thresholds of Interpretation*, Gérard Genette describes dedications, epigraphs, and all that surrounds the body of the text in a written publication, what he terms the "paratext," as a threshold of interpretation. More than just a boundary or sealed border, according to Genette, the paratext is a zone of transaction, "a privileged place of a pragmatics and a strategy, of an influence on the public, an influence that … is at the service of a better reception for the text and a more pertinent reading of it" (1–2). He defines each paratextual element by determining its location, the date of its appearance, its mode of existence, the characteristics of its situation of communication—that is, its sender and address—and the function that its message aims to fulfill (Genette 4). Due to his interest in literary— rather than academic—texts, Genette does not address acknowledgments. At the same time, his ideas are useful for understanding what aims acknowledgments often seem to fulfill. Like dedications, acknowledgments are performative, in that they constitute the act that they are supposed to describe. They recognize and thank those who contributed—through feedback, as an intellectual interlocutor, or via emotional support—to the writing of the text, but in doing so they also tell the reader that they are recognizing these people as contributors, and they are telling the person that they are recognizing that their gratitude is a public one. The acknowledgments are thus a demonstration and exhibition of affiliation. They proclaim relationships, whether intellectual or personal, and these proclamations, like those of dedications, are thought to be at the service of the book itself.

How, exactly, they are at its service is not obvious, however. To many, they appear ancillary to the reading of the text, perhaps even decorative and unnecessary. When conducting research, it is common to follow the footnotes, to check out the primary and secondary sources cited in the text's body. While some of those named in the acknowledgments are undoubtedly cited again in the text itself, many, if not most, are not. Their influence, then, is not obvious or palpable. And, unlike the dedicatee, an individual thanked in the acknowledgments is but one of many and is thus only minutely responsible for the work she has supported. The service that acknowledgments offer the work, thus, is not so much to be tied to singular relations between the author and a supporter of hers. Instead, they provide an idea of the tenor of the context within which the text was written and a sense of the breadth of its intellectual support and influence. They recognize that our ideas are not developed in isolation but through discussions with friends, acquaintances, and colleagues. And, accordingly, they demonstrate that our ideas do not come out fully fledged and perfectly crafted. Instead, our thoughts become clarified through elaborate processes of drafting, conferencing, receiving oral and written feedback, rewriting, and editing. In suggesting this discursive process, acknowledgments thus humanize the text, subtly revealing the labor and affection that go into the work we do.

Because acknowledgments illuminate the interconnectedness of academia and offer a rebuke to the image of a scholar working alone in the cold, dark bowels of a university library, it would only make sense to study them as linked documents rather than as solitary texts. More specifically, it would be beneficial to conceive of them as a network of recognitions and, in studying them, to draw upon the methodologies of network analysis. In doing as much, we join the growing number of scholars who make use of network analysis, a trend spurred both because our technological and economic systems have become increasingly reliant on tremendously complex networks and because network terminology and visuals have become part of everyday life thanks to widely popular social media tools. In fact, some scholars have already turned to network analysis to better understand the contours of academia. As an example, one might look to a website like *Eigenfactor.org* (University of Washington), which points out that "scholarly literature forms a vast network of academic papers connected to one another by citations in bibliographies and footnotes" ("Overview"). Accordingly, the site allows visitors to visualize this network in a number of ways, examining how journals and papers map into various research fields.

Eigenfactor.org is typical, though, in that its focus remains solely on citations. Citations, after all, are a major focus in the ongoing quest for impartial academic evaluation, being used to assess journals and academic programs, not to mention the productivity of individual scholars. Unsurprisingly, then, *Eigenfactor.org* states that one of its primary missions is to use network analysis to evaluate "the influence of scholarly periodicals." Because acknowledgments are viewed as less practical, in that they cannot easily be re-appropriated to measure and rank academic work, they have been subject to less scrutiny. Moreover, in the rare cases in which acknowledgments have become the focus of network analysis, the work has been largely exploratory and limited to scientific papers. In "Towards Building and Analyzing a Social Network of Acknowledgments in Scientific and Academic Documents," Madian Khabsa, Sharon Koppman, and C. Lee Giles note, to their dismay, that "books have more variation in their acknowledgement format than papers," thus making analysis ungainly (360). However, it is precisely this "variation" of book acknowledgments that intrigues us, as it opens new possibilities for thinking about academic relationality.

To study book acknowledgments as networks and to unlock these new possibilities, we first collected 28 queer studies books released over the span of four years (see Appendix). Next, we manually entered the acknowledgments sections into NodeXL, a social network analysis template for Microsoft Excel. Once the information was in the program, we began the process of visualizing the data. The graph below begins to reveal several things (see Fig. 2.1). For one, we can quickly see a few of our authors— including Elizabeth Freeman, Scott Herring, and the late José Esteban Muñoz—clustered in the middle of the graph, an arrangement that gives us a sense that these scholars are relatively important within the network. Additionally, it is easy to notice where acknowledgments are reciprocated, the highlighted edges indicating, for instance, that Ann Cvetkovich thanks David Eng, and vice versa. This visualization of the data demonstrates that, while academic influence in recent queer studies scholarship radiates out in many directions through a confluence of myriad lines, repetition nonetheless happens. Affinities, other than institution and affiliation, group scholars together. This visualization, when coupled with the relative intimacy of the language of most of these acknowledgments, suggests that there could be a kinship structure to queer studies alternative to that of institutional family lines.

GENEALOGY, QUEER KINSHIP, AND ACKNOWLEDGMENTS

Kinship is a concept central to queer studies, because the excessive repetition of the heterosexual family structure has normalized this particular set of relations, in turn making others unimaginable. As Freeman writes in "Queer Belongings: Kinship Theory and Queer Theory," "Heterosexual gender norms ... 'make' kin relations, in that they regulate human behavior toward procreation while appearing to be the result of some primal need to propagate the species. Meanwhile, whatever the connections forged by

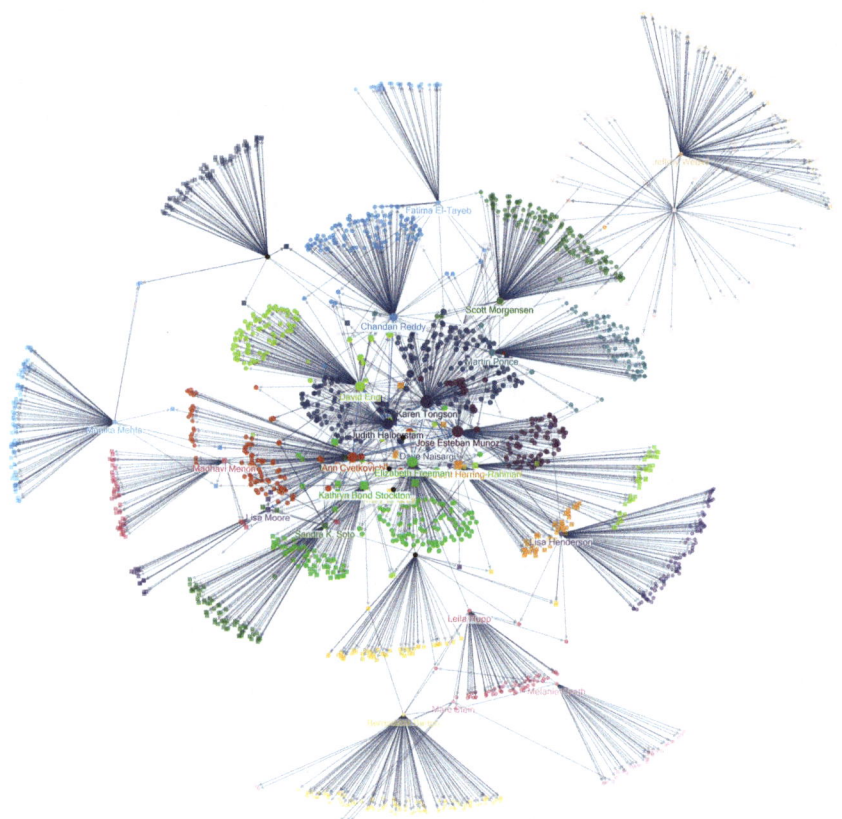

Fig. 2.1 Queer studies network

queer gender performances and other embodied behaviors 'make' remains unintelligible as kinship" (297–298). Queer studies' approach to kinship, then, is more than an advocacy of gay and lesbian politics' "chosen family," which appropriates and then transforms heterosexual kinship but emphasizes individualistic choice and presumes a range of racial, economic, gender, and national privileges in doing so. Queer studies, meanwhile, pursues entirely other ways queer people have created kinship, outside of families, and emphasizes the *doing*, rather than *being*, of kinship—normative or otherwise (304–305). While heterosexual kinship reproduces itself, queer kinship sustains and transforms physical and emotional attachments over time.

This renewal is not the same as a recreation of self, which again would be grounded in identity. Instead, it responds to our needs for connection, opens more possibilities for connection between people across time, and grants these connections a future, albeit with uncertainty and openness in form (299).

In *Queer Phenomenology*, Sara Ahmed provides an account of how kinship structures and one's iteration of or deviance from their norms through sexual orientation come with a nearly physical sense of adherence or divergence, respectively. Following genealogical lines is one way we navigate the world around us. Heterosexual orientation is what keeps us on course. And yet, in following its lines, the lines erase themselves, such that *how* we have arrived where we have seems to have disappeared from view. Reproducing these lines in turn puts some objects (such as marriage, family, a house of one's own) within reach and makes those out of reach inaccessible. It is the same with lines of thought. Paying greater attention to influential texts' acknowledgments might be one way for us to remind ourselves of this. We did not come to our objects of study, methodologies, or approaches by way of solitary thought or inspiration. We have been directed to where we are by the work of many scholars who came before us, and in pursuing our own scholarship we may eventually be directing that of those—students, other mentees, and strangers alike—who come after. However, as the complex networks of acknowledgments sections show, the family tree fails to account for variations to this experience and the many people, other than our advisors, who have influenced the directions we have gone and participated in our orientations. There are certainly ways in which academia, much like genealogy, works to keep scholarship "in line." However, how successful it is at doing so and what sort of lines it in fact creates, through such repetition, is not so straightforward.

In the case of the family tree, the vertical lines of descent seamlessly meet the horizontal lines between husband and wife and between siblings, and with the hope that "the vertical line will produce a horizontal line, from which further vertical lines will be drawn" (Ahmed 83); any relations other than that of the couple and their biological children are concealed. Figured as a family tree, like those on *The Academic Family Tree*, academia can be seen as pridefully begetting lines of scholars, which in turn beget others. Through this strong and direct association with advisors, presumptions about our fields of study and methodologies are made, and we gain entry into nominalization, such that we are spoken of as "Foucauldians" or "Deleuzians." We are presumed to have learned disciplinarity in an institutional fashion, and it is expected that we will then go on to pass this learned practice on to our own students later. However, neither sexual subjects nor scholars always follow the lines laid out before them. Sometimes our orientation directs us to other lines and, in following those lines, new objects come within reach. "Queer," Ahmed reminds us, "is, after all, a spatial term, which then gets translated into a sexual term, a term for a twisted sexuality that does not follow a 'straight line,' a sexuality that is bent and crooked" (67). Just as following a straight line provides access to certain "straight" objects, queer people are those who, because of their orientation, see the world slantwise and act out of line with others, which in turn allows different objects to come into view (107). Seeing orientation not as an identity but as a process, Ahmed claims that reorientation takes work (101). It requires reinhabiting one's body, and it affects what we can do and how we are perceived in what we do; it affects how we navigate public space (101). Queerness, as a process of reorientation, is not merely about one's sexual relation to others, but one's relation to a heterosexually oriented world (102).

In their proliferation of lines that radiate out in many directions, connecting scholars in unexpected ways, the maps we have produced of academic networks through queer studies acknowledgments sections appear quite queer themselves. They make a mess of our neatly ordered "intuitive" family trees. What to make of this mess? What objects, if not academic reproduction, are made palpable? In addition to providing network visualizations, the software also offers metrics that quantify what we see and what can be used to determine which of the scholars are key nodes within the network. Two of the centrality measures that it offers for analysis are the in-degree and out-degree numbers, which tell us both how many times a person is acknowledged and has acknowledged others. In-degree, as the name implies, gives us the former; it lets us know the number of times a given scholar is mentioned. Both Lisa Duggan and Muñoz, for example, have ten mentions, followed closely by Ann Pellegrini with nine. These high numbers are probably explained, at least in the case of Muñoz and Pellegrini, by them having served as general editors of the NYU Press Sexual Cultures series. Out-degree, meanwhile, lets us know how many people each author thanks. This reveals quite a wide range in acknowledgment practice, with Karen Tongson thanking 176 people and Marc Stein thanking 7. While some scholarship is undoubtedly more collaborative, this difference most likely also signals an attitude toward the acknowledgment process, whereby some reserve such official thanks for those with most direct influence on the writing of the text and others make fewer distinctions and give credit to all. This choice to thank many, rather than just a few, could be considered a "queer move" in that it quite consciously refuses the premise that scholarship is an isolated process with clearly demarcated lines of intellectual influence and instead offers a much more collective conception.

The same software offers centrality measures that put greater attention on who exactly is being thanked. That is to say, it calculates the importance of a particular node in a network not just by looking at how many connections it has, but also whether it is connecting to other nodes with many connections. One such calculation is eigenvector centrality. By that measure, we can assess the most "important" scholars of our sample as being Tongson, Muñoz, Jack Halberstam, Freeman, Eng, Cvetkovich, Kathryn Bond Stockton, and Chandan Reddy. While this calculation naturally tends to skew toward scholars who thank more people than do others, it is not always that simple. For example, we can observe that Gayatri Gopinath has the ninth-highest score even though she does not have a book in our database and thus has an out-degree of zero. Instead, her high score is driven by being thanked by several other scholars who have high numbers. Martin Manalansan also scores very high despite having an out-degree of zero. A related calculation to eigenvector centrality is PageRank, an algorithm made famous by Google and described by network theorists David Easley and Jon Kleinberg as "a kind of 'fluid' that circulates through the network, passing from node to node across edges and pooling at the nodes that are the most important" (359). Therefore, even though Reddy and Freeman have almost identical in-degree and out-degree numbers, Reddy rates higher on PageRank, thus suggesting he is slightly more influential within this network because he is linked to more highly connected individuals than Freeman.

This sort of investigation into queer studies networks mostly follows along the path established by the previously mentioned network analysis studies, whose primary goals appear to revolve around questions of status and impact within specific fields. However, if we are to argue for acknowledgments' reorientation of academic kinship away from the model of the family tree, we should perhaps not fixate on questions of influence and importance, in the process reifying hierarchies. Fortunately, there are other ways to approach acknowledgments sections through network analysis. To begin, we can examine the network as a whole. One typical way to do so is to look at a network's density, which in this case is the ratio of the number of connections between scholars in the network to the total number of possible connections between all pairs of scholars. This number can then help us determine just how closely connected our network might be. Looking at our queer studies network, that number is incredibly low—just 0.0006. However, such a low number is to be expected given how many of our nodes are people named by scholars who do not have their own works in the database, thus giving them no chance to form connections with other nodes. If we limit our network just to scholars whose books have been entered, then the number jumps to 0.07, though that remains a relatively low number and perhaps indicates that queer scholarship is only loosely connected. We also have the option to break down our networks into even smaller networks using other variables. For instance, we can split our network into smaller groups based on publisher. Once we do this, we can see the density take an even more noticeable jump. NYU Press, for example, has a density of 0.1. Duke University Press, meanwhile, has a density of 0.22. A scholar's publisher, then, seems to be indicative of relatively strong sub-communities. This can also be seen visually if we separate out the Duke and NYU authors (see Fig. 2.2). We can imagine performing similar exercises by creating sub-groups based on research interests. Such efforts could potentially help us locate where academic kinship is strongest.

Another possible approach might begin by trying to network the life of an individual scholar. Here it is important to distinguish between the different types of acknowledgments sections found across academia. Whereas the acknowledgments sections in the types of journals being studied by other scholars tend to be rather straightforward, a typical acknowledgments section in a queer studies work, as exemplified by Tongson's acknowledgments, reads like a life story. Not only are editors, advisors, and departmental colleagues thanked, but so are friends, partners, and family (and, in Tongson's case, childhood teachers, friends from "da club" only identified by initials, and a cat), all of whom have influenced the events that have culminated in the completion of the manuscript. A "queer move" in that it not only reveals the scope of academic influence, but also signals the breadth of kinds of influence within this scope, with Tongson's acknowledgments indicating that her project came out of research in non-academic communities. Acknowledgment sections, then, are more than just lists—they contain narratives that reveal how scholars come to be who

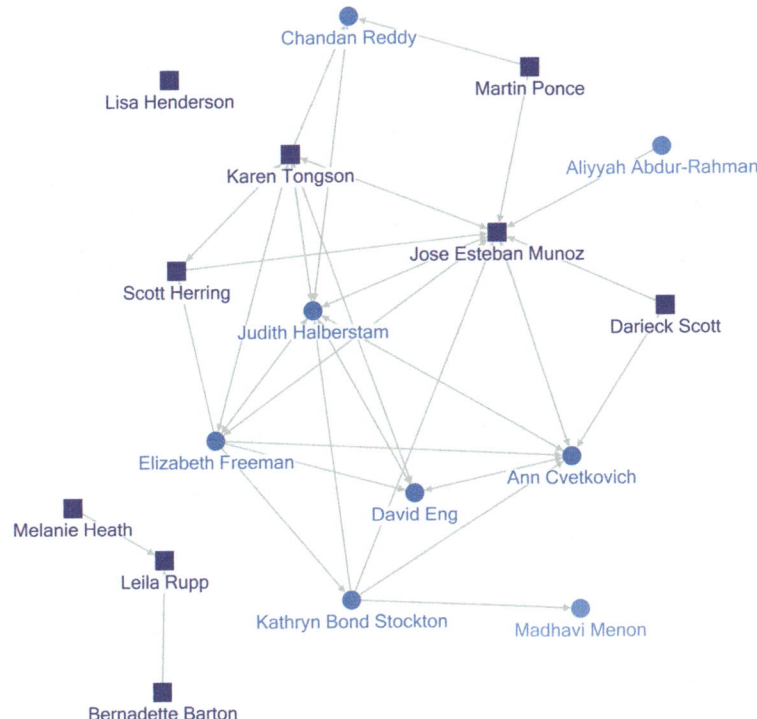

Fig. 2.2   A visualization of Duke and NYU authors

they are. They also could be read for indications of what sort of future relations for academia their authors would like to create or sustain. In isolating just Halberstam's network, which produces a type of graph referred to as an ego network (see Fig. 2.3), we could further explore clusters that appear and attempt to determine whether they might come from previous teaching appointments, shared time in grad school, or instead through less-institutionalized friendships of various kinds. For every scholar, a narrative lies beneath these lines and nodes—intellectual narratives that cannot be contained by the romance of academic procreation implied by the family tree.

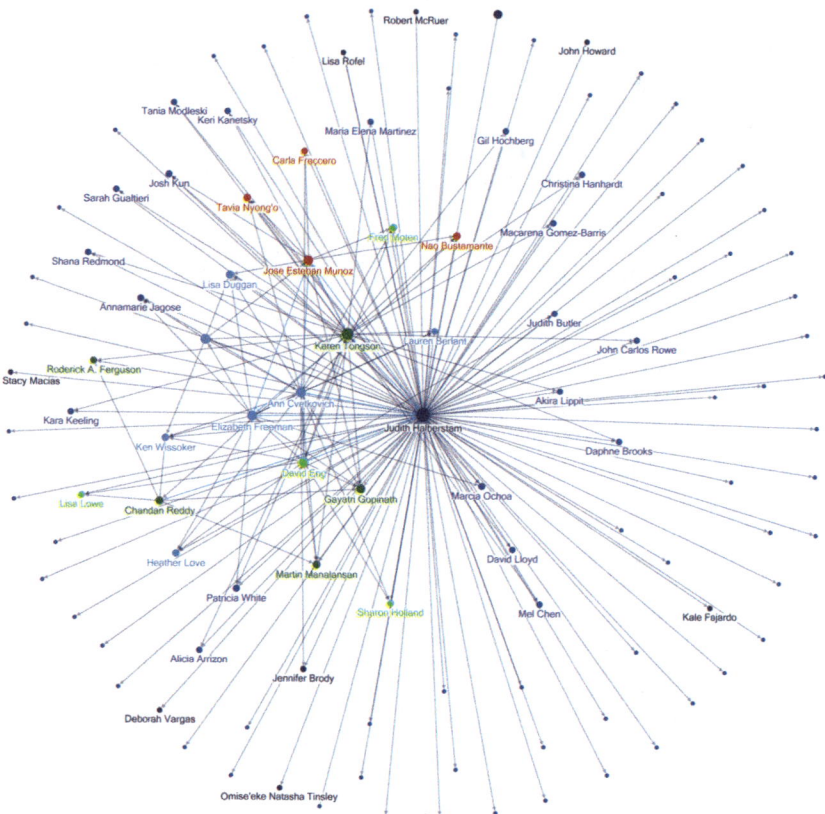

Fig. 2.3 Ego network for Jack Halberstam

MATERIAL MATTERS

While the sections above have described how network analysis provides new ways to understand academia, it should also be noted that network analysis has been subject to critique. In his software studies work *Protocol*, for example, Alexander Galloway tackles at length the concept of the distributed network—a network that lacks centralized hubs. Rather, each node within the network is independent and can link to any of the other nodes. As Galloway further explains, the "perfect example is the rhizome described in Gilles Deleuze and Felix Guattari's *A Thousand Plateaus*," linking together many autonomous nodes "in a manner that is neither linear nor hierarchical" (*Protocol* 33). Therefore, the distributed network shuns concepts of trees and roots, much as we do in reorienting academic kinship away from the traditional model of the family tree. As the analyses of our sample above demonstrate, however, many network analysis metrics within the NodeXL software attempt to assess influence and importance and thus reinforce hierarchies. Furthermore, the algorithms that plot the graphs pictured throughout this chapter naturally center more connected nodes. Thus, there exists tension between the rhizomatic ideal of the distributed network and attempts to analyze networks using network analysis software.

Perhaps even more importantly, though, in *The Interface Effect* Galloway suggests that network visualizations often obscure more than they illuminate. For instance, Galloway asserts that network visualizations hide their inertness—that is, their inability to provide us any true sense of orientation—behind "candy colored lines and nodes" (*Interface* 98). According to Galloway, this inability to see gets to a larger problem of being unable to represent the control society—this "control society" terminology referring back to Deleuze and Guattari's conception of the contemporary condition (91). This is a hard argument to dispute, for the ubiquitous nodes and links of network visualization always divorce us from the material and ideological realities of networks. The most common network visualization, for example, might be those produced out of the data from social networking site Facebook. When we "friend" someone on Facebook, though, it is not a mere matter of two circular "friend" nodes being connected via a new straight line. Rather, our connection is facilitated by way of an apparatus that mines our information and packages it for any number of advertisers. Moreover, our connection on the site is routed through any number of servers whose material existence is always effaced from network visualizations. Similarly, the graphs included above hide any number of material realities behind their seductive "candy colored lines and nodes." For instance, the maps do not consider whether scholars might be tenured or, alternatively, working as adjuncts—a divide that speaks not just to financial security but to academic freedom as well.

We need to consider not only the limitations of network analysis as a methodology but also the ways in which conceptions of queer kinship delimit what relations we take into consideration in our study of acknowledgments. While kinship and its immediate intimacies have been central to the development of queer studies, scholars, including many of those whose book acknowledgments are mapped out above, have more recently begun to think about generations and cross-temporal queer relations on a historical scale that truly tests the limits of kinship sans genealogy. In recent studies, Freeman, Muñoz, Christopher Nealon, Carolyn Dinshaw, Heather Love, and others pursue how entire historical periods might relate to one another. Together, they are interested in the queer historical impulse to engage with gay and lesbian and pre-gay pasts to extend community-building resources across time. Recognizing that sexuality is historically determined and thus different now than it was at the turn of the century, in ancient Greece or the 1970s, these scholars explore how queer people today nonetheless turn to these moments and commune with them and their subjects through archives, media, and art. In so doing, Dinshaw's and Nealon's historiographical models, with their interest in the affective, resemble friendship or community. For Freeman and her "erotohistoriography," lesbian pasts become like lovers, opening themselves to our touch. Love, however, is critical of the ways in which so often the pain and negativity of queer living gets positioned as solidly in the past, such that those of us in the present reject stories of violence and oppression as irrelevant to our experiences or try to rescue those who suffered by concocting linear progress narratives. Such friendship, Love claims, is an impossibility, not because of the obvious separation of time but because much of queer historical experience is characterized by isolation and untouchability. Rather than a historiography that characterizes queer self-recognition as consoling, she pursues those that shatter and argues that these negative or ambivalent identifications can "serve to disrupt the present" (45). Such historiographical conceptualizations of queer kinship reveal the limited temporality of most models of kinship, which focus on contemporary relations and flounder when asked to expand across generations without making genealogical claims of descent or inheritance.

The limitations of network analysis and queer kinship are worth noting, but they are also not reasons to abandon network analysis and queer kinship, thus foregoing the types of insights described in the previous sections. To that point, one of the most frequently enunciated concerns within the digital humanities is the need for humanists to become involved in the design of the digital technology of which they make use in their research. Anne Burdick et al.'s *Digital_Humanities*, for example, explains that much of the software currently being used by digital humanists was originally created for business purposes or for the use of social scientists. These origins, then, craft the types of data that can be used, the types of questions that can be asked of that data, and the types of answers that will be received by the researcher. Thus, the authors call on digital humanists not just to articulate these shortcomings but also to articulate how exactly the software might better serve their purposes. Speaking more specifically on the topic of visualization, for example, the authors write, "Visualizations designed to specifically address the communication needs of humanities research will only be created if humanists become actively engaged in their design" (Burdick et al. 42). Galloway's criticism in mind, then, we might ask how we can better design network analysis software to consider material realities and account for the inequalities within academia. Similarly, if our queer method of mapping and analyzing acknowledgments through computing tools were to be pursued and expanded to broader periods of knowledge formation, queer historiographical models, such as those of Love and Freeman, should be taken into consideration to account for a researcher's own relation to the acknowledgments she studies.

Conclusion

In deviating from the typical modes and means of research by using social network analysis software to map out those named in acknowledgments sections, previously invisible lines of connection, association, and exchange become apparent. Acknowledgments both reveal these lines and, like family trees, produce acknowledgments. Analyses of them suggest that some people seem to have great influence on the field, and some of these, such as Halberstam, are clearly scholars who have made substantial intellectual contributions to queer studies and over the years have mentored, edited, and debated the work of many others. This is not, however, necessarily the same thing as a top-down form of influence, but, as the visualizations also suggest, a cooperative and multidirectional process. Furthermore, not all nodes are the same in scale or status, and some may appear in any such mapping quite routine, while others are unexpected. Queer studies has grown to be quite interdisciplinary, always attempting, if not perfectly successfully, to remain outside the system of disciplinarity by drawing on many methodologies and fields of research. The acknowledgments sections we sampled certainly reflect as much. When queer studies appears to replicate the prevailing conceptions of academic structures, as in the centrality of esteemed scholars within our network, these instances simply suggest that queer kinship intersects with and works through ongoing structures. Through this tension, acknowledgments offer a site for rethinking the most quintessential elements of academia, such as mentorship and publishing, how we do such things most productively, and how we might think about doing them differently. Approaching academic kinship by paying closer attention to the maps made by acknowledgments sections could itself bring different objects—including creative and critical texts, affects, approaches, and modes of thinking—within reach. Taking up acknowledgments as a site of such potentiality and mapping out its many lines of influence suggests that academia has been for quite some time already fairly queer. Perhaps it's time we acknowledge as much and begin acting out of line with others.

Appendix

Abdur-Rahman, Aliyyah. 2012. *Against the Closet: Identity, Political Longing, and Black Figuration*. Durham: Duke University Press. Print.

Barton, Bernadette. 2012. *Pray the Gay Away: The Extraordinary Lives of Bible Belt Gays*. New York: New York University Press. Print.

Batra, Kanika. 2010. *Feminist Visions and Queer Futures in Postcolonial Drama: Community, Kinship, and Citizenship*. New York/Abingdon: Routledge. Print.

Cvetkovich, Ann. 2012. *Depression: A Public Feeling*. Durham: Duke University Press. Print.

Dave, Naisargi N. 2012. *Queer Activism in India: A Story in the Anthropology of Ethics*. Durham: Duke University Press. Print.

El-Tayeb, Fatima. 2011. *European Others: Queering Ethnicity in Postnational Europe*. Minneapolis: University of Minnesota Press. Print.

Eng, David L. 2010. *The Feeling of Kinship: Queer Liberalism and the Racialization of Intimacy*. Durham: Duke University Press. Print.

Freeman, Elizabeth. 2010. *Time Binds: Queer Temporalities, Queer Histories*. Durham: Duke University Press. Print.

Gray, Mary. 2009. *Out in the Country: Youth, Media, and Queer Visibility in Rural America*. New York: New York University Press. Print.

Halberstam, Jack. 2011. *The Queer Art of Failure*. Durham: Duke University Press. Print.

Heath, Melanie. 2012. *One Marriage Under God: The Campaign to Promote Marriage in America*. New York: New York University Press. Print.

Henderson, Lisa. 2013. *Love and Money: Queers, Class, and Cultural Production*. New York: New York University Press. Print.

Herring, Scott. 2010. *Another Country: Queer Anti-Urbanism*. New York: New York University Press. Print.

Mehta, Monika. 2011. *Censorship and Sexuality in Bombay Cinema*. Austin: University of Texas Press. Print.

Menon, Madhavi. 2011. *Shakesqueer: A Queer Companion to the Complete Works of Shakespeare*. Durham: Duke University Press. Print.

Moore, Lisa L. 2011. *Sister Arts: The Erotics of Lesbian Landscapes*. Minneapolis: University of Minnesota Press. Print.

Morgensen, Scott Lauria. 2011. *Spaces Between Us: Queer Settler Colonialism and Indigenous Decolonization*. Minneapolis: University of Minnesota Press. Print.

Muñoz, José Esteban. 2010. *Cruising Utopia: The Then and There of Queer Futurity*. New York: New York University Press. Print.

Ponce, Martin Joseph. 2012. *Beyond the Nation: Diasporic Filipino Literature and Queer Reading*. New York: New York University Press. Print.

Reddy, Chandan. 2011. *Freedom with Violence: Race, Sexuality, and the US State*. Durham: Duke University Press. Print.

Rupp, Leila J. 2010. *Sapphistries: A Global History of Love Between Women*. New York: New York University Press. Print.

Scott, Darieck. 2010. *Extravagant Abjection: Blackness, Power, and Sexuality in the African American Literary Imagination*. New York: New York University Press. Print.

Soto, Sandra K. 2010. *Reading Chican@ Like a Queer*. Austin: University of Texas Press. Print.

Stein, Marc. 2012. *Rethinking the Gay and Lesbian Movement*. New York/Abingdon: Routledge. Print.

Stockton, Kathryn Bond. 2009. *The Queer Child, or Growing Sideways in the Twentieth Century*. Durham: Duke University Press. Print.

Symons, Caroline. 2012. *The Gay Games: A History*. New York/Abingdon: Routledge. Print.

Tongson, Karen. 2011. *Relocations: Queer Suburban Imaginaries*. New York: New York University Press. Print.

Weeks, Jeffrey. 2011. *The Languages of Sexuality*. New York/Abingdon: Routledge. Print.

WORKS CITED

About The Academic Family Tree. 2017. *Academictree*. Web. 2 Oct 2014.

Ahmed, Sara. 2006. *Queer Phenomenology: Orientations, Objects, Others*. Durham: Duke University Press Books. Print.

Burdick, Anne, et al. 2012. *Digital_Humanities*. Cambridge, MA: The MIT Press. Print.

Deleuze, Gilles, and Felix Guattari. 1987. *A Thousand Plateaus: Capitalism and Schizophrenia*. Minneapolis: University of Minnesota Press. Print.

Easley, David, and Jon Kleinberg. 2010. *Networks, Crowds, and Markets: Reasoning About a Highly Connected World*. Cambridge: Cambridge University Press. Print.

Freeman, Elizabeth. 2007. Queer Belongings: Kinship Theory and Queer Theory. In *A Companion to Lesbian, Gay, Bisexual, Transgender, and Queer Studies*, ed. George E. Haggerty and Molly McGarry, 295–314. West Sussex, UK: Wiley Blackwell. Print.

Galloway, Alexander R. 2006. *Protocol: How Control Exists after Decentralization*. Cambridge, MA: The MIT Press. Print.

———. 2012. *The Interface Effect*. Cambridge/Malden: Polity. Print.

Genette, Gérard. 1997. *Paratexts: Thresholds of Interpretation*. Trans. Jane E. Lewin. Cambridge: Cambridge University Press. Print.

Hansen, Derek, Ben Shneiderman, and Marc A. Smith. 2010. *Analyzing Social Media Networks with NodeXL: Insights from a Connected World*. Waltham: Morgan Kaufmann. Print.

Khabsa, Madian, Sharon Koppman, and C. Lee Giles. 2012. Towards Building and Analyzing a Social Network of Acknowledgments in Scientific and Academic Documents. In *Social Computing, Behavioral – Cultural Modeling and Prediction*, ed. Shanchieh Jay Yang, Ariel M. Greenberg, and Mica Endsley, 357–364. College Park: Springer Berlin Heidelberg. *link.springer. com*. Web. 2 Oct 2014. Lecture Notes in Computer Science 7227.

Love, Heather. 2009. *Feeling Backward: Loss and the Politics of Queer History*. Cambridge, MA: Harvard University Press. Print.

Overview. *Eigenfactor.org*. Web. 2 Oct 2014.

CHAPTER 3

Queer Settlers in a One-Room Schoolhouse: A Decolonial Queerscape Pedagogy

Garrett W. Nichols

The US academy is a settler institution that relies on, promotes, and perpetuates the ideologies of settler colonialism, including the notions that the US has a "manifest destiny" to claim the lands, bodies, and knowledges of indigenous and non-white peoples for projects of white expansionism. Scholars and teachers who refuse to account for their participation in settler society perpetuate the traumas of settler colonization on the lands, bodies, ideas, and histories of colonized peoples. This is particularly true for queer scholars and teachers when one considers that, according to Scott Morgensen, "[w]hite settler heteropatriarchy creates queers who resolve their exile through land-based relationships to disappeared Native people" by staking imaginary claims to indigenous cultural and sexual practices (6). It is a practice that courses through queer theory, as well. Qwo-Li Driskill calls this an "old story within 'the new queer studies': Native people, Native histories, and ongoing colonial projects happening on our lands are included only marginally, when included at all" (*Asegi* 21–22). This refusal to acknowledge *and* centralize the experiences of Native people and Native histories in queer theory, Driskill argues, means that queer theory's critiques risk reinforcing the settler colonial "master narratives" that justify

G.W. Nichols (✉)
Department of English, Bridgewater State University,
Bridgewater, MA, USA

© The Author(s) 2018
E. McNeil et al. (eds.), *Mapping Queer Space(s) of Praxis and Pedagogy*, Queer Studies and Education,
DOI 10.1007/978-3-319-64623-7_3

violence against Native people simply by refusing to acknowledge Native bodies in the first place (*Asegi* 27).

In imagining what a queer pedagogy might look like, I cannot help but consider how imbricated settler colonial histories and logics are in the academy, as both a physical and ideological institution. I worry about the violence a queer pedagogy might perpetuate by failing to make Native and Queer/Two-Spirit teachings central to its practice.[1] In this chapter, I propose a decolonial queerscape pedagogy, one that recognizes and challenges the heteronormative assumptions that permeate our classrooms and understands how these assumptions are central to the projects of settler colonization. Decolonization, writes Driskill, refers to "ongoing, radical resistance against colonialism that includes struggles for land redress, self-determination, healing historical trauma, cultural continuance, and reconciliation" ("Doubleweaving" 69).[2] A decolonial queerscape pedagogy centers the contributions of Native and Queer/Two-Spirit activists/scholars to practice "a decolonial work that is responsible to the land and lives it builds itself on" (*Asegi* 37). I respond to Driskill's call by proposing a decolonial queerscape pedagogy that asks teacher-scholars to ally with Native claims to sovereignty in order to challenge the invisibility of alternative sexual identities and histories in the settler classroom.

Settler Classrooms

Every institution of higher education in the US has a settler history. As Janice Gould points out, "It is obvious that there is not a university in this country that is not built on what was once native land" (81). From the beginning of colonization, educational projects, especially Indian boarding schools, were a key tool in forcing Natives to cut ties with their communities and assimilate into settler culture, often with the goals of creating docile laborers. Deborah Miranda's analysis of boarding school educational materials shows that these schools "had, at the center of their curriculum, no intention of educating American Indians for anything but vocational and subservient positions in the lowest strata society" (214). Insofar as they reside on contested lands gained through the actions of settler history and insofar as they reproduce settler ideologies through the production of traditionally Western forms of knowledge, universities and colleges are settler institutions. Native scholar and rhetorician Malea Powell refuses to ignore the lived and recurring histories of violence and oppression upon which the academy is sustained. She shows how settler histories continue to shape academic discourse when she writes:

I believe that rhetoric as a discipline has been and continues to be complicit with the imperial project of scholarship in the United States. I believe that rhetoric as a discipline does not see the foundation of blood and bodies upon which it constitutes itself. I believe that many of us who work within the discipline participate daily in un-seeing, in denying, and, in doing so, perpetuate the myth of the empty continent. I believe that scholarship in America can never be staked forth on neutral ground. (Powell, "Blood and Scholarship" 11)

Powell makes clear that imperial logics are more than just an unfortunate chapter in the history of the American academy. They continue to structure and inform our personal and professional actions as academics. That they do so without our knowing it is perhaps a hallmark of the strategies of settler power. As Morgensen aptly notes, "Settler colonialism is naturalized whenever conquest or displacement of Native peoples is ignored or appears necessary or complete" (16).

As an outpost of colonial power, the academy sets the terms for how we theorize our world. Settler educational systems rely on the production of a specific form of knowledge meant to bolster Western imperial conceptions of how the world is ordered. As Linda Tuhiwai Smith argues:

Imperialism provided the means through which concepts of what counts as human could be applied systematically as forms of classification, for example through hierarchies of race and typologies of different societies. In conjunction with imperial power and with "science," these classification systems came to shape relations between imperial powers and indigenous societies. (25)

The division of humanity into hierarchies is carried through the systematic organization of knowledge found in the universities. The methodologies and knowledges of the West are placed at the top of the hierarchy, categorized as rigorous and objective, while non-Western ways of knowing are debased as primitive, superstitious, biased, or subjective. Within the settler colonial research paradigm, indigenous knowledges are replaced by supposedly more advanced approaches. "Deeply embedded in these constructs," Smith points out, "are systems of classification and representation which lend themselves easily to binary oppositions, dualisms, and hierarchical orderings of the world" (55). These classificatory constructs constitute what she calls "research 'through imperial eyes' ...[,] an approach which assumes that Western ideas about the most fundamental things are the only ideas possible to hold, certainly the only rational ideas, and the only ideas which can make sense of the world, of reality, of social life and of human beings" (Smith 56). What is knowable, in other words, is that which is organizable according to Western precepts.[3] Anything outside of these formulations is not true knowledge. This categorization also enacts a colonial violence. Tony Castanha has demonstrated that current academic research, especially when applied to Native peoples, communities, and histories, is rooted in the Christian "doctrine of discovery" that justified colonial expansion across the globe and continues to enact violence against Native peoples. He writes, "It plays out not only in particular, important ways— such as the continuous violations of religious freedom occurring when Native descendants are chided and belittled when claiming Native burial remains and sacred sites, but also in how American Indian and indigenous peoples in general continue to be publicly viewed and treated" (59). As Powell remarks, "We have cut the wholeness of knowledge into little bits, scattered them to the four winds and now begin to reorganize them into categories invented to enable empire by bringing order to chaos and civilization to the savage" ("Listening" 15).

The academy, and by extension the classroom, constitute, in part, what I call a "settlerscape," a visual and ideological horizon upon which the settler gaze is fixed, surveying, quantifying, and organizing according to the logics of settler colonialism (which are also, but not the only, logics of white supremacy and heteropatriarchy). Within the classroom, a microcosm of the settlerscape is recreated, sometimes consciously, sometimes subconsciously, as a group of settler and colonized subjects join to reenact and practice settler colonial rhetorical strategies that they will later employ in their "natural" progression from the university to the colonial marketplace.

One way in which the university classroom mirrors the larger settlerscape of the university is through the conscious construction of distance (read as objectivity) within the classroom. Smith points out that the concept of distance in research "is most important as it implies a neutrality and objectivity on behalf of the researcher. Distance is measurable. What it has come to stand for is objectivity, which is not measurable to the same extent" (56). Under this view, personal attachment and overt historical and socio-political ties to one's research agendas lead to questions about one's ability to remain "objective" in relation to one's research, a standard which creates an unfairly steep barrier for researchers engaged in understanding and dismantling histories and systems that have subjugated and oppressed them and their communities.

This preoccupation with distance and objectivity extends to the university classroom as well. bell hooks notes that the classroom has become a place in which eros/passion is actively discouraged, leading to spaces of disengaged pedagogy that fail to provide transformative education for students. hooks argues that teachers who actively value their students and privilege the classroom experience are viewed with suspicion by an academic community that places research and publication at a premium over teaching:

> Some of the suspicion is that the presence of feelings, of passions, may not allow for objective consideration of each student's merit. But this very notion is based on the false assumption that education is neutral, that there is some "even" emotional ground we stand on that enables us to treat everyone equally, dispassionately.... To allow one's feelings of care and will to nurture particular individuals in the classroom—to expand and embrace everyone—goes against the notion of privatized passion. (hooks 198)

hooks's observations about the dispassionate classroom reflect the intransigence of settler ideologies in the academy, from the field to the archive to the classroom. In the dispassionate classroom, the imperial center is again reconstructed, such that, as Smith explains, "Distance again separated the individuals in power from the subjects they governed" (55).

In the classroom, we may think of these "subjects" as both students and fields of study. A distance emerges between the student-subject and the instructor in the settler classroom. Instructors maintain an "objective" and dispassionate space between themselves and their students, allowing students little glimpse into their personal lives, with no acknowledgment of the passions and preoccupations that must necessarily blur the lines between the instructor and their other identities beyond the classroom. The instructor exists solely as the conveyor of information/knowledge and the cipher through which to evaluate the progress and/or failure of each student to synthesize properly the information conveyed within the classroom.

We physically maintain this objective distance, as well. Within the settler classroom, we are trained (sometimes explicitly, sometimes through our own experiences as students) to lecture from a position of visibility, demonstrating our knowledge, when necessary, on boards or screens positioned at the eyeline of students. The setup is one of masterful gaze: we command the attention of every student; we direct our attention to each student; we recognize and police the attentions a student may direct elsewhere, often calling the attention of the entire class to the student in the process. This setup may remind us of Foucault's theory of the panopticon in *Discipline and Punish* as an organizing principle to create docile bodies who internalize the gaze of an authority figure. Yet, it should also remind us of the imperial trope of surveillance, outlined by David Spurr in *The Rhetoric of Empire*. Surveillance, or "the commanding view," Spurr writes, "is an originating gesture of colonization itself, making possible the exploration and mapping of territory which serves as the preliminary to the colonial order" (16). Through the panoptic implementation of surveillance, the classroom is surveyed, mapped, and explored, all means to the end of a controlled and "objective" academic experience for students and instructor alike.

The subjects of what we study, and how we divide our studies into "fields," also reflect colonial attitudes about the value of certain frameworks of knowledge. Smith writes that, from an indigenous perspective, Western research is "research which brings to bear, on any study of indigenous peoples, a cultural orientation, a set of values, a different conceptualization of such things as time, space and subjectivity, different and competing theories of knowledge, highly specialized forms of language, and structures of power" (42). This "cultural orientation" directs the colonial division of the world into various branches of knowledge, or disciplines, which Foucault argues "appeared when man constituted himself in Western culture as both that which must be conceived of and that which is to be known" (*Order* 345). Essentially, disciplinary boundaries exist to reflect and justify Western conceptions of modern humanity. The fact that indigenous and non-Western forms of knowledge are not accepted within this framework is because they reflect non-Western conceptions of humanity and the world.

The settler classroom is born out of this creation of the "governed subjects" of disciplinary knowledge. Each course promises students exposure to a specific form of knowledge or methodological approach to understanding the world. Within the classroom, the instructor is in control of this knowledge-subject, dictating what, how, and why it will be studied in the class. As in the first of the double meanings of "subject," the instructor again fulfills the role of the colonial administrator, displaying mastery of the knowledge-subject and demonstrating the appropriate critical "distance" one must keep within the academy. The students might be seen as "administrators in training," learning through repetition and example how to engage with and manipulate the subject in ways that support the advancement of empire.

QUEERSCAPES AND QUEER COLONIZATION

Part and parcel with settler ideology is the promotion of white supremacy and heteropatriarchy, not as separate though aligned ideologies, but as entwined and central to the perpetuation of settler culture. Necessarily, white supremacy and heteropatriarchy are not promoted *as* ideologies but, rather, as natural and self-evident, a move that makes it deliberately difficult to challenge and dismantle them for decolonial purposes. Scholars working to decolonize queer theory, like Driskill, Morgensen, and Mark Rifkin, have demonstrated that decolonial work must account for the heteropatriarchal logics that undergird settler colonization and that responsible queer theory must account for the ways in which homophobia and heteropatriarchy are inextricably tied to settler colonization. "Heteronormativity," writes Rifkin, "is a key part of the grammar of the settler state.... [C]ompulsory heterosexuality can be conceptualized as an ensemble of imperatives that includes family formation, homemaking, private propertyholding, and the allocation of citizenship" (37). The "allocation of citizenship" requires that subjects, queer and non-queer alike, promote the tenets of the settler state to receive the recognition of the settler state. The implication of this for queer studies, as Morgensen puts it, means that:

> The problem is not that white, class-privileged, national inheritors of settler colonialism have been central to queer accounts. The problem is that all conclusions drawn from such accounts fail to explain not only all who are excluded from them but also all who are *included*: because the only possible explanation of queerness under white-supremacist settler colonialism is one that also interrogates that condition. Queer studies must examine settler colonialism as a condition of its own work. (26)

A responsible queer pedagogy must also account for the histories and realities of settler colonization. If the contemporary classroom represents a microcosm of the settlerscape, then it would follow that it would also be sustained by white supremacist and heteropatriarchal logics. It would also follow that the continued invisibility of these logics is central to the unchallenged perpetuation of the classroom settlerscape.

Such logics may become visible if we look to the spatial rhetorical strategies that queer communities have used to carve out spaces for community and sexual expression in homophobic society. Gordon Brent Ingram has theorized the construction of queer space in response to homophobic marginalization and repression. Sexual marginalization, he argues, leads to alienation, which, in turn, leads to the development of alternative social networks, which can lead to more marginalization. Together, the "cumulative interactions and the associated environmental constraints and opportunities" that arise in relation to these queer spaces form what Ingram calls a "queerscape" (Ingram 28–29).[4]

Public space can often be a space of danger and hostility for queer people. In response to the oppression and policing of public spaces by a homophobic society, queer communities have responded to homophobia by making "oppositional use of public space" in ways that reconstruct these spaces for queer use over the top of the existing heteronormative uses of space. Ingram writes:

> A queerscape is also an aspect of the landscape, a social overlay, where the interplays between assertion and marginalization of sexualities are in constant flux and the space for sexual minorities is "decentered," in terms of increasingly supporting stigmatized activities and identities. Queerscapes embody processes that counter those that directly harm, discount, isolate, ghettoize, and assimilate. A queerscape is, therefore, a cumulative kind of spatial unit, a set of places, a plane of subjectivities constituting a collectivity, which involve multiple alliances of lesbians, gay men, bisexuals, and transsexuals and which support a variety of activities, transactions, and functions.... Like the landscape, the queerscape is a cultural construct that provides a territorial basis for considering opportunities for and persistent disparities in access to public space and various respective services and amenities, as well as options for personal and collective expression. (40–41)

As Ingram describes it, queerscapes embody imaginative responses to systematic homophobia. Queerscapes are not necessarily "safe spaces" for queer action, but they do provide strategic spatial alliances for queer communities to engage in personal and communal queer expression.

In theorizing the queerscape, Ingram is not proposing a new construction of space but, instead, attempting to make sense of existing queer uses of space. His failure to account for Indigenous and settler colonial histories in his theory, while disappointing, reflects the settler imaginaries created by many queer activists as they struggle for inclusion within the settler state.[5] Though Ingram sees queerscapes as alternatives to the "processes ... that directly harm, discount, isolate, ghettoize, and assimilate," his description of this alternative is remarkably similar to the processes of settler colonization. For example, he claims that with many queer-identified people, "there is a 'queering' of adjacent environments in terms of a limited safety in numbers as a means of countering repression and developing more diverse and dependable relationships" (Ingram 41). Though developed to provide the resistance to homophobic oppression that strength-in-numbers provides, this process mirrors the processes of settlement practiced on Native lands and territories by the US government. Indeed, Ingram himself evokes this possibility when he describes the "territorial basis" for communal resistance that the queerscape provides, an implicit recognition of the nationalistic imperatives embedded within queer political rhetoric that fails to address the underlying colonial structures upon which they are built (41). As a result, queerscapes have the potential to recreate the very structures of colonial oppression that perpetuate the heterosexism they seek to undercut.

Opening queerscapes to the critiques of queer Indigenous scholars and activists creates the possibility of a decolonized future broader than the aims of any single political group. Queer activists can learn much from the expertise of queer Indigenous people who "have been under the surveillance of white colonial heteropatriarchy since contact," write Driskill et al. in the concluding chapter of *Queer Indigenous Studies* (212). "Queer Indigenous critiques," they point out, "do not look for recognition from the nation-state for our pain and suffering because of identities, but seek to imagine other queer possibilities for emancipation and freedom for all peoples" (Driskill et al. 213). As Driskill argues elsewhere, "For Native Two-Spirit/GLBTQ people and our allies, part of imagining our futures is through creating theories and activism that weave together Native and GLBTQ critiques that speak to our present colonial realities" ("Doubleweaving" 70).

Decolonial Queerscape Classrooms: A Practice of Alliance and Resistance

Revealing queerscapes in the classroom creates pathways for challenging notions of access in the academy as they relate to race, gender, sexuality, class, and colonization. Because queerscapes overlap with "normative" spaces, revealing and/or forming queerscapes in the classroom can be a productive way for students and teachers from multiple perspectives to understand the always-personal histories of privilege and marginalization that are systematically enforced in settler culture, specifically the settler classroom.

But queerscapes also reflect the contours of the landscapes in which they are formed. Because the academy and classroom are also settlerscapes, a queerscape classroom may easily become a colonial queerscape classroom that uncritically resides on the lands and ideas appropriated by settler colonialism. When we queer our classrooms without accounting for these histories and realities, we risk constructing what Malea Powell terms a "prime narrative" that covers over difference to promote the illusion that we are "held together by the sameness of our beliefs" ("Down by the River" 57). In reality, settler heteropatriarchy affects Native and non-Native queer subjects differently, and if we want to challenge heteropatriarchy in the classroom, we need Native and non-Native alliances to "spur one another on to even more disruptive tactics" (57). Thus, when Ingram writes that "a queerscape is essentially a sum total of subjectivities, some more closely linked, for a time, than others," we have to push on this lest we rest on a "prime narrative" of multiculturalism that erases the colonial experiences of Natives and queer Natives on settler lands (43). We need to incorporate alliances (between queer and non-queer, between Native and non-Native) into this "sum total of subjectivities" so that the focus is more on the "closely linked" than the "sum total."

Decolonizing the classroom is an endeavor fraught with many seemingly insurmountable obstacles, not least of which is the fact of the classroom's location within the university system, which, in addition to being housed on stolen Native lands, is also situated within regional and national accreditation systems steeped in settler colonial legacies. As long as we are required to evaluate students using normative grading systems, match institutional benchmarks, or justify the value of our classes by the number of students we can attract to them, and as long as these classes take place on contested lands, we are participating in a colonial structure. In positing a decolonial queerscape pedagogy, I propose the emergence of what Ingram describes as "a plane of subjectivities constituting a collectivity" within the settler university, "a cumulative kind of spatial unit" composed of, and centering, the specific histories, practices, and identities of all subjects in the classroom, settler and non-settler alike (41). As I envision it, a decolonial queerscape classroom begins at the intersection of three contested realities within the settler classroom: space, knowledge, and bodies.

Queerscapes emerge from within contestations of space and embody "constellations of sites of various habitudes and utilities" (Ingram 41). In the settler classroom, that space incorporates not only the classroom but also the surrounding environs and lands upon which the classroom/

academy rests. These are spaces designed to ignore or discourage the intrusion of bodies and identities that threaten settler colonial authority. But because "the existence of the oppressed is necessary" to the existence of the oppressors (Freire 58), these unwanted subjectivities are often lumped together into an undifferentiated mass under the guise of multiculturalism, which can be "highly problematic for any minority group, and particularly for Native communities who are not necessarily seeking equality so much as working to maintain literal and rhetorical sovereignty" (King 211). Challenging settler space in the classroom requires both a vociferous acknowledgment of the contested lands on which the classroom is located and vigilance toward the construction of space within the classroom. Without this constant awareness, queerscape classrooms may perpetuate the "imaginaries of indigeneity" that queer non-Natives often pursue in making claims for settler recognition (Morgensen 227).

Acknowledging contested lands requires that we situate our classes within a space larger than the classroom but specific to the immediate environment. At the most basic level, this means we need to know the history of the lands on which we teach, a history that includes the stories of all the land's inhabitants. Rather than seeing our classes as a zero-point from which learning begins anew each semester, we should make use of institutional histories that have resulted in the specific spaces in which we teach. In *Asegi Stories: Cherokee Queer and Two-Spirit Memory*, Driskill challenges us to know the ongoing histories of colonization in the spaces we inhabit:

> Whose land are you on, dear reader? What are the specific names of the Native nation(s) who have historical claim to the territory on which you currently read this book? What are their histories before European invasion? What are their historical and present acts of resistance to colonial occupation? If you are like most people in the United States and Canada, you cannot answer this question. And this disturbs me. (23)

These questions, always important, are critical if we wish to challenge the settler imperatives undergirding our pedagogies, especially if we hope to fight cissexism and heterosexism in our classrooms (and institutions, communities, and societies). In asking ourselves these questions (and then asking how we learned the answers if we know them and why we did not learn them if we do not), we should also ask, "How can I incorporate these questions into my classrooms in ways that further the course and institutional objectives?"

I have tried (not always successfully) to do this in my own teaching. When I was a graduate instructor at Texas A&M University, for example, my students and I conducted archival research into the histories of marginalized communities in the university and surrounding communities. In doing so, we fulfilled university requirements for conducting primary research and practicing rhetorical techniques in the advanced composition course I taught, but we also learned how research methodologies and rhetorical strategies are shaped by histories of contested space in the region. These questions are easier to incorporate in some classes than in others, but they are always germane to any subject, especially when that knowledge is being taught as part of curriculum structured by settler colonial institutions such as universities.

Bridgewater State University, my current institution, resides on Wampanoag ancestral lands in southern Massachusetts. The courses that I teach here, ranging from First-Year Writing to Technical Writing to Writing Our Heritages (an historiography and archives course) to Queer Rhetorics, have all touched on our spatial and historical relationship to colonization and the Wampanoag people, frequently in a way that encourages students to see themselves as participants in that history. By examining treaties and legal documents, researching genealogies, or visiting local sites of queer and Native history (such as the Plimoth Plantation), we explore together the ways settler projects have been written onto these spaces and the bodies that inhabit them.

We must be vigilant about the contestations of space that happen within the classroom as well. As sites of privilege, classrooms have historically been cordoned off to all but a few of the most privileged in settler society. Even with the removal of official barriers to admission, unofficial barriers exist, and higher education continues to be largely populated by members of privileged groups. The classroom, then, when populated by students and instructors from marginalized communities and backgrounds, is a contested space. As a contested space, we must be critically engaged with how we fill this space. How does the class physically align itself in relation to the classroom, for example? Because queerscapes make use of marginal spaces, we should seek to identify the marginal spaces in our classrooms.

At my university, I often teach in a "standard" classroom with five or six rows of desks, a podium, and a whiteboard at the front. In this room, the marginal spaces tend to emerge as the less visible desks situated near the back or side of the classroom. As a white male instructor, I notice that the seats near the front and center are largely populated by apparently white students, students who, through the course of the semester, tend to speak more in class and feel more comfortable challenging me and engaging the other students in discussion (whether invited or not). Students of color, working-class students, and queer students, on the other hand, disproportionately populate the marginal spaces. The students in these spaces tend to contribute less in class discussions, but I also notice that they tend to engage more personally and creatively with the subject matter when writing classroom projects.

Each semester, I reveal my sexual orientation as a gay man to my students. When I do this, I sometimes sense a shift in the physical and emotional dynamics of the classroom. Many times, the "front and center" students become more comfortable challenging me or calling out my "agenda" as a queer teacher. The students in the marginal spaces, on the other hand, do not always contribute more to my prompts in class, but I do notice that they will engage with the "front and center" students more, often challenging their assertions and providing alternative rationales based on their personal histories and experiences.

I attribute this shift not to a greater acceptance of my sexuality from the students in the marginal spaces but to a recognition of the shifting contestations of space in the classroom. As a white male, my authority in this space is often unchallenged, and even supported, by the students who try to sit as close as possible to me in the classroom. After coming out to my students as queer (as well as working class and as someone with mental illness), the space that I occupy in the classroom is suddenly revealed to be a contested space to students of privilege in the class, though marginalized students may have been aware of it as a contested space well before I came out.[6]

These vectors extend beyond our classrooms, too. Scott Lyons has argued that key to Native sovereignty is a relationship with the land that is "made truly meaningful by a consistent cultural refusal to interact with that land as private property or purely exploitable resource. Land, culture, and community are inseparable" (458). To decolonize our classrooms, we must realize that our classes do not end at the walls of the classroom; we and our students are responsible to our communities in which we live and the land on which we teach, work, and study. Morgensen says that "[h]aving questioned desires to belong to the settler state or to possess Native history, non-Native queers can consider the groundlessness that follows critiquing settlement as a condition of their existence" (226–227). This "groundlessness," he argues, can be a productive space from which alliances between Native and non-Native queers can be formed. Likewise, facilitating this groundlessness in our classes can open up our classes, and the academy, to decolonial alliances in which we work together for decolonization.

The construction of space and land, and the limitations to access in these spaces, is tied to access to knowledge within the academy. Access to knowledge (and access of knowledge) is key to challenging the forces that separate the "plane of subjectivities" that constitute a queerscape from the privileges enjoyed by hetero-colonial subjects. As I discussed above, colonial cultures construct what counts as "knowledge" in Western culture to affirm colonialism's conception of humanity and the privileged role of the settler subject in the world. In a decolonial queerscape classroom, we should be open to other forms of knowledge, such as those drawn from personal experiences, that are formed as a community, and that are temporally relevant or have *kairotic* value. This means that we must be open to the possibility of students becoming the providers of knowledge within the classroom. When students engage their wealth of personal knowledge, and when they pool their knowledges together, they are better positioned to take advantage of the "personal and collective expression" offered by the queerscape (41). As Paolo Freire writes in *Pedagogy of the Oppressed*, power inculcates self-doubt and denial in the oppressed who are taught to believe that only the "professor" has the knowledge. "Almost never do they realize that they, too, 'know things' they have learned in their relations with the world and with other women and men" (63).

Finally, a decolonial queerscape pedagogy accounts for the contestations of bodies within the classroom. This requires, first, recognizing that there *are* bodies in the classroom, and importantly, that these bodies can form erotic alliances. hooks argues that the de-eroticization of the classroom perpetuates the binaristic separation of the mind from the body, and discourages enthusiasm and passion within the classroom. Noting that the erotic is not merely confined to sexual drives (though these should not be ignored) but, rather, constitutes a force that propels us to self-actualization, hooks writes:

> Given that critical pedagogy seeks to transform consciousness, to provide students with ways of knowing that enable them to know themselves better and live in the world more fully, to some extent it must rely on the presence of the erotic in the classroom to aid the learning process.... Understanding that eros is a force that enhances our overall effort to be self-actualizing, that it can provide an epistemological grounding informing how we know

what we know, enables both professors and students to use such energy in a classroom setting in ways that invigorate discussion and excite the critical imagination. (194–195)

hooks argues that teachers need to be open to allowing passion to emerge in their classrooms, first from themselves and then from their students. In the process, "the classroom becomes a dynamic place where transformations in social relations are concretely actualized and the false dichotomy between the world outside and the inside world of the academy disappears" (hooks 195). In allowing the erotic and the passionate to emerge in the classroom, the erotic alliances of the queerscape can begin to form, and the class can begin to interrogate (passionately!) the "landscape of erotic alien(n)ations" that constitutes every classroom but cannot be examined without the revelation of the queerscape (Ingram 27).

These three contested realities of the settler classroom—space, knowledges, and bodies—are interwoven, and deciphering the settler colonial ideologies that inform one requires that we decipher them all. Restricted access to space limits access to certain forms of knowledge, while the colonization of other spaces may lead to the theft of other knowledges. The bodies we inhabit, and the erotic attachments we form with them, may be used against us to discredit our knowledges or deny us access to lands, to places, to learning, or to community. By revealing the queerscapes formed in relation to the settlerscapes of the classroom, we move closer to understanding and reclaiming these contested realities in the classroom and in our lives.

NOTES

1. "Two-Spirit" is an "intentionally complex" term employed by many Native GLBTQ people. Driskill writes that "*Two-Spirit* is a word that itself is a critique.... It claims Native traditions as precedents for understanding gender and sexuality, and asserts that Two-Spirit people are vital to our tribal communities" ("Doubleweaving" 72–73).

2. Decolonial critiques and projects differ from "postcolonial" critiques whose theories and stories reflect a different reality than that faced by Native people who still live on lands occupied by settler colonists. In *Decolonizing Methodologies*, Smith illustrates this tension when she quotes Aboriginal rights activist Bobbi Sykes's response to a conference on postcolonialism: "What? Post-colonialism? Have they left?" (24).

3. Michel Foucault traces this practice back to the "Classical Age" of Western culture, which divided all of knowledge, or the *episteme*, "in terms of the articulated system of a *mathesis*, a *taxinomia*, and a *genetic analysis*" (*Order* 74). This articulation and division, he argues, informs Western analysis and research. "The sciences always carry within themselves the project, however remote it may be, of an exhaustive ordering of the world; they are always directed, too, towards the discovery of simple elements and their progressive combination; and at their centre they form a table on which knowledge is displayed in a system contemporary with itself" (74).

4. One strategy to centralize power in the hands of settler subjects is by making invisible competing identities, ideologies, and histories without actually removing them, because settler society requires non-settler ways of being to convince itself that it provides a superior alternative. Often, these very categories are created to assert cultural and social divisions, which are then used to justify exclusion from the benefits of the settler state. For example, as Siobhan Somerville has demonstrated in *Queering the Color Line: Race and the Invention of Homosexuality in American Culture*, scientific discourses of racism and sexual perversity in the US developed together to make sense of "cultural anxieties about 'mixed' bodies, particularly the mulatto, whose symbolic position as a mixture of black and white bodies was literalized in scientific accounts" (37). Further, as Cathy Cohen has noted in "Punks, Bulldaggers, and Welfare Queens: The Radical Potential of Queer Politics?" this development has led to the queering of non-normative bodies and lives, outside of a simple white/non-white binary, that limits "the entitlement and status some receive from obeying a heterosexual imperative" (442). Settler colonialism provides the terms of discourse for these alternatives lest they speak their own realities in a way that threatens to undermine settler society's supposedly self-evident claims to existence. In essence, settler colonial ideology pulls a bait-and-switch, acknowledging that non-settler forms of socialization threaten the settler state, while describing as threatening the very parts of those alternative forms of socialization that are either non-threatening or do not even exist.

5. Ingram does make reference to colonialism and empire, though he does so in a way that implies colonialism has ended: "Most of these conditions are regulated in terms of the overlapping vestiges (the societal artifacts) of colonialism and empire, as well as today's flows of globalizing capital" (36–37).

6. My experiences and tactics are not meant to be generalizable beyond my own classroom. As an able-bodied, white, male teacher, I can access privileges many other instructors, queer and non-queer, may not when identifying and teaching toward marginal spaces. Where I hope this example is useful is in making visible the vectors of power and privilege that converge in my body, the bodies of my students, and the space we call the classroom.

WORKS CITED

Castanha, Tony. 2015. The Doctrine of Discovery: The Legacy and Continuing Impact of Christian 'Discovery' on American Indian Populations. *American Indian Culture and Research Journal* 39 (3): 41–64. Print.

Cohen, Cathy. 1997. Punks, Bulldaggers, and Welfare Queens: The Radical Potential of Queer Politics? *GLQ* 3: 437–465. Print.

Driskill, Qwo-Li. 2010. Doubleweaving Two-Spirit Critiques: Building Alliances between Native and Queer Studies. *GLQ* 16 (1–2): 69–92. Print.

———. 2016. *Asegi Stories: Cherokee Queer and Two-Spirit Memory*. Tucson: University of Arizona Press. Print.

Driskill, Qwo-Li, Chris Finley, Brian Joseph Gilley, and Scott Lauria Morgensen. 2011. The Revolution Is for Everyone: Imagining an Emancipatory Future through Queer Indigenous Critical Theories. In *Queer Indigenous Studies: Critical Interventions in Theory, Politics, and Literature*, ed. Qwo-Li Driskill, Chris Finley, Brian Joseph Gilley, and Scott Lauria Morgensen, 211–221. Tucson: University of Arizona Press. Print.

Foucault, Michel. 1970. *The Order of Things: An Archaeology of the Human Sciences*. New York: Random House. Print.

———. 1977. *Discipline and Punish: The Birth of the Prison*. Trans. Alan Sheridan. New York: Random House. Print.

Freire, Paulo. 1993. *Pedagogy of the Oppressed*. 1970. New York: Continuum. Print.

Gould, Janice. 1992. The Problem of Being 'Indian': One Mixed-Blood's Dilemma. In *De/Colonizing the Subject: The Politics of Gender in Women's Autobiography*, ed. Sidonie Smith and Julia Watson, 81–87. Minneapolis: University of Minnesota Press. Print.

hooks, bell. 1994. *Teaching to Transgress: Education as the Practice of Freedom*. New York: Routledge. Print.

Ingram, Gordon Brent. 1997. Marginality and the Landscapes of Erotic Alien(n) ations. In *Queers in Spaces: Communities, Public Places, Sites of Resistance*, ed. Gordon Brent Ingram, Anne-Marie Bouthillette, and Yolanda Retter, 27–52. Seattle: Bay Press. Print.

King, Lisa. 2012. Rhetorical Sovereignty and Rhetorical Alliance in the Writing Classroom: Using American Indian Texts. *Pedagogy: Critical Approaches to Teaching Literature, Language, Composition, and Culture* 12 (2): 209–233. Print.

Lyons, Scott Richard. 2000. Rhetorical Sovereignty: What Do American Indians Want from Writing? *College Composition and Communication* 51 (3): 447–468. Print.

Morgensen, Scott Lauria. 2011. *Spaces Between Us: Queer Settler Colonialism and Indigenous Decolonization*. Minneapolis: University of Minnesota Press. Print.

Powell, Malea. 1999. Blood and Scholarship: One Mixed-Blood's Story. In *Race, Rhetoric, and Composition*, ed. Keith Gilyard, 1–16. Portsmouth: Boynton/Cook. Print.

———. 2002. Listening to Ghosts: An Alternative (Non)argument. In *ALT DIS: Alternative Discourses and the Academy*, ed. Christopher Schroeder, Helen Fox, and Patricia Bizzell, 11–22. Portsmouth: Boynton/Cook. Print.

———. 2004. Down by the River, or How Susan La Flesche Picotte Can Teach Us about Alliance as a Practice of Survivance. *College English* 67 (1): 38–60. Print.

Rifkin, Mark. 2011. *When Did Indians Become Straight? Kinship, the History of Sexuality, and Native Sovereignty*. New York: Oxford University Press. Print.

Smith, Linda Tuhiwai. 1999. *Decolonizing Methodologies: Research and Indigenous Peoples*. London: Zed Books. Print.

Somerville, Siobhan. 2000. *Queering the Color Line: Race and the Invention of Homosexuality in American Culture*. Durham: Duke University Press. Print.

Spurr, David. 1993. *The Rhetoric of Empire: Colonial Discourse in Journalism, Travel Writing, and Imperial Administration*. Durham: Duke University Press. Print.

CHAPTER 4

Queering the First-Year Composition Student (and Teacher): A Democratizing Endeavor

Mark McBeth and Tara Pauliny

Calling Students Queer

In Spring 2008, I walked into my second-semester freshman writing course, and once again greeted the same students I had taught the semester before. In our previous writing class, we had studied New York City homeless organizations and, in addition to reading scholarship about homelessness advocacy, students also did at least eight hours of community work in local soup kitchens, food banks, or shelters. During that semester, their experiences dispelled many of the myths that they had about the homeless, and they gained a richer and far more nuanced understanding of an often over-determined and stereotyped urban identity. I wanted the next semester to extend this idea of the "Other" and public misperceptions but, first, I wanted students to identify the "Other" within.

Since this group of students and I were already well acquainted and were comfortable working together both in and out of the classroom—they had, after all, met my partner on class outings and, while I may never have said, "I'm Gay," they certainly acknowledged the trail of glitter that figuratively

M. McBeth (✉) • T. Pauliny
Department of English, John Jay College/CUNY,
New York, NY, USA

© The Author(s) 2018
E. McNeil et al. (eds.), *Mapping Queer Space(s) of Praxis and Pedagogy*, Queer Studies and Education,
DOI 10.1007/978-3-319-64623-7_4

swirled at my feet—the semester launched itself on a particularly perky note. Once greeted and settled into our new classroom, I told students that I had a directed freewriting prompt for them; knowing my classroom practices, they sat with pens, paper, and/or keyboarding fingers at the ready. Without a preamble of any sort, I asked them, "How are you Queer?" Nearly simultaneously, pens and laptop screens went down and hands went up.

"But, Mark," they asked, "what if you're not Gay?"

"I didn't ask you anything about your sexual identity," I responded. "I asked you 'How are you Queer?'"

For a moment, this prompt felt unsettling for my students. If words make things happen, the word "Queer" made my students cease and desist, halt and resist; they stammered. And while "Queer" did not necessarily misfire for them, it did not make them entirely felicitous either. To cite one of my own professors, I think Eve Sedgwick might have responded to their confusion by telling them that "Sexual identity is one of the things that 'Queer' can refer to…. Again, 'Queer' can mean something different…. [A] lot of the most exciting recent work around 'Queer' spins the term outward along dimensions that can't be subsumed under gender and sexuality at all…. [T]he term 'Queer' itself deepens and shifts" (8–9). And this, indeed, is a version of what I told them. Our resulting conversation turned to the definition of Queer and how it could denote and connote in our lives. And although their initial balk at my provocative inquiry illustrated a certain type of fear of Queer by association, my students did not have a fear of a Queer planet: they knew we were here … they knew we were Queer … they had gotten used to it. What they had not considered and, maybe, could not bear to know was how they might relate to Queerness and feel comfortable within its implications.

I have argued elsewhere that all the students I have encountered are Queer: at my urban, commuter, public university, many of my students baffle me with their odd literacy strategies, their unconventional but incredibly rich language usage, and their customary habits of mind that often battle for time with full-time jobs, an arduous commute, and family obligations. My students may not identify as one of the letters in LGBT, but they certainly are the two Qs that have popped up at the end of that acronym. With all their odd habits, unconventional educational contexts, and quirky strategies, I do not see how they could be Queerer. While I might not know the self-proclaimed sexual identities of my students, their educational bio-political struggles certainly shape them as academic "Others." Consistently, I hear media coverage and public opinion which disparages them for this Queer academic Otherness, and I think to myself, how can I help them understand their educational otherness, not as a shaming characteristic, but, instead, reveal it as an optimistic force that should inform their subjective positions within school and compel them to engage with these agonistic (and antagonizing) forces? How can I help them use writing and research to acknowledge, confront, and embrace their Queerness and share in its connotations and conundrums? Ultimately, how can I make Queerness democratic? How can I invite everyone to share in the definition of that word and to feel a part of its resulting, oddball community?

My answer to these questions is to embrace this Queerness, make it visible, and ask students to approach it rather than run away from it. However, despite this democratizing and welcoming impulse, whenever I have told this story about Queering my freshmen, someone always has had a shocked look and asked, "What did they do?" with a tone that assumed that either they or I had immediately burst into flames when I posed my *queery*. Even a reviewer of this chapter commented that when a teacher posed the same question to the students in his prison program, a riot nearly erupted.[1] Judiciously, instructors would need to gauge the Queer-ability of their students and how this sometimes shocking approach would help or hinder their writing process and progress. In the privileged urban safety of my New York City classroom, however, I knew that my students and I could negotiate a definition of Queer that could help them generate some rich, productive thinking about feeling "outside the box." So, after much discussion, I posed my question in other ways: When or where have you felt the effects of normativity? What or who has made you feel Queer? What "forces" made you feel weird? To push the question even further, I also asked them to peruse my course description, which read as follows:

> People often seem torn between the desire to conform and be part of a community and, on the other hand, to stand out as an individual. Most often when people struggle with issues of conformity and individuality, they must make decisions about the normality of their personal identity and how much they want to invest in it. If someone invests completely in "the normal,"

how does this limit their creativity, their pleasure, or their achievements? After all, some of our most prominent artists, scientists, and even world leaders haven't been what one could call "normal."

If someone completely denies "the normal," how does this strain relationships to family, community, or society? Many who have shirked normalcy have been shunned by society and, in some cases, rubber-roomed. Frequently, societies or governments enforce normalcy, and that puts into question a citizen's right to free expression, pursuits of happiness, and civil rights. Do citizens have the right to be weird?

In this course, students will explore the non-normative, considering what role it plays in the progression of society, the undermining of values, the risk of civil rights, the sustainability of culture, and whatever other issues students can uncover in this forum of the weird, whacky, Queer, and quirky. Through the varying perspectives of psychologists, artists, filmmakers, sociologists, scientists, and historians, we will negotiate the often-turbulent waters between normal and strange.

As a result of my Queer questioning, students in this class wrote papers about a variety of non-normative subject positions: feeling like an inadequate college student who once claimed top honors in high school or feeling like a suburban bumpkin while on the streets of "sophisticated" New York City. One woman even came out as a lesbian in a Muslim family whose story overturned and nuanced the homophobic stereotype of the Islamic reaction to homosexuality. Despite their particulars, all of their stories highlighted how prevalent the sense of non-normativity is among undergraduate students and, for me, underscored a strange contradiction—that being/feeling Queer is, in fact, pretty universal and normal.

At the risk of provoking (or bursting into flames), in this chapter, we would like to flirt with the idea that all students in the first-year writing class are Queer, consider the theories that might support such an agenda, and illustrate some moments where the non-normative already prevails within the Academy. To embark on this odd adventure, we ask these questions: What if we proposed to our students that they are all, in fact, Queer? What if we suggested to them that as first-year composition students, they are all a bit out of place, all working within a space of shifting identities, and all, therefore, just a little out of the ordinary? Then, what if we proposed this theory to them within the context of their first-year composition course and asked them to explore (rather than resist) this non-normativity? We offer students this Queer orientation into Academia (and its weird ways), because the first year of college can be so disorienting.

Nancy Sommers and Laura Saltz have suggested that the first year of college acts as a liminal space where students "leap forward—or linger at the door" (133). It is just this Queer, liminal space of the freshman year, where students often confront conundrums about their place in Academia, their feelings of (dis)identification with the work done there, and a burgeoning sense of self that often feels "out of fashion" in their new situation (Sommers and Saltz 133). In *Queer Phenomenology*, Sara Ahmed theorizes that:

> Even in a strange or unfamiliar environment we might find our way, given our familiarity with social form, with how the social is arranged. This is not to say we don't get lost, or that at times we don't reach our destination. And this is not to that in some places we are not shocked beyond the capacity for recognition. But "getting lost" still takes us somewhere; and being lost is a way of inhabiting space by registering what is not familiar: being lost can in its turn become a familiar feeling…. The work of inhabiting space involves a dynamic negotiation between what is familiar and unfamiliar, such that it is still possible for the world to create new impressions, depending on which way we turn, which affects what is within reach. Extending into space also extends what is "just about" familiar or is "just about" within reach. (7–8)

Ahmed's statement resonates with Mary Louise Pratt's contact zones (note: "dynamic negotiations") and shimmers with Lev Vygotsky's zones of proximal development (note: "what is 'just about' familiar or is 'just about' within reach"); it reminds us that, if we were to point at and make incoming freshman aware of the actual Queer educational phenomena that happen to them and to give them some language to discuss these occurrences, that their metacognition might actually offer them a contact zone of proximal development—a place where they encounter unfamiliar academic culture but still feel uncannily safe(r).[2] In the end, this attentive scrutiny of liminal Queerness allows such counter-productive feelings of disenfranchisement (and defeatist victimization) to parlay instead into productively optimistic moments of learning.

Using the triangulated frameworks of Queer theory, performance studies, and composition/rhetoric research, we provoke our students (and our readers) to consider how their own non-normative positions have shaped their intellectual abilities, how these studied experiences can evoke interconnections with other people's differences, and how these investigations can become an undertaking in identity deconstruction/reconstruction. We demonstrate how many of these discoveries occur in composition classrooms where students do not just absorb information from unilateral lectures but, instead, where they construct knowledge through self-generated, dynamic language that expands their boundaries of knowing and know-how. And, we know that while incoming students often wrangle with ideas that they heretofore could not bear to know (Britzman), they can also gain a greater sense of the futurity of their own becoming (Halberstam; Muñoz). Ultimately, we flirt with the idea that when everyone considers their "Queerness" in a personal yet socially grounded context, democratizing sensibilities may emerge through writing, and a greater investment in equality and justice may occur.

Ideally, this proposition of Queerness should be made to students at a much younger age. By the time someone is in their first year of college, they have already been pressured to accept normality. In *Sex, Death, and the Education of Children*, Jonathan G. Silin struggles with and tries to make sense of education's "passion for ignorance" with young people, unpacking how "preferred ignorance," like knowledge, "is allied to a specific regime of truth, one that privileges conformity over distinction, the Caucasian over the person of color, the heterosexual over the homosexual" (170). He further confronts the compulsory ignorance of school, stating:

> Ignorance is negotiated as we actively conspire not to address certain topics, maintaining a foundational set of open secrets. It is these secrets, with their critical information about acceptable and scandalous behavior, that provide the structural underpinnings of social life and the thematic material of cultural production. Silence is itself a performative speech act and becomes essential pedagogy, a way to remain not implicated, to teach nonresponsibility. (Silin 171)

Within an educational system of open secrets, students waste years of their life conforming to the boundaries of Academia; right and wrong, black and white … specifically, in the writing classroom context, the grammatically correct over the awkwardly inspired, the established answer over the questioning, and the expected over the risk-taking. Students become obsessed with this need to find the right answer and not their own answer. Since overhauling the entire American schooling system would be quite difficult, college may be the next best place to inform students that they have no predetermined mold to fit. Allowing the student to inquire within themselves and incorporate that into their intellectual endeavors will only help them to mold *themselves*. Allowing students to embrace and proclaim their differences allows *normalness* to be illuminated. Changing this mindset will not only improve upon the student's rhetoric but shift their perspective on themselves, others, and all the offerings of the world at large.

GETTING TO KNOW YOUR QUEER SELF

Proposing that students are Queer and out of the ordinary helps them realize their identities as they grow into adults. Doing this also makes for an interesting class. Exploring these abnormalities can make students become critical thinkers, analyzing everything that surrounds them as well as their own life's events.

While first reading this section's epigraph, one might expect it to emerge from the pages of the theoretical work of Deborah Britzman yet, somewhat surprisingly, the quote comes directly from a first-year student who responded to a prompt about the relationship between Queerness and classroom work. In the way that a seasoned theorist might address nonnormativity, so did this student. In fact, Britzman's work supports the introspection of this student when she writes:

> A queer pedagogy is not concerned with getting identities right or even with having them represented as an end in themselves. The point is to read—in radical ways—the insufficiencies of identity as positivity and to examine and to refuse "cases of exorbitant normality" whether such cases take the form of heteronormativity, racisms, gender centerings, ability hierarchies, and so on. (94)

Both Britzman and this student agree that, rather than consider identity a foregone conclusion ("a positivity"), it should instead be considered a process—a Queer pedagogical process that allows students to engage in its alternative possibilities of growth. Likewise, in much of his performance studies scholarship, José Esteban Muñoz discusses a Queer futurity that steps away from an identitarian idea of Queer *being*, instead prioritizing Queer *doing* (which, in effect, may induce a fresh sense of being); like the work of the student and Britzman, this Queer futurity concerns itself with "a modality of doing and being that is in process, unfinished" (99). Similarly, in "The Novice as Expert: Writing the Freshman Year" (what now appears as a classic text in composition), Sommers and Saltz remind us of the (Queer) spaces and time where students once again become "unfinished," where they seem to lose footing in their own sense of (writerly) identity because of the in-between space that they inhabit in college. Sommers and Saltz assert that

Thresholds such as these, of course, are dangerous places. College students, for example, are asked to leave something behind and to locate themselves in the realms of uncertainty and ambiguity. It doesn't take long for most first-year students to become aware of the different expectations between high school and college writing, that something more is being offered to them and, at the same time, asked of them. The defining academic moment of the first semester is often the recognition, as one freshman put it, that "what worked in high school isn't working anymore." The first year of college offers students the double perspective of the threshold, a liminal state from which they might leap forward—or linger at the door. (125)

While Britzman, Muñoz, and Sommers and Saltz acknowledge these issues of uncertainty, ambiguity, and double perspectives, the university setting often does not allow for such desirable space of undirected (inductive) exploration. Queer theory, however, because it has based its theories on these shifting terms, underscores and revitalizes how we may think about students' writing and learning. And, as a parallel to the theories of composition and rhetoric that have developed over the past four decades, Queer theory (and Composition Studies alike) thwart the over-determinations that come with final products. Such a conceptualization allows for the belief in the possibilities of students' intellectual growth and that, as instructors, we can act as "scouts" to facilitate the Queer future development of the less-experienced writer (read: the writer who develops). Or in Muñoz's terms, we are "Reading for potentiality ... [and] scouting for a 'not here' or 'not now' in the [writerly] performance that suggests a futurity" (99).

In *In a Queer Time and Place*, Halberstam further examines "the Queer temporalities that are proper to sub-cultural activities" (such as freshman-year composition within the culture of Academia) and proposes "that we rethink the adult/youth binary in relation to an 'epistemology of youth' that disrupts conventional accounts of youth culture, adulthood, and maturity." She continues, asserting, "Queer subcultures produce alternative temporalities by allowing their participants to believe that their futures can be imagined according to logics that lie outside of those paradigmatic markers of life experience—namely, birth, marriage, reproduction, and death" (Halberstam 2). Or, substituting for these larger socio-cultural benchmarks, the university sets normative paradigms of admission, progress, mastery, and graduation.

Another student who responded to our prompts about their Queering in the freshman composition classroom stated:

> Everybody exhibits some level of "Queerness." This ... has little to do with sexuality [and more to do with the fact] that college is a space where identities shift as we continuously read, contribute to research studies, and write about certain topics. While in this phase, we enter an atmosphere where our mind's eye is trying to look in every direction; sometimes our attention will be caught by an author, or a subject and we will move to that field of study either for a short time (until our attention is caught by something else) or for the rest of our lives.... [I]f a freshman college student did not explore their non-normativity (a.k.a., strengths) it would be a shame because then they are missing the sheer joy of embracing something that they would be extremely ... passionate about.

This student's commentary on identity exploration and intellectual discovery reminds us that disorientation is powerful; those moments of "looking in every direction," where our attention is pulled from one shiny idea to another, are also the moments of discovery and wonder. Perhaps even more importantly, they are also moments of pleasure or, as this student puts it, "sheer joy." However, these moments of "sheer joy" often lie few and far between for students. In the longitudinal study *Rehearsing New Roles: How Students Develop as Writers*, Lee Ann Carroll remarks that students often remain novice writers as they advance in their degrees, often in a process of periodic regression as well as progression of their writing abilities. Commenting upon the educational dynamics of students and faculty, she remarks:

> [Students] may not understand the expectations of the professor and may need more fully developed assignments, guidelines for performance, models, specific feedback, and opportunities for improvement. Their writing gets better in that they do learn to write differently, but they do not fulfill the fantasy of mastering one kind of literacy, an idealized version of academic writing, which improves consistently over time. (Carroll 60)

While she may not articulate as such, Carroll acknowledges a Queer futurity of student writing, a not-quite-there-yet, but also recognizes the potentialities of their progress or fruitful regress. In contrast, "[m]any faculty members, however, assume that this generic form of writing could or should be mastered in first-year English courses and complain bitterly when students who have already completed their composition requirements 'still can't write'" (60). This pedagogical vexation and disappointment often trickles down in the economy of classroom practices. Both the teacher and student lose the opportunistic joy inherent in such a seductively Queer teaching/learning process—what we have historically called the "teachable moment."

Several of Mark's students highlight this connection between Queerness and pleasure. For them, non-normativity does not simply lead to confusion or abjection; rather, it encourages creativity, personal growth, and self-expression. One student, for example, writes that:

> The idea of becoming aware of my Queerness and non-normative personality has made a significant impact on me. It allowed me to realize that as much as I strived to become everyone's definition of normal, I am far from it.... By acknowledging that I have grown through abnormal experiences, I have been able to realize that these attitudes were in fact positive. They haven't hindered me in any way from achieving anything. Rather, I embraced everything non-normative about me and used it as a weapon to succeed.

Another student is even more pointed in her response to Mark's *queery*. "To propose that each and every student is Queer would be non-conventional to say the least," she writes. "The move would be an optimal chance to widen the thought paradigms of students who have been previously drilled into creative submission. If we were to explain to students that they were indeed eccentric, out of the ordinary, non-normative, I can only see positive results." She continues, noting that encouraging students to connect the personal to the academic makes for a useful learning experience. She notes:

> I know the hindrances and constraints that accompany concepts of conformity and narrow paradigms. I can personally testify that understanding and acknowledging my differences helped me accept my own academic quirks and utilize them to my benefit. Having first year students venture into their own minds to extract their individual quirks and have those students use their respective non-normativity would be an excellent challenge. I feel that it is preferable for students to make use of their personal abilities and qualities, rather than to suppress them in order to fall in line with the order.... It would be the optimal choice to allow these assets to shine, and not simply rot.

This student's use of the two terms "shine" and "rot" offers up an interesting inter-relationship between two words that are not exactly antonyms. To shine something, you must purposefully attend to it; to allow something to rot, you must purposefully ignore it. This choice of terms underscores the fact that an instructor can encourage a student to explore and celebrate their nonconformity or, on the other hand, to deny or hide it, ultimately to decompose.

Widening from the personal, this pedagogical strategy also has the effect of building community. For example, another of Mark's students notes that even though she identified as Queer before taking this course, bringing the concept into her academic work broadened its scope from the personal to the communal. Queer became more than an identity category; it also became a means of connection with other students. As she tells us:

> The proposal of Queer into my identity is not something new to this course. Throughout my life, Queer has been a part of my identity, a part of me that I have explored and accepted. It was not a new thing to dive into the "weirdness" and "non-normality" of my persona, and I have found I quite like writing about my quirkiness. I think that having a course dedicated to exploring non-normality in ourselves allows us to write more freely and openly about ourselves, without the threat of backlash or judgment. Especially in a class of people we know and trust, I feel that I can dig deeper into my Queerness and not fear what others might think or say, because we are all sharing personal things about ourselves. Exploring what makes us Queer together, and learning that we have had similar experiences and thoughts, brings us closer together, I believe, and allows us to explore Queerness in a better learning environment.

Being Queer, another student writes, is "not an idea that I would resist in any sense ... because it offers me a sense of belonging ... where before I had felt persecuted or ridiculed for how I approached any and all composition course-related feats." And yet another student reports that:

> If it were to be proposed to me that I was in fact Queer, I believe that I would have to simply agree.... I would also agree that as a first year composition student I am a bit out of place; I often feel under or overwhelmed with how I go about completing particular [composition] assignments or projects. It is with this course, currently, that I have felt open to creatively pursue what had previously separated me from my peers and colleagues. I find it rather exhilarating to be able to explore or dive into what others may perceive as Queer or non-normative, but what I have always found at home with and semblance in.

PRACTICING TO ACT QUEER

As Mark's students' work has shown us, when students are offered the opportunity to embrace and explore their Queerness, they do not fully accept the Queer marker, but as Muñoz would tell us, they identify, counter-identify, and disidentify with the term. Thus, not being constrained by their preconceived notions of it, some students welcome its connection to sexuality, while others connect more to the outsider status it confers or the celebration of otherness it engenders. However, as they take up the term, it is the process of dis/identification that is important, because it is the point at which students position themselves in relation to the assignment, to the class, and thus to the academy at large that they learn their Queerness. Through the scaffolded and procedural work of this course, students see themselves as non-normative and equally recognize this oddity as a strong point of departure. As Sara Ahmed reminds us, "The hope of changing directions is that we don't always know where some paths may take us: risking departure from the straight and narrow makes new futures possible, which might involve going astray, getting lost, or even becoming Queer" (21). It depends on how we teach it.

Acknowledgment Tara and Mark would like to thank the students in Mark's Spring 2013 ENG 201 Honors course for their willingness to entertain these questions and for their insightful and thoughtful comments. This chapter could not have been written without them, and we hope we do justice to their ideas.

NOTES

1. This is not surprising since such a response can certainly be read as reasonable in the homosocial situation of a prison, where the definition of Queer needs to retain its sexual connotations precisely because inmates lose sexual autonomy when they enter this institution. It is also an understandable response since inmates often make situational sex choices, rely on stable gender roles for survival purposes, and behind bars, "Queer" takes on entirely new, and potentially precarious meanings. Queer, obviously in this scenario and others, demands rejection and cannot take on any democratic or collective meaning.

2. This pedagogical metacognition or self-awareness may also remind faculty of how counter-intuitive and bizarre the habits of Academia can feel when first encountered. It seems that once enculturated into the habitudes of college, its members fall into Oddness Denial Syndrome (ODS), which apparently erases all memory of their once-novice, less masterful beginnings.

WORKS CITED

Ahmed, Sara. 2006. *Queer Phenomenology: Orientations, Objects, Others.* Durham: Duke University Press. Print.

Britzman, Deborah. 1998. *Lost Subjects, Contested Objects.* Albany: SUNY Press. Print.

Carroll, Lee Ann. 2002. *Rehearsing New Roles: How College Students Develop as Writers.* Urbana: CCCC/NCTE. Print.

Halberstam, Judith. 2005. *In a Queer Time and Place: Transgender Bodies, Subcultural Lives.* New York: New York University Press. Print.

Muñoz, José Esteban. 1999. *Disidentifications: Queers of Color and the Performance of Politics.* Minneapolis: University of Minnesota Press. Print.

Pratt, Mary Louise. 1991. Art of the Contact Zone. *Profession* 33–40. Print.

Sedgwick, Eve Kosofsky. 1993. *Tendencies.* Durham: Duke University Press. Print.

Silin, Jonathan G. 1995. *Sex, Death, and the Education of Children: Our Passion for Ignorance in the Age of AIDS.* New York: Teacher's College Press. Print.

Sommers, Nancy, and Laura Saltz. 2004. The Novice as Expert: Writing the Freshman Year. *CCC* 56 (1): 124–149. Print.

Vygotsky, Lev. 1978. *Mind in Society: The Development of Higher Psychological Processes.* Cambridge, MA: Harvard University Press. Print.

CHAPTER 5

Queering the Campus Gender Landscape Through Visual Arts Praxis

Libby Balter Blume and Rosemary Weatherston

INTRODUCTION

At the entrance of the gallery space of the Women's and Gender Studies Biennial Art Exhibition *behind the mask: Women, Men & Masculinities,* the same scene played out over and over. Alone or in groups of two or three, students entered the gallery and looked straight ahead, scanning some of the closer exhibits; they looked left, taking in the space in its entirety; they looked right and stopped dead in their tracks. From this point on, the direction of their gazes was unpredictable. Some eyes were quickly averted, while others stared motionlessly. The students in groups often exchanged glances of incredulity, amusement, or disgust. A few sought out the gallery assistant's eyes, perhaps searching for reassurance. Most glanced around the room to see if any other visitors were watching them look.

They were looking at two portraits by artist Molly Marie Nuzzo titled *Noah* and *Cristy.* These are large, almost life-size oil paintings of transgender bodies. The subjects are partially or fully unclothed and stare back at

L.B. Blume (✉) • R. Weatherston
University of Detroit Mercy, Detroit, MI, USA

© The Author(s) 2018
E. McNeil et al. (eds.), *Mapping Queer Space(s) of Praxis and Pedagogy,* Queer Studies and Education,
DOI 10.1007/978-3-319-64623-7_5

71

the students with calm, direct gazes. The rich, dark background colors in both paintings provide strong contrasts to the pale flesh tones. This highlighting effect drew the students' eyes inescapably to the subjects' exposed bodies, while the subjects' direct gazes disrupted the comfortable hierarchy of viewer and viewed.

Noah's body stretches across a partially draped sofa, evoking the languid curves of odalisque portraiture. At the same time, *Noah*'s flat chest with its red surgical scars undermines that iconic imagery (Fig. 5.1). The subject of *Cristy*, in contrast, sits upright, wide-legged, with arms thrown behind head (Fig. 5.2). *Cristy*'s masculine stance aligns with the subject's short hair, large muscles, and the man's tie knotted tightly around the neck. The large breasts between which the tie hangs and the ambiguous denim-clad genitalia to which the tie points sent the students' gazes rebounding between *Cristy*'s head, upper torso, and lower body in an attempt to resolve seemingly incongruous parts into an integrated whole.

These are "queer" images in the most basic sense of the word: they overtly destabilize conventional binaries of male/female, masculine/feminine, and gay/straight. They are also "queering" images, however,

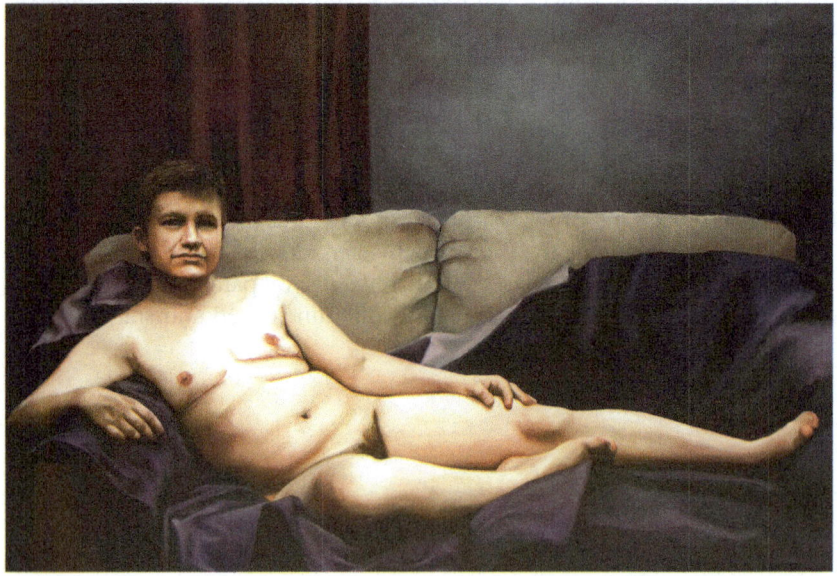

Fig. 5.1   *Noah*, oil on wood panel, 48" × 33" © Molly Marie Nuzzo

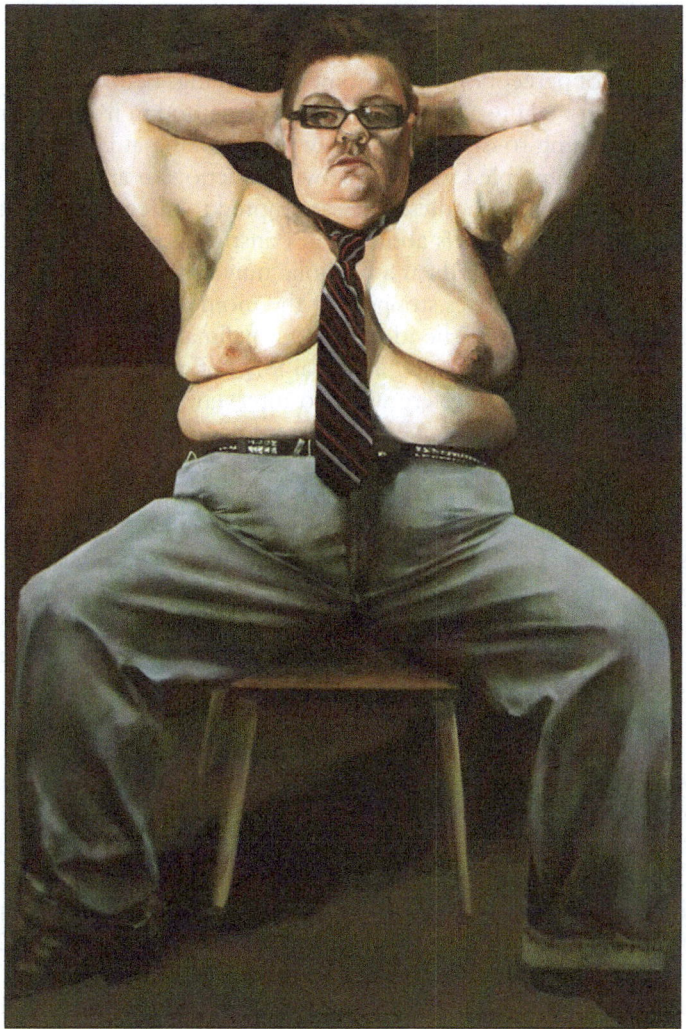

Fig. 5.2 *Cristy*, oil on board, 40" × 60" © Molly Marie Nuzzo

activating in their viewers a complex, relational process of identification and disidentification that also undermines the boundaries between margin/center, subject/object, fluid/stable, universal/particular, self/other, and aesthetic/academic.

Nuzzo's portraits stop viewers at what Amelia Jones describes in *Seeing Differently: A History and Theory of Identification and the Visual Arts* as "the moment of perception," the moment of seeing, before reacting, giving meaning, and taking action (220). Students stood in front of Nuzzo's paintings struggling to determine if they were looking at portraits of men or women. They grappled with their own attraction to and/or repulsion from the subjects' naked bodies. They attempted to integrate these images into their pre-existing beliefs about what constitutes art and what constitutes proper subjects of study at a Catholic university.

Although Jones discusses stopping at the moment of perception in the context of the visual arts, the idea is also a hallmark of queer pedagogy, which in this essay we define as "a radical form of educative praxis implemented deliberately to interfere with, to intervene in, the production of 'normalcy' in schooled subjects" (Bryson and de Castell 285). This definition is broader than the idea of queer pedagogy as specific practices used to teach queer content, but deliberately narrower than a definition that would include any nontraditional educative practice.

This definition also embodies two other important characteristics. First, it allows an understanding of "schooled subjects" as both specific disciplinary knowledges and as individuals participating in educational systems. Second, in its use of the term "normalcy," it underscores the importance of understanding "queer" as a site-specific and process-based term. What constitutes interference or intervention in one context may very well represent complicity or normalcy in another. The strategy, thus, of holding schooled subjects at the moment between perception and interpretation or action, as a means of interfering with or intervening in the re/production of what is normal, accepted, stable, or proper, is a strategy that is, itself, unpredictable, processual, and context-specific.

In this essay, we analyze the pedagogy and praxis of queering the specific gender landscape of an urban, Catholic university campus through 12 years of international juried fine arts exhibitions co-curated by Women's and Gender Studies faculty. Past exhibition themes have included (re)visioning gender, embodiment, gender politics, gendered space/s, masculinities and feminism, and (trans)itions. These campus interventions have combined the use of visual arts, poetry, performance, environmental installation, interdisciplinary lectures, and course work to interrogate gender and sexuality as socially constructed, relational categories, and to deconstruct binary models of identity in academic space.

In our analysis, we utilize both social science and humanities frameworks of "queering" to examine intersections between art works, binaries, pedagogies, and academic and religious discourses. Drawing on Amelia Jones's concept of identification and interpretation in art and visual culture as a "queer feminist durational" process, we discuss the pedagogical and political implications of engaging students, faculty, and staff in self-reflexive interactions with queering images, texts, and spaces (i). Finally, we address both the potential and limitations of using the curatorial space of the exhibitions to engender change as well as reflection.

Each of the sections that follows takes as its starting point one of the categorical binaries we posit have been queered on our campus by the intersections of art, artists, audiences, and space occasioned by our six biennial WGS art exhibitions. Although each section references particular works of art, we do not mean to imply these works are the only pieces relevant to the discussions in each section. Rather, we see them as moments in an ongoing interrogation that transverses the 12 years the shows have been intervening in campus conversations about gender, sexuality, identity, and meaning.

Margin/Center

A biennial is an exhibition of contemporary art occurring every two years. Biennials redefine the boundaries of contemporary art as they shift between "multiple works, multiple worlds, and multiple audiences" (Gioni 176). According to visual art theorists such as Chin-Tao Wu, to understand the power implications of biennials it is necessary to look at the representation of artists from varied social locations. Since our first biennial, *[re]:GENDER: through the eyes of women*, in 2004, we have exhibited 85 artists from three countries, 20 US states, and the District of Columbia. The exhibitions are free and open to the public. This exposure to a diversity of feminist artistic perspectives has engaged not only students but also faculty, staff, and administrators with artistic re/productions of gender discourses. Consistent with feminist and queer praxes, such self-reflections and campus-wide interactions are intended to encourage biennial visitors to "see difference" as they view the exhibitions and to examine critically the multiple intersections among gender, race, class, and sexualities as they return to their respective academic areas.

The primary location of the biennials has been an exhibition space in the School of Architecture building, a place that many students rarely, if ever, experience. The very entrance into this unfamiliar world of visual and environmental interventions is "queer" to them and sets up a condition of nervous expectation as they encounter the exhibitions. Many visitors attend the opening receptions, thereby protecting themselves through participation in the normalcy of a campus event, accompanied by familiar friends and colleagues. However, as people wander through the gallery and read the artist statements placed prominently beside each work, they discuss their reactions with others, raise questions, or engage the artists themselves in conversation. For example, at the *Gender Politics* opening reception, several students noted with apparent surprise that one of the participating artists was a Sister of Mercy. We have adopted the curatorial policy that each artist is accepted based on his or her expressed critical feminist position as much as on the aesthetic quality of his or her art work. Previously marginalized on a campus with no art department, the artists in the exhibition are now at the center—as is the gender theme of the biennial, such as embodiment, masculinities, or gendered spaces.

As multiple audiences enter the exhibitions, they encounter not only the world of the artists but also must "attend to affect, sensation, unprocessed data, and collective identity[ies]" (C. Jones 198). The WGS biennials, in this sense, have served to deconstruct the binary of margin/center as the exhibitions foreground the intersectionality of gender, race, class, sexuality, ethnicity, age, and status.

In the 2012 biennial *behind the mask: Women, Men & Masculinities*, textile artist Bren Ahearn presented a series of framed cross-stitched mottos that evoke familiar wall decorations in many households. Yet his embroidered sayings also elicit uncomfortable reminiscences of childhood as viewers identify with the gender constraints he dealt with growing up, such as "When Daddy dresses me in my blue uniform, I become a man" and "When I refuse to fight, I am called a pussy" (Fig. 5.3). When students approached his oversized sampler stitched with the saying "I guess the flowered lunchbox was the wrong choice" and slowly realized that the petals of the flowered pattern are formed out of footballs, they may have vicariously experienced the dialectical tension at play when non-gender-conforming or gay people are marginalized by their peers (Fig. 5.4). Although there is an active Gay-Straight Alliance student organization on our Catholic campus, many students and faculty still are not comfortable discussing, much less disclosing, queer sexual orientations. Including Ahearn's work in the exhibition provided a safe opportunity for both identification and disidentification with the childhood socialization of American men—whether gay or straight.

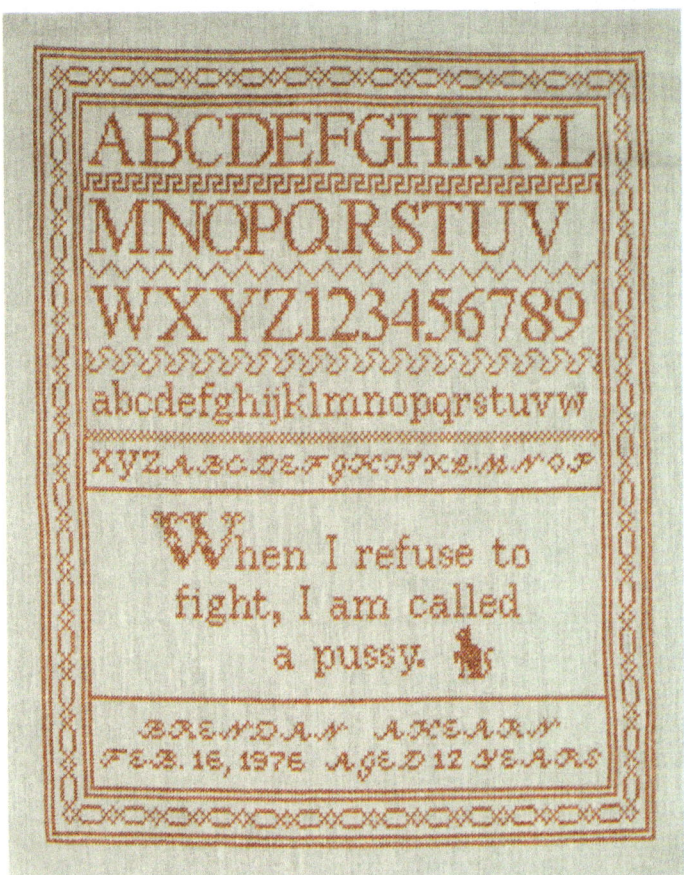

Fig. 5.3 *Sampler 1*, cotton, 19.75" × 15.5" © Bren Ahearn (Photo: Allison Tungseth)

Another significantly marginalized population on our campus is university women with young children. In the 2006 exhibition *Embodiment: gender + culture + action,* architect Danielle Hermann revised the decades-old anthropometric standards still used by environmental designers today. In a series of investigative images titled *BIGwomen,* her graphics reveal the continuing marginalization of a constant and rapidly changing pregnant female body (Fig. 5.5). All elements of these images, from their aerial view and strong colors, to their use of biometrics and incorporation of buttocks

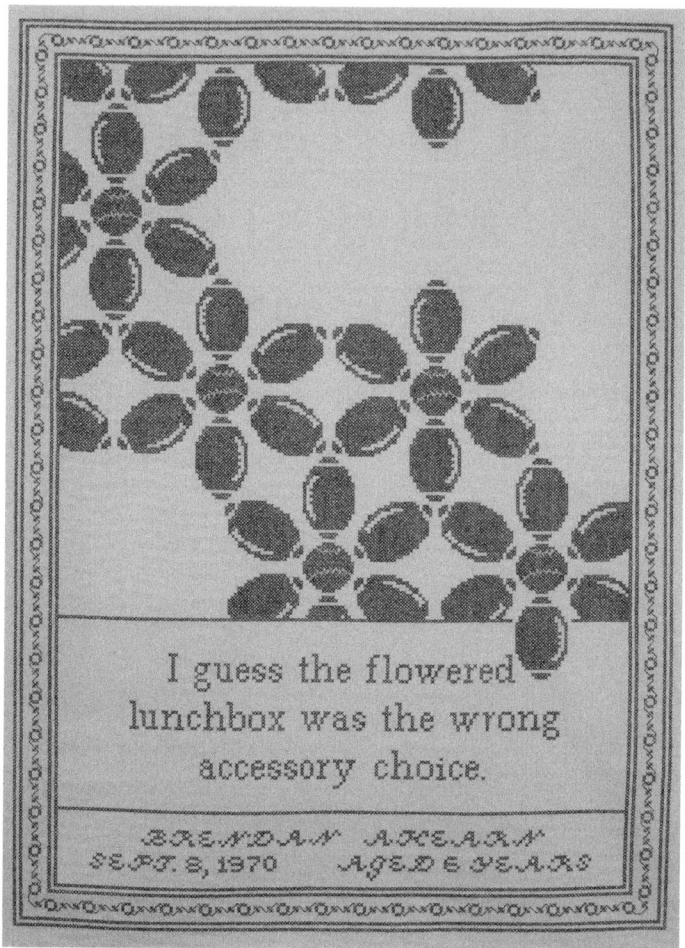

Fig. 5.4 *Sampler 9*, cotton, 88" × 60" © Bren Ahearn (Photo: Kiny McCarrick)

and breasts, as well as swelling belly, stand in stark contrast to the most common depictions of pregnant women on our once all-male campus: the expectant Madonna.[1]

Pregnancy, child care, and family leave policies remained largely unaddressed in 2010. Therefore, the curators of the biennial exhibition on *Gendered Space/s* invited UDM professor and social ethicist Dr. Gloria

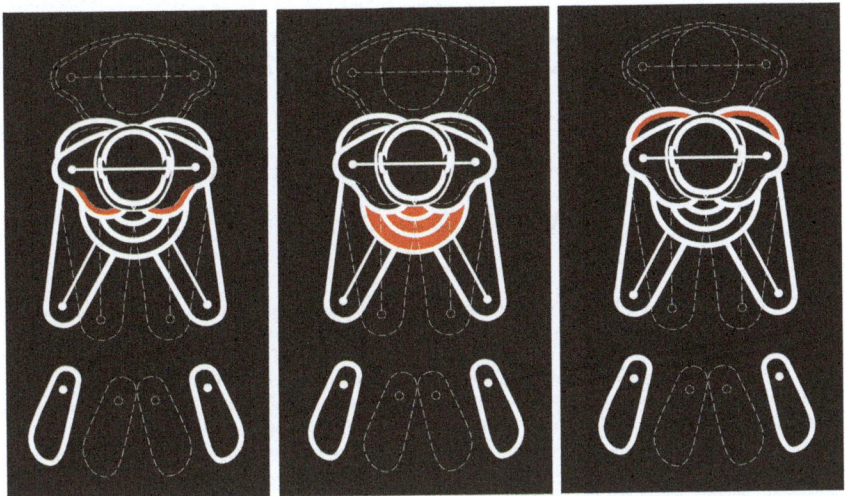

Fig. 5.5 *BIGwomen, Plans 1(boobs), 2(belly), 3(butt),* prints, each 4' × 8'
© Danielle Hermann

Albrecht and UDM administrator and community activist Donzetta Jones to help author a parody of the July 4, 1876, *Declaration and Protest of the Women of the United States by the National Women's Suffrage Association.* As an attempt to bring to the center our need for campus child care for both women and men, the installation titled *Declaration of Rights, 2010,* was a facsimile of the 1876 declaration, with the goal of drawing the attention of exhibition visitors to the needs of families. Although tongue-in-cheek, this gender praxis project was accompanied by a serious call to action: "If you are interested in supporting UDM students and employees who are seeking a gendered space on campus for nursing mothers and for family-centered child care, please sign the accompanying petition" (Fig. 5.6). Sixty-eight individuals signed the petition to support discussions of family policy with the university administration. The simultaneous repositioning of marginalized disciplines, politics, and peoples within the academic space of the campus both interfered with and intervened in the production of "normalcy" in these "schooled subjects."

DECLARATION AND PROTEST

OF THE

WOMEN OF THE UNIVERSITY

BY THE

WOMENS & GENDER STUDIES PROGRAM.

APRIL 6th, 2010.

While the University is buoyant with social justice, and all hearts are attuned to praise, it is with sorrow we come to strike the one discordant note, on this fourth anniversary of the Women's and Gender Studies Biennial Juried Art Exhibition.   When subjects of University Trustees, Presidents, and Deans, from the Academic World, join in our Gendered Space/s Jubilee, shall the women and men of the University refuse to lay their hands with benedictions on our campus?   Surveying the University of Detroit Mercy, surpassing in magnificence those of London, Paris, and Vienna, shall we not rejoice at the success of the youngest rival among women's studies programs?   May not our hearts, in unison with all, swell with pride at our great achievements as a University; our academic research, teaching, and service, and the rapid progress we have made in the law, dental, and health professions, libraries, liberal arts and education, business administration, engineering and science, architecture and the inventive arts?   And we do rejoice, in the success thus far, of our experiment of self-governance, the McNichols Faculty Assembly.   Our faith is firm and unwavering in the broad principles of the University, proclaimed in 1877, not only as abstract truths, but as the corner stones of a Jesuit and Mercy institution.   Yet, we cannot forget, even in this glad hour, that while all people of every race, and religion, and condition, have been invested with the full rights of membership, under our hospitable banner, all mothers and fathers of infants and children still suffer the degradation of the unavailability of campus child care and insufficient family leave.

Our history, the past 133 years, has been a series of assumptions and denials of the needs of families, in direct opposition to the principles of social justice, acknowledged by the University of Detroit Mercy at its foundation, which are:

First. The natural rights of each individual to a family.
Second. The exact equality of these rights for all male and female employees and students.
Third. That these rights include campus child care.
Fourth. That no person can ethically or morally ignore the needs of others.
Fifth. That the non-use of these rights does not destroy them.
And for the violation of these fundamental principles of our University, we arraign our leaders on this 6th day of April, 2010, -- and these are our
ARTICLES OF CAMPUS CHILD CARE.

Fig. 5.6   *Declaration of Rights, 2010*, photocopy, 11" × 14" © Libby Balter Blume

SUBJECT/OBJECT

As students, staff, faculty, and administrators have encountered gender images in the works of participating artists, they have experienced what Amelia Jones refers to as *queer feminist durationality:* "a potential, an idea.... it indicates the potential for doing something with artworks through interpretation" (174).

At the heart of Jones's concept of queer feminist durationality is a foregrounding of the temporal and processual nature of identity and meaning. Identity and interpretation both are recast as intersubjective processes of identification and disidentification. This strategy of interpretation draws on feminism's long history of "expos[ing] the circuits of meaning-making as inexorably productive of and supported by structures of power." It "queers" this feminist practice, however, by insisting on the provisional, relational, and incomplete nature of all meaning-making. "[I]n this context," Jones posits, "queer is that which by definition troubles the idea that we can know what we see and installs durationality, and its corollary qualities of undecidability and unknowability, at the heart of meaning. We could even argue that *queer is that which indicates the impossibility of a subject or meaning staying still*, in one determinable place" (174-5, emphasis in original). Jones notes the similarity between this definition of queer and Monique Wittig's association of queer with the insertion of "the diachronism of history into the fixed discourse of eternal essences" (qtd. 175). Importantly, Jones follows in the path of other theorists who refuse the full abstraction of the term queer. Queer, she reiterates, is always attached to particular bodies, sexual practices, and individuals. The queer of queer feminist durationality becomes "the potential of bodies, images, texts, performances in the visual field to unsettle by opening out the durationality of our desiring relationship to particular aspects of the world" (175).

It is this subversion of static identities and meanings and opening up of relationships that the Women's and Gender Studies biennials have attempted to activate in our attendees over the past 12 years. In this regard, we conceptualize the curator's responsibility to believe in the potential for positive transformation of audiences through aesthetic experiences (Zolghadr 279). Furthermore, questioning the conventional subject/object relationships of artist, work, and viewer involves re-imagining a reciprocal interaction among these three elements and leads to the possibility of queering gender.

In queer feminist durationality, audience members are active participants, recognizing gender not only in the cultural context of immediate apperception but also with respect to their own past experiences. This contemporary understanding of art includes participation as "relational aesthetics," which historian and curator Nicolas Bourriaud defines as "a set of artistic practices that take as their theoretical and practical point of departure the whole of human relations and their social context, rather than an independent and private space" (qtd. in Dumbadze and Hudson 202).

For example, in the 2012 *behind the mask: Women, Men & Masculinities* biennial, new media artist Vagner Whitehead queered the binary of subject/object with a video loop titled *Tango*, consisting of images of a solo male dancer digitally manipulated to appear as animated line drawings on the screen: "a dancer mirrored, reflected and refracted in varied configurations, to the point where its referent turns into abstracted patterns" (Fig. 5.7). Whitehead further explained, "The inspiration for this piece came about after I completed an artist residency in Argentina in Summer 2010, where many things unseen and untold kept tugging at my heart. Loneliness, melancholia, disconnection, and the reaching out to an other, aspects of my daily routine there, turned into longing upon my return." In the context of the University's vast exhibition space, the intimate personal display afforded viewers a private moment to experience the dancer/subject morphing into pattern/object and back again, and thus to consider the relational aesthetics of dance and performance.

In the same show, students encountered multi-media artist Owen Eric Wood in the gallery space sitting almost naked—wrapped in clear plastic from head to toe—cutting out paper dolls and clothes in view of his video titled *Clothes Make the Man* (Figs. 5.8 and 5.9). Obviously confused by the act of a subject *becoming* the object, they looked from the video to the

Fig. 5.7 *Tango,* single channel video, 17:21, still image © Vagner M. Whitehead

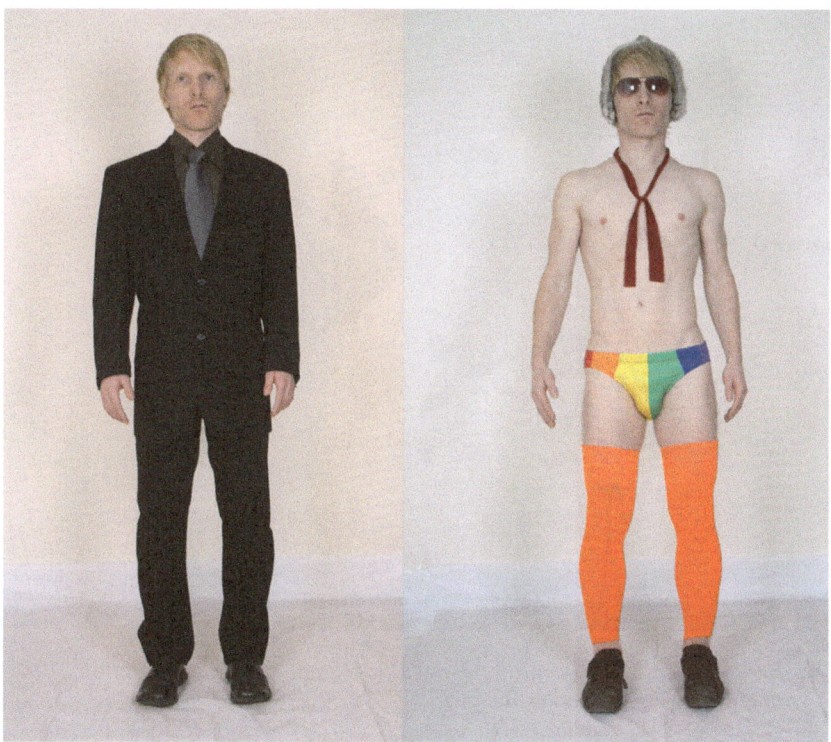

Fig. 5.8 *Clothes Make the Man*, video, 3:50, still image © Owen Eric Wood

artist and back again, talking to each other, and became involved in queering gender at a social relational level.

Also exploring the relational aesthetics of subject/object, an environmental installation by Alana Bartol was created during the opening reception of the 2006 biennial *Embodiment: gender + culture + action*. While students alternately watched Bartol's performance and looked at other works in the exhibition, the artist, dressed in a business suit, repeatedly applied red lipstick and kissed a prepared white wall, applying and reapplying lipstick marks in rows that were uniform, controlled, and precise (Fig. 5.10). Her artist statement read, "[In my performances] I attempt to sensitize viewers to an aesthetic that blurs the distinctions, that thins the borders, between the natural and the artificial, the self and the other."

Fig. 5.9 *Clothes Make the Man*, Owen Eric Wood, Opening Reception, 2012
© Women's & Gender Studies Biennial

In the essay "Imagining Otherwise: Performance Art as Queer Time and Space," cultural critic Cristyn Davies claims that performance art not only contests traditional theater, but also challenges our understandings of normative subjects. By allowing viewers to see her work being performed, Bartol implicated the audience in its creation. According to visual arts theorists Liam Gillick and Maria Lind, participation "not only reexamines the relationship between the 'viewer and the work' but also focuses on art that intentionally attempts to encourage or provoke varied levels of participation" (204). With this queer pedagogical goal in mind, we incorporated a poetry reading into the opening night activities of the WGS biennial in 2012. Steven Sherrill, whose paintings were exhibited in the show, is a published poet and professor of creative writing. He read from his book of poems titled *Ersatz Anatomy* (Fig. 5.11). A question and answer period followed his reading, attended by community members, students, faculty, and staff, in which Sherrill candidly revealed the

Fig. 5.10 *Dressage: 7,437 Kisses*, Alana Bartol, performance, 2006 © Women's & Gender Studies Biennial

permeability of his intersecting identities as poet, artist, musician, and teacher. One student asked the artist, for example, if the images in the paintings were memories of his own childhood. The audience was challenged to deconstruct the binary opposition of subject/object as they questioned the mutuality of relationships among Sherrill's painting, poetry, pedagogy, and creative processes. This opposition was further challenged when audience members turned the discussion to their own artistic processes and mediums, reframing Sherrill's reading as a conversation among peers, and their own role from that of consumers to producers.

Further interrogating the subject/object binary on campus, Sherrill gave a guest-lecture and second reading to a poetry class taught by Women's and Gender Studies faculty member Dr. Claire Crabtree. For the past decade, she has brought her creative writing students to the WGS

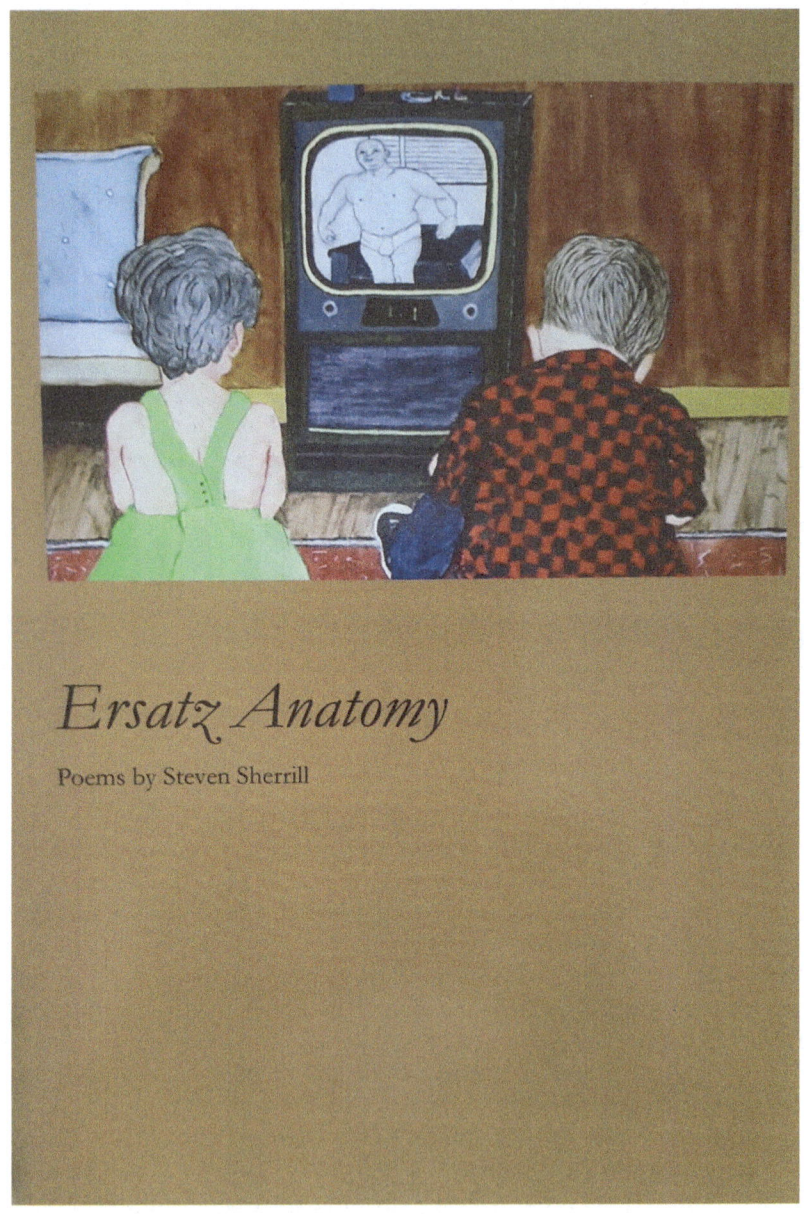

Fig. 5.11 *Ersatz Anatomy Cover Painting*, oil on cardboard, 14" × 18"
© K. Steven Sherrill

biennials and required that they write poems about their experience of the exhibitions. Held at the moment of perception by a process that is simultaneously participatory, reflective, and generative, these students utilized their personal reactions to queering works of art as the raw material of their own artistic productions. They thus oscillated between the positions of viewer, work, and artist in ways that undermined clear distinctions between subject and object, and "normal" pedagogical hierarchies of expertise and knowledge.

FLUID/STABLE

Queer theorist Eve Sedgwick has noted that "queer" can refer to "the open mesh of possibilities, gaps, overlaps, dissonances and resonances, lapses and excesses of meaning when the constituent elements of anyone's gender, of anyone's sexuality aren't made (or *can't* be made) to signify monolithically" (qtd. in A. Jones 176, emphasis in original). This resistance to stability, prominent in other understandings of queerness, such as Judith Butler's concept of performativity, has been reflected in works by a number of artists in the Women and Gender Studies biennials. In the 2012 biennial, for example, openly gay artist Owen Wood, whose gender performance was previously described, exhibited a second video titled *Made Up*. In this film, his facial features were transformed (off-camera) from male to female by a professional make-up artist, revealed on the screen by time-lapse photography (Fig. 5.12). The voice-over of the artist commenting on "acting gay" only added to the impact of drag. Wood's artist statement explained, "This controversial position is common on gay chat sites, where it is acceptable for men to state they are masculine and that they expect others to be the same." In the exhibition, many viewers of the video loop averted their gaze or moved away, appearing to be uncomfortable with the artist's enactment of overt gender fluidity in tension with his nuanced and ambiguous references to sexual orientation.

In many ways, similar tensions were also elicited by Molly Nuzzo's paintings, described earlier. Most of the gender confusion students shared when asking whether the subject of each painting was male or female likely represented their discomfort or lack of familiarity with transgender identities. As a challenge to the audience, the curators deliberately paired Nuzzo's two paintings to destabilize gender by reading male and female identities as fluid. Although the portraits were clearly titled *Noah* and *Cristy*, many viewers seemed resistant to the idea that a man would adopt

Fig. 5.12 *Made Up*, video, 4:20 © Owen Eric Wood

a classically feminine pose or that a woman would assume a typical masculine posture.

According to poststructural feminist theory:

> Transgender explodes the notion that male and female are discrete categories. Transgender people change sex or inhabit third (or multiple) sex, androgynous, or fluid identities…. Poststructuralist accounts can, however, entail denial of bodily limitations, erase transgender people's subjective experience, and overlook social and political factors, such as the importance of gender categories as a basis for identity politics. (Monro 3)

In 2008, painter Joyce Polance depicted, in *Coup*, a strong woman who has a "skirt" made of penises (Fig. 5.13). Accepted for the biennial exhibition on *Gender Politics*, this queer image transcends normalcy, focusing not so much on the binary of sexual difference as the fluid potential in all humans to become the "other." In her artist's statement, Polance explained that the woman growing her own penises "explores how women can take ownership of the assertive/aggressive energy often needed for political success without compromising their femininity and identities as women."

Polance's image undermines the hierarchizing, fetishizing gaze not simply by reversing it, but by sending it careening through shifting

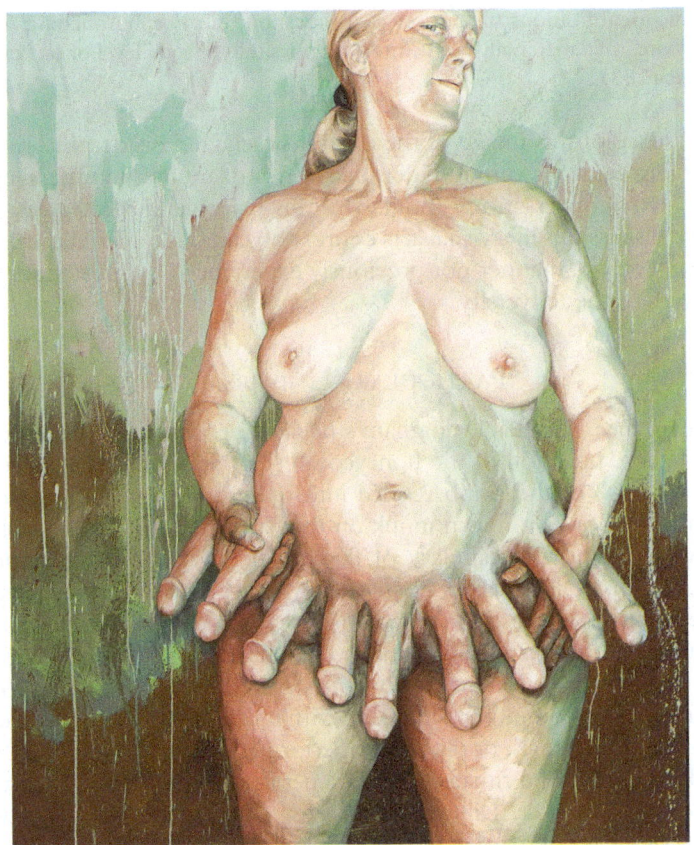

Fig. 5.13   *Coup,* oil on canvas, 40" × 30" © Joyce Polance Particular/Universal

refractions of sexual, gendered, corporeal, and visual power. Although not an image of female genitalia per se, the shock of Polance's painting to many of its viewers (mostly its male viewers) recalls Amelia Jones's description of the impact of some feminist cunt images:

> By enacting this kind of radical relationship in visual arts contexts, or at least offering the possibility of opening circuits of identification and disidentification, certain kinds of performances and representations of the female sex have the potential of affecting the bodies of viewers in a visceral (or perhaps more aptly vulvar?) manner, not necessarily or inherently tied to the anatomical or

psychic identifications of the viewer in question, but deeply touching us at the "core" of a materially constituted yet physically shaped level of our experience. (183)

The presence of this image in the exhibition elicited disidentification and revulsion in some viewers and identification and laughter in others, engendering many conversations about why this painting was selected. These reflexive discussions in a visual arts context on campus queered the campus environment in a manner not previously experienced by most students or employees of the university.

Particular/Universal

From a distance, Amanda Dillingham's *Blossoming Bodies* immediately evokes the geometric precision of the honeycomb (Fig. 5.14). Moving closer, the uniform "cells" of the comb resolve into unique, delicate sketches of red flowers. Each flower is drawn in ink on the flat, white surface of a communion wafer. Using a vocabulary of flowers, beeswax, honey, communion wafers, and ink, Dillingham's densely symbolic piece explores intersections between female body disciplines and imagery, the social organization of bees, and purification rituals in the Catholic church. Each of these, she writes in her artist's statement for the 2006 *Embodiment: gender + culture + action* biennial, "share a common relationship with intake and production" and the "common use of rituals, or repeatedly performed behaviors."

Both instinctive and ritualistic acts are performed according to prescribed orders. Here, however, Dillingham as artist determines the order and the meaning of the act of making and viewing her work: "*Blossoming Bodies* references ritual, but it was also created through a ritualistic act. The actual task of creating as well as the act of viewing each gives time for meditation. The artwork serves as both an object of engagement for the audience, and at the same time, evidence of my own ritualistic process of art making."

Golden Maze, East, Jane Lackey's mixed media depiction of the 2007 protest march by Burmese monks, nuns, activists, and students on the streets of Rangoon, also recasts the relations of time, the universal, and the particular (Fig. 5.15). Using tape, stickers, thread, and paint on kozo paper, Lackey "map[s] aspects of the imagined and actual space of this march, its coordination and protection in the midst of extreme suppression and opposition." A part of the 2010 *Gendered Space/s* biennial, both the materials and subject matter of *Golden Maze, East* emphasize "short-lived connections." Tape, stickers, and thread "are easily adhered and

Fig. 5.14 *Blossoming Bodies (detail)*, communion wafers and ink, 4' × 4' × 1"
© Amanda Dillingham

released as they mark direction, interaction and place." Lackey's mapping of real and imagined convergences of religious and political, militaristic, and economic actors during the protest march literally relocates the spiritual within the secular and the particular: Rangoon, Burma, 2007, and Detroit, Michigan, USA, 2010.

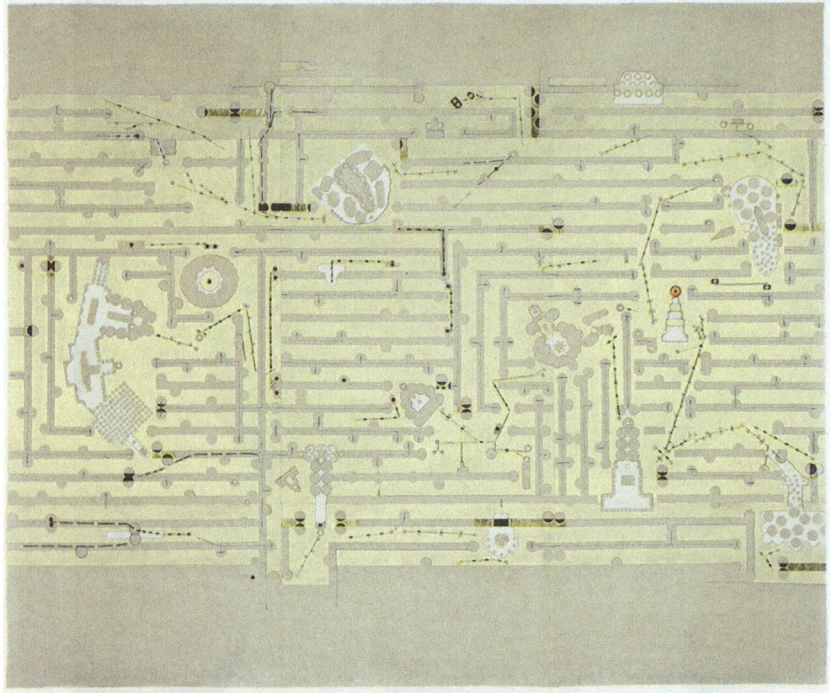

Fig. 5.15 *Golden Maze, East,* tape, stickers, thread, paint on paper, 45" × 54" © Jane Lackey (Photo: Tim Thayer)

Art works such as *Blossoming Bodies* and *Golden Maze, East* call specific attention to their makers and processes of production and more generally interrogate the processes by which gender, sexual, and religious meanings are produced. In emphasizing the durational, they "queer" these processes, bringing Wittig's "diachronism of history into the fixed discourse of eternal essences" and "linking the interpreting body of the present with the bodies referenced or performed in the past as a work of art" (A. Jones 174). On a Catholic campus, the introduction of the durational (and thus the processual, relational, and provisional) into issues of identity and meaning can have intense and unpredictable implications. Temporality in all its manifestations challenges notions of the knowable eternal and destabilizes the boundaries between the particular and the universal.

Today, the instability of the boundary between the binary particular/ universal is at the heart of a number of gender and sexual controversies dividing Catholic communities around the globe. These range from the church's doctrinal positions on contraception, homosexuality, and the ordination of women, to its cover-up of the sexual abuse of minors by Catholic priests and reprimands of Catholic nuns in the United States for promoting "radical feminist themes incompatible with the Catholic faith" (Congregation for the Doctrine of Faith 3).

It is the nature of that faith—whether it stems from fixed discourses of universal, eternal, knowable essences, or whether it partakes in and evolves over the particularities and vagaries of historical, human time—that is in question. To recast Catholic identity and religious meaning, too, as processes of identification and interpretation that are durational, relational, and never fully realized is liberating to some, anxiety-provoking for others, and, to still others, sacrilegious.

The WGS biennial exhibitions of art works that interrogate gender and sexuality as socially constructed, relational categories can be seen as part of this complex process of identification and interpretation. They are our deliberate attempts to interfere with and to intervene in the production of what is considered normal and universal on our campus.

SELF/OTHER

The Women's and Gender Studies Program's intention is that our biennial art exhibitions enact queer forms of pedagogy in both senses of the term— queer as attributed to specific bodies, practices, and subjects and queer as that which indicates the impossibility of *any* subject or meaning staying still. To what extent our choice to utilize the curatorial space of the exhibitions as a locus of queer pedagogy and to engender change as well as reflection has succeeded, however, is something that also needs analysis.

A number of factors would seem to undermine the biennials' ability genuinely to queer the gender landscape of UDM. First is the episodic nature of the exhibitions. It is unlikely students would attend more than two biennials over the course of their four- to five-year education at UDM. Second is the Women's and Gender Studies Program's sponsorship of the shows, which risks creating a limiting perception that these exhibitions, works of arts, and issues are relevant only to women or to the discipline of women's or gender studies. Similarly, the artistic focus of the shows risks creating a form of aesthetic containment of the works and ideas within them. We experienced this type of containment when we attempted to publicize our 2012 biennial on campus using Steven Sherrill's painting, *What I Did Last Summer*, as the background of our publicity poster (Fig. 5.16). The woman's exposed breast, while deemed acceptable within the context of an art exhibit, was considered an inappropriate image to display on posting walls in the university at large. Factors such as these push to reestablish normative boundaries between margin/center, subject/object, fluid/stable, universal/particular, self/other, and aesthetic/academic.

At the same time, however, as in all binary relations, the inherent instability of these boundaries can and has worked in support of our goals. To begin with, normative forces can be utilized in the service of queer agendas. Responding to the assertion that the female breast was an inappropriate image, we created another version of the poster that put a black

Fig. 5.16 *What I Did Last Summer*, oil on cardboard, 14" × 16" © K. Steven Sherrill

censorship bar—readily associated with pornographic images—over the woman's exposed nipple (Fig. 5.17). The incongruous juxtaposition of the older (read, therefore, "asexual") woman and the black "obscenity" stripe made the poster even more provocative and attention-catching, drawing visitors curious about the uncensored image to the exhibition.

The visual emphasis of the exhibitions also speaks directly to their potential for deconstructing binary models of gender, sexuality, identity, and meaning in academic space. Identity and interpretation, Amelia Jones writes, are distinctly visual phenomena. The "key structure of belief about how people [in Western cultures] identify" rests on the simultaneous conviction "that people 'appear' a certain way, can be visually identified and thus given meaning or positioned in the social order, and yet, that this meaning can at any moment betray the 'truth' of an internal, authentic identity" (A. Jones xvii-iii). With paintings, photos, drawings, sculptures, videos, installations, and performances that provide counter-stereotypical images

Fig. 5.17 *behind the mask: Women, Men & Masculinities*, poster, 11" × 14" © Women's & Gender Studies Biennial (Graphic design: Libby Balter Blume)

and evoke queer feminist durational interpretive experiences in their viewers, the exhibitions are queering the key structure of Western beliefs about
identity, self, and other.

Moreover, the academic, religious, economic, racial, sexual, political,
and ideological heterogeneity of the University of Detroit Mercy complicates any notion of "change" or "containment" in rich and challenging
ways. In the pages of our campus newspaper, students argue vociferously
over how central a role of religion should play in their education. The
development of an Islamic Studies program in our Religious Studies
department delights some and baffles others. External parties like the
Cardinal Newman Society denounce the existence of our Gay-Straight
Alliance student organization or our biennial productions of Eve Ensler's
play *The Vagina Monologues*.[2] Their fierce condemnation of UDM's "failure" to uphold Catholic teachings finds a sympathetic ear among some of
our students, faculty, employees, and alumni, but is rejected and criticized
by others.

Aesthetic/Academic

Simplistic binary oppositions of academic/religious, feminist/dogmatic,
or queer/Catholic fail to address the complex, fluid, and permeable nature
of these categories in the lived experience of individual members of our
community. A significant number of students, faculty, and staff experience
the exhibitions as forms of *confirmation* of their already "queered" beliefs
and identities or leave both surprised and pleased that the regular exhibition of such work is institutionally recognized as art and as constituting a
proper subject of study at a Catholic university. A male, Muslim WGS
student brings his friends to view the shows as his own intervention into
UDM's gendered landscape. A Sisters of Mercy faculty member raises
thoughtful, challenging questions about the role of spirituality in queer
scholarship. A physics professor regularly offers his students extra credit
for attending and responding to the exhibitions. Other faculty members
bring students from literature, writing, religious studies, philosophy, history, architecture, digital media studies, and psychology courses to view
and engage with the art works. The instructors report back to us on the
heated debates over gender, sexuality, academia, obscenity, aesthetics, and
religion that subsequently take place in their classrooms. Our 2012 biennial was co-curated and co-exhibited by faculty from the University of
Windsor in Canada, adding national borders to the boundaries destabilized

by the exhibitions.[3] Our 2014 biennial was co-curated and co-exhibited by faculty from Lawrence Technology University and exhibited in a gallery space in downtown Detroit, Michigan.[4] In these ways, we see the impact of the biennials moving beyond the walls of singular exhibition spaces and into the larger university, as well as other academic and civic communities.

In these examples, we also see enacted queer pedagogy as "a radical form of educative praxis implemented deliberately to interfere with, to intervene in, the production of 'normalcy'" (Bryson and de Castell 285). For our 2014 biennial *TRANS*, we used this praxis as the organizing framework of the exhibition, using feminist aesthetic works and practices to queer academic identity constructs and conventions.

TRANS explored the theme of "transitions" and highlighted transdisciplinary feminist art that deconstructed such binaries as movement/stasis, academic/activist, closeting/outing, male/female, marriage/divorce, life/death, thinking/doing, and being/becoming. The exhibition was co-sponsored by the School of Architecture and Design at Lawrence Technological University and featured a residency by two faculty members from Texas Tech University: Elizabeth Sharp, Associate Professor of Human Development/Family Studies and Women's Studies, and Genevieve Durham DeCesaro, Associate Professor and Chair of Theatre and Dance. Sharp and DeCesaro are collaborators on a feminist research project that re-presents qualitative social science datasets on women's negotiations of singlehood, marriage, and motherhood as choreographed performance. As they explained in their artists' statement, the performance, entitled *Ordinary Wars*, "fore-grounds liminality and troubles cultural expectations of women by using dance and theater to spotlight tensions of 'being' (single) versus 'becoming' (a wife)" inviting audience members to "experience the movement, both physically and metaphorically."

TRANS combined a gallery exhibition of feminist photography, video, sculpture, and mixed media; an artist symposium; and a theatrical performance of *Ordinary Wars* (see Fig. 5.18) with a guest talk by Sharp for students on the socio-historical context of marriages and weddings and a campus-wide scholarly symposium on transdisciplinary research. In her talk to multiple classes, Sharp presented her qualitative research on marriage and weddings as topics of co-investigation for her, the students, and their instructors. The students, recast as collaborative researchers of contemporary gender and sexual norms, dominated the conversation. This generated a far-ranging discussion of sexual and gender norms, marriage equality,

Fig. 5.18 *Ordinary Wars*, poster, 11" × 17" © Flatlands Dance Theatre (Graphic design: Keren Weaver Design, Inc.)

Catholic identity, feminism, and media representation. Similarly, in the transdisciplinary symposium, Sharp and DeCesaro used their collaborative feminist research to interrogate more generally the definition of "transdisciplinary," the relationship of the arts and sciences, the borrowing of analytic tools between disciplines, and the ethical dilemmas involved in the aesthetic reproduction of the words and experiences of living subjects.

In their entirety, the events of the *TRANS* biennial drew artists together with students, faculty, and administrators from two campuses into site-specific and self-reflexive interrogations of their academic as well as sexual and gender identities. Thus, rather than creating a limiting perception that the biennial was relevant only to women or to the discipline of women's or gender studies—or that the artistic focus of the show created a form of aesthetic containment of the works and ideas within it—*TRANS* utilized artistic explorations of gender and sexuality to call into question fundamental academic identity constructs such as "discipline," "research," "expertise," and "knowledge." This reversal of conventional context and content relations interfered with and intervened in the production of "normalcy" in a multitude of schooled subjects.

CONCLUSION

Eve Sedgwick asks in her essay "Queer and Now," "What if instead there were a practice of valuing the ways in which meanings and institutions can be at loose ends with each other? What if the richest junctures weren't the ones where *everything means the same thing*?" (6, emphasis in original). The biennial art shows serve as both junctures and a form of practice in valuing the generative ways in which different elements in our university are at loose ends with each other.

In this way, we see the biennials as opening new territories in the pedagogical and ideological landscapes of our institution by establishing new precedents of what constitutes proper subjects of study at our Catholic university. These new territories remain open after the biennials themselves have closed, becoming the clearings in which students, faculty, staff, and community members continue to engage in self-reflexive interactions with queering images, texts, and spaces. In the same year as our *behind the mask: Women, Men & Masculinities* biennial, for example, WGS, the Religious Studies and English Departments, and the student Gay-Straight Alliance co-sponsored a reading by lesbian author Kelly Barth. The reading was advertised to the UDM community as a celebration of LGBT History Month and National Coming Out Day.

Barth's memoir, *My Almost Certainly Real Imaginary Jesus*, traces her journey from the fear-driven fundamentalism of her childhood to the transformed spirituality and happy marriage to her female partner of her adult life. Her discussion of complex intersections of religion, faith, Christianity, authorship, love, sexuality, and queer identity held all her audience members at a moment of perception, asking them to reflect on the intersections and contradictions of their religious and sexual identities. After the highly successful talk, one student remarked that he was both surprised and unsurprised that an event like this was held on our campus. Surprised, because of the queer and religious subject matter; unsurprised, because he had been to the biennial earlier in the year and knew our reputation for sponsoring such events. Almost immediately after, a top administrator remarked how valuable it was that our university *was* seen by students as a place where such events took place. Over the last twelve years, the self-image of our institution has become overlaid, like a palimpsest, by the images and after images of the biennials.

We return to our chapter's opening images for a final reflection. In her artist statement accompanying the portraits *Noah* and *Cristy*, Nuzzo wrote:

> My continual interest in painting queer subjects, or queer bodies, is sparked and sustained by my own experiences and relationships with others whose identities fall outside these social norms. I view my representations of transgender bodies not simply as appropriations of the physical body of trans sexual subjects, but as honest and relatable portraits of people in my community.

As visitors to the exhibition stood in front of Nuzzo's paintings—held in the moment of perception, brought deliberately into awareness of identity as a process of identification and disidentification—would any viewer unfamiliar with Nuzzo's community have seen them newly, even temporarily, as *relatable* portraits, thus suggesting change as well as reflection? Are the students, faculty, staff, and administrators on our campus merely vicarious observers, or are they participants in queering gender and academia? We have found that our audience members cannot help but participate agentically in the cultural discourse surrounding works of art as they react, discuss, question—and even dismiss or reject—the gender images before them, both in and outside the gallery walls. In so doing, they queer the gender landscape of our urban, Catholic university campus.

APPENDIX: CURATORS

[re]:GENDER: through the eyes of women, 2004
Curators, Julie Ju-Youn Kim and Libby Balter Blume
Embodiment: gender + culture + action, 2006
Curators, Amy Green Deines and Libby Balter Blume
Gender Politics, 2008
Curators, Amy Green Deines and Libby Balter Blume
Gendered Space/s, 2010
Curators, Libby Balter Blume and Allegra Pitera
behind the mask: Women, Men & Masculinities, 2012
Curators, Libby Balter Blume, Allegra Pitera, and Veronika Mogyorody
TRANS, 2014
Curators, Peter Beaugard, Libby Balter Blume, and Allegra Pitera

NOTES

1. The University of Detroit, founded in 1877 by the Society of Jesus, was an all-male school until the 1970s, when female students began being admitted. The presence of women on campus was again increased with the 1990 consolidation of the University of Detroit and Mercy College, founded by the Sisters of Mercy of the Americas, creating the University of Detroit Mercy. Negotiations of the gender hierarchies occasioned by the consolidation continue to this day.
2. On the production of *The Vagina Monologues* on Catholic campuses, see Heather Hathaway, Gregory J. O'Meara, S.J., and Stephanie Quade.
3. Dr. Veronika Mogyorody, Assistant Provost, School of Visual Arts, and Associate Professor and Coordinator, Visual Arts and the Built Environment, University of Windsor, co-curated *behind the mask: Women, Men & Masculinities, 2012*. Following the UDM biennial, the exhibition toured to the University of Windsor Visual Arts Project Gallery.
4. *TRANS, 2014* was co-curated by Peter Beaugard, Director of the Graphic Design, Game Art, and Digital Arts programs, and co-sponsored by Amy Green Deines, Associate Dean of the School of Architecture and Design at Lawrence Technological University. The exhibition was held at LTU's Studio Couture in downtown Detroit.

Works Cited

Barth, Kelly. 2012. *My Almost Certainly Real Imaginary Jesus.* Pasadena: Arktoi Books. Print.

Bryson, Mary, and Suzanne de Castell. 1993. Queer Pedagogy: Praxis Makes Im/Perfect. *Canadian Journal of Education / Revue canadienne de l'éducation* 18 (3): 285–305. Print.

Butler, Judith. 1993. *Bodies that Matter: On the Discursive Limits of Sex.* New York: Routledge. Print.

Congregation for the Doctrine of Faith/Congregatio Pro Doctrina Fidei. Doctrinal Assessment of the Leadership Conference of Women Religious. *Doctrinal Assessment For LCWR.* United States Conference of Catholic Bishops. Web. 12 Mar 2013.

Davies, Cristyn. 2012. Imagining Otherwise: Performance Art as Queer Time and Space. In *Queer and Subjugated Knowledges: Generating Subversive Imaginaries,* ed. Cristyn Davies, Kerry H. Robinson, and Bronwyn Davies, 23–55. Oak Park: Bentham Science. Print.

Dumbadze, Alexander, and Suzanne Hudson. 2013. Participation. In Dumbadze and Hudson, 202–203. Print.

Gillick, Liam, and Maria Lind. 2013. Participation. In Dumbadze and Hudson, 204–213. Print.

Gioni, Massimiliano. 2013. Defense of Biennials. In Dumbadze and Hudson, 171–177. Print.

Hathaway, Heather, Gregory J. O'Meara S.J, and Stephanie Quade. 2012. Textual Deviance: *Eve Ensler's* The Vagina Monologues *and Catholic Campuses.* In *Jesuit & Feminist Education: Intersections in Teaching and Learning for the Twenty-first Century,* ed. Jocelyn Boryczka and Elizabeth Petrino, 203–233. New York: Fordham University Press. Print.

Jones, Amelia. 2012. *Seeing Differently: A History and Theory of Identification and the Visual Arts.* London: Routledge. Print.

Jones, Caroline A. 2013. Biennial Culture and the Aesthetics of Experience. In Dumbadze and Hudson, 192–201. Print.

Monro, Surya. 2012. Beyond Male and Female: Poststructuralism and the Spectrum of Gender. *International Journal of Transgenderism* 8 (1): 3–22. Print.

Sedgwick, Eve Kosofsky. 1993. Queer and Now. In *Tendencies,* 1–20. Durham: Duke University Press. Print.

Sharp, Elizabeth A., and Genevieve Durham DeCesaro. 2015. Modeling Innovative Methodological Practices in a Dance/Family Studies Transdisciplinary Project. *Journal of Family Theory & Review* 7 (4): 367–380. Print.

Sherrill, K. Steven. 2010. *Ersatz Anatomy: Poems.* Cincinnati: Word Tech Communications. Print.

Wu, Chin-Tao. 2009. Biennials Without Borders? *New Left Review* 57: 107–115, May–June. Print.

Zolghadr, Tirdad. 2013. Fusions of Powers: Four Models of Agency in the Field of Contemporary Art, Ranked Unapologetically in Order of Preference. In Dumbadze and Hudson, 277–286. Print.

CHAPTER 6

Safety in Numbers: On the Queerness of Quantification

Adam J. Greteman and Justin N. Thorpe

The landscapes surrounding American schools are littered with numbers. Numbers have become the dominant object used to represent contemporary school experiences. From scores on exams discussing school achievement, numbers on a scale grappling with the obesity epidemic, to the quantification of violence against queer bodies used to fight for legislation and the inclusion of lesbian, gay, bisexual, and transgender (LGBT) subjects, there has emerged a rather strange safety in numbers.[1] Numbers have come to be the objects that give us our lessons, reducing subjects in all their uniqueness, to objects that "generally" teach. Numbers have come to illustrate what Jane Gallop calls "logical eroticism": "an eroticism of control and power, striving in the spirit of Scientific Progress and the Technological Revolution toward the bigger and better" (75). The "dream of logical eroticism," as she argues, is one where "there is nothing more than that which can be measured by instruments rather than judged by a

A.J. Greteman (✉)
School of the Art Institute of Chicago, Chicago, IL, USA

J.N. Thorpe
Salt Lake Community College, Salt Lake City, UT, USA

© The Author(s) 2018
E. McNeil et al. (eds.), *Mapping Queer Space(s) of Praxis and Pedagogy*, Queer Studies and Education,
DOI 10.1007/978-3-319-64623-7_6

subject" (Gallop 75). These numbers wrapped in their scientism and the dreams of Enlightenment promise a better tomorrow, deferring the better to the future seen ever so in Dan Savage and Terry Miller's campaign "It Gets Better" where there, in the future, after high school, after progress is made on the front of gay and lesbian rights, after you have grownup things will be better. After the numbers have spoken, you too can live the storied lives of successful (white, upper class, cisgender) gay subjects.

In contemporary educational discourses, instruments and the data they produce have come to speak and judge the reality of experience in order to make political demands persuasive and set in place policies to make it better (see, e.g., Lorraine Daston, Ian Hacking, Theodore Porter, Nikolas Rose). Quantification promises progress in education and an end to any given crisis (e.g., obesity, anti-gay bias, achievement gap). Yet, such progress and the ending of crises are there, in the future, displacing the ways in which bodies meet in the space and time of the school presently. Numbers speak of the past quantifying in more and more complex ways the singularity of human existence to speak of a future that will be. However, in doing so, numbers come to speak of and for the present bodies in the here and now. Students come to know themselves, in part, as the numbers that are placed on them by test scores or by media attention of their plights as, for our interest, LGBTIQ youth. The future imagined, hoped for by such research, is founded on the idea that the numbers of the past speak to the present in a way that influences or alters the future viability of those subjects objectified by numbers.

We take to task specifically the quantification of anti-gay bias and violence as seen in the annual *National School Climate Survey* (*NSCS*) administered by the Gay Lesbian Straight Education Network (GLSEN). The space of schools has been viewed as homophobic for decades now, yet with the rise to prominence of GLSEN's *NSCS*, the public is shown how homophobic that space has become through numbers that inform us, for instance, that "84.9% of students heard 'gay' used in a negative way frequently or often" and "71.3% heard other homophobic remarks (e.g., 'dyke' or 'faggot') frequently or often" (Kosciw et al. xiv). For the purposes of our chapter, we will focus on *The 2011 National School Climate Survey: The Experiences of Lesbian, Gay, Bisexual and Transgender Youth in Our Nation's Schools*. This, in part, because it was the first survey to show decreases in anti-gay bias and increases in resources available to LGBT students in our nation's schools. It would seem it's getting better.

In looking to this report, we seek to explore the fetishization of numbers and the rhetorical use of quantification regarding the experience of LGBT students. Our project is not simply to negate the use of quantification or numbers, but to critically investigate how such numbers impact and produce the subjective possibilities of LGBTIQ students. Or put differently, how have numbers become the object of the lessons we want to teach regarding issues of gay, lesbian, bisexual, and transgender subjectivity and the limitations of who is included? And how do the object lessons of such numbers come to rely on the very institutions such subjects have been violated by in the first place exposing the neoliberal ruse of tolerance and protection? Does this landscape scattered with numbers limit the possibilities of coming into presence (Biesta, *Beyond Learning*)?

QUANTIFICATION'S TEMPORALITY

Queers and queerness have challenged education's relationship to the future. Queers and other marginalized populations' hostility to social norms have sought to undo education's socialization process. In the anonymous leaflet entitled *Queers Read This*, distributed during the 1990 Gay Pride March in New York City, the anger and hatred felt by queers was made explicit, particularly toward public education. As one of the anonymous writer(s) proclaimed:

> I hate that in twelve years of public education I was never taught about queer people. I hate that I grew up thinking I was the only queer in the world, and I hate even more than most queer kids still grow up the same way. I hate that I was tormented by other kids for being a faggot, but more that I was taught to feel ashamed for being the object of their cruelty, taught to feel it was my fault. (Anonymously by Queers 8)

Since the early 1990s, such challenges have been explored by queer educational research. This research has, in any number of ways, taken up the plight of queers in education. Cris Mayo, in her review of queer educational research, notes a shift of such work from the 1990s, which focused on gender bias, gender roles, and heterosexism as they contribute to homophobia, to the 2000s, which turned to challenge the trope of "gay-as-victim" in order to illuminate gay youth agency and subjectivity. Kristen Renn, in her assessment of the status of queer research in higher education, notes a significant paradox regarding such work. Higher education—where a significant amount of queer research is done—tolerates queer research while remaining a profoundly modern institution that maintains hierarchies and binary thinking. Taking a rather pragmatic approach, Renn calls for "increased use of queer theory and new research approaches" while also calling for "continuation of large-scale studies of campus climate that of necessity reinforce established categories of hetero/homosexual, cisgender/transgender" (138). It is necessary, it would seem, to grapple with the various modes of research and the stories it tells and opportunities it makes available or inadvertently occludes.

For the time being, queers and queer research continue to operate within rather contradictory spaces—seeking to survive the still homophobic and transphobic social space while searching for ways to innovate and thrive despite homophobia and transphobia. As such, numbers or the techniques of quantification used by reports such as those by GLSEN are not techniques to be given up, at least not yet. They "do" something, such as providing numbers, which helps make compelling arguments to politicians and policymakers. Yet, they also cover up the singularity of students and contribute to the use of sexuality as a means for the state to deploy its power over life, as Foucault has elucidated. The numbers reveal on the rhetorical level a belief that non-action is possibly a matter of life or death. Students, particularly LGBTIQ students, are being violated at high rates, and such violations contribute to the deaths of these students, be it physical or social. However, as the 2011 report illustrated, changes have occurred and "progress" is being made, particularly regarding a reported lessening of violence against LGBT students and a growing access to resources and support. Nowhere, though is there attention paid to the non-violated or thriving LGBTIQ students as their experiences are relegated to the silent side of statistics, a point we will explore in a bit.

Following what was called an "epidemic" in teen suicide and the immense amount of media attention focused on the gay-youth-as-victim trope, Laura Essig wrote,

> The fact that way more than five queer teens had an amazing month, had their first love, their first encounter with the richness of queer culture—from drag to politics—is not a story we want to hear as a culture. The fact that hundreds or even thousands of queer kids stood up to a bully, injected queer consciousness into a classroom or a family dinner, and generally lived technicolor lives over the rainbow rather than locked down in some black and white Kansas is lost in the news cycle. We prefer our queers as victims. They're easier to support and much less scary that way.

Responding to the hyper-vigilance of the media, LGBTIQ advocates, and schools Essig points out the lack of commentary on the aspects of queer youth not relating to their victimhood. Eric Rofes, in a similar vein, argued for the interrogation of such narratives to challenge them in order to offer a picture beyond the martyr-victim storyline. And as we noted via Cris Mayo, there was a shift in research in the 2000s that challenged this trope. Yet, such a trope still has sway. The gay-as-victim is still a compelling story; it is perhaps the story that we are affectively drawn to because stories of queers' amazing months are for some reason(s) unnerving.

The emphasis on the negative school climate for LGBTIQ students through quantification utilizes this victim trope to illustrate the continued assaults on queer time where homophobic violence cuts short the lives of queers (see Michelle Birket, Dorothy Espelage, and Brian Koenig; David Dupper and Nancy Meyer-Adams; Joseph Kosciew, Emily Greytak, and Elizabeth Diaz). Yet, in a landscape that is littered with bodies of dead queers, the constant emphasis on the victimized queers and the need for benevolent saviors (particularly armed with numbers) frames out the adversarial and thriving queers. But queers never go extinct. Our numbers might fluctuate, AIDS may have been an inexpressible catastrophe that decimated a generation or two of queer people and their knowledges, yet queers persist in what seems a never-ending quest against normativity. There is, of course, irony, since this quest against normativity—the anti-normative desires of queer theory—has been normalized itself in the institutionalization of queer theory and sexuality studies. Yet, the critical practices of queer theory continue to have their place in critical thought. And it is in this vein of queer thought that we challenge the use of quantification, following a list of other scholars who have long challenged the mystification that occurs with numbers.

The quantification that occurs within "large-scale" studies inevitably promises something, yet we want to propose that such promises need to be challenged. This challenge is pragmatic though for we recognize the political relevance of such large-scale projects. They tell a part of a story that we do not wish to deny. We only wish, or perhaps hope, that we might change the landscape of and for LGBTIQ students' lives ever so slightly to see possibilities for becoming that are not steeped in the victimist logic of GLSEN's annual reports taken up within the mainstream and significant portions of educational scholarship. This is, inevitably we might say, a move away from the protectionist agenda of GLSEN (to protect the victim from the perpetrator) and toward a promotionist agenda to promote the sensibilities of queers.

Framing GLSEN

Founded in 1990 as the Gay and Lesbian Independent Schools Teachers Network, and becoming the Gay Lesbian, Straight Education Network in 1995, GLSEN's mission has been one that "strives to assure that each member of every school community is valued and respected regardless of sexual orientation or gender identity/expression." This is done both in making it safe for teachers to be out and for students to have a school space that is safe and free from homophobic violence. Alongside other gay-rights organizations such as the Human Rights Campaign (HRC), the National Gay and Lesbian Task Force, and Parents, Families and Friends of Lesbians and Gays (PFLAG), GLSEN has arguably changed the landscape of American Politics and the necessity of issues of sexual orientation and gender identity being recognized and engaged. While there have been significant changes in LGBTIQ politics over the last few decades, of course, there have been trenchant critiques of these political organizations and their contribution to the normalizing project of neoliberalism (see Duggan; Spade; Vaid; Warner).

Of these organizations, GLSEN has most significantly focused on the climate of American schools and the well-being of both students and teachers. In addition to conducting the *NSCS*, which is the focus of this chapter, the organization also sponsors such events as the National Day of Silence, No Name Calling Week, and the Think Before You Speak campaign to create various types of activities and actions to assist creating safe and respectful school communities. Focusing on GLSEN's research in this chapter helps us think about the space of schools and the possibilities and problems that emerge with GLSEN's work exploring the climate of "our nation's schools." Initiated in 1999, the *NSCS* has documented "the school experiences of lesbian, gay, bisexual, and transgender youth" particularly "the prevalence of anti-LGBT language and victimization, the effect that these experiences have on LGBT students' academic achievement, and the utility of interventions to both lessen the negative effects of a hostile climate and promote a positive educational experience" (Kosciw et al. 3). We see at its emergence in 1999 a particular focus on LGBT identities, a focus that would not change until 2015, when Queer was added to the *NSCS*, with the authors noting, "we have explicitly added queer in this [2015] installment as a result of the increase in an observed self-identification of student as queer over time" (Kosciw et al. 3).

As the 2011 report states, the *NSCS* "remains one of the few studies to focus on the school experiences of LGB students nationally, and the only national study to focus on transgender experiences" (4). The Department of Education, the US General Accounting Office, and the Institute of Medicine have carried out related national projects. These governmental institutions look at issues relating to youth victimization, including, respectively, state-level anti-bullying laws and policies, the prevalence and effect of school bullying, and the health of LGBT people, showing a limited understanding and lack of mechanisms in place to assist in projecting LGB youth. Transgender youth continue to be absent from such research and the concerns it purports to have for youth health and safety.

GLSEN's annual *NSCS* and these other national attempts to understand the state of LGBT youth reveal a focus on victimization and legal policies (e.g., anti-bullying laws, anti-discrimination clauses that enumerate sexual orientation and gender identity) to protect LGB and sometimes T youth. While such a focus is understandable and reflects the quest for legal rights that is the dominant goal of mainstream LGBT political and educational organizations, this approach is limited. As Dean Spade notes in *Normal Life*, the law is limited because it cannot do everything that it is asked to do. The rise of the non-profit in the political landscape of the USA has done less to foment a critical social movement that addresses the intersections of injustice and instead has led to an emphasis on "single-issue politics" (Spade 66). "Through the rise of the non-profit form," Spade argues "certain logics that support criminalization, militarism, and wealth disparity have penetrated and transformed spaces that were once locations of fomenting resistance to state violence" (67). Wrapped up in its mainstream appeal GLSEN has contributed to the normalizing and conforming agenda seen in its own mission that "envisions a world in which every child learns to respect and accept all people, *regardless* of sexual orientation or gender identity/expression" (Kosciw et al.). Regardless of the vectors of difference, GLSEN proposes a landscape where students, particularly LGBT students, are protected from discrimination based on their sexual orientation and/or gender identity/expression, but this regardless of their difference *not* due to the contribution and importance of their difference.

GLSEN fetishizes numbers, yet this fetishization should not be read as merely a pathological focus on an object (numbers). As E. L. McCallum illustrates, there are things to do with fetishism. There are benefits to the fetish and the fetishization of numbers that GLSEN operates within has provided productive (albeit problematic) spaces to grapple with sexual orientation and gender identity within the conservative and reactionary realm of American Public Education. The fetish, like everything, has its limitations, as its limit is with engaging the subjects that are behind the object of interest. The fetish of numbers then has taught us lessons, particularly lessons that have provided political ammunition regarding the need to address issues of sexual and gender differences in schools. Yet, in doing so, it has captivated our attention and made us captive to the lure of its certainty. We move to disrupt and challenge the certainty of GLSEN's numbers fetish and its attempt to convert qualities into quantities.

GLSEN's Conversion

Descriptive statistics are not unfamiliar; if we were to look at the exposure to descriptive statistics we would find even in elementary school basic descriptive statistics are taught from an early age, including concepts like having children count how many of their classmates' favorite color is blue or making a pictograph of the numbers of dog owners in a class. Elementary-aged children are also exposed to such descriptions like finding the mean (average), the median (middle), or the mode (most). However, descriptive statistics continue well beyond elementary school, particularly in academic research and the writing and rhetoric involved in that research. Descriptive statistics aim at portraying things as they were, that is ascribing through some numeric analysis conditions in the past. For example, one type of descriptive statistic might be counting the number of deaths from pneumonia in 1918, the year of the influenza pneumonia pandemic. Or we might consider describing annual incomes in the USA by describing the average income, which is found through adding incomes and dividing by the number in the sample, or by using the median income, the fiftieth percentile of household incomes.

Education is also concerned with the use of these descriptive statistics. For example, we find that it is common to hear reports that count (often to be reported in percentages) the racial demographics that compose the school district, or schools counting the number of children that qualify for free or reduced lunch. We see in these reports a problem. While it is possible for individual children to be counted, the difficulty with this is the assumption that the qualities of these children can be converted into measures that accurately describe these qualities. For example, in creating a demographic variable called race, the assumption has already been made to establish an abstraction and classification of individual qualities. Or, in considering the counts of children who qualify for free and reduced lunch (which is often seen as a proxy in statistical analysis for socio-economic status), the quantification assumes that qualities and conditions of poverty can be abstracted based on an arbitrary formula which establishes a classification for poverty.

This educational system, one that relies on auditing standards that have been in place, also relies on descriptive statistics and reporting things like, for our interests, the percentage of youth who hear homophobic remarks made in school or the average number of times schools respond to reports of homophobia. The appeal of these quantified values is not difficult to see, as such percentages or averages allow for comparisons among schools and make it possible to determine the climate of America's schools. However, these "numbers" serve as a proxy for qualities related to school experience, such as the sense of safety in the classroom or the accountability of teachers and administrators regarding reports of homophobia. Thus, whether the description is that of homophobic remarks or that of comparing responses to student reports of homophobia, there are inherent problems of accurately mapping qualities through calibrated measures.

Another problem arises in the use of descriptive statistics: the comparisons of demographic subgroups based on reported descriptions. To return to the influenza pneumonia pandemic of 1918, there is a common rhetorical use to report this statistic as comparisons across groups, such as comparing the number of deaths in Great Britain as opposed to in the USA for the number of deaths of white versus black people in the USA. The numbers assume that individuals share common characteristics that can be used to label and classify. This assumption is problematic. The difficulty in this is that these deaths are individuals, with individual characteristics and qualities. These people have lived lives and have experiences that require more than simply summarizing them under the guise of a common demographic. It is possible to count (and report) the individuals who died because of the influenza, but this counting and reporting must itself be recognized for its rhetorical impact on how lives and deaths are understood.

In his *Trust in Numbers*, Theodore Porter provides a different perspective of the problems associated with converting qualities into quantities through descriptive statistics. He suggests that, although the motives of early statisticians might have been for improvement, the problem became that the rhetorical use of these descriptions was to highlight qualities in need of intervention and change, often classifying groups of people that the researcher had little desire to associate with personally (Porter 74). Much, probably most, statistical study of human populations has aimed to improve the condition of working people, children, beggars, criminals, women, or racial and ethnic minorities. The writings, especially private ones, of early social statisticians and pioneers of the social survey exuded benevolence and goodwill. In print, though, they generally adopted the hardheaded rhetoric of actuality, which permitted women as well as men to assume the role of the scientific social investigator, and not merely of an agent of charity (77).

Here, Porter is describing the use, particularly the rhetorical use, of quantification particularly in descriptive statistics that have been used historically to change conditions of those less fortunate, non-normals. Converting qualities into quantities became a rhetorical server of offering evidence for change. In describing these qualities, descriptive statistics also provides a sense of actuality and objectivity, which is perceived as authoritative. Descriptive statistics also allows for a dismissal of moral closeness in favor for impartial distances. Porter suggests that descriptive statistics were used to describe and investigate members of society "whom they did not know, and often did not care to know, as persons" (77). The use of descriptive statistics such as averages or percentages seems to gain favor as a vehicle for describing populations that lacked "strong and interesting personalities" (77).

However, the issue of this rhetorical deployment is that it is impossible to measure the qualities of these people. In the social sciences, the rhetorical norm is to consider human qualities as countable through calibrated measures. This is not to say that there are not things in education that are countable, such as the number of desks in the classroom or the number of text books provided or the amount of money used within the schools. These objects are countable without the ethical concerns of diminishing human qualities into quantities that can never accurately portray the qualities being measured.

Education's rhetorical use of descriptive statistics continues to be used in attempts to describe conditions within schools and classrooms. Later these descriptions are often interpreted as bases for inferences that portray conditions that need to be changed or altered. The deployment of descriptive statistics in education is used as a tool for summarizing the past conditions within schools or summarizing the past assessments of, as GLSEN's work shows, school climate.

GLSEN's Rhetorics

In writing about the rhetoric of quantification, we recognize that there are different ways that quantifications are portrayed in writing and presentation. We could consider the rhetorical use of quantification in predicting future conditions of LGBTIQ students based on the current conditions of those sampled, or said differently, forecasting the future based on the events of the sampled past. There is, in fact, much that could be said about this rhetorical deployment. Instead, we consider the rhetorical use of quantification as a description of what is in the LGBTIQ student community. One of the purposes of quantification is to describe how things are, allowing for audiences to view discrepancies and differences between groups.

It is in these descriptions that portray what life is like among LGBTIQ students that we focus the bulk of this chapter. We look at the portraits of school safety that are argued through the 2011 GLSEN School Climate Survey. We limit ourselves to looking at the rhetoric of conditions instead of the conditions of what is probabilistically implied. We find this helpful in discussing the safety that is found in using numbers to persuade and inform. The GLSEN reports are used as tools and evidence in suggesting current trends and necessary reforms. We recognize that this report is commonly used in shaping how educational safety is currently construed. Thus, in considering the ways that quantification is rhetorically used to describe what is, we recognize that this rhetoric also omits important other stories that could also be described as what is. The arguments use descriptive quantification as rhetorical tools to portray certain sides of events and glamorize areas viewed as needing improvement.

There are two important components of the GLSEN report: the executive summary and the full report. We recognize that the rhetorical use of descriptive statistics in citing GLSEN could come from either report. Both portray similar stories of the current conditions and trends of LGBT students in the USA. However, we recognize the full report portrays more details about the survey and the nuances of the survey. This chapter draws from both pieces of the 2011 report. In addition, the executive summary is highlighted as a convenient evidence source for those wishing to draw from GLSEN's data.

We consider the rhetoric of descriptive quantification through three different deployments of quantification: the rhetoric of descriptive comparabilities, the rhetoric of descriptive transparency, and the descriptive rhetoric of the jeremiad. In writing about these three rhetorical deployments of descriptive quantification, we are not suggesting that there is a problem with using quantification in writing about LGBTIQ issues. Instead we suggest that there has become a trust in using these numbers when writing for persuasive changes, especially when addressing audiences like policymakers and general readers.

THE RHETORIC OF COMPARABILITIES

In using descriptive quantification as a rhetorical trope in arguing about changes that should occur, quantification becomes a space where groups can be compared. We recognize that one of the steps in quantifying is the creation of arbitrary groupings and labels. The authors of this chapter claim ties to education, and an example from education might be useful in order to consider this rhetoric of comparabilities. In the GLSEN reports, (both the full and executive summaries) there are common uses of quantification as a comparison. The rhetoric of comparison requires taking the quantities and making them discrete into arbitrary categories, such as is found in the executive summary when the authors of the GLSEN reports suggest that there is a difference in the relationships between victimization based on the differences in sexual orientation and gender identity. The report considers two graphs, found on page 11 of the executive summary, which consider the relationship between depression and severity of victimization and self-esteem and severity of victimization. The graphs are line graphs showing two lines, one for sexual orientation and the other for gender expression and how these compare against sever and low victimization levels. We suggest that the reader take a moment to consider these graphs in the initial report.

Here the GLSEN report takes advantage of the rhetoric of comparison by highlighting the differences in victimization by gender identity and sexual orientation. Although we could write about the issues that come through comparing with sexual orientation and gender identity, we choose to highlight the arbitrary nature of the victimization levels. The report argues through this rhetoric that there is a difference between high and low victimization in both the measures of depression and self-esteem. This rhetoric assumes that it is possible to quantify the qualities of depression and self-esteem and then it is possible to assume a measurable difference between those who had high victimization against those who had low levels of victimization. The executive summary tells the audience that those who had high levels of victimization had lower levels of self-esteem and higher levels of depression. This is a rhetorical move to convince the audience of the reports that there is a necessary difference between victimization levels.

We contend in this rhetorical deployment that GLSEN's argument becomes a teller of what is bad in hopes to enact changes for the youth. The argument tells the audience what to notice in these comparisons, promoting a specific desired outcome. In this case, the authors purposefully choose to highlight in the report those students who were classified as highly victimized, suggesting a needed change in those who were highly victimized. We ask the question, what might happen if the comparisons that were reported were for those who had high victimization. Consider the finding that students with low victimization levels had lower depression and higher self-esteems. The rhetoric does not promote a needed shift, as there are LGBT students who are not depressed and have a high self-esteem. The marginalized LGBT students are now seen as not needing interventions in the classroom.

THE RHETORIC OF TRANSPARENCY

The second rhetoric we discuss comes as quantification is used rhetorically to clarify current conditions, often by relying on the quantification to portray a reality of how things are. We highlight that the reality is portrayed through the lens of the data, the lenses of the researchers, and the specific ending purpose of the argument. This rhetorical label is not magical but, as Biesta suggests, does carry connotations and associations (*Good Education*). This transparency is a particular rhetoric that deploys quantification to clarify positions and objectify reality. This rhetoric is couched in the trends of scientific investigation that promotes generalizability and objectivity, which have become a research cultural norm, especially in research that involves the human, such as the case of the research reported in GLSEN's *NSCS*.

Here we suggest that the safety of numbers can be deployed as mechanisms for transparency, clarifying, (of course, from the rhetor's perspective) the supposed truths about the current conditions within schools, particularly in the historically specific notions of quantifying the qualities of safety in schools. GLSEN uses the rhetoric of quantitative transparency to support the qualitative aspects, such as the interviews, that are found throughout the report. Consider the following from the full *NSCS* regarding harassment, which demonstrates this student's perception of school: "Bullying in our school is mostly verbal, but it hurts just as much as any physical pain…. Teachers rarely do anything about it" (Kosciw et al. 26). The rhetoric of quantitative transparency becomes one of showing that in "reality" the type of bullying occurring in schools is verbal harassment.

In the report, this rhetoric of transparency suggests what the reality is like for LGBT students in middle and high school grades: "An overwhelming majority (92.3%) reported being verbally harassed at some point in the past year," the report states, suggesting that the reality for LGBTQ students is one of being verbally harassed in the schools (Kosciw et al. 24). We see this deployment of quantification as offering authoritative support for the claims of the individual, particularly those in quoted statements. Is it not enough to quote the student who states that the majority of the bullying in that particular school is verbal harassment? We suggest that there is a safety in using numbers to make transparent the conditions of "reality."

THE RHETORIC OF THE JEREMIAD

We close this analysis by considering the rhetoric of the jeremiad. We take our understanding of the jeremiad from Sacvan Bercovitch's *The American Jeremiad*. Bercovitch analyzes a common rhetoric found within the USA, particularly in the works of Puritan sermons. This rhetoric is not only found in speaking from the pulpit but has become a rhetorical norm in political speeches, scholarly writing, and ultimately in writing for general readership. In this type of rhetoric, we find an ironic call to institute change on a scriptural basis, particularly on a promised blessing. We use the term scriptural lightly as not to be solely based in the Christian canon, but instead as an established norm. The form of the American jeremiad, Bercovitch suggests, is that the rhetoric establishes that some law or norm that is being broken, suggesting punishment or retribution or casualty that will come if the norm is not restored, followed by the distinctly US rhetoric of a promise of salvation and benefit from returning to the law or norm. In this rhetorical deployment there is a sense of punishment and fear for what might come if changes are not enacted.

We recognize that the rhetoric of the GLSEN report is embedded within a desire to change the conditions of LGBT (now Q) students within schools. Thus, the document becomes one of posed problems and posed solutions, allowing for the solutions to become a suggested norm within schools, especially for LGBT students and youth. The jeremiad then becomes one of writing about how school environments should be safe spaces for students; however, the quantification suggests that the promised blessings of learning in a safe, secure space are not being fulfilled. For example, the report provides suggestions of how to improve the lives of LGBT students and youth, providing promised blessings for those who enact the changes. Throughout the introduction, GLSEN offers suggestions to problems, backing the claims through quantified data. The authors trust in the rhetoric of the quantification to support the claims that there is no safety in the schools; however, if the numbers are to be believed and ultimately changed, then there is potential for schools that are "safe." Offering the following: "Taken together, such measures [outlined in the suggestions] can move us toward a future in which all students have the opportunity to learn and succeed in school" (Kosciw et al. xx). There is promised blessings that await those who adopt the suggestions supported by the measured qualities of experience in the lives of LGBTQ youth.

Concluding Remarks

Eve Sedgwick points out that the mainstream gay/lesbian movement has come to dominate the scene of America's sexual politics (*Weather in Proust*, 201). The mainstream gay/lesbian movement operates almost entirely through the work of non-profits like the HRC, PFLAG and, of course, GLSEN. Such non-profits have become less interested in radical social change and more interested in maintaining their social and economic privileges and relationships with major corporate donors. They operate we might argue through the status quo. These organizations might scoff at the queer critiques of their neoliberal agendas because at least they are "doing something." Relying on various rhetorical techniques they come to limn the frame of how LGBTIQ subjects might be understood. However, upon examination the something that they are doing is often at the expense of the most vulnerable because they work in single-issue politics. "Such a politics," Spade contends, "excludes queer and trans people who experience homophobia simultaneously with transphobia, poverty, ableism, xenophobia, racism, sexism, criminalization, economic exploitation, and/or other forms of subjection" (66). GLSEN's focus on students—including an attempt to address issues of race and class maintains both a separatist and assimilationist agenda—paradoxically. On this,

Sedgwick writes, "mainstream gay/lesbian politics ... is paradoxically both separatist and assimilationist. It is separatist in its sense of identity, but at the same time all its goals involve the uncritical assimilation of gay people into the institutions of a very conservative culture" (*Weather* 201). GLSEN advocates for inclusion and protection of LGBT youth by focusing on their minority status, while it negates the promises and potential of sexual orientation and gender identity/expression as legitimate sensibilities that operate far beyond the limiting logic of identity politics.

The landscape of American sexual and educational politics may seem rather straight and narrow, as it is a landscape littered with more and more numbers that attempt to clean up the messiness of lives while offering little by way of changes to that landscape. The safety of such numbers and their rhetorical uses claim to take the disparate experiences and create a manageable picture of the world so as to compare, to sermonize, and to clarify. And as such, these numbers also come to occlude and hide the contingent and unique subjects that seek to survive and thrive in these times. Yet, again, such statistics are important. Sedgwick writes, "I think everyone who does gay and lesbian studies is haunted by the suicides of adolescents. To us, the hard statistics come easily" (*Tendencies* 1). Citing the statistics from the late 1980s and early 1990s, statistics that were starting to tell the story of gay and lesbian adolescents' lives; the soft-spoken queen of queer theory highlighted the need for numbers. Hard statistics are not unimportant. They have purpose. However, they cannot tell the whole story. They cannot dominate the landscape and the stories told of queer youth/students because as that happens the numbers come to maintain the status quo.

It has been our attempt here, a rather modest attempt, to draw attention to the rhetorical use and normalization of "hard statistics" in foreclosing the "soft side" of the human story to open up space, to paint a slightly different landscape whose status is queer (Rofes). If the hard statistics that come easily to us help us make sense of the haunting deaths and violence of queer youth, then the simultaneous need is to create a world that challenges the hardness of such statistics and the violence they represent. Perhaps it calls for embracing the stereotypical "softness" attributed to queerness and queers to make space for their sensibilities and their ways of challenging the phobic worlds in which they invent their lives daily?

We end then where we began—with Eve Sedgwick. While not wanting to generalize about people doing queer work but recognizing "some effects [that] seem widespread," she writes and we agree, that:

[M]any adults are trying, in our work, to keep faith with vividly remembered promises made to ourselves in childhood: promises to make invisible possibilities and desires visible; to make tacit things explicit; to smuggle queer representation in where it must be smuggled and, with the relative freedom of adulthood, to challenge queer eradicating impulses frontally where they are to be so challenged. (*Tendencies* 3)

Sedgwick believes that "many of us feel the need to make, cumulatively, stubbornly, a counterclaim ... a claim that something about queer is inextinguishable" (188). The call to protect LGBT youth from the homophobic landscape of schools seen in GLSEN's work is commendable. Yet, its penchant for assimilation and contribution to the normalization of LGBTIQ issues at the expense of queerness raises concerns for the possibility of, not only, queer survival, but also thrival in the landscapes of our pluralistic society. The queer impulse developed in the perverse days of childhood where the imagination existed unencumbered by the practicalities of the world must maintain its impulsive needs to think the unthinkable. The imagination might ask, as we hope to have here, to create a safety in numbers. The queer safety in numbers cannot be a safety in numbers that is founded on the occluding work of the "number" developed in the objectification of statistics and quantitative work. Rather, the queer safety in numbers is a turn, perhaps return, to the safety in numbers of coalitional politics that advocates for a radical politics that is not separatist or assimilationist, but relational. Might the object lessons of numbers give way, make room for, the possibility of envisioning and creating daily a landscape that does not give up on the radical promises of queerness and its inextinguishable "something"?

NOTE

1. Acronyms around sexual and gender diversity are ever expanding. In this chapter, we use both LGBT and LGBTIQ. LGBT is used when referring to the *National School Climate Survey (NSCS)* since that is the language used by the Gay, Lesbian, Straight, Education Network (GLSEN). In making our own argument, we utilize the broader acronym LGBTIQ.

WORKS CITED

Anonymously by Queers. 1990. *Queers Read This*. New York: ACTUP New York, Zotero, November 26, 2011. Web. 23 Jan 2016.

Bercovitch, Sacvan. 1978. *The American Jeremiad*. Madison: University of Wisconsin Press. Print.

Biesta, Gert. 2006. *Beyond Learning: Democratic Education for a Human Future*. Boulder: Paradigm Publishers. Print.

———. 2010. *Good Education in the Age of Measurement: Ethics, Politics, Democracy*. Boulder: Paradigm Publishers. Print.

Birket, Michelle, Dorothy Espelage, and Brian Koenig. 2009. LGB and Questioning Students in Schools: The Moderating Effects of Homophobic Bullying and School Climate on Negative Outcomes. *Journal of Youth and Adolescence* 38 (7): 989–1000. Print.

Daston, Lorraine. 2007. *Things that Talk: Objects Lessons from Art and Science*. Brooklyn: Zone Books. Print.

Duggan, Lisa. 2002. *Twilight of Equality: Neoliberalism, Cultural Politics, and the Attack on Democracy*. Boston: Beacon. Print.

Dupper, David R., and Nancy Meyer-Adams. 2002. Low-Level Violence: A Neglected Aspect of School Culture. *Urban Education* 37 (3): 350–364. Print.

Essig, Laura. 2010. Queer Youth Not a Tragedy. *The Chronicle of Higher Education*, October 3, 2010. Web. 4 Oct 2010.

Gallop, Jane. 1988. *Thinking Through the Body*. New York: Columbia University Press. Print.

Hacking, Ian. 1990. *The Taming of Chance*. Cambridge: Cambridge University Press. Print.

Kosciw, Joseph, Emily Greytak, and Elizabeth Diaz. 2009. Who, What, Where, When, and Why: Demographic and Ecological Factors Contributing to Hostile School Climate for Lesbian, Gay, Bisexual, and Transgender Youth. *Journal of Youth and Adolescence* 38: 976–988. Print.

Kosciw, Joseph G., Emily A. Greytak, Mark J. Bartkiewicz, Madelyn J. Boesen, and Neal A. Palmer. 2012. *The 2011 National School Climate Survey: The Experiences of Lesbian, Gay, Bisexual and Transgender Youth in Our Nation's Schools*. New York: GLSEN. Print.

Mayo, Chris. 2007. Queering Foundations: Queer and Lesbian, Gay, Bisexual, and Transgender Educational Research. *Review of Research in Education* 31: 78–94. Print.

McCallum, E.L. 1999. *Object Lessons: How to Do Things with Fetishism*. Albany: SUNY Press. Print.

Porter, Theodore M. 1995. *Trust in Numbers*. Princeton: Princeton University Press. Print.

Renn, Kristen. 2010. LGBT and Queer Research in Higher Education: The State and Status of the Field. *Educational Researcher* 39 (2): 132–141. Print.

Rofes, Eric. 2004. Martyr-Target-Victim: Interrogating Narratives of Persecution and Suffering among Queer Youth. In *Youth and Sexualities: Pleasure, Subversion, and Insubordination In and Out of Schools*, ed. Mary Lou Rasmussen, Eric Rofes, and Susan Talburt, 41–62. New York: Palgrave. Print.

Rose, Nikolas. 1991. Governing by Numbers: Figuring Out Democracy. *Accounting, Organizations and Society* 16 (7): 673–692. Print.

Sedgwick, Eve Kosofsky. 1993. *Tendencies*. Durham: Duke University Press. Print.

———. 2011. *The Weather in Proust*. Durham: Duke University Press. Print.

Spade, Dean. 2011. *Normal Life: Administrative Violence, Critical Trans Politics, and the Limits of Law*. Brooklyn: South End Press. Print.

Vaid, Urvashi. 1995. *Virtual Equality: The Mainstreaming of Gay and Lesbian Liberation*. New York: Anchor. Print.

Warner, Michael. 1999. *The Trouble with Normal: Sex, Politics, and the Ethics of Queer Life*. Cambridge: Harvard University Press. Print.

Queer Out Here:
Public Bodies and Spaces

CHAPTER 7

Out There: The Lesbian in Literature

Amy Gall

I learned what a lesbian was through my father's porn. In his closet, tucked between the folds of his cardigan sweaters was a battered copy of *Letters to Penthouse*. It didn't matter that the "stories" in this collection were clearly fake (the boss's wife decides to go to their secluded hot tub and oops, the boss's secretary happens to already be in there, naked, and oops, she also happens to be on all fours masturbating), or that all the stories were written by men, for men, and that I was an 11-year-old girl. I wasn't reading these stories because I identified with them; at the time, I didn't even know there was something within me to identify. I was reading these stories because they made the backs of my knees sweat. They were my first understanding of desire. The desire moved in a circle: wanting, understanding that I couldn't have what I wanted, shame at wanting something I couldn't have, fear that my parents would come upstairs and find me wanting and shaming over something I couldn't have, and finally the story, pulling me back to want.

Usually, after a page or so, the boss came out of the bushes he was hiding in, and the women quickly forgot about each other and focused on the real prize: the man's penis. That these stories discounted and erased sex

A. Gall (✉)
Brooklyn, NY, USA

© The Author(s) 2018
E. McNeil et al. (eds.), *Mapping Queer Space(s) of Praxis and Pedagogy*, Queer Studies and Education,
DOI 10.1007/978-3-319-64623-7_7

between two women as much as they represented it was part of what made me so attracted to them. If lesbian sex time weren't always threatened with interruption or dissolution, it wouldn't have been so dangerous and mysterious. And because there was so little actual story to go on, I was also able to flex my own imaginative muscles and extend these scenes well beyond sex. If the boss's wife was, say, wearing a cowboy hat, maybe she actually worked at a dude ranch, and maybe when the wife and secretary weren't having sex with the boss, they were living on that dude ranch together, roping cattle, taming horses, their bodies covered in a thick layer of dust and sweat.

Still, desire unfulfilled is painful. In an interview with one of my favorite authors, Eileen Myles, I asked about her experience of reading as a queer child. "I think the act of reading is always identificatory. And it's surprising, I think there's always that moment when you're identifying with something and then you realize you're not that something. And what do you do with that?" The answer, for many lesbians who don't seem themselves reflected in any form of media, much less *Penthouse*, or in the heterosexual mass that surrounds them, is to create their own stories.

I don't know how I stumbled upon my first *Xena* or *Star Trek: Voyager* fan fiction website, but from the very first mention of Amazonian princess hands cupping leather-clad warrior breasts I knew I had found the stories I desired. Fan fiction is just what it sounds like: fictional stories written about pre-existing television shows or movies by fans. But it is far more than simply furthering a plot. In the case of *Xena* and *Star Trek*, the female television characters that the fan fiction writers were working with were not explicitly gay. They were best friends or partners or "close." They traveled and fought together, or shared long meaningful looks or even kissed, but the nature of their bond remained mysterious and tenuous and immediately broken whenever a man came on the scene. In fan fiction, however, these women became full-blown, nipple-biting, pussy-eating dykes. And these dykes did not just have sex or fall in love; they also went on adventures. They traveled to other planets, saved orphanages full of needy children, killed the God of War. These stories kept me reading long before, and long after the sex, for many reasons.

The characters had to go to great lengths to consummate their relationship or be together in peace. Half the time one of them was blinded, or dying from a poisonous arrow, or had their minds taken over by the Borg. They were beaten and tortured, or separated from each other for decades, or thrown into another time-space continuum. And only by the power of their love were they able to reunite. I was never physically attacked for being gay, but who I was constantly being discounted, by teachers who told their misbehaving students to quit being such faggots, by girls who would not come over to my house without a friend because they did not feel safe being alone with me, by friends who, after starting rumors that other students were gay, said they were doing me a favor because I needed to know what was in store for me if I came out. These fan fiction stories echoed for me the sense of danger and impermanence I felt as a young gay person, the only gay person, for most of my childhood, whom I knew. But they also provided a very concrete example of how that impermanence could be overcome.

What was most comforting about these stories was that the characters' attraction to each other wasn't the thing that kept them apart or caused them suffering. They lived in times of war, under repressive governments, or were threatened by alien forces, and everyone in that world was suffering just as much, if not more, than they were. It was those governments and gods and aliens who were the villains, not the lesbians. In fact, while everyone else was cowering in fear, the lesbians were not just rescuing each other, but whole villages, nations, whole planetary systems of people at the same time. And, during the time that these two were kept apart, the world suffered, nations crumbled, gods died, and evil alien forces took over. Their love and bond, then, was not only heroic; it was necessary for the very survival of goodness and human life. As Dorothy Allison writes in "Puritans, Perverts, and Feminists," discussing her own experience of being a young, lesbian sci-fi reader, "Justice happened in those books—justice, revenge, vindication, female bonding, sex—and what seemed to me a more humane, compassionate philosophy of life" (*Skin* 98). Gayness could not just exist, but triumph.

Since it was the Internet, people could not only read stories but comment on them, which sometimes turned into discussions with the authors about their stories, or sometimes turned into conversations about life. Though I never met the people whose stories I read, and whom I lusted after, these discussions let me know that there were other lesbians out there who existed in real time and who wanted the same things I did, even if, like me, they had to create their own stories to get it.

I came out when I was 14. I'm not saying that Internet fan fiction gave me the courage to do so, but it was a place I returned to often. I could escape from thinking about the countless straight girls I was pining after, and remind myself that I wasn't the only other woman who wanted to love a woman, or go on adventures, or have a community by whom they felt known. It also encouraged me to do my own writing: first imitations of the fan fiction I saw, and then other types of fiction, some that had lesbian characters in it and some that didn't. And eventually I was even able to write about the topic that scared me the most: myself.

* * *

When I interviewed writer Elizabeth Hand about her views on science fiction, she said the following:

> The American strain of 20th-century science fiction … was a lot about possibility, and I think whether or not the work was optimistic, some of the works could be very grim, it was all about exploding the paradigm. You know, exploding the notion of two sexes, two genders and the only union a heterosexual one within a nuclear family for the production of children…. I think sci-fi was a common language for people who were interested in expanding their notions of what it means to be human.

I was very curious about this idea and decided to re-visit science fiction as an adult, through Samuel Delany's *Dhalgren*. Though *Dhalgren* takes place in the traditional sci-fi setting of a post-apocalyptic town and many of the tropes of science fiction, unexplained natural disasters, super powers, are present throughout, the book's presentation of sexuality and humanity in general was far more nuanced and complicated than any Internet fan fiction or science fiction I'd ever read.

Kidd, the main character of *Dhalgren*, arrives in the mysterious town of Bellona, with no knowledge of why he came there, how he got there or even his name. Bellona has undergone an unexplained apocalypse where most of the people in the town died or left. But those who remain don't seem to be from Bellona, and most of them don't seem to know how they got there and why they chose to stay. Communities dissolve and reform, people disappear and reappear seemingly at random. Even the setting itself constantly changes. A whole house will be on fire one day and the next day it will be standing there untouched as if nothing ever happened. Street signs that were at one end of town will reappear at the other end of town ten minutes later.

Everything in Bellona actively resists being known or categorized. This, in itself, is a revolutionary choice. By presenting a place where there are no rules, Delany is also presenting a place where there are no rule breakers, gay or otherwise. And because the novel is over 800 pages, I was forced to look at the unknown at such length and depth that I found myself looking with less anxiety and fear at the unfamiliar ideas or people I saw in my own life.

The treatment of sexuality in *Dhalgren* is especially revolutionary. It is not measured on a moral spectrum; it is simply presented from such varied standpoints and with such depth and empathy that it became impossible not to question my own desires and the biases and fears I had toward other people's desires. Along with the relationships he has with women and men, Kidd is, at various times, attracted to the dead body of a young boy, a tree, and a car crash. But Kidd's realizations of his desires aren't met by panic or disgust or even confusion. He simply recognizes and accepts the feelings he has, and either acts on them or doesn't. No one in the town stops him or threatens him for these acts.

The language of sex in *Dhalgren* is also completely unselfconscious. The language of sex in fan fiction was fun, but also vague and imprecise. Vaginas, for instance, are called "pleasure mounds," "sensitive treasures," and, my personal favorite, "cum palaces." While this may have been an author's attempt to be creative, there's something about constantly obscuring sexual organs and what we do with them that feels embarrassing. It implies that those things need to be obscured, as if writing about sex with a direct or honest gaze is somehow even *more* embarrassing. But Delany not only uses straightforward language to talk about sex, he maintains the gaze of sex. When Kidd begins a relationship with a boy named Denny, Delany dedicates a full three pages to the first sexual encounter, and describes Kidd's climax with simple poetic clarity: "He … lay, with his mouth opened, his head back, each muscle loosening; Denny held Kidd's balls while he sucked; and that felt good. Kid held the boy's sides with his legs. And came. It was something like hot oil poured in cotton…" (Delany 398).

Unlike fan fiction, sex in *Dhalgren* is not the end point, but part of a fluid exploration of human relationships. After Kidd orgasms, he and Denny talk:

"When I blew you," Denny said, "were you thinking about her?"

"You'd like that, wouldn't you? No, I wasn't. I mean only a little at first."

"I don't care what you were thinking about," Denny said. "You think you know an awful lot about what I like, huh?"

Now Kid shrugged. "I think I like you. How's that?" Relaxing from the shrug, he began to laugh. "You want to suck it, sit on it, that's fine by me."

Now you're going to turn around and run off and look all scared and wide-eyed at me every time we see each other from now on huh? But I want to make love to you, sometime. Just you."

... "I'd like that." (Delany 400)

Within this conversation, there are moments of awkwardness, and mis-communication, but there is also a great deal of honesty. Kid acknowl-edges his desire for Denny and his fear that, because Denny hasn't had sex with a man before, he will become a symbol of the something fearful and therefore unspeakable. It's as if Kidd is saying to Denny, "You have the power, by not acknowledging what we did, to make me disappear." But Denny is not a naïve or unwilling participant. He admits his desire for Kidd, and the relationship that develops out of their first sexual encounter is a genuine one that lasts throughout the rest of the novel.

What makes *Dhalgren* even more important is that it critiques the same community for which it also shows great compassion. Tak Loufer, a gay man who has a swastika tattoo on his back that he won't talk about, gets into a fight with Paul Fenster, a black political activist. Fenster asks:

"—what *gives* you a black soul."

"Alienation. The whole gay thing, for one."

"That's a passport to a whole area of culture and the arts you fall into just by falling into bed," Fenster countered. "Being black is an automatic cutoff from that same area unless you do some fairly fancy toe-in-the-door work." Fenster sucked at his teeth. "Being a faggot does *not* make you black!"

Tak put his hands down on top of one another. "Oh, all right—"

"You," Fenster announced to Loufer's partial retreat, "haven't wanted a black soul for three hundred years. What the hell is it that's happened in the last fifteen that makes you think you can appropriate it now?"

"Shit." Tak spreads his fingers. "You take anything from me you want—ideas, mannerisms, property and money. And I can't take anything from you?"

"That you *dare*"—Fenster's eyes narrowed—"express, to me, surprise or indignation or hurt (notice I do not include anger) because that is exactly what the situation is, is why you have no black soul.... You can have a black soul when I *tell* you you can have one! Now don't bug me! I gotta go pee!" (Delany 294)

By Fenster calling Tak a faggot he disproves his own point about alien-ation because he invokes a word that is a symbol of alienation and one that has been used by straight people in relation to a history of violence and exclusion. And Tak—who, when Fenster is not around, uses the word "nigger" all the time—ignores the violent and dehumanizing history of being black in the USA, sees only the power black people had recently gained through organization and struggle, and immediately wants to take that power. But by being so defensive and accusatory, they are actually both expressing their longing not to be alienated. Gayness is not heroic, nor does a character's gayness mean they are not closed-minded in other ways.

It's also a very sci-fi moment. Bellona is such an unstable town with such limited resources that Tak and Paul, who under normal circumstances might never acknowledge each other or even meet, are thrust together and given the opportunity really to talk. Delany uses the fact that there is only one real bar, to provide another example of the power of honesty. That people have different viewpoints is precisely why they *should* be talking to each other in the first place. Tak and Fenster don't come to blows because they disagree; in fact, when Fenster is in the bathroom, Tak calls Fenster a good man, and once Fenster comes back, Tak concedes Fenster's point and they continue drinking together. So, just as *Dhalgren* makes no attempt to reason away the unfamiliar, it encourages the reader, through constant, unresolved, and frank discussions about sexuality and race, to make the unfamiliar familiar.

When I asked Elizabeth Hand about what the book meant to her, she said, "There was a period of time when I was in university in the '70s when I would give that book to male friends to read and I'm not making this up, there were like three or four of them who read that book and then proceeded to come out of the closet. And they were not people who were necessarily sci-fi fans.... I think at that time, science fiction really kind of opened a door for a lot of people that had been closed."

There is, however, a door in *Dhalgren* that remains closed. There are threesomes, gangbangs, and orgies, there is sex between a woman and a man, two men, a man and a tree, a man and a little blind boy who has red glass balls for eyes, but for all this, there is not one sex scene between two women. One peripheral character, Madame Brown, casually reveals that she is a lesbian at the very end of the book, but only after Kidd directly asks her about it—afterwards, the subject is immediately dropped, and nothing before that reveal had given any indication of Madame Brown's sexual orientation.

The one mention of a sexual relationship between two women, Filament and Black Widow, is less than a paragraph long:

> Always standing hand in hand, always sitting knee to knee whispering, running through the house giggling or asleep at any time in any room, one's head against the other's breast, one's breast beneath the other's hand, intense, innocently exhibitionistic, and almost wordless, they developed, within hours, a protective/voyeuristic (?) male circle that ran with them everywhere…. (Delany 694)

Black Widow leaves after a few weeks and Filament is described as "sad, but did not talk about her; then returned to older ways" (694).

The relationship is described in extremely childlike terms: the women giggle, whisper, sleep curled next to each other; if they have sex, it's never mentioned. The two women are also never alone; rather, they are constantly observed by a group of men, as if the male gaze itself is what makes their relationship exist at all. By being "exhibitionistic," they also desire and invite this male gaze, and by being "innocently exhibitionistic," they are too naïve to even know that they are doing so. The men, who are not so naïve, recognize the importance of their "voyeuristic" gaze and "protect" the women with it, as if, by leaving the women to their own devices, something dangerous would happen.

When Black Widow leaves, Filament is momentarily sad, but she wordlessly and immediately returns to heterosexuality, and in doing so, she is: "returned to older ways." The word "returned" implies that heterosexuality is permanent, a fixed point to which women always find their way back when they stray. And "older ways" implies that lesbianism is newer than heterosexuality, a new place to visit, a new place from which to return, but never in which to remain. Lesbianism can never be a home. We don't hear from Black Widow or Filament about their feelings on the matter, either. In this way, it is even worse than *Penthouse*: not even a shout and then a silence, just a deep absence of sound.

Arguably, it is not Delany's job as an author to represent every human being in existence. But why did he feel that he could authoritatively include the perspectives of a rapist, the woman he raped, a strong heterosexual woman, an asexual monk, people from every nearly every race, class background, sexual proclivity and gender representation, and not include even one word of desire spoken between two women? Why was a lesbian so beyond the scope of Delany's massive imagination? Why am I so unimaginable?

* * *

When I went to college, I started reading lesbian literature by actual lesbians: Jeanette Winterson, Myles, Rebecca Brown, and Allison. In these stories and novels, I found something I had never found in the waxed blonde Barbies of my father's *Penthouse* books, or the alabaster-skinned warriors pledging eternal love in the moonlight of sci-fi fan fiction, or the desexualized and infantilized lesbians in *Dhalgren*. What I found was lesbians who were ordinary. They had jobs, favorite foods. They fought with each other over petty things, they read books, they held each other, they went to movies, they lied, they told the truth, they took shits. I remember reading Allison's short story "A Lesbian Appetite" and getting goose bumps. The sex scene in it is good—really good—but what makes it so good is that prior to having sex, the two women are simply cooking a meal together and talking. The sex had slid out of a close, casual domesticity: one minute they are chopping eggplants and teasing each other, the next minute they are rubbing those eggplants on each other's nipples and orgasming on the floor, and the next minute they are back to chopping eggplants and teasing each other. Like the gay male and heterosexual relationships in *Dhalgren*, no apologies or explanations are necessary. But unlike *Dhalgren*, when the women leave the kitchen, they don't walk out into a post-apocalyptic ghost town; rather, they walk to their weekly Women's Collective meetings, to their mothers' houses, to their friends. They walk out into the real world. I didn't have to do any imagining or creating to see myself and my friends in these women's lives. I simply read and felt recognized.

Rebecca Brown's short story "Nancy Booth, Wherever You Are" was similarly revolutionary. The story is narrated by a 13-year-old girl who realizes that she has a crush on her camp counselor, Scuff. The narrator is on the cusp of understanding that both she and Scuff are lesbians, though the narrator doesn't quite know what a lesbian is. They talk every night after lights out. I kept expecting their conversations to be about flirtation or about sex, but instead, they talk about books or music or who they would be if they could be one person in history. At the end of the summer, the narrator asks for Scuff's address and they write letters back and forth to each other for years. Again, they are not romantic letters, but letters of friendship and guidance. Scuff never tells the narrator how to be a lesbian. She teaches her a much more powerful lesson: that lesbians are people, that they are not defined by sex or sexual attraction, and that can, not only survive, but thrive. Scuff eventually stops writing. The narrator, now an adult, reflects on the impact of her letters: "Sometimes, I still think of her. I think of her kindness, what she gave me, her example.... I also want to tell her that a tomboy she met years ago, a girl, like any girl, with her own set of pains and fears and mysteries was helped by her. I want to tell her I survived and I am happy now. I want to tell her I am grateful" (Brown 50).

I thought here of dinners at my high school girlfriend's house with Aunt Linda and Aunt Sarah. They sat next to each other at the head of the table with wry smiles on their faces.

"Have you seen *Personal Best?*" Aunt Sarah asked.

"Yes," I said.

"Ha!" Aunt Linda pounded the table with her wine glass. "And how does it end?"

"Obviously, Muriel Hemingway leaves the older lesbian for a man." I sighed, a world-weary sound that only a sixteen-year-old would make. "Just like all lesbian movies."

They looked back at each other over their matching wire rim glasses and shook their heads. "I guess she knows everything. I guess there's nothing else we can teach her."

But they did teach me. They taught me by holding down jobs and having a home together and raising children that the life I wanted to lead was possible, that I had a future. And like *Dhalgren* they also taught me about the duplicity of sexual attraction. Aunt Linda's first serious relationship was with a man. They dated all through high school and even got engaged.

"Did you love him?" I asked.

"I did," she said.

"But you're a *lesbian*."

She smiled at me and raked a hand through her salt and pepper hair. "I am."

I was incredulous. That sexuality and love were fluid did not seem possible. How could she call herself a lesbian if she'd been attracted to a man, even once? Wasn't identity something that never changed? Leaving room for fluidity when it came to lesbianism and love made me nervous, like the boss from the *Penthouse* story had just stuck his erection between

Aunt Linda and Aunt Sarah's love. But stories, at their best, do not just show us what we want to see; they also show us what we don't want to see, what we are afraid of seeing. They show us the very core of our fear. They remind us that there is never anything completely solid or unchanging in this world. Gay, straight or otherwise, people are attracted to individuals, not whole populations of people. And though words like gay and straight are umbrella terms that group large populations together for the sake of community building and political organizing, figuring out how you identify is a highly personal act. Aunt Linda loved Sarah, and she loved the man she almost married, and neither thing canceled the other out or made her any more or less a lesbian. And when it came down to it, no one could tell me who I was then or was going to be later, not even myself.

I needed the reality of all these stories just as much as I needed the fantasy of fan fiction or science fiction. Reading and hearing about the normal, and often contradictory parts of being a lesbian made me feel like I had more options for how I could live my life. I could define myself as much by my sexual desires as by my interest in mask making or writing or going on picnics. And my sexual desires didn't have to be steadfast either. Fluidity didn't mean I would disappear; it meant that I would have greater freedom to be myself. What a simple and yet completely revolutionary idea.

Offering a fluid, liberating orientation, Eileen Myles's writing straddles many genres—poetry, fiction, personal essay—and covers a wide range of subjects. Her most recent book, *Inferno*, deals specifically with finding one's identity as a woman, poet, and lesbian, and the ways that reading and writing play a part in that identification. The book opens with a young "fictional" Myles staring at her writing teacher's ass: "With each movement of her arms and her hand delicately but forcefully inscribing the letters intended for our eyes her ass shook ever so slightly. I had never learned from a woman with a body before. Something slow, horrible and glowing was happening inside of me. I stood on the foothills to heaven. She opened the door" (Myles, *Inferno* 1). There is an explicit link between desire, shame, queerness, words, and a redemptive sense of self.

In our interview, one of the first questions I asked Eileen was how she experienced the link between queerness and shame as a child:

Eileen: When I was growing up it was more about not being a lady. There
was this great phobia around something that I *was* being by not being
that … like "not being a lady" was covering something that was much
more awful…. So there was a message right away that I was humiliating
myself by some kind of leakage, and I needed to seal it down. I feel the
first thing we're told about our queerness is to stop it immediately
because we're bringing shame upon ourselves and our house.

Me: And even saying, you need to be more of a lady doesn't really get at
what people don't like or don't want from you. Which makes it worse—

Eileen: Which makes you totally paranoid—

Me: Because you don't even know what is wrong with you.

Eileen: Yes, you're like a ship where the crew is running around and they
know that the ship is sinking and they don't know why. (Myles, Personal
interview)

What strikes me about this comment is that despite our age gap (Eileen is
61 and I am 26), the messages we received about the shame of being a
lesbian were strikingly similar. The taunts that were thrown at me, particularly when I was younger and hadn't come out, were not fag or dyke; they
were that I was manly. As if having a deep voice or wearing blue sneakers
or laughing out loud was something that only men got to do. And, by
doing so, we weren't just being ourselves. We were actively trying to take
away men's identities and had to be shamed into stopping. As if a person's
identity is so tenuous that the only way for it to exist is to make other
people exist less.

Clearly, most girls' bodies and behaviors have been policed in this way
whether they are gay or not. But after I came out, my supposed "manli-
ness" was also the explanation for my attraction to women. Many of my
high school friends said things like, "I don't even think about you being
gay, I just think of you as a dude." So then I tried to be "a dude" in as
many aspects of my life as I could. I wore a baseball hat and baggy shirts
that said things like "Hos to lay and suckers to spray." I talked to girls like
I was a little bit better than them, teased and tickled them, got into their
personal space without asking. I made jokes about how stupid women
were, about bitches and their feelings. There was privilege in this position.
Presenting myself this way made straight men and even most straight
women comfortable and more willing to accept me. But, while straight
women were happy to flirt, or be picked up and spun around or cuddled
drunkenly at a high school party, when it came to going on a date or
having sex, their answer was always, "If only you were a man." And while

straight men and women were fine having a gay friend, I couldn't talk about the loneliness or confusion I felt because they didn't see how I could be feeling so lonely and confused. And how could I expect them to understand this loneliness and confusion when I spent so much time trying to make my life as a lesbian seem full and easy and clear cut?

Like Eileen, I was constantly scrambling to present my sexuality and my gender in a way that was socially acceptable, but internally, it didn't work. Eileen said that as a child she "just prayed to God to make me wake up as a boy." Being boys meant our desires would be encouraged, not ridiculed. Eileen pointed out that it isn't just the desire for women that would have been encouraged, but the desire to be a writer, a desire that for most women carries many of the same roadblocks as being a lesbian.

As a child of the 1950s and early 1960s, Eileen had even less access to queer media or people than I did, so literature was essential to her understanding and acceptance of herself. She told me about the effect Yukio Mishima's book *Confessions of a Mask* had on her as a teenager:

> *Eileen:* It's an amazing book and I took this amazing class in college called "The Adolescent in Literature" and it was taught by this guy Lee Grove, who's a queer. He introduced us to … a whole array of classic coming of age books that touched on gender constantly and one of them was Mishima, and it was about a boy seeing a picture of Joan of Arc and being alarmed that it was a woman and that alarm being the beginning of something opening for him in his sexuality. And I just remember, it was the first time I ever read anything like that….
>
> *Me:* Was that a part of feeling right in your body or right in your sexuality? What was that opening for you?
>
> *Eileen:* Well, the confusions that felt like the most familiar places in my psyche were connected to other people's confusions. So if someone else was confused, like this boy, there would probably be another person and another person who was confused, and it's like once I saw it reflected in print, I knew that it was true. (Myles, Personal interview)

For Eileen, as for me, reading opened up a whole world. Not only did she know there was someone else who was confused; she also knew that it was possible to voice that confusion on something as permanent and far reaching as a page. Books are not just being read by one person. They are being read by many people. Part of the thrill of reading something with which I identify is knowing that other people will read it and know a part of me, and if *they* identify with it, I will know a part of them.

Being able to read yourself also means being able to write yourself. For Myles, this meant taking all the messages she'd received about lesbians and women writers being fearful, ugly, or incomplete and holding those messages outside of herself, exposing them: "I think writing is a way of detraumatizing the witnessing that already occurred. So often I feel like my writing is a soundtrack to the visual silence of my childhood, and also my adulthood…. It's like I want to be whole, I want to be present, but it's just a bumpy road. So writing isn't fixing that, but kind of opening it somehow and making a different kind of whole."

I want to be whole too, which is why I continue to read and write. Reading allows me to see myself in a variety of settings and people, who I think am, who I could be, who I've always wanted to be. Reading connects me to a community, and I take that community with me when I do the personal, solitary work of writing. I write because I want other people to see me, but I also write because I want them to see themselves and know that they too are just as real and important as anyone else. As Myles says, writing can't erase the silence of the past, but when I write, whether the stories are real or imagined, gay or straight, they cut through the silence, they make a noise, even if that noise only lasts until I turn off the computer or put down my pen.

WORKS CITED

Allison, Dorothy. 1988. A Lesbian Appetite. In *Trash*. Ithaca: Firebrand. Print.

———. 1994. Puritans, Perverts, and Feminists. In *Skin: Talking about Sex, Class and Literature*. Ithaca: Firebrand. Print.

Brown, Rebecca. 2003. Nancy Booth, Wherever You Are. In *The End of Youth*. San Francisco: City Lights. Print.

Delany, Samuel R. 1977. *Dhalgren*. Boston: Gregg. Print.

Hand, Elizabeth. Personal interview. 15 Jan. 2012.

Myles, Eileen. 2010. *Inferno (A Poet's Novel)*. New York: OR. Print.

———. Personal interview. 11 Nov. 2011.

CHAPTER 8

Work This Cunt Bucket: Knowledge, Love, and De-containment in Sapphire's *Push*

Michael Angelo Tata

Admittedly, the language of Sapphire's *Push* is raw, rude, and offensive in almost every way known to readers and writers alike: brilliantly descriptive passages about sex, body, rape, ravishment, locomotion, curvature, flesh, odor, nutrition, and comestibility are a shock to even the most enlightened communities, making the novel the fantastic achievement that it was and continues to be, and placing Sapphire herself in the enviable position of being a dangerous writer. Sure, Oprah will turn her book into a movie, but when will she ask her Book Clubbers to engage Sapphire's language on the page, placing her by the side of William Faulkner and Toni Morrison? Through the power of her anguished and agonistic language, among whose accumulations and dispersals a word like "cunt bucket" creates jarring electric discharge, Sapphire becomes monstrous in her own right, and can only haunt popular culture as bad girl, Ebonic phantom, and urban legend, legendary for producing a *mythos* no urban center will ever own up to: such is the nature of her queer disruptiveness and its utter monstrosity. For who could ever claim to have a part in the New York City of Claireece Precious Jones, to own incest, retardation, disability, and the nightmare cycle of welfare dependence making it possible for

M.A. Tata (✉)
Coral Gables, FL, USA

© The Author(s) 2018
E. McNeil et al. (eds.), *Mapping Queer Space(s) of Praxis and Pedagogy*, Queer Studies and Education,
DOI 10.1007/978-3-319-64623-7_8

fiends like Mary Johnston and Carl Jones to direct the development of the innocent? Balls to the wall, Sapphire crosses multiple and supernumerary boundaries of decorum, holding up a funhouse mirror contorting the present into a mangled dystopia where Freudian family romance meets lost Dickensian foundling.

Yet among all the words and expressions Sapphire uses to bring her protagonist Precious's precarious situation to light, from this astounding collection of words and phrases that comes to constitute a Monster Language in its own right, the strange compound noun "cunt bucket" is, to me, the most critical in her twisted lexicon; as an expression, it best encapsulates the epistemological and pedagogical states in which Precious finds her thrown-ness thrown. The term is certainly too hot for Tyler Perry and Oprah, surviving as buried expletive that continues to throb off-camera, posing too much of a challenge to Hollywood and its tinseled surfaces: I cannot employ the word "too" enough when it comes to the cunt bucket, as comparatives and superlatives multiply around this queer center of ignorance and rehabilitation. While the film *Precious* (2009) does its best to import the feel of violation, entrapment, and abuse which Sapphire so carefully uses to create Precious's world, the palliative involvement of Perry and Oprah causes some of the most vicious aspects of Sapphire's vivid, visceral, and vulgar language to disappear: it is among these casualties of respectability that the cunt bucket reigns queerly as stilted queen, too ugly to be repeated, too ripe to be appreciated, and yet an adhesive string of letters that sticks in my mind and throat, unable to be dislodged. The cunt bucket obsesses me, and I can only exorcise it by devoting myself to it, engaging its function as both vivacious piece of literary language and poetic manifestation of the cultural tendency to seal off the psyches of various women, rendering them impermeable to knowledge and illumination. And as knowledge itself invokes the amorous relation of lover and beloved, particularly as this state has been vitrified by the discipline we call *philosophy*, I can think of no better way to interrogate the scene of knowledge-production which eventually becomes Precious's proper matrix than to take this cunt that is also a bucket but can never carry wisdom because, at best, it can only dominate a mundane technique of filling and emptying, and undo it philosophically as commentary on pedagogy.

Although there is clearly a homosocial network in place in *Push*, to use the term coined by Eve Sedgwick in her classic investigation *Between Men*, along with the inferred presence of lesbian desire, via the lesbian character Blue Rain, whose orientation is never in question, yet is a site of curiosity and interest among the members of her community, and in the end, essentially connected with the liberatory thinking only an outsider could give, the queerness I attribute to the cunt bucket transcends configurations of carnality or sexual gravitation, and is more the equivalent of the word *seltsam* as Ludwig Wittgenstein uses it in so much of his philosophical writing: that is, as the inception point of philosophical puzzlement, the spot where the ordinariness of ordinary language loses its customary transparency, and we are quite simply left to ponder as the inexorability of a mathematical truism like $2 + 2 = 4$ slips through our fingers.[1] We *wonder* because a situation or phenomenon has revealed a new aspect to us: a duck suddenly becomes a rabbit, or a rabbit becomes a duck, or perhaps a Necker Cube reveals the presence of a second competing cube within its lines, causing us to marvel at the emergence of a once hidden order: in short, the queer moment is that rarefied point in time when the utter strangeness of a destabilizing novel dimension throws into relief the sense of comfort we expect to experience as we take refuge in the ordinary, relieving us of the various complacencies and comforts which have blinded us to the existence of all that transcends the nullifying stases of normalcy—even when that normalcy is profoundly abnormal. The cunt bucket is one such node, pulverizing language, biology, and philosophy, queer to the core, and speaking to the ways in which knowledge-production itself is anything but the simple amassing of material within receptacle, the famously repurposed Platonic *chora* of Luce Irigaray, Julia Kristeva, and Jacques Derrida, ceasing to function as boundary, border, or membrane, and revealing the amorous roots of sapience, in general, which might be housed in a brain yet which transcends location, traveling outside of itself into the ether as perhaps its greatest illusion: such is the course my engagement of the cunt bucket's queerness and its geometrical salvation will take as I parse the an-epistemology of Precious and attempt a thetic dissolution of the many stupidities and ignorances that inform and structure this grim picture—grim, but certainly not hopeless.

Let the urban *Symposium* begin.

This Ain't No Container Store

For this project, I take the semantic unit "cunt bucket" coined or at bare minimum popularized by Sapphire—for its history must in some way be determined, much in the way that Jim Dawson's *The Compleat Motherfucker* gives the motherfucker its genealogical due—and engage it both linguistically and existentially, tying it to Precious's epistemic journey along her own Divided Line from subject of a paralyzing ignorance leaving her alone in the gutters of the Harlem Renaissance to rebirth as cupbearer of the liberating light of knowledge. In placing and displacing the cunt bucket, my personal homage to Sapphire, I look at the role it plays in the poetics of *Push*, along with how, as a metaphor of the female body, in particular, when that body is rendered monstrous, it speaks to the place allotted to women within that love of wisdom we call philosophy, the amorous tendency that, if we follow Platonic metaphysics, makes women of men in the cycle of degeneration at the core of the cosmology in his *Timaeus*.[2] Outside of the occasional Diotima, who must necessarily be a foreigner, women are read as receptacles or vessels, places where materials pass without being causally connected with either container or containment—particularly when that matter is epistemic in nature, turning the feminine into a Receptacon—inert, automatic, and thoughtless.

In her *Revolution in Poetic Language*, psychoanalyst and critic Kristeva famously conceives of the pre-linguistic mind of the infant as a *chora* or place where a chaos of sense data semiotically destabilizes the infant, who rides the chaos of the various desires and impulses assaulting it, buffeted about by the fluxion of the material world, which has not yet become the social site of symbolization for it.[3] Kristeva borrows the term *chora* from Plato's *Timaeus*, where it is called a *hypodoche* and described as being a host or receptacle for primordial matter, exhibiting the contradiction of helping to create matter while somehow remaining outside materiality itself, fundamentally and radically heterogeneous to it: it authors matter, but is not matter. Since Plato genders the *hypodoche* as female, an attributory act that Kristeva does not dismiss, Kristeva's dilemma becomes that of the principle of receptivity identified with the chora and feminized by Plato, who views it as something of a nurse or mother, marks an epistemological turn in which the feminine and the empty become synonymous. While Kristeva will view this emptiness—productive as it is—as the foundation of poetry and revolution, assimilating the chora to maternal materiality in the most optimistic way possible, it still leaves female receptivity intact, causing problems within a society for whom reception is read all too readily as a kind of non-productive, ideal passivity devoid of materiality, yet uterinely bound to it.

Within the grammatological and pharmaceutical,[4] this particular formulation of the chora is also critical to Derrida's deconstruction in

Dissemination, as he seeks to carve out a space for the inchoate within a culture seeking to pin down meaning and inexorabilize it through the literary management of presence and absence. For him, the chora will become less of a causeway to the cunt bucket and more the ungenderable commitment to absence that every writing project takes as its cause, wither consciously or despite itself. And yet again, the idea of the chora is taken up by Queer Theorists like Irigaray in her *Speculum of the Other Woman* and Judith Butler in her *Bodies That Matter*, as they seek to undo the deleterious trend of identifying women with conduits, places where male knowledge rains down, filling their emptiness with positive content always external to it: a veritable chorus of *chorae*. With regard to Sapphire, and the strange and beautiful life of her greatest creation, the cunt bucket, what I am arguing here is that the cunt bucket is another way of articulating "chora," and consequently examining instances when people treat Sapphire's character Claireece Precious Jones as receptacle, all in an effort to reveal the many ways in which assimilating her to a Receptacon have hurt her, as in the sperm receptacle her father makes of her: for when women are viewed as receptacles, when the chora of semiotic possibilities becomes recast as the space where male knowledge and ideas proliferate symbolically and socially, then women lose their access to agency and volition, becoming mere instruments put to the use of male machinists, who inseminate them with flagellates and information. This filling and ordering takes place for "average" and monstrous bodies alike: *Push* merely uses an outré instance to permit the exception to illuminate the conditions of possibility of the rule.

In conjunction with the chora of Plato, Kristeva, Derrida, Irigaray, and Butler, and yet departing from them productively, Sapphire reveals through Precious and the literal and metaphorical readings of her anatomy embodied by the word "cunt bucket" that the concatenation of genitalia and container limits drastically what women—and particularly women of color—can be expected to achieve, and hence must not merely be emptied, but dissolved. Furthermore, Plato's reflections on the relation between container and form, place and production in his *Timaeus* are preceded by his theories of intellectual midwifery and the transmissivity of knowledge in his *Theaetetus*, the dialogic spot where Socrates most powerfully formulates his self-identity as one who possesses no positive knowledge but helps others give birth to their own, technically making him a second-generation midwife, or *maia*, the philosophical equivalent and heir to his mother, the "burly" Phaenarete.[5] Like Socrates, Blue Rain, Precious's mentor, herself a gateway to *anamnesis*, or recollection, does not so much instill positive content within Precious's mind as much as she teaches her how to think and remember for herself. In doing so, Blue Rain uses Socratic dialecticality, while also leveraging a kind of educational reform initiated centuries after Plato by Paolo Freire, whose approach to learning and education in *Pedagogy of the Oppressed* veers away from the domesticity and docilization of bodies so frequently imposed by grammar, canon, and the institutions protecting them against erosion, invasion, or contamination. Transforming Precious from cold metal pail to warm and pulsing center of ideas, concepts, and *rêverie*, Blue Rain is the exact kind of Socratic-Freirian teacher who does not impart positive content, but instead exposes the foundations of educability through a benign queer maieutics coming closest to that dialogic ideal, the conversation, which if we believe Richard Rorty, is the cornerstone of philosophy, and if we follow William Blake, the spot where internecine chaos gives way to friendship.

It is with this palette of ideas in mind that I take Sapphire's wonderful word, a bit of urban sass eluding cinematic recuperation, and examine what it has to say about Kristeva, Derrida, and Plato and their ideas about these cosmologies of knowledge which determine how our own possibilities play out in a world where, as Wittgenstein aptly notes in his *Philosophical Investigations*, our metaphors so often mislead us, compelling us to take a picture for reality. Along with him, I want to urge: "A *picture* held us captive. And we could not get outside it, for it lay in our language and language seemed to repeat it to us inexorably" (Wittgenstein §115). Here, the inexorable or *Unerbittlichkeit* is the exact opposite of the *seltsam*, which rather than stabilizing our epistemic impulses via cultural homeostasis, confuses them, throwing them into chaos and queering their scrutabilities. I would certainly argue that taking the vajayjay as a repository has created a trope that has led us to mistake women as vaults waiting to be filled and appreciate the ways in which Sapphire has attempted to lead us out of the quagmire by showcasing its contemporary form in a particularly monstrous case. In essence, this piece of writing could only be a meditation on the intransigencies of translation: primarily the semantic challenge posed to us by the cunt bucket, which I am translating from contemporary street to philosophical Greek. But it also scrutinizes the difficulties involved with hewing the cunt bucket from its literary context and translating it from small to large rectangle, page to screen: its inscrutability is obvious, as are the various resistances it sparks.[6]

What presents itself is a series of reflections on the refrangibility of neologism, on the demands a new word makes upon us, especially when it speaks to us from across the divide of idiomatic or cultural difference, queering not only our lexicon, but our syntax, the order we impose upon words comprising our world. Ultimately, I am declaring a kind of synonymic equation between the cunt bucket and the chora, since for me, and I would argue for Sapphire, yet perhaps neither Oprah nor Tyler, the cunt bucket is the most current version of the chora in existence, a myth that demands direct address. And as the ghetto-fabulousness of Precious depends upon her coming-to-consciousness of the fact that she is anything but a cunt bucket, I must historicize the concept of the chora, if only so we might come to an understanding of the social mythology in play in Precious's Harlem, within the educational system she must conquer, within a familial constellation in which her mother views her as a rival rather than a victim, and in her own relation to fame and glamour, as evidenced by her bright and vivid daydreams of beauty and celebrity, and her own ascension to star of literacy, one who, when the going gets rough, is sheltered by Langston Hughes's home, which felicitously and non-allergically receives her, like housing like:

> But you know where I stay? Ms Rain got friend who is caretaker or something at Langston Hughes' house which is not but around the corner, it's city landmark. I SPEND ONE NIGHT IN LANGSTON HUGHES' HOUSE HE USED TO LIVE IN. Me and Abdul in the Dream Keeper's house! (Sapphire, *Push* 79–80)

For if Precious begins her journey as a queer monster presence, star of her own Creature Feature in this never-ending Halloween of hypothalamic freakishness and fleshy excess, she finally comes to a place where she can be both beautiful and articulate, a subject who makes decisions and not an object ruled by blind, cruel determinisms of class, race, and gender. She gets one night with Langston, which is one more than most of us ever have the good fortune to receive. Langston's guest, honoree inducted into the Harlem Renaissance, site of literary hospitality, Precious does finally make it out of the cunt bucket trap, learning how to learn, and in doing so becoming a completely different kind of receiving principle, host or *hospis*.

CUNT BUCKET, CUNT BOX, PECKERWOOD: ILLUSIONS
OF BEING AND HAVING

In an untitled poem that is a masterpiece of minimalism, the poet Lorine
Niedecker succinctly and poignantly writes:

> Remember my little granite pail
> The handle of it was blue.
> Think what's got away in my life
> Was enough to carry me thru. (7)

As I am embarking upon a literary project aimed at unearthing the meanings, uses, and abuses of an expression like "cunt bucket," I am instantly
drawn to the only other literary pail I know, Niedecker's. And yet the
move from Sapphire to Niedecker, poets with huge stylistic and cultural
differences, is neither random nor gratuitous, as the two combine to raise
important questions about gender, containment, memory, loss, and possibility in a pataphysics I am attempting to turn into a metaphysics—
queerly, the only way it could be done. For how can one be sustained by
all that has overflowed the boundaries and limits of retention? Does the
sensual material that escapes me mnemonically come to constitute a gravi-
tational core structurally similar to Freud's primally repressed *bolus* as it
continues to influence psyche, despite the fact that it is essentially no—or
elsewhere—and if so, then what lies outside Precious's pail, exerting
spooky-action-at-a-distance? If for Lorine this implement for storage manifests as a childhood artifact standing at the juncture of things held onto
and things swallowed by the abyss, for Sapphire it will become an entirely
different kind of vessel, one concerned with the positive contents of epistemology and pedagogy and with how the metaphorical rendition of gendered bodies within society delimits who can fill and who gets filled—in
essence, ordering the sequence "filling" for monsters and regular folk
alike. Memory will also be involved in this second birth, primarily as it ties
to the notion of positionality, or thetism: that is, the ability of Precious to
take her place within the social-symbolic, using experience and memory to
anchor herself within time.

Reading Precious's implement against Niedecker's, unconventional as
this move might be, allows a series of perhaps unanswerable questions to
emerge. For example, if there is a cunt bucket, is there also a cunt pail? In
Push, there is a cunt box, so why not other cunt structures? Does the cunt
function as a kind of lexeme, giving birth to accessory implements that all
share a verbal relation with it pointing to further structural correspondences

within the tools designated by the items in a Cunt Series? The logic of the cunt seems to demand its attachment to satellite nouns demarcating the packaging and partitioning of space, its obsidian and obsidional transformation into a shiny besieged polygon separating an inside from an outside, contents from dis-contents:

> Everybody call me Precious. I got three names—Claireece Precious Jones. Only motherfuckers I hate call me Claireece.
> "How old are you, Claireece?"
> White cunt box got my file on her desk. I see it. I ain't that late to lunch. Bitch know how old I am. (Sapphire, *Push* 6–7)

Is the cunt box a variation of a cunt bucket, a square version of a cylindrical original, or is it, in fact, some other cunt formation, another take on the logic of containment? From the perspectives of Heideggerian handiness (*Zuhandenheit*) central to the existential disentanglement recommended by *Being and Time* or the Sartrean staple of the hodological map in its charting of self, space, and Other, we are led to ask what respective instrumentalities the cunt bucket or cunt box possess, which functions they facilitate, if they diverge or converge on a kind of essence or *eidos*. In the world of instruments and instrumental-complexes/hodologies, does a bucket differ from a pail, in general, and if so, how do the various vaginal versions of "bucket" and "pail" play out within an urban American mythology that seems to give them their *raison d'être*? Lastly, are there positive and negative uses for the cunt bucket—that is, using it to hold memories of lived experience via *mnésis* versus storing the wisdom of others hypomnesiacally?[7]

In addition, what is the relation between the compound "cunt bucket" and the compound of choice Sapphire uses to denote various males, the peckerwood, as in Precious's exchange with her math teacher, Mr. Wicher?

> I say, "Motherfucker I ain't deaf!" The whole class laugh. He turn red. He slam his han' down on the book and say, "Try to have some discipline." He a skinny little white man about five feets four inches. A peckerwood as my mother would say. I look at him 'n say, "I can slam too. U wanna slam?" (Sapphire, *Push* 4–5)

Like cunt bucket, peckerwood is a derisive term refracted through the lens of Precious's mother, Mary Johnston, who, true to the workings of the chora, becomes the first linguistic barrier encountered by a Precious on the verge of articulacy and the ultimate site of monstrosity, place where deformed body produces queer body. Part of Mary's linguistic body, the cunt bucket and the peckerwood must be assimilated and ultimately rejected by Precious if she is to individuate, taking her place among the symbols of the unfolding social scene. Also like the cunt bucket, the peckerwood is something one is, not something one has; it is an identity or totality, not the identification of a part that can take on a relation to possession. Pretending to partake of no mereology, it claims on the surface to truck solely with entities that are entireties, even though they represent the conflation of whole and part that produce the metonymies and synecdoches constructing social reality. One is, not "has," a peckerwood or cunt bucket in Precious's Harlem, just as down on the Jersey Shore, one *has* a Christian Audigier trucker cap, but *is* a douchebag, or when, in the gastroenterology clinic, one *has*, not *is*, a colostomy bag, linguistic situations recalling the primal Lacanian drama of the phallus, which women curiously are and men only *seem* to possess, "penis" and "phallus" never coinciding, the latter always overflowing and escaping the former, opening up every imaginable possibility of pursuit.[8] In light of these questions, I wonder: must metaphors of "pail" and "bucket" be removed entirely, displaced from the scene of memory and knowledge such that the cunt becomes some other entity—perhaps a fountain, as in the Blakean adage, "The cistern contains: the fountain overflows" from his *The Marriage of Heaven and Hell*? Or dare I veer away from thalassography entirely, decoupling "wisdom" from "water," despite the history of their conjunction within the Western tradition of liquid intelligence?

Clearly, it is time to turn to *Push* and the very concrete and specific instantiations of the word "cunt bucket," so that I might better discern what exactly the word means to Sapphire, and why I should take it as a microcosm of the macrocosmic state of affairs representing Precious's queer present. Although I have identified it as a critical hotspot, and in many ways placed the entire weight of Sapphire's Monster Language upon it, I have not done so because of its frequency but rather because of all Sapphire's iterations, it is the one which best encapsulates what's wrong with both the educational institution and the system of gender relations available to Precious, who finds herself drastically and fatally limited by containment and its metaphors, as they liquidate her possibilities. In fact, "cunt bucket" only appears twice, both times toward the book's beginning, presumably closer to semiosis and further away from symbolization:

She look at me like I said I wanna suck a dog's dick or some shit. What's with this cunt bucket? (That's what my muver cal women she don't like, cunt buckets. I kinda get it and I kinda don't get it, but I like the way is sounds so I say it too). (7)

"Fat cunt bucket slut! Nigger pig bitch! He done quit me! He done left me 'cause of you. What you tell them motherfuckers at the damn hospital? I should KILL you!" she screaming at me. (19)

In the first instance, Precious meets with her school counselor Mrs. Lichenstein, who informs her that her recent pregnancy is the cause of her suspension from school; here, "cunt bucket" is clearly a female version of the peckerwood, as it, too, applies to white authority figures who make up for what they lack in stature or physical beauty by the authority they represent and wield, roadblocks along Precious's way. In the second instance, Precious's mother attacks her for releasing the name of her baby daddy to the authorities at the hospital, where she gives birth to the differently abled Little Mongo, since by identifying her father as Mongo's parent and Mongo as her sister-daughter, she has jeopardized his freedom and, by extension, Mary Johnston's love life. In particular, the second instantiation of "cunt bucket" reveals a certain nominal gravity at work within Sapphire's *Sprachspiel*, as nouns agglomerate wildly, clotting literary space with staccato combinations of mono- or di-syllabic particles: *cunt bucket slut nigger pig bitch*, as the current series reads, unpunctuated. These words, each one a bomb, are strung together in a detonative sequence blowing up publishing house, library, and literary history with machine gun precision.[9]

Apart from the phonetic texture of the cunt bucket, with its inherent slant rhyme and assonance, is also the issue of how a contemporary audience would use the word, which illicit syntaxes it would be employed to fill in the production of meaning—and, to me, at least, it is clear there are no *licit* uses of the cunt bucket, which always destabilizes space and place every time it appears, as if by incantation or homeopathic magic. *Urbandictionary.com*, the best source for tracking all the strange and curious words that will most likely never make it into Merriam-Webster but which are used and employed each day on the physical streets and in the electronic corridors of communal space, offers seven definitions of "cunt bucket," along with six definitions of "cuntbucket," all of which bear relevance to Sapphire's use of the term and which, when summed, raise important issues about how the word is to be spaced, and what these spacing choices signify; I present them all in exactly the language in which they're written, bearing in mind the special problem of the word's dual existence as fused (one word) or dispersed nominal compound (technically two words read as one), leaving the question of what exactly keeping the space intact between the two words-become-one has to say about the relation between "cunt" and "bucket," if, for example, it represents a species of proximity, or is instead the very place where the two words threaten to come apart and veer off along their own tangential odysseys. Of all the definitions supplied, I omit only the first one under "cuntbucket," solely because it is an advertisement for a fictitious product, The Cunbbucket™, an item billed as "a new storage device tailored specifically to women."

Apart from this fantasy item, which, even in its fictitiousness, capitalizes upon a receptacle-like quality that Sapphire has through the character of Precious challenged in her undoing of the Kristevan chora, the various definitions provided are:

cunt bucket
1. A great saying used by people who rule
2. (1) A car marketed to and driven by a woman
   (2) An SUV going annoyingly slow in a parking lot
3. Big saggy vag, a real wizard's sleeve
4. A word used when referring to idiots
5. Group of nasty smelling, sloppy looking, vaginas. Which no guy wants to stick his dick in.
6. A bucket full of chopped up cunts. Namely over 5 or 6 cunts.
7. What one bar patron calls another bar patron that bumps into them

cuntbucket
2. Someone who is annouying
3. A XXL vaginal hole
4. An utter bucket of cunt
5. Characteristical name from one of the species commonly found in the nastiest bars, dressed "to kill" LITERALLY in her best of 80's motif accompanied with poofy hair hanging on anyone from 5–95 years old often used by drunk belligerent men to retain sperm in a bucket like way in their femalian genitalia hence referred to as cunt bucket
6. Vulgarly or seductively excessive (*Urban Dictionary*)

In both Sapphire's and the Internet's urban dictionaries, places where every queer expression imaginable becomes normalized, in a sense—and I would have to argue that Sapphire's comes first, indeed that someone like Sapphire necessitates the existence of a lexical collection of street terms in a publicly accessible and popular place—the cunt bucket is clearly a derogatory term speaking to the worst aspects of stereotyped femininity, and yet the word continues to generate meaning, much in the way that its twin "motherfucker" remains vibrant, long after we dispel illusions of incest and fantasies of the voracious MILF, denotation influencing yet underdetermining connotation, which exceeds it brilliantly. *Urban Dictionary* is particularly salient to the fate of the cunt bucket primarily because the definitions it lists are provided by various subscribers to the site, most of whom are presumably prefect representatives of street lingo, the very robust and energetic bastard, illegitimate, "nothic" language Sapphire uses in *Push* to characterize Precious and her world.[10] That "annoying" is rendered "annouying" or that "female" becomes "femalian" are critical, in that these textual and grammatical misfires—specifically, a misspelling and an improperly elongated, double adjective—provide a definition of the cunt bucket from within and not without, in many ways increasing definitional credibility by virtue of the closeness of the actual definition to one who might actually use the word in daily communication, as cuntbucket definition 5 manifests, conjuring an image of Saturday night bar fights and the Reality TV lens capturing them as entertainment for Andy Cohen, all images informing Precious's own *seltsam* sense of celebrity.

Is Precious "annoying"? The world certainly does act as if it has some kind of allergy to her, much in the way that none disturbs my peace of mind more than the victim I victimized, the abject body I declare to be monstrous. Clearly, to her mother, she is an inconvenience, a nuisance and a rival; in many ways, she is also a blight upon an educational system seeking to exert an orthopedic influence upon her intellectual development. What about a potential biological dimension to the cunt bucket, as we see in cunt bucket #3—"a real wizard's sleeve"—or cunt bucket #3—"A (not *an*) XXL vaginal hole?" Does the word trace back to a physical aberration, a supervagina with an exaggerated opening, and hence the capacity to take more action than a regular, regulation-size vagina? It could be a Vagina Dentata, or *vagine* (defined by *Urban Dictionary* as "third-world pussy"). Carl's pillow talk is rife with the language of craters: "Orgasm in me, his body shaking, grab me, call me Fat Mama, Big Hole!" (Sapphire, *Push* 111). During her final social services interview with Ms. Weiss, Mary Johnston, much to Precious's mortification, spills the beans a little too freely, commenting upon her body with a mixture of carnival consternation and maternal ignorance. In the interview, Mary explains that Carl's sexual relations with Precious are rooted in the fact that both he and Precious shared her mammary glands, his sucking causing her lactation to continue until Precious is a toddler, their milky effusions generously bottled for Precious by a mother charged with two mouths to nurse: "'I give him tittie, Precious bottle. Hygiene, you know?'" (135). Nonplussed, Mary continues:

> "So he on me. Then he reach over to Precious! Start wif his finger between her legs. I say Carl what you doing! He say shut your big ass up! This is good for her. The he git off me, take off her Pampers and try to stick his thing in Precious. You know what trip me out is it almost can go in Precious! I think she some kinda freak baby then. I say stop Carl stop! I want him on *me*! I never wanted him to hurt her. I didn't want him doing *anything* to her. I wanted my man for myself. Sex me up, not my chile. So you cain't blame all that shit happen to Precious on *me*. I love Carl, I love him. He her daddy, but he was my man!" (135–136)

Earlier, Mary had described Precious in terms of an excessive growth outdistancing her peers: "Her teef, everything. Teef growing like Bugs Bunny or something!" (134). Her teeth, everything—but even her vagina? Does this post-natal developmental extravagance in some way account for the eventuality that Precious would become a freak baby whose genitals could accommodate penetration by a fully grown man?

Whether or not Precious is in possession of this wizard's sleeve, the fact remains that each of these definitions is in some way evocative of lethal attitudes toward women, who are either turned into voracious sluts whose bodies can never be satiated, irritating presences demanding a smackdown, fallen creatures whose only relation to knowledge is one of total oblivion and disinterest, even radical alterity, as they fill with everything that knowledge is not, spinning heedlessly toward reincarnation as land animals: alcohol, germ cells, hostility, and the unbridled ignorance of those held hostage by their bodies. Like the chora, the cunt bucket is matter that can never matter, the kind of thing that only bastard reasoning can grasp obliquely and inferentially, and about which only a plausible or likely tale can be told, especially when *Urban Dictionary* is doing the telling—and who else would take on the task? Yale?[11] Its production is the vicious counterproduction of Gilles Deleuze and Felix Guatarri: a kind of making that unmakes making, a fabrication that unravels, a second site of making where what is produced is inimical to what *has* been produced elsewhere in this system of creation and progress. It would almost be apt to deem the cunt bucket a hive of antimatter, a Crab Nebula where what is produced destroys other productions directly on contact, the two types of particles at war from the get-go.

THRESHOLDS OF ARTICULACY: SEMI/OSIS, LIMINALITY, MAIEUTIC STRAIN

In order to trace the cunt bucket back to the choral prototype I am arguing produces it in the an-epistemology of silence and stupidity inflicted upon the monstrous body and mind of Precious and ultimately reversed by the lesbian Blue Rain, who, as Sapphire underscores, is a bit idealistic for this GED-geared program of calculable intelligence, I return to Kristeva, who has more than anyone else transported the mythical account of materiality at the heart of Plato's *Timaeus* into the realm of linguistic awareness, where it has flourished as a repository of extra-semantic functioning, gateway to the twinned and intertwined revolutions of poetry and psychosis.[12] While she certainly refashions Plato's *hypodoche* to suit the purposes of the schema of subject-formation she develops, her repurposing has the advantage of making the issue of the receptaclization of women a relevant topic, one touching upon issues of poetry and revolution as much as knowledge-production and ignorance, and, in fact, intimating that the female might already be a monstered entity ever before she swells to the size of a Presh. In Kristeva's version of language acquisition and *assujetissement*, the two, of course, being inseparable, and insuperable, the subject's immersion in the symbolism of language occurs as an interruption in the wild chaos of the semiotic, an inchoate and *jouissance*-suffused zone where the id-like infant, like Levi-Bruhl's primitive, knows no law of contradiction, but proliferates violent and brilliant mental and physical scenes of desire and play under the plenum of the mother's body, its only regulating principle.

As echo of the maternal body, it becomes the crucible, where fragments and figments interact outside the useful and employable pairings of signifier and signified, or the compulsion to generate meaning semantically and syntactically—to GET-R-DONE. As such, the chora becomes the feminized receptacle that subjects itself to the limitations imposed by the social-symbolic in order for the individual psyche-in-process to achieve legibility, audibility, and scrutability in the very public, intersubjective game of communication which is denied monsters and other queer creations, who are spoken at, or about, but never to. As such, the chora is a-thetic, or non-positional, commencing well before the infant embarks upon what Kristeva terms the Thetic Phase, or the point when the infant can situate itself *somewhere* because it has finally come to comprehend and apply concepts of self and space and is thus able to enter society properly, placefully:

> We shall distinguish the semiotic (drives and their articulations) from the realm of signification, which is always that of a proposition or judgment, in other words, a realm of *positions*. This positionality, which Husserlian phenomenology orchestrates through the concepts of *doxa, position,* and *thesis,* is structured as a break in the signifying process, establishing the *identification* of the subject and its object as preconditions of propositionality. We shall call this break which produces the positing of signification a *thetic* phase. (Kristeva, *Revolution* 43)

For Kristeva, the problem with philosophy is that it does not account for the ways in which the I arrives as center of positions, propositions, and positings, erecting it as monumental and eternal; hence, her critique of Husserl, whom she believes never subjects the self to the kind of Semiotic Reduction that would reveal the various stases and motilities that mark its path.[13] The Kristevan move is to, via the special kind of bastard reasoning we call *psychoanalysis*, regress the self to the conditions of its possibility, using the chora as philosophical analogue to the conflictual, storm-buffeted, fuzzy materiality of all that precedes the concept of selfhood. The sem/iosis of this choral creature—semi, partial, and contradictory, anything but solid, whole, or holistic—must limit itself, if there is to be any positionality at all, causing the maturing infant to trade semi/osis for symbology and symbiosis, the social and communal activities it will use to come to thetic awareness and mastery via a shared linguistic project with equals. Outside of thetic consciousness, there is no chance of reflection or recursion, no opportunity to construct a *cogito* or take up a position against abuse and incursion, and so the chora gives way to the *agora*, that space the monster can never enter positionally.

Central to thetism and to thetic cognizance is the idea of time, ultimate marker of where and how we locate ourselves in relation to other minds and bodies with whom we share ecosystem, economy, *oikos*. As Platonic *maia*, she whose uterus carries no fetus yet who can elicit births from her constituency, Blue Rain, whose sexuality can be no accident, becomes the occasion for Precious's thetic development, using the stability and irreversibility of time as a way for her to uproot herself from the Monster position and select a healthier place to call her own. Throughout their educational exchanges, it is the sexual outsider Blue who constantly encourages Precious to date her journals, underscoring the indispensability of Precious's learning to situate herself on life's calendar in a spot that is hers—not one assigned to her by outsiders, but one she assumes and inhabits herself. At the novel's beginning, Precious displays only an external awareness of the passage of time, one about as far removed from the lush Proustian flux of minutes, hours, years, and decades that is the literary epitome of thetic temporalization: "I'm in the kitchen two hours, I know that, even though I don't tell time so good, 'cause man on the radio say four o'clock, tell some news, play music, and by the time I'm fixing Mama's plate man say six o'clock" (Sapphire, *Push* 19). For this Precious, past cannot detach from present: "I'm twelve, no I *was* twelve, when that shit happen" (21). Outside of time, even unable to mark it, Precious finds herself in league with ghouls and demons haunting human life:

> I big, I talk, I eats, I cooks, I laugh, watch TV, do what my muver say. But I can see when the picture come back I don't exist. Don't nobody want me. Don't nobody need me. I know who I am. I know who they say I am—vampire sucking the system's blood. Ugly black grease to be wipe away, punish, kilt, changed, finded a job for. (31)

De-centered—and not in the fun postmodern way—Precious can only access her existence in terms of horror, brain-dead zombie on the fringes of a world she supposedly drains of vital life force.

To re-orient her to the space and time of the human, Blue Rain insists that Precious see herself as *intemporal*: "Dear Precious, Don't forget to put the date, 1/18/88, on your journal entries" (70); "Don't forget to put the year, '88, on your journal entries" (71). Under the spell of Blue, Precious finds herself at long last caring about time: "Time, I want to learn to look at round clock and tell time" (88). Eventually, it is Precious who will temporalize Blue when she forgets to do so: "Dan frget rite day Ms R" (72). Through temporal thetism, Precious gives birth to both herself and the worldliness of the world, all via poesis:

Rita ask me do I want another hot chocolate. I do but don't want to be greedy. Even if boyfriend do give her money she got better things to spend it on then Precious. She hug me and ask waitress, "Could I have another hot chocolate and cappuccino." I like how Rita is, she know the world, how to act and stuff. Sometimes I don't have a clue! (131)

Through Blue, the partial structures of semi/osis give way to a thetic ordering according to which the parasitic existence of the vampire gives way to the symbiosis of self and society that constitutes the best version of articulacy.

In Kristeva's schematic, the infant escapes parasitology through the logic of what Freud terms *Verneinung*, or negation, in his 1925 paper by the same title; later in her career, Kristeva will ally this pulsation with *abjection*, and tie it to the machinations of horror, but for now, it is the self's ability to reject or expel undesirable contents from an inside which is to remain inside that marks its ascension to the types of individuality capitalism demands. In the case of Precious, she begins her tale as incapable of rejecting anything or anyone, taking in more than she ever should, and giving back nothing, cunt bucket sapping the resources of a fiscal order including her only as exclusion, just another Monster Mom in an American Culture of Fear, taking her place by the side of the Octomom, another Monster Procreator with a monster bod.[14] But if she begins as that which is rejected, and ejected, repelled and expelled, she will not end there; the temporal and thetic awareness that Blue Rain installs in her, a development transcending mere literacy or test-taking ability, teaches her to be the subject, not object, of rejection and refusal, thereby saving her from a life as the refuse and offal of family and educational conveyor belt. For Kristeva, rejection itself mirrors the phenomenon of negativity, which for her, as for Hegel, does not denote absence or eradication, but rather the positive presence of something corrosive, mordant, or alienating, referring to the process by which solidity is dissolved and loosened positively in the permanent flux of motility and stasis. Rejection is fundamentally expulsive, eliciting associations of anality and sadism, since it is through the anus that the first acts of expulsion and separation occur, as we know from the psychoanalysis of the gift:

> Before the body itself is posited as a detached alterity, and hence the real object, this expulsion of objects is the subject's fundamental experience of separation—a separation which is not a lack, but a discharge and which,

although privative, arouses pleasure. The psychoanalyst assumes that this jubilant loss is simultaneously felt as an attack against the expelled object, all exterior objects (including father and mother), and the body itself. (Kristeva, *Revolution* 151)

Beyond Precious's own relation to anality encapsulated by the smearing of feces on her face after her father is through raping her—"Afterward I go bafroom. I smear shit on my face. Feel good" (Sapphire, *Push* 111)—the salient Kristevan fact is that, until Precious learns to stop being rejected and abjected by others and to mark her own flows with the violent scissions of *Ausstossung* (expulsion), she'll never produce the very "third-degree rejection" that for Kristeva constitutes poesis, liberatory, and bright (*Revolution* 146).

Aside from the many rejections Precious must un- and re-do, the center of the cunt bucket controversy resides in the monstrosity of her body, supersized presence placing her squarely on the side of the abject, or that fundamental Kristevan dynamic that determines how health and filth are cordoned off from one another in the social hygiene of accepted and rejected torsos, bodies that matter, and bodies whose matter is the stuff of legend, mythos, and nightmare.[15] In the language of Elizabeth Grosz, hers is a volatile body, which, like all volatile bodies, reveals the vicious domestication at work within the social-symbolic, as it castrates, clitorectomizes, deforms, and debases the various corporealized entities it must subject to civilization, *volonté générale*, or grammar in this topology of sustained damage and torsion. In the Preface to her *Bodies That Matter*, Judith Butler beautifully summarizes the sketchy position of those bodies which find themselves expelled from this aesthetic and sexual order, contained within society in a kind of shadow box, bubble, or curio cabinet framing their excesses to neutralize them:

Given this understanding of construction as constitutive restraint, is it still possible to raise the critical question of how such constraints not only produce the domain of intelligible bodies, but produce as well a domain of unthinkable, abject, unlivable bodies? The latter domain is not the opposite of the former, for oppositions are, after all, part of intelligibility; the latter is the excluded and illegible domain that haunts the former domain as the spectre of its own impossibility, the very limit to intelligibility, its constitutive outside. How, then, might one alter the very terms that constitute the necessary' domain of bodies through rendering unthinkable and unlivable another domain of bodies, those that do not matter in the same way? (xi)

For Butler, a queer body such as Precious's speaks to the fundamental drama of Platonic choral matter, as it either forms the substrate to materiality proper, and hence falls outside it, as a kind of neutered base and eccentric center, or else is inherently a part of materiality, participating in its phases and transformations vitally, there being no outside to the scene of atoms and atomic propositions, which comprise and constitute the great Sigma of everything. The construction of Precious, her "performativity," if we revive the playful language of Butler's *Gender Trouble*, is troubled by the schizoid bifids surrounding her like an unleashed apiary we have shaken just enough: thin/fat, rich/poor, white/black, light/dark, laffin' ugly/cryin' ugly, however we enumerate the dual poles of her many virgules. And yet the question robustly remains: is she the inhabitant of the denigrated slot of a bipole, or, rather, the inert ground on which various paired opposites reveal themselves as split, her body the cold earth where carnivorous plants take root and flower wildly?[16] Is her unintelligibility the result of her being the ground of intelligibility, and hence a choral presence giving shape, form, and meaning to matter without mattering herself? And lastly, what do we gain by stereotyping her, freezing her in the position of Welfare Queen, BBW, or Receptacon, arresting her motion in the spot where obesity and poverty combine in the bolstering of the racial phantom of American urban myth and spectacle?

Part of the scandal of Sapphire is that she makes us inhabit the *unlivable* body of Claireece Precious Jones, with the excesses she is forced to endure in the various influxes of foreign matter (food, cum) she is made to receive against her will—for example, the kilocalories she must eat to keep up with her mother, who clearly does not want to be Circus Size all by herself:

> I go back to the kitchen and fix myself a plate. Mama holler, "Margarine! Bring me some margarine and hot sauce." So I bring her the margarine and the hot sauce. Then I go git my plate and sit down with her. Greens, corn bread, ham hocks, macaroni 'n cheese; I eat 'cause she say eat. I don't taste nothin'. The pain in my shoulder is throbbing me, shooting up my neck. Some white people is smiling and kissing on television. "Oh ain't he cute!" Mama going ape over black guy in beer commercial. I don't like beer. "Git me some more." Mama push her plate toward me. "'N git you some more—." (Sapphire, *Push* 20)

Precious tells the tale of her own abjection, Kristevan and cruel, in a language revealing just how she has been constructed as monster body, chicken bucket Godzilla, fat bitch at the furthest reaches of intelligibility, and *all the things she is not*, roles she is compelled to assume so that others may manage their own borders through the erection of a monstrous Other. Learning to temporalize herself via rejection, Precious becomes her own historian, pushing her way to rebirth urged on by the gentle yet unshakeable goading of her midwife, making *Push* far more than *bildungsroman*, cautionary tale or urban horror story.

FROM CHORA TO ISTHMUS: A SECOND PLATONIC GEOGRAPHY

Since I have traced the cunt bucket back to the chora, largely through *Urbandictionary.com*, which has helped define the cunt bucket, and Kristeva, who has helped illuminate its apositionality through a theory of thetic awareness that suggests a recuperative strategy of orientation, it now seems that the only place I can turn to complete the cunt bucket's redemption is to the only other meaningful spatial metaphor to figure within the *Timaeus-Critias* continuum which has set up the current discussion, the isthmus, second piece of geography threatening neat notions of discrete, self-identical space and place, counterpoint to the chora, and golden parachute for Monsters everywhere (no, this is not a Lady Gaga song). At once host and place, receptacle and space of gifting, the chora or *hypodoche*, isolated and alone, as intimately connected with the production of matter as it is separated radically from contact with its creations, is counterbalanced by another critical spatial feature co-eval with the chora, this one more geographical and less metaphysical, the land mass represented by the *isthmos*—strip of earth connecting masses that would otherwise remain disjoined, part of neither but facilitating their cleavage at the same time that it gives rise to their junction-at-a-distance. *Timaeus* and *Critias* are textually connected by an invisible isthmus of missing words yoking Timaeus's cosmogony with Critias's history of bellicosity: the two form a shattered whole we can only re-construct inferentially but which we must hold in our consciousness, however tenuously, if we are to connect cunt bucket with chora, ignorance with illumination, white snow blindness with bluest Blue Rain. Politically, the isthmus leads us from Athens to Sparta, then to the world beyond, where Atlantis reigns long before it is drowned. Essentially *im*material, the isthmus bonds, unites, connects, substituting proximity for distance, and existing at the heart of world map and cosmogony, conceptually integral to land and body, self and nation, law and international policy/polity. If only Atlantis had had one.

Within the cosmogony of *Push*, it is this movement away from the chora and toward the isthmus that is the redemptive moment, the turning point, the switch. If the chora is the figure of figuration, the immaterial matter, which colors Western views about feminine receptivity and produces the cunt bucket as its metaphorical representative, then the isthmus is that kind of matter which is so material that it is not clear how to chart it when the time for drawing boundaries arises. The isthmus is the very figure of "that third thing," material connection uniting fire and earth at the dawn of time, primary bond that through its thirdness makes firstness and secondness communicate:

> But fire is required for the creation of anything visible, and solidity for anything to be tangible, and earth for solidity. It follows that the god began to form the body of the universe out of fire and earth. But it's impossible for any two things to form a proper structure without the presence of a third thing; there has to be some bond to mediate between the two of them and bring them together. (Plato, *Timaeus* 31c)

This bond, identified as "correspondence," is isthmic in structure, looking forward to the strip linking brain with passion in the human body:

> Piety kept them from polluting the divine soul with these things, short of the direst emergency, and so they lodged the mortal soul in separate quarters, elsewhere in the body; and they built an isthmus to distinguish the region of the head from that of the chest, by placing the neck between them, to keep them apart. So they bound the mortal soul within the chest—the thorax, as it is called. (69d-e)

Here, the isthmus—literally a neck—permits reason and passion to communicate, connecting them via anatomical land bridge, one which largely depends on the kindness of strange waters that either reveal or conceal it. Like that strange mirror that becomes the liver, its function is to allow the mind to dominate appetite by keeping track of it, placing it "within hearing of reason" (70a) and the dictates of the Acropolis.[17]

Within the myth of Atlantis described briefly in the *Timaeus* and elaborated somewhat in the *Critias*, before the text breaks off abruptly, the geographical neck appears again within the context of national sprawl:

> Then again, the old stories about our land are reliable and true; above all, in those days its border was formed by the Isthmus and, in relation to the rest

of the mainland, our territory extended as far as the hills of Cithaeron and Parnes, and went down to the coast, with Oropus on the right and the Asopus forming the border on the left. (110e)

In this tale, a story not told under the guise of the *eidos lokos*, yet not entirely under the authority of Solon and the oral history of patriarchs, and hence the occasion for an application for critical leniency from the audience of experts who will hear it, the Isthmus of Corinth forms the ancient southern Athenian border, carrying citizens as far as they can go before the land becomes another territory, the Peloponnesus, site of ancient enemy Sparta and its allies.[18] Beyond the isthmus, there is no civilization, or another civilization: another place, where different rules and values apply, where the proclamations of the Acropolis fall on deaf ears of those monsters we refer to as Barbarians. The isthmus is the Athenian limit, the furthest one can go before another world begins, the kind of matter that leads one from *terra firma* to matter which does not concern it.

Within the logic of Platonic geography, and in light of the choral nature of the cunt bucket, I end this chapter with the isthmus because of its fundamental difference from the chora and its relevance as alternate physical/metaphysical geography, another way of conceiving the inter-relations of matter. For Precious, disconnected and abject, submerged and Atlantan, it is the figure of the isthmus which carries the greatest geophysical resonance in this Platonic battle for epistemic access: she must learn to connect heart with head, language with world, body with bodies, and it is these very isthmic linkages which the poetic literacy inspired by Blue Rain help her to recognize (literally, to re-cognize, or conceive anew). If we remain within the cartography, chemistry, and anatomy central to Plato's cosmogony, then it is not the radical outside to matter, maternalized by Socrates, which can be Precious's buoy, but instead the land bridge bringing polis into contact with extra-polis, the neck supporting the head, and giving body and mind the chance to communicate, the third thing without which no chemical bond or materiality would be possible, a kind of Higgs Boson making matter sticky and hence able to accumulate and cohere primally: matter's matter. Isthmus to Atlantis, the *Critias* bridges the temporal and chemical gap of lost land and history, redrawing *Mappa Mundi* and friendship.

Like Atlantis, Precious must find a way to release what has been submerged, to rise from the ocean, Botticellian and resplendent, thetically aware, and in charge of her borders. Without its neck, the Peloponnesus would be only John Donne's island, isolated and inhuman. The island, that is, Claireece Precious Jones finally finds its isthmus, materializing from the deep in a kind of reverse Ice Age. While we can never be sure what will happen to the newly created poet, we find encouragement in her love of her healthy son Abdul and desire to make him literate: "He my shiny brown boy. In his beauty I see my own. He pulling on my earring, want me to stop daydreaming and read him a story before nap time. I do" (Sapphire, *Push* 120). Finally able to constitute herself as beautiful bride of truth ("I do"), Precious is not the desolate island of ignorance and sexual desire that her parents and schoolmates have made her out to be: coming into her own, she can now begin the delicate business of thriving. Her Thyroid Isthmus no longer pulsing with hunger, Precious is free to glut herself on knowledge, wed to that one existential modulation of time that opens the human to possibility, the future. Of course, we will have to wait nearly two decades for Sapphire's *The Kid* to discover where her new fluency will lead her, Mongo, and Abdul, but it's alright: we've got her radiance to distract us. The rubric is not queer pedagogy: rather, it is the queerness of knowledge and pedagogy, in general, for all bodies and minds, not just those that have been abjected in the formation of identities without which the institution of society, correctly deemed *imaginary* by Cornelius Castoriadis, might cease to function. What we must realize is that this society functions best when Precious writes poetry and Beth Ditto models Gaultier, when the chora becomes a voluminous fountain and not little granite pail. For Precious is that point of Wittgenstein puzzlement where philosophy truly begins and where, in the philosophy of gender, difference performs the work of inspiring knowledge-production, as we reverse the Monster dynamic and are motivated to investigate the origins of ALL knowledge, especially those facts that seem to force themselves upon us with the hopelessness of inexorability.

NOTES

1. Wittgenstein's word "seltsam" in books like *Philosophical Investigations* or *Remarks on the Foundations of Mathematics* is generally translated as "queer" by G.E.M. Anscombe. Of course, there are no sexual connotations to the translation or to the word "seltsam" as it is used in the German language, and yet I myself find it striking that this ultra-famous homosexual philosopher whose sexuality NEVER ceases to be seltsam for his biographers and commentators should be the only one to use this word with

such regularity and frequency: the proper adjective for THAT kind of queer would be the informal and pejorative Schwül. Ever investigating philosophical puzzlement in the wake of inexorability or *Unerbittlichkeit*, Wittgenstein is the queer Queer who regresses thought to the queerness of a philosophical confusion structurally similar to the epistemological chaos inaugurated by the inscrutable body. It is in this spirit that I use him as one way of making sense of Sapphire, for whom knowledge is also profoundly queering.

2. Here, rebirth bears the metaphysical traces of correspondence, as each instance of regeneration within Platonic metempsychosis produces "an animal of a kind determined by the principle that it should resemble the kind of wickedness it displayed" (*Timaeus* 42c). The chain of degradation proceeds as follows: men, woman, birds, land animals, snakes, fish, and crustaceans. Later on in the dialogue, *Timaeus* will blame the generation of women on a hedonism I can only read as homoerotic: "Some men, once they had been incarnated, lived unmanly or immoral lives, and it's plausible to suggest that they were reborn in their next incarnation as women. That, therefore, was when the gods invented sexual desire, a living being that they formed, though different in men and in women, and endowed with a soul" (91a-b).

3. In the Kristevan schema, the two relevant psychic zones are the semiotic and the symbolic. The semiotic, marked by the chora and assimilated to the maternal body, is "a nonexpressive totality formed by the drives and their stases in a motility that is as full of movement as it is regulated" (Kristeva, *Revolution* 25). A-thetic, or non-positional, the chora is what must be transcended as one enters language, the space of the social-symbolic. It recurs later, via poetry and psychosis.

4. In "Plato's Pharmacy" (*Dissemination*), Derrida analyzes the word *pharmakon* and the way it pulses between "poison" and "remedy" in the dialogue *Phaedrus*. "Grammatological" is clearly a reference to his *Of Grammatology*, my point being to add chemicals and grammar to the choral mix.

5. See *Theatetus* 149a.

6. Here, I have in mind, from Willard Van Orman Quine, *Word and Object*, the idea of the "inscrutability of reference" within the program of radical translation he outlines, my point being that even Analytic Philosophy has something to say about what might happen with the cunt bucket in terms of both correspondence and lateral movement.

7. I take the distinction between *mnésis* and *hypomnesia* from Derrida, "Plato's Pharmacy" (*Dissemination*). In a nutshell, *mnésis* refers to the organic act of actively remembering, while *hypomnesia* results when one externalizes an inactive memory by erecting a monument—for example, a

Cancer Survivor's Park, or if we turn to grammatology, writing itself, which covers over absences insisting on being remembered. In *mnésis*, memory is organic, intimate, warm and pulsing with life; in *hypomnesia*, however, memory is inorganic, alien, and cold as a categorical imperative.

8. The paradox of giving that which one is not in possession of is not lost on Derrida, who begins his *Given Time* with a reference to the Lacanian donative paradox: "Lacan says of love: it gives what it does not have, a phenomenon whose variations are ordered by the *Écrits* according to the final and transcendental modality of the woman inasmuch as she is, supposedly, deprived of the phallus" (2).

9. Sapphire's *Black Wings & Blind Angels* contains further brutal examples of the Machine Gun aesthetic I identify in *Push*.

10. "Nothic" refers to the *nothos*, or bastard son, who interrupts proper generation and filiation/*ekgonos*. I take it from the bastard logic according to which the chora is apprehended in the first place by Timaeus, who can do no more than provide a "likely" or plausible (*eidos logos*) cosmogonic report to Socrates, Critias, and Hermocrates (*Timaeus* 52b).

11. "We'll have to be content if we come up with statements that are as plausible as anyone else's, and we should bear in mind the fact that I and all of you, the speaker and his judges, are no more than human, which means that on these matters we ought to accept the likely account and not demand more than that" (*Timaeus* 29c-d).

12. Precious reads from her own file, pilfered from Ms Weiss, to her friend and fellow student, the "Harlem Butch" Jermaine: "'The teacher, Ms Rain, places great emphasis on writing and reading books. Little work is done with computers or the variety of multiple choice pre-G.E.D. and G.E.D. workbooks available at low cost to JPTA programs'" (Sapphire, *Push* 119).

13. The traditional reductions of Husserlian phenomenology as presented in his *Ideas* are: (1) eidetic, (2) transcendental, (3) phenomenological. I add a semiotic reduction to the series in light of Kristeva's desire for phenomenology to de-transcendentalize the I, which is more of a provisional structure than something fixed and permanent, something continually negotiating its relation to loss and absence.

14. See Barry Glassner, "Monster Moms: On the Art of Misdirection."

15. Abjection does not arise as a concept in Kristeva's *Revolution in Poetic Language*, arriving eight years later in her *Powers of Horror: An Essay on Abjection*. Still, the stage is clearly set in her analysis of rejection (as typified by Freud's Rat Man), expulsion, disavowal (as typified by the Wolf Man) and denial (*dénégation*), waiting only for a special name to be given to the fundamental negativity central to the hygiene of selfhood.

16. "I hear kids at school. Boy say I'm laffing ugly. He say, 'Claireece is so ugly she laffing ugly.' His fren' say, 'No, that fat bitch is crying ugly.' Laff laff" (Sapphire, *Push* 12).

17. "They made the liver dense, smooth, bright, and sweet (but with some bitterness), so that it would act as a mirror for thoughts stemming from intellect, just as a mirror receives impressions and gives back images to look at" (*Timaeus* 71b). As such, the liver communicates via reflection, a kind of visual isthmus allowing the basest instincts to be subjected to rational control via photoelectric telepoesis.

18. "I'm not suggesting that anything in your speech was less than excellent— how could anyone in their right mind presume to do so?—but I do want to try to show that what remains to be said is actually more difficult, and therefore calls for more leniency" (*Critias* 107b).

WORKS CITED

Blake, William. 1982. *The Marriage of Heaven and Hell*. In *The Complete Poetry and Prose of William Blake*, ed. David V. Erdman. New York: Anchor. Print.

Butler, Judith. 1990. *Gender Trouble: Feminism and the Subversion of Identity*. New York: Routledge. Print.

———. 1993. *Bodies That Matter: On the Discursive Limits of Sex*. New York: Routledge. Print.

Dawson, Jim. 2009. *The Compleat Motherfucker: A History of the Mother of All Dirty Words*. Port Townsend: Feral Books. Print.

Deleuze, Gilles, and Felix Guattari. 1987. *A Thousand Plateaus: Capitalism and Schizophrenia*. Trans. Brian Massumi. Minneapolis: University of Minnesota Press. Print.

Derrida, Jacques. 1997. *Of Grammatology*. 1967. Baltimore: The Johns Hopkins University Press. Print.

———. 1981. *Dissemination*. Trans. Barbara Johnson. Chicago: University of Chicago Press. Print.

———. 1992. *Given Time: I. Counterfeit Money*. Trans. Peggy Kamuf. Chicago: University of Chicago Press. Print.

Freire, Paolo. 1993. *Pedagogy of the Oppressed*. Trans. Mary Bergman Ramos. New York: Continuum. Print.

Freud, Sigmund. 1925. Die Verneinung. In *Sigmund Freud, Gesammelte Werke XIV: Werke aus den Jahren 1925–1931*, 11–15. Frankfurt: S. Fischer Verlag, 1968. Print.

Glassner, Barry. 1999. *The Culture of Fear*. New York: Basic Books. Print.

Grosz, Elizabeth. 1994. *Volatile Bodies: Toward a Corporeal Feminism*. Bloomington: Indiana University Press. Print.

Irigaray, Luce. 1985. *Speculum of the Other Woman*. 1974. Ithaca: Cornell University Press. Print.

Kristeva, Julia. 1982. *Powers of Horror: An Essay on Abjection*. Trans. Leon S. Roudiez. New York: Columbia University Press. Print.

————. 1984. *Revolution in Poetic Language*. Trans. Margaret Waller. New York: Columbia University Press. Print.

Niedecker, Lorine. 1996. *The Granite Pail: The Selected Poems of Lorine Niedecker*. Frankfort: Gnomon Press. Print.

Plato. 1987. *Theaetetus*. Trans. Robin H. Waterfield. New York: Penguin Classics. Print.

————. 2008. *Timaeus and Critias*. Trans. Robin Waterfield. Cambridge: Oxford University Press. Print.

Precious. Dir. Lee Daniels. Lionsgate. 2009. Film.

Quine, Willard Van Orman. 1964. *Word and Object*. Cambridge, MA: The MIT Press. Print.

Sapphire. 1996. *Push*. New York: Vintage. Print.

————. 2000. *Black Wings & Blind Angels*. New York: Knopf. Print.

————. 2011. *The Kid*. New York: Penguin. Print.

Sedgwick, Eve Kosofsky, and Wayne Koestenbaum. 1985. *Between Men: English Literature and Male Homosocial Desire*. New York: Columbia University Press. Print.

Urban Dictionary. N.d. Web. 12 Dec. 2014.

Wittgenstein, Ludwig. 1953. *Philosophical Investigations*. Trans. G.E.M. Anscombe. New York: Macmillan. Print.

CHAPTER 9

"Modern" Is as *Modern* Does: *Modern Family* and the Disruption of Gender Binaries

Bruce E. Drushel

Even before commercial television series began regularly featuring openly gay and lesbian characters, in the 1970s, writers suggested them through character behaviors that were violations of conventional gender norms. The coding of the effeminate male and the masculine female character permitted representation *sans hominem*, thus allowing more sophisticated viewers in on the secret that the program had breached a cultural taboo, while simultaneously allowing otherwise easily offended audiences to laugh at characters who were sight gags merely because of their non-normative speech, vocations, and mannerisms. Eventually, the love that dared not speak its name achieved a voice, yet remained gender-bound. Even supposedly ground-breaking series such as NBC's *Will & Grace* made its gay male lead acceptable through its opposition to the more effeminate Jack sidekick. Sissies and butches thus abounded, from the limp-wristed Marty of *Barney Miller* and the comically pixieish Jody Dallas of *Soap* to *ER*'s uber-serious Dr. Weaver and the pants-wearing Ellen Morgan of *Ellen*. In each case, the characters also were those who most

B.E. Drushel (✉)
Miami University, Cincinnati, OH, USA

© The Author(s) 2018
E. McNeil et al. (eds.), *Mapping Queer Space(s) of Praxis and Pedagogy*, Queer Studies and Education,
DOI 10.1007/978-3-319-64623-7_9

169

visibly challenged traditional gender binaries on their respective series and seldom were allowed behaviors in any of their lives' domains that were exceptions: once a sissy, always a sissy; once a butch, always a butch.

The current ABC situation comedy *Modern Family* distinguishes itself through its willingness to develop characters that freely depart from these binaries, most notably the gay male couple Mitch and Cam. While a surface-level view of the pair suggests the continuation of at least an approximation of traditional couple gender roles—Mitch as the masculine breadwinner complete with beard and conventional masculine appearance and background, and Cam as the feminine stay-at-home nurturer and domestic problem-solver—episodes reveal more sophisticated and multi-dimensional types: the nurturer was a farmboy, can drive an 18-wheeler, and stave off the menace of a gas station bully, while the breadwinner can be insecure, bitchy, and cowed by a bully.

This chapter examines in detail the gender behaviors of the Mitch and Cam characters from *Modern Family* and contrasts them with those of characters represented as lesbian or gay among both recent US television sitcoms and those of past characters represented as lesbian, gay, or at least queer. Among the issues to be addressed are the presence/absence of strategies evident in the construction of the Mitch and Cam characters and whether the characters appear to be part of a revolution in representations of gender and sexuality, or whether, like the Roger and Beverly characters from *All in the Family* decades before, they are merely encouraging anomalies.

TV Families as Behavior Models

The significance of media representations of gender and sexuality owes to the reality that "The mass media become the authority at any given moment for what is true and what is false, what is reality and what is fantasy, what is important and what is trivial" (Bagdikian xviii). Television, as the most pervasive of the media, mass or otherwise, is a powerful ideological system operating, as Todd Gitlin puts it, to "certify reality as reality" (2). Among those certifications are those for gender stereotypes and gender behaviors of the society in which viewers live (see F. Earle Barcus, Robert M. Liebert, and Joyce Sprafkin). Moreover, according to Beth Olson and William Douglas, the characters in TV families provide an historical record of gender roles over time and may be used as an indicator of changing societal attitudes toward gender (409–427).

Representations of families on television offer a prime opportunity for the examination of gender, not just because the interactions between male and female adult characters in the home often highlight contrasting gender roles but also because the family frequently serves as an incubator in which those roles are both debated and modeled. Family-based drama on television has been a staple on broadcast network and cable/satellite television schedules (e.g., CBS's *Lassie* and NBC's *Bonanza* in the 1950s and 1960s; CBS's *The Waltons* and ABC's *Family* in the 1970s; ABC's *Life Goes On* in the 1980s; ABC's *My So-Called Life*, NBC's *I'll Fly Away*, and FOX's *Party of Five* in the 1990s; and The WB's *Seventh Heaven* and *Everwood* in the 2000s). But besides the popular family dramas, Marvin L. Moore found that 85 percent of prime-time TV family depictions between 1947 and 1990 were in situation comedies (41–60). The prevalence of sitcoms featuring families is due, undoubtedly, to the durability and popularity of the domestic sitcom genre but also perhaps is because comedies allow for the treatment of otherwise sensitive and controversial themes as gender roles, changing cultural mores, and child-rearing with less risk of indignation among audiences. According to Serafina Bathrick, these episodic comedies situate the viewer by offering some of the subject positions men and women inhabit so that they may make sense of their own lived gender relations.

Television is thought to be quite pervasive in its influence on gender norms. Exposure has been shown to change the ways in which audiences think about real families, including the institution of marriage (and divorce) (Brown, Childers, Bauman, and Koch). It even is thought to influence stereotypes regarding gender appearance among family members, including appropriate weight and body shape, which are communicated both through modeling by characters and through verbal reinforcement in character dialogue (Fouts and Burggraf; Toro, Salamero, and Martinez).

A review of scholarly studies by Olson and Douglas led them to conclude that portrayal of family roles on television may be especially influential for children (411). That phenomenon appears to be true both in nature and magnitude. Terry Frueh and Paul E. McGhee found that extensive time spent watching television was associated with stronger traditional sex-role development. This is not surprising, since children select "television characters as people they want to be like when they grow up" and, to the degree possible, emulate the behaviors and attitudes they see modeled (Miller and Reeves 85).

Class and gender are interwoven in complex and multi-faceted ways on television, and particularly in situation comedy. According to Joan Wallach Scott, domestic situation comedy has been persistently and overwhelmingly middle class, with only a few households headed by manual laborers or by the very wealthy (390). Plot lines in episodes of domestic comedies frequently are characterized by conflict between males and females. Richard Butsch found working-class families in domestic situation comedies often feature men who, by at least some measures, are failures and women who fill the vacuum thus created. Among depictions of middle-class families, fathers do a better job of meeting the masculinity standard (Butsch). Even so, and particularly in shows about middle-class families, the father was unchallenged as the authority figure (Rowe 81).

The Changing Face(s) of Gender

While certainly it is the case that gender as both a social construction in the unmediated world and a representation of identity in the television world is subject to continual refiguring, reconsideration, and contestation, there is evidence to support two contentions: that traditional masculine and feminine stereotypes were most entrenched in the 1950s and most in upheaval in the 1970s (Scott 391). The families television revealed to viewers in its first decades consisted of middle-class fathers who were successful and part of a functional parenting team with mothers; both were represented as less childish than the offspring they were attempting to rear (393). The middle-class mothers occasionally could be buffoonish but middle-class fathers never were (395).

By the 1970s and 1980s, middle-class fathers occasionally could be depicted as more fallible (393), but there likely was more difference in depictions within decades than between them. Olson and Douglas have concluded there has been less change in television depiction of equality, similarity, and dominance in gender roles on television than actually occurred in the non-mediated world, and, in fact, if they changed at all during television's first 50 years, it was only to return in the 1990s to much what they were in the 1950s (422).

That said, two characters in television situation comedy history frequently are mentioned as challenging traditional gender roles in their respective eras: Mary Richards (*Mary Tyler Moore Show*), whom critics accused of conforming to traditional proscriptions (Dow, "Hegemony"), but whom many viewers felt was an inspiration and represented independence (Byars 289–303), and Murphy Brown (*Murphy Brown*), whose feminism often created cultural discomfort on the show (Press), whose traditionally masculine traits made her professionally successful but personally less so (Dow, "Femininity"), and whom viewer mail suggested was seen as a role model for a broad array of women, reflecting approval of her nontraditional gender-based attitudes and particularly her aggressive verbal behavior (Collins).

MEET THE *MODERN FAMILY*

While it might be claimed that other leading and supporting characters from situation comedies in the decades since *The Mary Tyler Moore Show* and *Murphy Brown* have further revolutionized gender performance (e.g., Karen Walker and Jack McFarland from *Will & Grace*), arguably the most complex performances may be found in the characters of Mitch Pritchett and Cam Tucker from the ABC series *Modern Family*. The Mitch and Cam characters depart from the expected television convention of gay characters as flamboyantly effeminate (e.g., Peter Barnes, a recurring character on *Ellen*) or vaguely yet pervasively masculine (e.g., Will Truman from *Will & Grace*) by representing distinct, interwoven tapestries of masculine and feminine.

Modern Family is a domestic situation comedy with an ensemble cast produced in the style of a mock documentary. It chronicles the lives and foibles of the extended Pritchett family, who are middle class and who live in an unidentified US city. It is an American adaptation of the French comedy series, *Fais pas ci, fais pas ça* (roughly, "Don't do this, don't do that") and includes both scenes in which the cast members interact only with each other and those in which they address an unseen interviewer. The family patriarch is Jay Pritchett, who is remarried to a much younger woman, Gloria, with whom he has a young son, Manny. Jay's daughter Claire is married to a real estate agent, Phil, and they are rearing three children, Haley, Alex, and Luke. Jay's son Mitch, an attorney, is in a domestic partnership with Cam, with whom he is rearing an adopted daughter, Lily.

The series debuted in September of 2009 and quickly was acknowledged as a success, both among critics and audiences. Average audiences grew each of its first three seasons to an estimated 16.71 million viewers by May 2012. The series frequently is among the most-watched scripted programs of the week and even has been credited with reviving the situation comedy genre in the twenty-first century, much as *The Cosby Show* was credited with doing 25 years before. In its first three seasons, it received 45 Emmy nominations and won in 16 categories, including Outstanding Comedy Series all three years.

The series has not been without its critics. Michelle Haimoff has observed that *Modern Family* is one of several popular situation comedies to represent male characters as professionally successful and female characters as unemployed or professionally struggling (neither Gloria Pritchett nor Claire Dunphy works outside her respective home). And LGBT activists have complained about a lack of display of affection between the Mitch and Cam characters, while the other two couples have been shown as more physically intimate. The producers responded by explaining the lack of affection as a symptom of Mitch's discomfort with public displays of affection (Guider). A social media campaign by activists ensured, and the pair eventually were seen in an on-camera kiss (Poniewozik).

CONSTRUCTION OF GENDER: MITCH AND CAM

Even among an ensemble of characters carefully constructed to have distinct and compelling personalities, the Mitch and Cam characters have proven particularly popular among viewers and have figured prominently in the series' plot lines. Thus, numerous episodes provide opportunities for examination of how the two characters perform their gender tapestries. Even so, three episodes–"Fizbo" from season one, "Halloween" from season two, and "After the Fire" from season three—are singularly illustrative.

"Fizbo"

In this episode, it is revealed that Cam once performed as a clown, Fizbo, whose name presumably was a parody of the acronym for "for sale by owner." Cam had promised Mitch, who apparently does not like clowns (and, as is suggested in a subsequent episode, may even fear them) that he would give up performing as Fizbo, but reneges on his vow to entertain at the birthday party of Mitch's nephew, Luke. En route to the party, they stop at a gas station, where Mitch is bumped by the SUV of an aggressively masculine male stranger.

Mitch: Um, hey!

Man: Hey, yourself. Move!

Mitch: You kinda just bumped me with your car.

Man: I don't think so.

Mitch: No, no, you did because, um, yeah, see, I got grease on my pants and then, also, I felt it.

Man: Call an ambulance.

Mitch: Okay. I just thought you might want to know in case you wanted to be a decent human being and apologize, but...

Man: (Shrugs)

Mitch: No? Okay ... (After man has turned away) Ass!

Man: (Abruptly turns to confront Mitch) What did you say?

Mitch: Forget about it, all right?

Man: Listen, Carrot Top, I didn't touch you, so do the smart thing and shut your hole, (shoves him) get in your car, and drive away.

Cam: (Steps between them, still in clown regalia) Is there a problem here?

Man: What the hell are you?

Cam: I'm the ass-kickin' clown that'll twist you like a balloon animal.... I will beat your head against this bumper until the airbags deploy ... so apologize to my boyfriend (emphasizes his words with sharp pokes to the man's collarbone) right ... now!

Man: (Startled) Apologize? Boyfriend?

Cam: (Shoves him) Apologize!

Man: Okay! (To Cam) I'm sorry....

Cam: (Points to Mitch)

Man: (Turns to Mitch) I'm sorry. (Retreats to his SUV)

Cam: (Pulls out his oversized clown alarm clock) Let's go. We're going to be late. (Corrigan, Walsh, and Winer)

Of the two characters, Mitch is the one whose gender performance is the most conventionally masculine: he is a successful attorney and the breadwinner of the household; when the two travel by car, Mitch assumes the traditional "husband" role and drives. He wears a neatly trimmed beard and his taste in clothing is muted and tasteful. While he can trade wisecracks best described as "bitchy" with Cam, his demeanor is as subdued as his dress, and he tends to provide the voice of reason in the relationship. Physically, however, he is smaller and slighter than Cam (or the other adult male cast members), he seems to share an emotional bond with the other adult female cast members, Claire and Gloria, and he looks forward to one-on-one get-togethers with them.

In this episode, Mitch finds himself face to face with an unfamiliar male of similar age but greater physical stature and is intimidated by his aggressively masculine and even bullying behavior. The crisis is resolved by Cam who, dressed as he was in clown makeup, ill-fitting and discordant clothing (including a hat with an oversized flower suspended from it), and oversized shoes and takes on an uncharacteristically masculine stance, invading the physical space of the stranger and displaying behavior that was both verbally and physically aggressive. The humor of the sequence is heighted by the irony of Cam's appearance and the startled reaction of the bully (and, likely, the audience) to the spontaneous, oddly natural, and convincing forcefulness of Cam's response to a perceived threat against a loved one.

"Halloween"

Equally complex and nuanced is the couple's behavior in the second season's Halloween episode (Richman and Spiller), in which we see both the contrast in the nominal roles of Mitch and Cam—professional provider and domestic nurturer, respectively, but also shifts in the attitudes of the two: Mitch's move from ineffectual victim to resolute actor and Cam's move from calming problem-solver to powerless observer, and finally to self-involved drama queen. In the episode, Mitch recently has been hired at a new law firm and is eager to fit in. When he overhears two colleagues talking about costumes they plan to wear to work for Halloween, he mistakenly assumes it to be widely observed organizational custom and dutifully arrives for work in a snug-fitting Spiderman costume, augmented with foam-rubber muscles. He quickly discovers he is one of only three employees in costume–and that the other two are not looked on favorably.

Mitch: There are exactly three people in costume here … a tool, a douche, and me. And I don't have time to go home and change….

Cam: Calm down. Did you bring in the drycleaning from last night?

Mitch: Are you really getting on me about the dryclean…. Oh! I have suits in the trunk!

Cam: Look at that. Yesterday's lazy cures today's crazy.

Here, Mitch begins to resemble the paternal failure common to situation comedies of the 1980s and 1990s, and Cam is the maternal backstop, cradling a child, while stirring a saucepan, but still not too busy to solve a minor workplace crisis. When Mitch later tries to get rid of the squeaky costume he continued to wear under his suit, he instead ends up in a toilet stall and the street clothes he has temporarily removed are taken by a janitor.

Cam: Hello?
Mitch: I'm trapped in a men's room and all I have on is a Spiderman costume....
Cam: Hot! Who is this?
Mitch: I have another suit in my trunk but I can't get to the car without going through the office.
Cam: You know what's ironic? Who could really help you right now is Spiderman.
Mitch: (Looks at himself in the mirror, adjusts his posture, and looks to a window) He's here.

As he realizes he possesses the physical skills necessary to extricate himself from his predicament, Mitch's stature is discernibly straighter and more upright and his attitude is more robust. Still in the Spiderman outfit, he climbs out the small window of the second-floor restroom and down the spouting to the ground and makes his way, superhero-like, to his car where, this being a situation comedy, he promptly sets off the alarm and is unable to find his key.

Recurring throughout the episode were both the Dunphy family's elaborate preparations for Halloween night and Cam's references to an apparently scarring experience he had while trick-or-treating as a child. Eventually, Claire attempts to persuade him to abandon his dramatic allusions to the event (accompanied by deep breaths and glances heavenward) and simply describe it.

Claire: What happened that was so awful that you, simultaneously, can't speak of it and yet can't stop talking about it?
Cam: (Dramatically) I can't. It's too emotional.
Claire: Okay. Some other time....
Cam: I was ten. Dressed as Quasimodo on a front porch with my best friend, Timmy Regler, a Ghostbuster. There was a bucket of candy with a sign ... said, "Take one." Timmy took the entire

bucket and put it in his bag. Timmy didn't play by the rules. It's what I liked and ... feared ... about him. Then the bag broke as a crowd of kids rounded the corner, saw the pile of candy, and Timmy said, "Cam did it!" [...] Timmy started running. I wanted to run, too, but my hunch got stuck on a rosebush and that's when I fell. I fell hard. [...] And everyone was screaming, "That's him! Get Quasimodo!" (becomes more emotional) And then the townspeople started chasing me ... and that's when ... I wet my pants! I wet my pants (sobbing) ... I wet my pants....

This sequence reveals a more typical mainstream stereotype of a gay man: feminized, trivialized, and self-obsessed. From the episode's opening minutes, Cam provides breathless allusions to a childhood trauma connected to Halloween, effectively begging fellow cast members to ply him for details, but then denying resolution of the story, either because dismissive cast members interrupt or because he claims ultimately that it is too troubling to discuss further. The effect is heightened expectation on the part of the audience (if not the rest of the cast) and a continual effort to re-direct attention from Claire's elaborate and obsessive rehearsals for greeting trick-or-treaters from the neighborhood. When Cam finally reveals the source of his childhood trauma, the audience reacts with amusement both because of the universality of the *schadenfreude* of wetting oneself in public and because the "trauma" is overplayed.

"After the Fire"

Cam directly addresses the issue of the mainstream's gender stereotyping of gay men in an episode from the series' third season. A fire has destroyed the home of a neighboring family, and the extended Pritchett family is pitching in to help. When Jay injures his back, he reluctantly agrees to let Cam drive the delivery truck from his home improvement business so the family can transport its remaining belongings. Cam reminds skeptics in the family that his experience of growing up on a farm (and operating tractors and combines) amply equipped him for the task. The Dunphy daughters, Alex and Haley, accompany him and offer to help when the truck becomes wedged between cars in a parking lot. Cam refuses their help, and the truck ends up stuck in a pile of gravel and tipped perilously to one side.

Haley:	Why couldn't we have just asked for help?
Cam:	Because I'm teaching you girls a very valuable lesson. That gay men can do anything straight men can do.
Haley:	Yeah, we know that! Do you think you're the only gay guy we know?
Alex:	Yeah, my soccer coach is gay.
Haley:	Oh, he is for sure....
Alex:	And my Latin tutor....
Haley:	Nerd! Our electrician....
Cam:	Well then why were you so surprised when I said I could drive a truck?
Haley:	Not because you're gay ... because you're you!
Alex:	And by the way ... you can't!

Cam apologizes to his nieces, explaining that he had been fighting cultural stereotypes of gay men all his life. He is interrupted by Haley, who spots a trucker she had seen earlier:

Haley:	Oh, hey there's that trucker that I talked to you.... Oh, hey! Excuse me! Hi! Could you give us a hand, please?
Trucker:	Sure thing, sweetie!
Cam:	Oh, like *she'll* be able to help us!

In the end, the serious intended lesson of the sequence–a gay man indeed can and *does* drive a truck and fails only because of his own overconfidence (itself perhaps a stereotypically masculine gender trait) is rescued by Cam's hypocrisy. He may be able to drive a truck but another effeminate male–this one an authentic trucker–cannot.

GENDER PARODY

As Butler has discussed, gender parody is performative and challenges ideas of core gender identity. That gender and sexuality should find themselves intertwined with situation comedy is perhaps inevitable since, according to Frances Gray, humor, like sexuality, is a social construction subject to the influences of changing temporal, geographic, and cultural contexts. By the 1990s, as Robert Hanke has noted, the boundaries between masculine and feminine domestic spheres had become permeable at least for members of the white professional middle classes (79). Since comedy relies, at least in part, upon the ironic or the unexpected, one might suppose that such permeability would render matters of gender less humorous, since fewer attitudes and behaviors would remain in the realm of the expected, in this instance, tacitly accepted binaries. But instead it could be argued that such humor only would need to become more nuanced or sophisticated, or perhaps implicate sex and sexuality as well as gender.

Indeed, Jerry Palmer reminds us that comic narrative is simultaneously plausible and implausible; that implausible actions or events reinforce a given discourse, while plausibility attacks the discourse by making actions seem absurd. Thus, once a viewer accepts the implausibility, at least according to traditional mores, of an otherwise effeminate man being able to draw upon a conventionally masculine set of reactions in a given situation, the plausible situation of his being called upon to aggressively defend his partner from a bully or to maneuver a delivery truck into a tight parking space reveals the latent (and heretofore unrealized) absurdity of the text, and thus its hilarity.

Comedy, as William F. Fry, Jr., has noted, entails the communication of a paradox. Here, the paradox seems to be characters whose humor derives, at least in part, from their ability to successfully challenge stereotypes the situation comedy form traditionally has applied to marginalized groups and to gay males, in particular. The more audiences believe they understand Mitch and Cam when they perform gender in ways dictated by mainstream culture and reproduced by television, the greater the pleasure they realize when the pair performs it differently. Whether the gender performance is dictated by situation and circumstance or whether it owes to the personality symbiosis necessary to maintain a successful domestic partnership in real life (and, hence, a believable one in television life), it challenges the viewer to comprehend the complexity of the characters, as they evolve with each episode and season and perhaps, in so doing, challenges the hold those very stereotypes maintain on culture.

Works Cited

Bagdikian, Ben H. 1987. *The Media Monopoly*. Boston: Beacon. Print.

Barcus, F. Earle. 1983. *Images of Life on Children's Television*. New York: Praeger. Print.

Bathrick, Serafina. 1984. *The Mary Tyler Moore Show*: Women at Home and at Work. In *MTM: "Quality Television,"* ed. Jane Feuer, Paul Kerr, and Tise Vahimagi, 99–131. London: British Film Institute. Print.

Brown, Jane Delano, Kim Walsh-Childers, Karl E. Bauman, and Gary G. Koch. 1990. The Influence of New Media and Family Structure on Young Adolescents' Television and Radio Use. *Communication Research* 17 (1): 65–82. Print.

Buerkel-Rothfuss, Nancy L., and Sandra Mayes. 1981. Soap Opera Viewing: The Cultivation Effect. *Journal of Communication* 31 (3): 108–115. Print.

Butler, Judith. 1990. *Gender Trouble: Feminism and the Subversion of Identity.* New York: Routledge. Print.

Butsch, Richard. 1992. Class and Gender in Four Decades of Television Situation Comedy: *Plusça Change....* *Critical Studies in Mass Communication* 9: 387–399. Print.

Byars, Jackie. 1987. Reading Feminine Discourse: Prime-Time Television in the U.S. *Communication* 9: 289–303. Print.

Collins, Claudia. 1997. Viewer Letters as Audience Research: The Case of *Murphy Brown.* *Journal of Broadcasting and Electronic Media* 41 (1): 109–131. Print.

Corrigan, Paul, and Brad Walsh, writers, and Jason Winer, dir. Fizbo. 2010. *Modern Family.* Twentieth Century Fox, Hollywood. November 25, 2010. Television.

Courtney, Alice E., and Thomas W. Whipple. 1983. *Sex Stereotyping in Advertising.* Lexington: Lexington Books. Print.

Dow, Bonnie J. 1990. Hegemony, Feminist Criticism and *the Mary Tyler Moore Show. Critical Studies in Mass Communication* 7: 261–274. Print.

———. 1992. Femininity and Feminism in *Murphy Brown. Southern Communication Journal* 57: 143–155. Print.

Fouts, Gregory, and Kimberley Burggraf. 2000. Television Situation Comedies: Female Weight, Male Negative Comments, and Audience Reactions. *Sex Roles* 42 (9/10): 925–932. Print.

Frueh, Terry, and Paul E. McGhee. 1975. Traditional Sex Role Development and Amount of Time Spent Watching Television. *Developmental Psychology* 11 (1): 109–114. Print.

Fry, William F., Jr. 1987. Humor and Paradox. *American Behavioral Scientist* 30 (1): 42–71. Print.

Gitlin, Todd. 1980. *The Whole World Is Watching: Mass Media in the Making and Unmaking of the New Left.* Berkeley: University of California Press. Print.

Gray, Frances. 1994. *Women and Laughter.* Charlottesville: University Press of Virginia. Print.

Guider, Elizabeth. 2010. 'Modern Family' Actors Practicing Gay Kiss. *Entertainment Weekly*, August 28, 2010. Web. 21 Jan 2016.

Haimoff, Michelle. 2012. Not So Modern Family: Top Sitcoms Make for Sexist, Inaccurate Television. *Christian Science Monitor*, January 27, 2012. Web. 21 Jan 2016.

Hanke, Robert. 1998. The 'Mock-Macho' Situation Comedy: Hegemonic Masculinity and Its Reiteration. *Western Journal of Communication* 62 (1): 74–93. Print.

Liebert, Robert M., and Joyce Sprafkin. 1988. *The Early Window: Effects of Television on Children and Youth.* 3rd ed. Elmsford: Pergamon. Print.

Meadowcroft, Jeanne M., and Mary Anne Fitzpatrick. 1988. Theories of Family Communication: Toward a Merger of Intersubjectivity and Mutual Influences Processes. In *Advancing Communication Science: Merging Mass and Interpersonal Processes*, ed. Robert P. Hawkins, John M. Wiemann, and Suzanne Pingree, 253–275. Newbury Park: Sage. Print.

Moore, Marvin L. 1992. The Family as Portrayed on Prime-Time Television, 1947–1990: Structure and Characteristics. *Sex Roles* 26 (1–2): 41–61. Print.

Olson, Beth, and William Douglas. 1997. The Family on Television: Evaluation of Gender Roles in Situation Comedy. *Sex Roles* 36 (5/6): 409–427. Print.

Palmer, Jerry. 1987. *The Logic of the Absurd: On Film and Television Comedy.* London: British Film Institute. Print.

———. 1994. *Taking Humor Seriously.* New York: Routledge. Print.

Poniewozik, James. 2010. Modern Family Watch: Lips Service. *Time*, September 30, 2010. Web. 21 Jan 2016.

Press, Andrea L. 1991. *Women Watching Television: Gender, Class, and Generation in the American Television Experience.* Philadelphia: University of Pennsylvania Press. Print.

Reeves, Byron, and Mark M. Miller. 1978. A Multidimensional Measure of Children's Identification with Television Characters. *Journal of Broadcasting* 22 (1): 71–86. Print.

Richman, Jeffrey, writer, and Michael Spiller, dir. 2010. "Halloween." *Modern Family*. Twentieth Century Fox. Hollywood, October 26, 2010. Television.

Rowe, Kathleen. 1995. *The Unruly Woman: Gender and the Genres of Laughter.* Austin: University of Texas Press. Print.

Scott, Joan Wallach. 1988. *Gender and the Politics of History.* New York: Columbia University Press. Print.

Skill, Thomas, and James D. Robinson. 1994. Trend: Four Decades of Families on Television: A Demographic Profile, 1950–1989. *Journal of Broadcasting & Electronic Media* 38 (4): 449–464. Print.

Toro, Josep, Manual Salamero, and Esteve Martinez. 1994. Assessment of Sociocultural Influences on the Aesthetic Body Shape Model in Anorexia Nervosa. *Acta Psychiatrica Scandinavica* 89: 147–151. Print.

Villarreal, Yvonne. 2011. 'Modern Family': Savior of the Sitcom. *Los Angeles Times*, October 30, 2011. Web. 21 Jan 2016.

Zuker, Danny, writer, and Fred Savage, dir. 2011. After the Fire. *Modern Family*. Twentieth Century Fox. Hollywood, November 15, 2011. Television.

CHAPTER 10

Online Romeos and Gay-dia: Exploring Queer Spaces in Digital India

Rohit K. Dasgupta

In June 2008, queer organizations in three major Indian cities—New Delhi, Mumbai, and Chennai—held simultaneous Gay Pride protest marches, with a total turnout of approximately 1000 persons, a very significant number at that time. While queer groups in Kolkata have sporadically organized such annual marches since 1999, this was the first time that it occurred on a national scale protesting against Section 377 of the Indian penal code. Instituted in 1860, Section 377 was driven by a Victorian purity campaign to regulate sexuality in the colonies. The law reads:

> Whoever voluntarily has carnal intercourse against the order of nature with any man, woman or animal, shall be punished with imprisonment for life, or with imprisonment of either description for a term, which may extend to ten years, and shall be liable to fine.
>
> Explanation: Penetration is sufficient to constitute the carnal intercourse necessary to the offence described in this section. (Narrain and Eldridge 9)

On July 2, 2009, the Delhi High Court ruled that Section 377 of the Indian penal code which criminalized "carnal intercourse against the order

R.K. Dasgupta (✉)
Institute for Media and Creative Industries,
Loughborough University, London, UK

© The Author(s) 2018
E. McNeil et al. (eds.), *Mapping Queer Space(s) of Praxis and Pedagogy*, Queer Studies and Education,
DOI 10.1007/978-3-319-64623-7_10

of nature" violated the country's constitution guaranteeing dignity, equality, and freedom to its citizens (Narrain and Eldridge 9). The judges read down (limiting the meaning of the words in the legislation) Section 377, decriminalizing consensual sex between adults of the same sex in private. This landmark judgment overturned a 150-year-old law that for years had denied queer citizens the right to be open about their sexuality.

Scholars have argued how queer identities dismantle the "purity" of an Indian nationhood by disorienting the idea of commonality which ties all citizens together within this mythic national citizenship (Bose and Bhattacharya x). As Judith Butler and Gayatri Spivak note, "If the state is what binds, it is also clearly what can and does unbind. And if the state binds in the name of the nation, conjuring a certain version of the nation forcibly, if not powerfully, then it also unbinds, releases, expels, banishes" (4–5). It is therefore important to complicate and understand queerness in India through the prism of the state and the idea of belonging.

I begin this chapter by examining India's media history. India's media history runs parallel to its social history and plays a significant role in understanding and interpreting India's changing social landscape. I trace this to the post-liberalized phase of India's media history which started in 1991. I also explain the role of mass media in the development of a universal Indian subject which itself was authored and created along colonial subjectivity. It is imperative to critique this notion of a universal nationalism which is based on a presumptive commonality. As I argue elsewhere (Dasgupta and Gokulsing 6), the history of queer sexuality in India is complicated, and modern homophobia is a remnant of the complex postcolonial modernity of the country. Thus, negotiating Indian-ness with queer-ness becomes a complex discourse on politics of nationalism. India's global power stems from its digital development; therefore, this chapter goes on to acknowledge the development of this new media and finally examining how the queer male community in India have used these online opportunities to test their identities, connect and construct communities, and mobilize political change through a critique of nationalism and the hegemony of national identities. This chapter addresses the politics of queer male sexualities in contemporary India by exploring its manifestation in digital spaces. I shall demonstrate how such spaces have been used by the queer male community to test their identities, connect and construct communities, and mobilize political change through a critique of nationalism and the hegemony of national identities.

MEDIA LIBERALIZATION AND QUEER MEDIA, 1991–2012

Colonialism and nationalism have a very intrinsic relationship with mass media. During British colonialism, the establishment of media institutions like the All India Radio were specifically created to carry out the propaganda of the British government against the Indian National Congress and the axis powers (Athique 25). With the end of colonial rule, the anti-colonial movement set about to create their version of a "nation state" with the backing of a state-owned media.

The development of modern media was in direct contravention to Gandhi's ideals of austerity and simplicity. His ideal of a traditional preindustrial society as a model for modern India did not reconcile with the urban medium of media (in this case, cinema). However, Nehruvian politics differed vastly from Gandhi's ideals and was in favor of advancing India's scientific and technological objectives (Athique 18–21). India's national rhetoric which was based on tradition and the rewriting of a precolonial past was underpinned by historicist notions which ranged against neocolonial advent of modernity which Western media and technology represented. The legitimacy of media was only included within the political discourse in 1959, when television made its appearance in India through a gift from Philips supplemented by a UNESCO grant. This led to the establishment of "tele-clubs" in middle- and lower-middle-class localities of Delhi followed by a roll-out rural program. The first regular daily service was started in 1965, and by 1967, the most popular daily service was *Krishi Darshan*, a program on agricultural development (Gokulsing 8). K. Moti Gokulsing argues that whilst media development in India was intended to provide a platform for dialogue between the government and the people, by the 1970s, it became the political voice of the government, which they used less for dialogue and more for "talking to" the people in India (14–15). Adrian Athique points out that a liberalization period in Indian media started in 1991, which marked the transition "from an era of statist monopoly ... to an era of popular entertainment, cosmopolitan internationalism" (69). This then became a time for "individualism and for the expression of a list of desires that were long suppressed in the name of national integration" (Athique 69).

The first phase of this liberalization was the deregulation of Indian television which followed the rapid growth of private entertainment-based television stations against the state-owned Doordarshan in 1991 followed by the growth of regional television and print media. But as Gokulsing and Wimal Dissanayake remind us the presence of regulatory bodies under the Ministry of Information and Broadcasting, of the Government of India, still have the power to rate and review audio visual materials meant for public consumption (159). This is exercised very stringently by the Central Board of Film Classification (CBFC) which was constituted by the Cinematograph Act of 1952 and the Cinematograph Certification Rules, 1983, for Indian films (Gokulsing and Dissanayake 160). The guidelines governing this body is so wide that the "State can, if it desires, restrain any film from public viewing on grounds of security or morality or some other issue" (160). The CBFC has a strong record of denying certification to films with queer storylines. Gokulsing and Dissanayake as a case in point refer to Sridhar Rangayan's 2003 film, *Gulabi Aina* (The Pink Mirror) which is about transsexuals. The film was denied certification on the grounds that it had vulgar and offensive content. The filmmaker appealed twice but failed to obtain a censor certificate without which films cannot be distributed or screened for commercial purposes. However, in the last five years, a few films with queer storylines and queer characters (*Dunno Y Na Jane Kyun, My Brother Nikhil, I Am*) have received censor certification and been screened for adult audiences.

Queer media in India can be found in various mediums and in various languages. In this section, I have chosen to look at both the print and visual medium. I recognize trying to document the entire media coverage related to queer issues since 1991 would be too vast for the purposes of this chapter and thesis, I have therefore chosen to provide some representative examples from three areas—the English language print media, Indian cinema, and television. These in turn will lead to an entry point to look at digital queer spaces.

Mainstream press coverage related to queer-related issues in India can be traced back to the early 1990s. Parmesh Shahani provides a few interesting examples of the tone these articles take. He argues "some of these articles were positive and almost evangelical in their tone," on the other hand, there were also articles which were "uninformed, replete with negative stereotypes about homosexuality and gay men; and downright silly" (175). Sandip Roy notes that the English language media in India started as a "Gay 101 story" which featured an interview with a psychiatrist, quotes from queer people with changed names, and finally an activist intervention. However, publications such as *Times of India* (Gupta), *The Telegraph* (Basu), and *Society* (Roy and Sen) have in recent years published several opinion pieces arguing for acceptance of queer people within the

Indian society. The *Society* piece, for example, interviews parents of LGBT children and their concerns about their children's sexuality. Many have written about their struggle with society and acceptance of their children. Of course, not all coverage has been positive. There is also an element of sensationalism which drives coverage of queer-related issues. Examples of this include the 2006 media coverage of police-aided harassment of the queer community in Lucknow, when the papers offered variations on what the *Hindustan Times* reported as "Cops Bust Gay Racket." The sensational coverage revealed names and addresses of all those who were involved in the "racket" which included "chatting with gay members at an Internet site" and "meet for physical intimacy." However, running parallel to this form of homophobic media was also the establishment of queer publications such as *Bombay Dost* by Ashok Row Kavi, in 1990, which ushered queer revolution in queer media, followed quickly by other magazines and ezines such as *Gaylaxy, Pink Pages India,* and *gaysifamily,* to name a few.[1]

Indian television has also played a huge role in the public perception of queer people in India. Chat shows such as *Kuch Dil Se* (From the Heart), telecast in 2004, *Zindagi Live* (Life), and *We the People* in the last two years have time and again invited queer-identified people on their panels as guests and have been sympathetic toward queer-related issues. In fact, Barkha Dutt, host of *We the People,* proudly declares that it was one of first television shows that has tirelessly advocated for the decriminalization of homosexuality in India.[2] Reality television shows such as *Big Boss* (Season 1, 2006) which featured the openly gay actor Bobby Darling further tried to push queer consciousness within the domestic space of India; however, his departure within the first week is a testimony to the passive homophobia of both contestants and viewers who decided to vote him off over the other participants. A recent Hindi soap, *Maryada: Lekin Kab Tak* (Honour: But for How Long? 2010) is credited for being the first national prime time soap to feature a gay storyline. This was a watershed moment as previous soaps such as *Jassi Jaisi Koi Nahin* (No One Like Jassi, 2003, an Indian version of *Ugly Betty*) and *Pyaar Ki Ek Kahaani* (This Is a Story About Love, 2010) featured queer characters as a stereotype to provide humor or a subplot to the main story. Similar changes can also be noticed within regional television; Kaushik Ganguly's Bengali television film *Ushnatar Jonnyo* (For Her Warmth, 2002), a homoerotic story about two female friends, signals this magnitude of transformation that Indian television has been witnessing in the last decade. However, incidents such as the sting attack carried out by the Hyderabad television channel *TV9* last year exposing gay men on social networking sites have drawn widespread criticism from both queer activists and mainstream media.

It is, however, the film medium in India which has been the most significant influence in establishing the public consciousness about queer identities and issues. Deepa Mehta's film *Fire* (1996), which drew the ire of the Hindu right wing for portraying a lesbian love story, also opened up lively debates around female sexuality and queer identities in India. Naisargi Dave argues how a new social world of lesbian activists emerged in India around the text of a sign reading "Indian and Lesbian" which was used during the counter protest demonstrations for the film (1). Gokulsing and Dissanayake writing about Indian popular cinema argue that "the discourse of Indian Popular Cinema has been evolving steadily over a century in response to newer social developments and historical conjunctures" (17). Cinema in India participates in the continual reconstruction of the social imaginary. In addition to being a "dominant form of entertainment," Indian cinema also represents the interplay of the global and local (Gokulsing and Dissanayake 15). While popular Indian cinema has a long history of featuring cross-dressing male stars in comic or song sequences, films in the 1990s and the 2000s, such as *Mast Kalandar* (Intoxicated, 1991), *Raja Hindustani* (Indian King, 1996), *Dulhan Hum Le Jayenge* (We Will Take the Bride, 2000), *Mumbai Matinee* (2003), *Rules Pyar Ka Superhit Formula* (Rules: The Superhit Formula for Love, 2003), and *Page Three* (2004), saw a shift from the stereotypical effeminate gay characters in the earlier films to more complicated layered gay characters in the later ones. This was followed by Onir's path-breaking film *My Brother Nikhil* (2005), which for the first time featured a HIV-positive gay character in the main role. In addition, two other films, *Kal Ho Na Ho* (If Tomorrow Never Comes, 2003) and *Dostana* (Friendship, 2008), using the trope of "mistaken identity" and "misreading," represents and stages homoerotic play and queer performativity. Rajinder Kumar Dudrah questions whether these films simply offer cheap thrills and comedy, or if they engage meaningfully with queer representations and possibilities. Recognizing the "secret politics of gender and [queer] sexuality in Bollywood," Dudrah writes that "These codes and their associated politics are attempted to be spoken, seen and heard cinematically that little bit more loudly; not yet as radical and instant queer political transformation, but as implicit and suggestive queer possibilities that are waiting to be developed further" (45, 61). In addition to these and numerous other mainstream Bollywood films, there are also significant queer films being made in regional film industries such as Bengali, including *Memories in March* (2010), *Arekti Premer Golpo* (Not Another Love Story, 2010), and *Chitrangada* (2012), to name a few. There is also a very strong non-commercial film sector in India spearheaded by queer film-makers such as the late Riyad Wadia, Nishit Saran, Sridhar Rangayan,[3] and others. The establishment of several queer film festivals across India are a testimony to the growing number of such films being made each year.

On Online Queer Spaces

As the above sections demonstrate, media representations of queer people in India have not had a linear development; it has changed over time due to societal and political change. While some sections of the media have been sympathetic to queer people, other sections of the media, fueled by jingoistic nationalism, have castigated and portrayed queer people in a very negative light. These have been major factors and a driving force behind the emergence of an alternative social space offered by the Internet. Identities as we are aware are contextualized within the various scapes (Appadurai 5) within which we inhabit. These range from home, nation, and community to gender and sexual preferences. My discussions in this section will turn and overturn these space terrains. Benedict Anderson in his famous narrative analysis of nationhood, *Imagined Communities* contends that a nation exists because people believe in them. Membership to this community is governed through a collective common origin, characteristics, and interests. The space of home, community, and nation has at its foundation a shared commonality. Stuart Hall contends that there are "people who belong to more than one world, speak more than one language and inhabit more than one identity, have more than one home" (206). Hall's insightful writing dislocates the notion of homogeneity, replacing it with heterogeneous identities in a new global world. Thus, the idea of home is in constant flux. The idea of home becomes more problematic when dissonant identities, in this case queer identities, conflict with the heterogeneity of a national identity.

The emergence of the Internet has had a profound impact on human life. By destabilizing the boundaries between the private and public, new spaces have opened for social interaction and community formation.

Thomas Swiss and Andrew Hermann examine the Internet as a unique cultural technology, where several complex processes come together: "The technology of the World Wide Web, perhaps *the* cultural technology of our time, is invested with plenty of utopian and dystopian mythic narratives, from those that project a future of a revitalized, Web based public sphere and civil society to those that imagine the catastrophic implosion of the social into the simulated virtuality of the Web" (2). The idea of a utopian world being created through the Internet envisages cyberspace as a safe and accommodating sphere, where communities can interact and grow. The concept of an online community was first advocated by Howard Rheingold in 1993 when he coined the term "Virtual Community." Taking on Anderson's idea of an "imagined community," Rheingold writes, "virtual communities require an act of imagination to use ... and what must be imagined is the idea of the community itself" (54). Radhika Gajjala and Rahul Mitra suggest that cyberspace is not a place, it is a locus around which modes of social interaction, commercial interests, and other discursive and imaginative practices coalesce. The emergence of the Internet in the context of community has resulted in several scholars arguing about the differences between real life and the virtual world. However, writers like Shahani see them as integral to one another: "I do not find this virtual versus real debate useful or productive. People do not build silos around their online and offline experiences—these seep into each other seamlessly" (64). Concurring with Sharif Mowlabocus, who also sees "the gay male subculture as being something that is both physical and virtual" (2), I suggest queer male digital culture in India be seen within the larger context of the social history of the country. The need for safe space is probably the single most important factor that underlies the formation of digital queer spaces. The engagement of queer people using the Internet and other digital spaces reveal one of the many forms of "expression of the personal self within the public sphere" (Pullen 1).

In his study of the relationship between sexual identity and space, Randal Woodland shows how spaces shape identity, and identities shape space. He writes that "the kinds of queer spaces that have evolved to present queer discourse can be taken as measure of what queer identity is in the 1990s" (Woodland 427). In his study of four distinct queer cyberspaces which include private bulletin boards, mainstream web spaces, bulletin board systems (BBS), and a text-based virtual reality system, shows that all these spaces deploy a specific cartography to structure their queer content. However, "one factor that links these spaces with their historical and real life counterparts is the need to provide safe(r) spaces for queer folk to gather" (Woodland 427). The need for safe space is probably the single most important factor that underlies the formation of digital queer spaces, and this will lead toward understanding the queer cyberculture better. Mowlabocus points out that this relationship between the online world created by new media technologies and the offline world of an existing gay male sub-culture complicates the questions concerning the character of online communities and identities. He argues that "the digital is not separate from other spheres of gay life, but in fact grows out of while remaining rooted in, local, national and international gay male subculture" (Mowlabocus 7).

Mowlabocus's statement about the digital being rooted in the local gay male sub-culture is important in understanding queer cyberspace. I shall argue that while anti-discrimination laws exist on a national level in the UK, some countries in Europe, and parts of the USA, sodomy laws still exist in most parts of the world, and until as recently as 2009, homosexuality was criminalized in India.[4] It is within this hostile space that I situate queer men using the Internet. Mowlabocus's study of *Gaydar*, a popular British gay cruising site, also points to the similarity of multiple queer digital spaces. He goes on to say that "Many of these websites may in fact be peddling the same types of bodies and the same ideological messages as each other" (Mowlabocus 84). However, queer space does not exist solely on queer-identified sites (e.g., *Gaydar*, *Guys4Men*, and *PlanetRomeo*— PR); rather, queer individuals' encountering one another via mainstream websites, such as *Facebook*, *MySpace*, *Twitter*, and *Orkut*, have added another dimension to discussions on queer identity and its representations on the Internet.

The Foucauldian idea of space and its subversive potential can be harnessed in the context of the queer cyberspace, which can be read as a Foucauldian heterotopia—a place of difference. Michel Foucault describes it as "something like counter-sites, a kind of effectively enacted utopia, in which the real sites, all the other real sites that can be found within the culture, are simultaneously represented, contested and inverted" (24). The alternative queer cyberspace can be considered heterotopic, where the utopic place is not only reflected but reconfigured and revealed. Affrica Taylor writes that the "other" spaces of the gays and lesbians destabilize their own territories and meaning just as much as they destabilize the territories of heterosexuality.

At this point, I would like to examine the issue of identity within a postcolonial digital space. The postcolonial approach suggests that subjects position themselves within the narratives of the past and see themselves in relation to it. Treading a similar trajectory, online queer identities are articulated as a position against the hegemony of a singular imagined past. While the queer identity is a point of entry into mainstream politics around restriction and discrimination, it also makes distinctions between identities shaped by culture and geography (the West and the East), social conditions (class structures), and personal identities—ones that we construct on our own. The important point being that identity is constantly reshaping. Jeffrey Weeks calls identities "necessary fictions" that need to be created "especially in the gay world" (98). If we concur with Weeks, then identity can be seen as sites of multiplicity, where identities are performed and contested and constantly reshaped. Identity is at the core of digital queer studies, as Nina Wakeford, in her landmark essay "Cyberqueer" (1997), also notes, "The construction of identity is the key thematic which unites almost all cyberqueer studies. The importance of a new space is viewed not as an end in itself, but rather as a contextual feature for the creation of new versions of the self" (31). While I recognize that our social and cultural lives are determined by a universal heteronormative code that validates heterosexual signifiers, the cyberqueer identity recognizes multiple sites (in cyberspace) and discourses that give rise to alternative readings of identity and allows one to read the multiplicities and complexities within individual profiles.

Mowlabocus asserts that "If gay male digital culture remediates the body and does so through a pornographic lens, then it also provides the means for watching that body, in multiple ways and with multiple consequences" (81). The Internet does not just allow the browser to be a passive participant but an active one. The participation can be in variety of ways. There are websites which feature coming out stories, which invite the reader to add their own. There are websites such as PR, *Guys4Men*, and *Gaydar* which are cruising/dating sites, and finally there are websites which have a more political and health-related output. The subject of online identity is a complex and shifting one. Like every other element of cyberculture, identity is centrally bound to the use of language, from the choice of a name to the representation of the physical self.

What we see here are certain unsettling gestures. Working from a marginalized position and beyond the bounds of that marginality, cyberspace challenges the existing boundaries with which identity is contained, yet presuppositions such as the individual wanting to be "the center of the social universe" are also harnessed. In this sense, while it acts as an erasure of differences by putting all the profiles (and by extension the identities) on the same plane, it also rearticulates the difference and otherness. Virtual communities offer the opportunity for identity testing, preparation for coming out, if one chooses to do so, and a support system throughout the entire process. The Internet thus provides the queer youth with tools to create and refine their queer identities from dating and sexual bonding to politics and activism.

The Internet is entering a phase remarkably linked to the concept of identification. With the proliferation of sites such as *Facebook* and *Twitter*, the garb of anonymity which dominated the Internet in the first decade is slowly lifting, when users were translated as stock information which was hidden by a username and information that is endorsed through their registration.

In the discourse of the cyberqueer community, the virtual space, community, identity, and voice of the individuals are all inextricably linked. Woodland points out that "community is the key link between spatial metaphors and issues of identity. By helping to determine appropriate tone and content ... community identity also informs the voice and ethos appropriate to members of that community" (Woodland 430).

While early work by scholars see the utopic possibilities of the Internet offering new spaces for political and ideological formations through debates about power, identity, and autonomy and heralding the beginning of a new democracy which is not impinged by race, color, and socioeconomic status, later scholars, such as Tsang, dismiss such utopic declarations. He writes, "Given the mainstream definition of beauty in this society, Asians, gay or straight are constantly reminded that we cannot hope to meet such standards" (Tsang 436). As an example, he states the case of a college student from Taiwan who after changing his ethnicity to white "received many more queries and invitations to chat" (435). Gajjala, Natalia Rybas, and Melissa Altman, writing about race and online identities, critically note, "Race, gender, sexuality, and other indicators of difference are made up of ongoing processes of meaning-making, performance, and enactment. For instance, racialization in a technologically mediated global context is nuanced by how class, gender, geography, caste, colonization, and globalization intersect" (1111). The primary reason for setting up virtual queer communities might have been to create a "safe" space, where people could freely express their identity, "over time such spaces also became sites where identities are shaped, tested, and transformed" (Woodland 430).

QUEERING THE CYBERSPACE IN INDIA

Following the discussions above, it is not surprising that the queer community in India has turned to the Internet and other digital forms of communication to "create a sense of community and solidarity" that are "unbounded by geography." Gayatri Gopinath articulates how sexual minorities of Indian origin, citing the case of South Asian Lesbian and Gay Association (SALGA), were denied representation at the Annual India Day parade in New York City in 1995 claiming that the group represented "anti-nationalist" sentiments (5). Thus, it would be safe to assume that the brand of Indian nationalism currently espoused by the State of India systematically denies and has been denying queer citizens representation and voice. Arvind Narrain and Gautam Bhan, in their landmark anthology *Because I Have a Voice*, point out: "It is not just Section 377 that affects queer people—laws against obscenity, pornography, public nuisance and trafficking are also invoked in the policing of sexuality by the state and police. One also has to pay heed to the civil law regime where queer people are deprived of basic rights such as the right to marry or nominate one's partner" (8–9). In this section, I turn to the creation of online queer spaces in India (and the diaspora) which engage with a new form of queer geography. These spaces act both as a point of resistance to the hegemony of patriarchal heterosexual Indian values and at the same time as a response to "the desire for community" (Alexander 102).

The early 1990s marked the beginning of the information age charac terized by economic liberalization and computer technologies. Manuel Castells, one of the leading theorists of globalization marks this as a new social order driven by the rise of informational technology and political processes.[5] This new form of networked society is driven by the exchange of knowledge. Given the ambitious aim of Nehruvian politics of advancing India's technological and scientific objectives, it is not surprising that India's postcolonial elite made their way to Silicon Valley and other "nodes" of information and technological revolution. However, before being accused of creating an elitist and utopic digital world for India, I should clarify that India has also remained a country of deep divides and contrast. The growth of Internet usage in India has been in depth and not in spread. This is to be expected in a highly stratified society like India, the penetration of Internet among urban Indians being around 9 percent and among all Indians about 2 percent. Athique gives three reasons for the low penetration of the Internet in India, that is, the slow growth of computer ownership, capacity shortage in telecommunications, and lastly the content of the Internet being delivered in English (103). However, there has been a huge surge of mobile phones in developing countries around the world, especially in places like India, Sri Lanka, and Bangladesh. For 2013–2014, the Telecom Regulatory Authority of India (TRAI) reported an overall mobile density of 75.23 percent of the total Indian population (4). These figures are very encouraging, though poor network connectivity and 3G intake means that it will be some time until Internet access is available to most mobile phone users.

South Asian presence has not been very visible on the Internet in the last two decades. The Internet remains a domain of privilege to which most South Asians have little access. Linda Leung, in her research on online geographies of Asia, remarks that "one of the main limitations of the study of Asian online identity and activity is that it has been confined to a narrow socioeconomic demographic" (7). While the Internet is not as white as it once was, it remains restricted to those who have the socioeconomic means to access it. Leung further points out that "Access to cyberspace requires the use, if not the ownership, of a computer, a modem, a telephone service and an Internet provider. These resources are surely not equally distributed amongst the diverse groups of lesbians, gay men, transgendered and queer folk" (Leung 22).

It is, therefore, not surprising that those who have been part of the South Asian diaspora, and more specifically the Indian diaspora, were among the first to inhabit cyberspace, because of their economic standing, in contrast to their counterparts back home. Radhika Gajjala and Venkataramana Gajjala argue that some of the earliest roles played by the Internet for the Indian diaspora were in relation to the establishment of call centers, the proliferation of Bollywood and Indian cinema, and finally helping to arrange marriages.

The Internet began in India in 1995, while online queer presence of South Asians can be traced back to the establishment of the Khush List[6] which was founded in 1992, and which is one of the "oldest and most established discussion spaces for LGBT-identified South Asians" (Shahani 85). With the establishment of the Khush List, other similar lists, such as SAGrrls and desidykes (a women-only group), emerged in quick succession. Roy, editor and, later, *Trikone Magazine* board member, writes that Trikone was the first ever queer South Asian website hosted online, in 1995.[7] One respondent explains:

> I am glad the internet is there, without it I would have been lost. My entire
> self-discovery (of being gay) has been possible because of the internet and
> sites likes Planetromeo. At home my brother is very homophobic, he always
> makes very bad remarks about homos. I am always scared to talk to anyone
> there and don't feel safe. The same for school, but having Planetromeo has
> opened up the world for me. I can sit in my chair and talk to other gay boys
> all the time and they understand me more.

The emergence of the Internet in the context of community has resulted
in several scholars arguing about the differences between real life and the
virtual world. However, writers such as Shahani see them as integral to one
other: "I do not find this virtual versus real debate useful or productive.
People do not build silos around their online and offline experiences—
these seep into each other seamlessly" (64).

The need for safe space is probably the single most important factor
that underlies the formation of digital queer spaces. As my respondents
have demonstrated, their public lives be it within the confines of home or
school and work are in constant conflict with their queer identities, and it
is within the space of PR that they try to create and recreate spaces of relative safety, identity formation, and belonging. These are men who are not
only marginalized because of the oppressive impact of homophobia but
whose opportunities for self and community formation are constrained
because of the lack of social acceptance.

Online sites such as PR represents a space where personal opinions with
political overtones and consequences are articulated and shared—a space
that is outside the purview of the state. Gajjala and Mitra argue that the
connection between voice and space becomes particularly critical when
such a space is denied in the real life through marginalizing forces, and a
new space needs to be carved out. Spaces such as PR constructs a new
Indian public sphere suggesting media activism and alternatives to state
responses by gathering together non-recognized actors and giving them a
voice. At the same time, it also allows a variety of queer desires to be recognized and acted upon. As one of my respondents, Jasjit, puts it:

> I am not an activist. I don't use Planetromeo to *andolanbaazi* [for activism].
> I'm more interested in having sex and that is primarily what I use it for. It
> takes care of having to speculate who is gay or not and then the whole dat-
> ing process. This is faster and instantaneous. In a click I have everything I
> need to know about him—his likes, dislikes, if he likes to party, his body
> stats as well as sexual fetishes.

Roy states that the Internet was invaluable for those growing up in small towns that did not have an active queer community. The anonymity offered by the Internet, and the possibility of meeting people from other parts of India and even the world, provided impetus for those queer men using the Internet in these small towns. Gajjala and Mitra writing about Indian queer men living in the rural and small towns of India critically point out that "Even gay men in the smallest, least industrialised, most rural towns of Indian heartland scout for tricks online.... Email and guys4men.com is a great way to make their presence felt in their tiny district (and even though they probably never imagined) in cyberspace" (416). From this homogenizing perspective, cyberspace can be seen as a force that erases the difference of queerness by setting up a dialectic between Indian and queerness, and challenging the assumption of anti-queer nationalism. The cyberspace thus not only allows for alternative communities to form and social interactions to take place but also offers discussion boards for political and social changes relevant to the queer community. While online new media might seem to offer a democratic scope for queer men to engage with issues around subjectivity and identity, we must also remember that this is fragmented and disconnected. The online space cannot just be viewed as an emancipator or all encompassing; rather, issues such as class, gender, and the socioeconomic background of the users play a vital role in the voices that are heard and those that are not. The birth of the cyberqueer in India has opened a vital space for dialogue, activism, and self-exploration.

NOTES

1. These are available at http://www.gaylaxymag.com, http://www.pink-pages.co.in, and http://www.gaysifamily.com, respectively.
2. See http://www.youtube.com/watch?v=x5_1aXfyw74&feature=share&list=SPE77B5BBB6220A28F, November 4, 2012.
3. *Bomgay* (1993), *A Mermaid Called Aida* (1996), *Summer in My Veins* (1999), *Pink Mirror* (2006), *Yours Emotionally* (2007), *68 Pages* (2007), and others.
4. In South Asia, homosexuality is currently illegal in Afghanistan, Bangladesh, Bhutan, Pakistan, and Sri Lanka. It was legalized in Nepal in 2007 and India in 2009 (pending Supreme Court decision). Seven countries—Iran, Saudi Arabia, UAE, Nigeria, Mauritania, Sudan, and Yemen—punish homosexuality with the death penalty.
5. See, for example, *Networks of Outrage and Hope* (2012).

6. Khush List is a bulletin board (http://dir.groups.yahoo.com/group/khush-list). At the time of writing this chapter, the last activity/message posted on the Khush List was February 9, 2012.
7. Trikone and *Trikone Magazine* (started in 1986) are based in San Francisco. Trikone is one of the earliest South Asian LGBT support groups.

Works Cited

Alexander, Jonathan. 2002. Homo Pages and Queer Sites: Studying the Construction and Representation of Queer Identities on the World Wide Web. *International Journal of Sexuality and Gender Studies* 7 (2): 85–106. Print.

Anderson, Benedict. 1991. *Imagined Communities: Reflections on the Origin and Spread of Nationalism.* London: Verso. Print.

Appadurai, Arjun. 1996. *Modernity at Large: Cultural Dimensions of Globalisation.* Minneapolis: University of Minnesota Press. Print.

Athique, Adrian. 2012. *Indian Media.* London: Polity. Print.

Basu, Arundhati. 2008. Breaking Free: Indian Gays Are Getting Organised and Boldly Coming Out. *The Telegraph,* August 31, 2008. Web. 4 Nov 2012.

Bose, Brinda, and Subhabrata Bhattacharya. 2007. *The Phobic and the Erotic: The Politics of Sexualities in Contemporary India.* Kolkata: Seagull. Print.

Butler, Judith, and Gayatri Spivak. 2010. *Who Sings the Nation State?* Kolkata/London: Seagull. Print.

Castells, Manuel. 2012. *Networks of Outrage and Hope: Social Movements in the Internet Age.* Cambridge/Malden: Polity Press. Print.

Cops Bust Gay Racket, Nab SAT Official, 3 Others. 2006. *Hindustan Times,* January 5, 2006. Web. 4 Nov 2012.

Dasgupta, Rohit K., and K. Moti Gokulsing. 2014. *Masculinity and Its Challenges in India: Essays on Changing Perceptions.* Jefferson: McFarland. Print.

Dave, Naisargi. 2011. Abundance and Loss: Queer Intimacies in South Asia. *Feminist Studies* 37 (1): 1–15. Print.

Dudrah, Rajinder Kumar. 2012. *Bollywood Travels: Culture, Diaspora and Border Crossings in Popular Hindi Cinema.* London: Routledge. Print.

Foucault, Michel. 1986. Of Other Spaces. *Diacritics* 16: 22–27. Print.

Gajjala, Radhika, and Venkataramana Gajjala, eds. 2008. *South Asian Technospaces.* New York: Lang. Print.

Gajjala, Radhika, and Venkatrama Gajjala. Introduction. In *South Asian Technospaces,* ed. R. Gajjala and V. Gajjala, 7–24. New York: Peter Lang. Print.

Gajjala, Radhika, and Rahul Mitra. 2008. Queer Blogging in Indian Digital Diasporas: A Dialogic Encounter. *Journal of Communication Inquiry* 32 (4): 400–423. Print.

Gajjala, Radhika, Rahul Mitra, Natalia Rybas, and Melissa Altman. 2008. Racing and Queering the Interface: Producing Global/Local Cyberselves. *Qualitative Inquiry* 14 (7): 1110–1133. Print.

Gokulsing, K. Moti. 2004. *Soft-Soaping India: The World of Indian Televised Soap Operas.* Staffordshire: Trentham. Print.

Gokulsing, K. 2012. *Moti and Wimal Dissanayake. From Aan to Lagaan and Beyond: A Guide to the Study of Indian Cinema.* Staffordshire: Trentham. Print.

Gopinath, Gayatri. 2005. *Impossible Desires: Queer Diasporas and South Asian Public Cultures.* Durham: Duke University Press. Print.

Gupta, Poonam. 2011. Do Desi Parents Accept Their Gay Children? *Times of India,* July 11, 2011. Web. 4 Nov 2012.

Hall, Stuart. 1995. New Cultures for Old. In *A Place in the World? Places, Cultures and Globalization,* ed. Doreen B. Massey and Pat Jess, 75–213. New York: Oxford University Press. Print.

Leung, Linda. From 'Victims of the Digital Divide' to 'Techno-Elites': Gender, Class and Contested 'Asianness' in Online and Offline Geographies. In *South Asian Technospaces,* ed. R. Gajjala and V. Gajjala, 7–24. New York: Peter Lang. Print.

Medhurst, Andy, and Sally Munt, eds. 1997. *Lesbian and Gay Studies: A Critical Introduction.* London: Cassell. Print.

Mowlabocus, Sharif. 2010. *Gaydar Culture: Gay Men, Technology and Embodiment in the Digital Age.* Farnham/Burlington: Ashgate. Print.

Narrain, Arvind, and Gautam Bhan. 2005. *Because I Have a Voice: Queer Politics in India.* New Delhi: Yoda Press. Print.

Narrain, A., and M. Eldridge. 2009. *The Right That Dares to Speak Its Name: Naz Foundation vs. Union of India and Others.* Bangalore: Alternative Law Forum. Print.

Pullen, Christopher. 2010. Introduction. In *LGBT Identity and Online New Media,* ed. Christopher Pullen and Margaret Cooper, 1–13. London: Routledge. Print.

Rheingold, Howard. 1993. *The Virtual Community: Homesteading on the Electronic Frontier.* Cambridge, MA: The MIT Press. Print.

Roy, Sandip. 2003. From Khush List to Gay Bombay: Virtual Webs of Real People. In *Mobile Cultures: New Media in Queer Asia,* ed. Chris Berry, Fran Martin, and Audrey Yue, 180–200. Durham/London: Duke University Press. Print.

Roy, Piyush, and Mamta Sen. 2002. I Want to Break Free. *Society,* October 2002. Web. 4 Nov 2012.

Shahani, Parmesh. 2008. *GayBombay: Globalisation, Love and Belonging in Contemporary India.* New Delhi: Sage. Print.

Swiss, Thomas, and Andrew Hermann. 2000. The World Wide Web as Magic, Metaphor and Power. In *The World Wide Web and Contemporary Cultural Theory,* ed. Andrew Hermann and Thomas Swiss, 1–4. London: Routledge. Print.

Taylor, Affrica. 1997. A Queer Geography. In *A Lesbian and Gay Studies Reader,* ed. A. Medhurst and S. Munt, 3–19. London: Cassell. Print.

Telecom Regulatory Authority of India (TRAI). 2015. *Annual Report 2013–14.* Web. 22 Jan 2016.

Wakeford, Nina. 1997. Cyberqueer. In *A Lesbian and Gay Studies Reader*, ed. A. Medhurst and S. Munt, 343–359. London: Cassell. Print.

Weeks, Jeffrey. 2011. *The Languages of Sexuality.* New York/Abingdon: Routledge. Print.

Woodland, Randal. 2000. Queer Spaces, Modem Boys and Pagan Statues: Gay/ Lesbian Identity and the Construction of Cyberspace. In *The Cybercultures Reader*, ed. David Bell and Barbara M. Kennedy, 417–431. London: Routledge. Print.

CHAPTER 11

Femme Is a Verb: An Alternative Reading of Femininity and Feminism

Sarah Murray

It's not if you qualify; it's if you identify!
—Personal mantra of S. Murray and J. Beckmann[1]

In Manchester, England, spring 2011, I realized how queer I had become.

We were walking down a city center street, my friend and I, looking for either the Ashton or Rochdale canal, I can't remember which. We had just spent the entire day walking several miles in the countryside, and for some godforsaken reason, once we got back to the city, we decided we had more energy to keep exploring.

We're bumbling down the streets, looking lost, when we notice smoke rolling out of a window of the top floor of some apartment building. The smoke's not intense; it's more white than gray, sort of consistent, and

---

Title engendered by S. Bear Bergman's *Butch Is a Noun*.

Note: This chapter was composed when the author was 21 years old and no longer accurately reflects the views of the author, who never had authority over the text's signification anyway.

S. Murray (✉)
Covina, CA, USA

© The Author(s) 2018
E. McNeil et al. (eds.), *Mapping Queer Space(s) of Praxis and Pedagogy*, Queer Studies and Education,
DOI 10.1007/978-3-319-64623-7_11

there's something gentle about it that keeps us in a state of fog. So we watch it for a while to see if it'll die down, trying to figure out if someone just ruined their dinner, or if it really is an emergency. I pull out my phone, debating whether or not I should call 999, until we think to go and talk to the apartment receptionist, if there is one.

We head toward the building, circling it for a while before we find any doors to the place. The doors are made of glass, and through them we can only see some mailboxes, a set of stairs, and a couple of people at the top. They're dressed in outrageously high heels, with their hair elaborately curled, and they've got on these sleek evening dresses and a shit ton of makeup. I immediately don't want to talk to them; I'd rather brave my phone anxiety and call the fire department. I start to pull out my phone again when my friend starts giggling.

"What?" I ask him.

Laughter is so far from my mental state that it takes me a second to process.

"Transvestites," he says.

Trans? I get excited.

Queers?

I go back to the door, and sure enough, they're drag queens. My fear evaporates like *that*, and I knock on the glass to talk to them, pulling my friend with me. One of them comes out to speak to us, and I immediately begin explaining the situation. She offers to go up and check, agreeing that the fire's a bit odd, and I'm so grateful to her in more ways than one as she struts away in shoes that could pop a balloon.

It doesn't hit me until later, way later—after I've slapped my friend upside the head, after we've found the canal, have had dinner and pints and are so exhausted that we collapse on the bus, after we've parted ways and I've walked home alone—that there had been something odd about the situation. It struck me as odd that I should be afraid of straight women in high femme, but completely relieved at the first sign of queerness.

It seemed, in that moment, that I had made a distinction between femininity, femme, and women; it was electric, yellow and pink and organic. I haven't really been the same since. It's probably a terrible thought, and I do hope that everyone was alright, but I've never been happier to see something burn.

* * *

I entered feminism from a point of queerness. Before that, as a Latina from a private Catholic school, I knew nothing of women. I knew that they sometimes were treated like vases, and I knew that sometimes they were forced to wear dresses and stockings when they might have preferred to wear pants, but there was never any point in my life where I had learned what gender equality meant. If it was mentioned in my classes, it was glossed over, or presented in a way that said, "Yes! Women fought for the right to vote, and now they have it, and the world is a much better place." Or they said, "There are women in other countries who cannot even leave their houses without male escorts, so consider yourselves lucky."

What they didn't tell us was, "You are going to spend the better part of your childhood agonizing over what you look like, smell like, laugh like, walk like, eat like, sleep like, breathe like. Your skin will stretch to cover you as you grow, but everything underneath will feel wrong. Your muscles will feel bulbous, green and infected as they slick over the white, white bones God gave you. You are going to be conflicted, because you will like people, but they will not know what you are."

What they also didn't tell us was, "You are going to leave this place of walls and enter a place of windows, and the light that shines through will be rainbow. When you leave, and start your life as an adult, people will take the time to talk to you, and listen, and they will sometimes close their eyes because they love the sound of your voice. They will teach you the value of your gender and your body and your self, and you will feel more privileged than you ever have in your life, so privileged that you will barely be able to stand it."

And this was how the queer community first taught me words like construct, transgender, patriarchy, intersex, misogyny, and oppression. They swam like shiny fish in my head. I learned what feminisms were, who feminists were. It took me four years, though—almost my entire college career—to identify as one.

* * *

I am not a lesbian.

It's important that you know this. It's important that you understand who and what you're dealing with. I am a cisgendered woman, a Chicana, a queer heterosexual,[2] and an activist and ally within the queer community.

I am going to tell you of my experiences, offer myself up freely to you, because I want to be able to give back, and I also want to grow the community that has opened itself to me, helped raise me, and allowed me to exist as however and whoever I am. My greatest fear, in this moment, is denying someone else's identity by trying to accept my own, because what does it mean to be a lesbian if a straight woman can be femme?

Kate Bornstein once said, in a roundtable discussion at my undergrad university, "We don't want allies. We want *members.*"[3] She caught my gaze in that moment, and I knew she was telling me to get up and flip the metaphorical table that was masculinity/femininity. It was more than permission; it was a call to arms.

That is why this story is so personal. This story is not about the *hows* or the *whys*; it's about the *whos*. It is not a definition of "femme," for it defies universal definition. It is a subscription. An enlistment. This is a thank you letter.

* * *

She is a disruptor of heterosexuality, a presence standing outside the conventions of patriarchy, a hole in the fabric of gender dualism. She cannot be contained within these institutions; she exposes their gaps and contradictions; she signifies a radical absence. Her desire functions as excess within the heterosexual economy. Hence she positions herself outside these institutions, or creates space within them. She also creates a narrative or textual space in which she interrogates accepted norms of textuality and sexuality, and constitutes herself as subject. Within that space she also creates a lesbian relationship between self and other. She is the metaphorical lesbian, *the* lesbian-as-sign.—Bonnie Zimmerman, "Lesbians Like This and That"[4]

When I wake up in the morning and decide how to dress, how I want to put my makeup on, it feels like writing. People will look at me and read. They will read my body, my clothing and my hair, my body language, and my words will tie bows on my dress sleeve. It is a constant process of editing and revising. Queers broadly do that with gender and sexuality, femmes more specifically with femininity. Performance is narrative, and I have become a feminist text. And when I, or anyone else disrupts the heterosexual economy (that is to say, when we *choose* queerness, regardless of who we sleep with, or when we prioritize that relationship between self and other), we are most definitely indicating a desire that is excessive. We are indicating that *queer is desirable*. We are exerting an agency, not outside or within a heterosexual narrative, but *over* it.

* * *

A friend of mine once asked me if I had a uterus. There were several of us, LGBTQIA activists out to lunch, eating Indian food. We sat at a long table so that we could all see each other's faces, with only empty plates between us. Our discussions, as always, generally swerved in and out of the silly and the politically charged, and it was within this context that my friend had expressed some menstrual discomfort, as you do. Somehow the conversation got turned around to me, probably because I had refrained from contributing to the relatable experience, and that's when she asked me.

There were a few giggles at the table, mostly due to the presupposed ridiculousness of the question: they all knew I was cisgendered. I had never explicitly stated it, though; there had never been a conversation between myself and any of these people about my gender, only minor, quick ones about my sexuality as a straight woman within the queer community. Perhaps this was why I felt such intense discomfort? I didn't find it funny, although I tried to play it off that way.

The table quieted as my friends watched me squirm. I wasn't saying anything, just looking at my friend. A line had been drawn between Me and Them, and I was staring down a chasm, unsure how to answer. I sat still, my hands on the table, studying their faces, when a couple of people spoke up for me. "That's a really personal question," they said.

I ended up answering yes, after my skin stopped tingling. I felt obligated to, plus I wanted the conversation to move toward a different topic. And that's exactly what happened; we laughed to shake off the cloud, and everything continued as normal. But it cost me something to say it, and I couldn't stop thinking about it for a few days afterward.

It took me years to figure out why that moment was so traumatic to me. At first, I thought it was because my friend assumed the answer was simple, assumed it was non-damaging to ask because I am not queer, couldn't possibly be queer as a straight cisgendered woman with no history of queerness. Maybe it was because, if I was anybody else, she probably wouldn't have asked. In one fell swoop, she denied my membership within the community we were both part of, a community I had fought in the trenches with, a community of glitter and mustaches and tears. I even briefly wondered if it was because of my own brand of gender dysphoria. Ultimately, I was uncomfortable because it felt like she called me out on something I had been trying to hide for years: my insecurity as a woman.[5]

It's important to me to explain that I wasn't, am not, offended. I was just so confused. A flush overtook me, too much heat, and I felt keenly aware of my clothes, trying to avoid an awareness of my body, my holey denim jeans, my shirt too tight over my stomach, obscured by a vest, my dirty Vans scuffing the floor in an awkward beat, *1...2.... 1...2...3....*

* * *

The identity of Woman has also generated serious controversy over issues of ownership and identification. Some women have begun refusing the identity, particularly when it seems to draw—consciously or unconsciously—on middle-class, Eurocentric, feminine norms with the ironic effect that "women" are now opposing the unintended political effects of the very feminism working to liberate them.—Riki Wilchins[6]

When you look at me, I do not want you to see just a straight woman. Just a brown woman. Just a woman. As your eyes land on my face, my limbs, I want you to nod your head and say, "I see." What you will see is an effort to erase, correct, destroy a Privilege that drips off my body and leaves puddles in my wake for other people to step in. What you will see is malleable, currently morphing, revising, intentional, and it comes in powders, liquids, and cloths. Haircuts. It is a yellow neon sign, attracting, inviting onlookers.

It is still me. I cannot change the building blocks I have to work with. But I can paint them, rearrange them. I can cut them, glue them, sand them, sculpt whatever I want. I am a textual collage, work of art in progress, an opportunity to transgress, break, soothe. A resolute text. The person, the identity, the performance, and the behavior are all contained within the person, wrapped up into something like a demolition ball.

"Femme" is a verb not only because the identity itself is a radical and violent stand against gender constructs and their economy, but also because the core of femme is the way it interacts with its surroundings, the characteristic of *movement*. Femme means a new economy, awareness of invisibility, and an embrace of intersectionality; it resists hegemony, and this strain of femininity no longer has any obligation to follow hetero feminine norms in a linear fashion. There is a break from the linear expectations of less to more feminine, as well as a break from a linear structure of school to work to marriage to kids. This queer movement means that femmes can literally jump from space to space, queer to hetero, stealthily if they wish. And it means that femme is a part of speech that invites anyone to be femme, a part of queer language that does not require any agreements.

* * *

I'm the type of femme who opens the doors for gentlemen.
        I'm the type of femme who will blush, pleased,
                if you call me a gentleman.
I will also blush, pleased, if you call me a lady. Compliment my dress, or necklace, or shoes.
                I'm the type of femme who knows
                  how to use power tools.
Who puts down the toilet seat.
                  I can shoot a gun. Well.
I enjoy hard labor, working with my hands. I've done a bit of construction with my father, using at first pink gloves, and now green.
           I'm the type of femme who enjoys cooking.
        If you walk through my door, I will want
              to feed you. I will not, however,
        want to do the dishes afterward. But I will.
I'm the type of femme who does yard work.
          I'm the type of femme who buys her own dinner.
            But you can buy me a drink if you like.
I'm the type of femme who enjoys face paint. Preferably vines and flowers. Or a dragon. Or dragonfly.
        I will go to the Renaissance Faire. Or a drag show. Or a bar.
Listen to music. Like, really listen. Shh.
                  Play pool.
I'm the type of femme who plays poker and takes your money.
And then buys you ice cream, and maybe a book.
        I'm the type of femme who likes to hold hands.
      If my hand's on the bottom, I'll swing our arms.
        If my hand's on the top, I'll pull you close.
I'd rather if you pulled me close, though.

I'm the type of femme who looks better in purple than in red.
I'm the type of femme who has a thing for bowties.

And vests.

No really, I own eight vests. It's a problem.[7]

But also a solution.

* * *

My femme body:
It moves between heteronormative space and homonormative space. It jumps between state lines, between California and Arizona. It moves between cities, Los Angeles and Manchester, Phoenix and Amsterdam, and London and Dublin and Edinburgh. It jumps between suburbs. It moves between countries. And when it moves, that new place becomes the new center, and everything shifts. I may walk differently. My speech patterns may change; my accent may adjust. In some places, there are queers; we see each other, know each other, smile. In some places, there may not be queers; when that happens, I am alone. Sometimes I cannot see them, can't find them, see only skins, and no bones.

* * *

"Woman is to drag—not as Real is to Copy—but as Copy is to Copy. Gender turns out to be a copy for which there is no original. *All* gender is drag. All gender is queer" (Wilchins 134).

* * *

Femme Ninja[8]

There was a time in my life where I tried to pass as a lesbian.

It was never a conscious decision. I never asked my mirror, "Does this look lesbian?" as I figured out my outfit for the day. I never tried to change my walk into a strut, never altered my speech patterns. But at the time, I was inhabiting more queer space than I was hetero space, always in the office where we queers would organize, mobilize, discuss, and it felt very natural to me that people should think I was a lesbian, even if I wasn't one.

It came up every so often, within that space: I'd be introduced as the "token straight girl," or a woman would ask me out without knowing, but I tried never to bring up my straightness; it was like a blemish I couldn't rub off, an oddly-shaped birthmark for people to point and stare at. Something no one ever let me forget. *We don't need you, we don't want you, you don't belong here, go away.* And of course I'd own up to it if someone called me out on it. But every time someone asked me, "So you're not a lesbian?" and I had to say no, it felt like regression, like a wrong answer I couldn't help. As if I was undermining something by being straight. I'm not ashamed of being a cisgender heterosexual. But I am ashamed of everything attached to it, the Privilege.[9] Passing as a lesbian seemed like a salve for my insecurities, cool and soothing to the touch.

Being femme for me is not like that. It doesn't feel as if I'm trying to solve my own problems or guilt with identity, presentation, or performance. It's bigger, and more natural. In "Gender Is Burning," Judith Butler alludes to an anxiety and neuroticism that results from the impossible attempt to maintain "heterosexual" gender (85), to treat the Copy as Original. Breaking the neurotic gender cycle and embracing instead a gender collage allows for possibility outside the heterosexual possibility: revision, subversion, access to feminism inclusive of trans*folk, touch, community, movement, and most importantly, action. All things I found inaccessible when restrained by gender policing.

Let me reset your bones.

* * *

You [femmes] *fight homophobia in a way that I never could. Some of them think I am queer because I am undesirable. You prove to them that being queer is your desire.*—Ivan Coyote[10]

I first read *Stone Butch Blues* by Leslie Feinberg as a sophomore in college. Through the eyes of a butch, it was my very first taste of femme, of what femme meant, looked like, was, could be. What femmes could do, and *how they could make others feel.* If queer narrative and theory has shown me one thing, it is how much of a difference a femme can make to a butch, yes, but also any other queer. That idea of Queer Comfort. It was a gift I was given once, a gift I am continually given. That recognition of self in others, that immediate sense of ease, camaraderie, solidarity.

This is the ultimate power of the femme: to carry Queer into heterosexual spaces, un-queer-friendly spaces, and offer an extension of queer comfort and community. We turn our desire into space.

* * *

Activism is like water for a fire. It quenches, balances, and cleanses. It has a strong current, and when you get swept up in it, it washes you clean. Every time you protest, every time you research, every time you plan and write and fight, it's like taking a big gulp after days of coughing up sand, which you had tried swallowing before, but it hadn't worked.

It's the sand that kills you. It gets in everything. It gets in your sandwiches, it gets in your shoes. Every time you walk, you feel it pressing into the arch of your foot. It's so dry, it sucks the life out of you. And you watch your friends step in it, sink in it, claw at the surface, and you watch their families look on, no idea what to do, so they grab a rope to toss but choke themselves with it.

You watch this whole process, and you think, if only I could grow my arms out. If only they were tree branches; I could extend them long and far, dip down in the sand, grow roots, be strong, not budge; "Hold on, I'm coming." But you need water to grow, so you search, keep searching, until you hit this giant reservoir, and the people there are all lapping it up, the most delicious water in the world, and they say, "Here, have some, we'd love to share." So you drink for days, and you say, "Aha, I can grow now. Aha."

I am still trying to shake off the sand. I can feel it sometimes, scratching me through my pajamas as I toss and turn in my bed at night. When I put on my glasses, I can see the marks it has left on the lenses. Sometimes when I shake people's hands without washing mine first, I can tell that I've left grains in between their fingers. That's what bothers me the most: when I am the one, I am the source, perpetuating and spreading the desert. And no one can tell, no one notices that anything is wrong, because the sand is the same color as my skin, just like it's the same color as theirs.

My identity as a femme, while not inherently radical, is something that I'm making radical. You may not be able to see me ever, but I am there. I blend in with the sand, soak in, but I am the water. I am getting rid of the sand, brushing it off. I may never be able to get rid of it; I'm not sure yet. I may have swallowed too much of it. I still look like it, will most likely always look like it. But I am becoming the water.

* * *

Going abroad, constantly traveling, and being on the move for five months was like jumping into an ice-cold lake without knowing how to swim:

your lungs freeze up, your stomach muscles cramp, your skin feels like insufficient covering, too light and thin for the heaviness of your bones, which have transformed themselves into weights that you can only carry because of the endorphins, because if you *drop them, don't drop them* or they'll shatter. and that lightness in your head, that detaches your eyes and your ears and your mouth and your tangled hair from your weighted arms and your acid stomach and your mechanical legs. and your fingers tingle, and you wiggle them to make sure they still move, because they're the only bones you have that don't feel like iron, but more like plastic, lighter but not as sturdy. even your jaw feels heavy, so heavy that you let it drop open, you'll never be able to pull it back up, and your tongue flops around, with nothing to protect it, and your tonsils ring in sympathy, in freedom, like bells.

The shock it sent to my system kept me up for three days straight; the sirens from the hospital across the street kept me company. I couldn't eat, didn't know where to find food. I didn't have a map or phone, so I would wander down the street in different directions, zigzagging to and fro, memorizing the street signs so that I could find my way back. I'd stand outside bus stops, memorizing the maps as best I could, because the streets were small, so small, like tiny veins of the city that were taken for granted until you got stuck in an alley. I'd walk into different shops, ask people to point me in the right direction, and eventually I'd calm down, and make friends with other international students who were in the same boat. Bonded by our displacement, our youth, and our confusion, we all stumbled along together. It was a very strange time for me, and it put a lot of things in perspective, and it was in this environment, with these people, that I first learned how to let go.

A few months in, I finally got the courage to ask one of these friends to go makeup shopping with me. I didn't own any, never had. Several years earlier, I had experienced some forced feminization after I was asked to prom by a boy at my high school. Not yet comfortable with feminine clothing, I was made to critically examine my body through others' eyes as I was taken dress shopping, to get my eyebrows waxed. I cried after my mother forced me inside a nail salon; when I came home, my fingers and toes found wanting and painted over, no longer my own, my father laughed. But in Manchester, I felt far enough away from my past, from my mother's hawk eyes, from my old friends who knew me too well and would want to make a big deal out of it, from my family's cooing sounds, to try. This friend in Manchester wouldn't know, or care, that I had no idea what I was doing; she was a no-nonsense kind of person, kind, with a bright smile, and she was more than willing to help me out.

I lived far from everyone, so we met at the city center and went straight to the mall. A couple of makeup stores with dark interiors and sultry atmospheres, music promising sex, reminded me too much of the USA, too much of home. To walk inside one would have been like walking straight into a pressure chamber, claustrophobic. I wanted nothing to do with them; I wasn't ready for that yet. We found a store with dull fluorescent lighting, small, and aisles of eye shadows, mascaras, foundation, and lipstick. Art supplies. Walking in there didn't feel quite as much like a commitment, quite as much like I was signing over my soul. It was more natural, more every day, and the clean white walls and scuffed tile floors made me feel like I could breathe a little easier.

I was looking for eyeliner, and maybe a little eye shadow. Something simple, something to start me off gently. We started at the far-left wall, and every dazzling color was there to greet me, all in little tiny containers. It seemed a shame for some reason, those containers, but I didn't consider why. She helped me look for some earth tones, neutral things, rubbing powder on her own finger and smudging them over my eye for me to see which ones suited me best. She almost poked my eye out at one point, and when we laughed, the air that *swooshed* into my lungs was so fresh, it made my whole body tingle. I felt good. A little dizzy, but good.

I paid for my pencil and palette, shoved them into my bag. As we left the store, I could feel them heat up the side of my leg, chasing away the English chill. I breathed in the bright gray sky, the soft clouds. *Yes, this is what I came here for.*

Postscript:
Untitled

shopping cart, red as the apples of our cheeks, as the
lipstick residue on your jaw, side of your throat, a good
place for a body to become undone,
            unwrapped, invitation for rope, perfume

to say nobody owns you is to say that you are a gift—

fingers, the sites of touch, little spiders
inching
with impatience, my love, across—

and the eyes! how could we forget: telescopes, one, two, they sit
atop mountain ridges, ocean mouths open wide to swallow our enemies down,
where they live in our bellies, happily ever after,
little watermelon seeds from which fruit grows

Notes

1. The author still believes in the essence of this, which is the desire for queer-ness and the dismantling of the Gender Police, but would like to state that it is problematic to invite yourself into someone else's house (I'm looking at you, Rachel Dolezal).
2. The author is demisexual these days.
3. Bornstein visited Arizona State University's Tempe campus in March 2010 to discuss and present on gender anarchy and, at the time, her upcoming memoir, *A Queer and Pleasant Danger* (2012).
4. 4.
5. Part of what made this so painful was being asked to confront my cis privi-lege at a time when I still hadn't come to terms with what it meant to be female in American society. Unpleasant but necessary. Currently, the author is working through what it means to be brown and femme in the Cheeto Age (also while maintaining many privileges), which is likewise unpleasant and necessary.
6. 124.
7. Queer Tip: Learning to sew is part of the resistance.
8. Author would especially like to acknowledge this term is appropriative as fuck.
9. The author acknowledges this moment as Fragile Heterosexuality.
10. Coyote performing at Speak Up! on April 10, 2010.

Works Cited

Bergman, S. Bear. 2010. *Butch Is a Noun*. 2006. Vancouver: Arsenal Pulp Press. Print.

Bornstein, Kate. 2012. *A Queer and Pleasant Danger: A Memoir*. Boston: Beacon. Print.

Butler, Judith. 1993. Gender Is Burning: Questions of Appropriation and Subversion. In *Bodies That Matter: On the Discursive Limits of "Sex."* New York: Routledge. Print.

Coyote, Ivan. 2010. *To All of the Kick Ass, Beautiful Fierce Femmes Out There....* YouTube, Uploaded by Pancake Heart, 12 Apr 2010. https://www.youtube.com/watch?v=2Q7IzwUa_kI

Feinberg, Leslie. 2003. *Stone Butch Blues.* New York: Alyson. Print.

Wilchins, Riki. 2004. *Queer Theory, Gender Theory: An Instant Primer.* New York: Alyson. Print.

Zimmerman, Bonnie. 1992. Lesbians Like This and That: Some Notes on Lesbian Criticism for the Nineties. In *New Lesbian Criticism: Literary and Cultural Readings*, ed. Sally Munt, 1–16. New York: Columbia University Press. Print.

Enspiriting, Living, Teaching Queer

CHAPTER 12

Intersextionality: Embodied Knowledge, Bodies of Knowledge

Stacey Waite

In *Teacher Narrative as Critical Inquiry: Rewriting the Script,* Joy
S. Ritchie and David E. Wilson write:

> The development of a professional identity is inextricable from personal
> identity and when personal and professional development are brought into
> dialogue, when teachers are given the opportunity to compose and reflect
> on their own stories of learning and of selfhood within a supportive and
> challenging community then teachers can begin to resist and revise the
> scripting narratives of the culture and begin to compose new narratives of
> identity and practice. They can begin to author their own development. (1)

To take this work seriously—to take narrative seriously—means, for me, to
enact and enmesh the lived world with theoretical practice. I often find
myself asking questions about the narrative that leads to the classrooms I
shape now. What is the story of this teacher I am? What is the story of the
person who searches for a queer pedagogy? How is intersexuality an intersectionality whereby the teaching body might continuously come into
being? This essay is an attempt of one queer teacher and scholar to "author
their own development."

S. Waite (✉)
English Department, University of Nebraska–Lincoln,
Lincoln, NE, USA

© The Author(s) 2018
E. McNeil et al. (eds.), *Mapping Queer Space(s) of Praxis
and Pedagogy,* Queer Studies and Education,
DOI 10.1007/978-3-319-64623-7_12

* * *

All the children are laughing. The two first-graders, Lucy Cavaro and Craig Larson, have rocks. Lucy is taunting, "Are you a boy or a girl? Boy or girl?" I don't say anything. I keep doing what I do whenever I feel cornered like this. I look off through the green fence and picture myself as capable of movement. I picture myself faster than I am, as fast as a boy, I suppose. I see myself leap the tire swing and head for home. But Lucy won't quit. She hurls one of her rocks at my feet. "Can't you even talk?" she wants to know. I can't rid myself of the fire rising in my small round belly. There's a pasty coating on my tongue and the lump in my throat is growing, expanding like a party balloon. I can't breathe. When Miss Sherri finds us, she's angry. When I tell her Lucy does this to me, she wants to know why I don't answer. "Tell her you're a girl," she says. But I can't think of what to tell—the way I can't think of any sins to tell the priest during confession. I saw a face of contradiction, I was frozen, unnamed.

* * *

I had never had a male teacher, so going into the third grade you can't blame me for my suspicion. Let me explain. Mrs. Guarino taught kindergarten, and in those days I wore my father's flannel shirts as smocks; I painted green trees around the suburban house. Mrs. Guarino was heavy and jolly, deep-voiced and tender. I had the sense I was different, but the other kindergartners couldn't put their fingers on it. They were still learning difference, still playing the "find what doesn't belong" games in the *Highlights Magazine*. My best friend was Robby O'Reilly. He hadn't punched me in the face yet, but he would. One hot summer day when I tip the bucket in which we keep the garter snake, the snake gets away. Robby punches me in the face. That's it. First grade was Mrs. Killian. She lets me take home the class gerbil on weekends. She's old and fragile and thinks of me as the caretaking kind—responsible and sound in judgment. She catches me and Jillian Becker trading kisses in the jacket room. She tells my mother I am "confused about my role—perhaps it's the four older brothers," she says, and she's kind and gentle enough for my mother not to be threatened or alarmed, but my mother does begin to dress me more gender appropriately, crying one morning when I refuse the dress and barrettes. Second grade, Mrs. Walsh. I remember her very little. She did not like my handwriting and was the first "B" grade—penmanship. I spent second grade failing at the alphabet sheets, not touching my capitals to the top line, missing the cursive "z" over and over. I cry at the bus stop. My mother says, "No one's perfect," and signs the report card with alacrity. My father leaves my mother for his nurse. He leaves a note on her pillow that says he "went with plan B." My mother drinks second grade away.

* * *

It seems to have started quite early—the idea that some things that I found so strange and terrifying were, to others, quite obvious and comforting. There was, however, some consensus like the idea that I should accept the invitation to join the third grade "Gifted and Talented Reading Group" at Forest Brook Elementary School. I don't remember any of the books we read in that group except one—*Call It Courage*, by Armstrong Sperry, about a young boy whose mother was killed by the sea in a hurricane. Of course, the young boy, Mafatu, was terrified of the sea and felt cast out by his community, which valued courage above all things. As narrative would have it, Mafatu goes out to sea alone to face his fears. Mrs. Sullivan, the beautiful librarian who painted on her eyebrows and drove a gleaming red car, chose me for the reading group. I had been a library aid for two years, and I suspect while my grades weren't always strong, she chose me because of the sheer number of books she had watched me check out. To this day, I am not exactly certain if I read any of them. But *Call It Courage* I did read. I read it on the school bus, on the way to Little League practice, late at night when just enough hall light (which I insisted be left on) shined through the bedroom door. I was obsessed with Mafatu's fear, and with the idea that there seemed to be no one else in his entire community who feared the sea. I had a hard time believing this, and when I told Mrs. Sullivan that there was no way no other kid was afraid of the sea except Mafatu, she said that even though we lived on Long Island we had no concept of how close Mafatu lived to the sea. And living so close, she explained, the sea was just part of everyone's life, so it is believable that no one living that close to the sea and looking out to the sea each day would be afraid of it in the way that Mafatu was.

What I loved most about Mrs. Sullivan was after school hours, when I'd stay to laminate book covers in the back room—a job given to only the most careful and efficient library aid. Mrs. Sullivan had taken to a nickname she called me only in private. She'd come to the back room and say, "How many books covered, Sir?" She'd say it in this military way as though we were performing some wartime version of book covering. Or sometimes she'd walk me out to the late bus and say, "See you tomorrow, Sir." And we'd both smile. Something seemed fitting about it. I liked it. It didn't feel judgmental in the way it did when rude old ladies asked my mother if I was a boy or a girl, or the way it felt when the other kids teased me. It felt right. I didn't need to defend myself, or my "womanhood," against this claim. Sometimes I had dreams I married Mrs. Sullivan next to the ocean. And I was a man, and I was dressed in that perfect black suit the way I had seen my father dressed a few times. And I was wearing a tie, the blackest, shiniest tie.

* * *

My relatives were always trying to give me my gender in the form of dollhouses, Hello Kitty blankets, pink things, yellow things, Barbies, the beloved Cabbage Patch Dolls. I wanted them to give me another version of gender, and sometimes, usually in private, someone would. My mother: a hockey stick. My grandfather: a baseball hat. My brother: advice. "This is how you punch back," he says. "Right. Like this. This is how."

* * *

In third grade, I distrusted Mr. Shellhorn right away—his dark mustache, his hard, full chest, and thick-rimmed glasses. I never raised my hand to sit on his lap during "John Brown Jalopy." I didn't raise my hand to turn the pages of afternoon stories. No matter how hard the other children laughed at his character voices, no matter how many times he praised my drawings and even my handwriting, I would not budge. I would not, as it were, love him. Then the science fair. And I hate the other students—their maps of constellations lighting up on cardboard, their mud mound volcanoes erupting over the desktops. I don't want to make anything. I don't want anything to explode or light up. I don't want the bad-smelling oak tag, the construction paper dry against my fingers. I would rather make up math problems sitting on the radiator. For a few days, Mr. Shellhorn leaves me there. He doesn't ask what my project will be. But by the time the light-up planets begin to show he's back there with black construction paper and a handful of orange tissue paper. He folds the black paper in half and cuts for what feels like a half hour, moving the big "teacher scissors" in curves and inside-out holes. And when he opens the paper, it's wings. He glues the orange tissue paper behind them. "It's a monarch," he says. "They are perfectly symmetrical. Do you know what symmetrical means?" And I'm still not budging. "I don't care," I answer, directing my stare through the back window toward the school lot where the cars are lined up in a green blur. I do care. I want to know what symmetry means. I like the sound of it, how his teeth joined at the "s," his lips touching at the "m" and curling together to end on the "try" of the word. I do love him, you understand. I do make five more butterflies when he goes. And as for symmetry, the dictionary says, "Match exactly."

* * *

I did try to be a real girl. In the eighth grade, I swore, to my father's new wife, that I would give up my brother's old jeans, that I would stop swearing, that I would blow dry my hair in the mornings and stop tucking it back underneath what she and my father called "a ball cap." I couldn't bear it very many days. The kids at school were not so willing to let me change identities before their eyes. "You look weird," Greg Blackstein said. "Where's your Yankee hat?" Jodie Lipkin asked. They wanted to know where I had gone. They wanted the rules of my old identity, one I didn't so much shed as I left back at the house, tucked away, where it was safe. I am not yet aware that years later I will read books from a discipline called "queer theory." I do not yet know that Judith Butler will write, "That my agency is riven with paradox does not mean it is impossible. It means only that paradox is the condition of its possibility" (3).

* * *

At age 17, a close friend says to me, "If you want to be a teacher you better take off those freedom rings and stay in the closet. You can't be queer around kids. People don't like that." And later in college, an education professor gives me advice about my student teaching experience: "Especially for you, Stacey, it's important you keep your classroom and office door open, and do not touch your students for any reason."

* * *

I'm not a good teacher. I make messes where there is supposed to be order. I trouble boundaries—my authority performance some kind of

All-American-Boy-Gone-Feminist-Not-Quite-Man vibe. I give impossible assignments. I stand before my students, an unknowable body in context (the classroom) where the assumption is there is something to be known, some body of knowledge (me, or the subject of the course) to be ingested, understood. But I (not surprisingly) became a teacher of writing, and in this landscape there both is and is not a body of knowledge at hand. Writing as subject: the body of knowledge a kind of moving process.

The phrase "body of knowledge" is most familiar to us as institutional, a set of sanctioned practices—this body of knowledge is understood to be located outside the self. It is something we can grasp toward, something we can know, something we can teach, but it is not, however, something that we are. In this model, I have the body of knowledge; my students do not. However, even as I *have* this body, this does not mean I *am* this body or can ever be it. Our bodies are forbidden to *be* this body of knowledge; our bodies are meant to be outside, separate from this body. What we know, then, is not supposed to be at all about embodiment. The body of knowledge replaces the body, substitutes institutional sanctions in its place, intending to forever codify and compartmentalize what we know from what we do, from what we are, from the lived experience of our bodies. The political stakes of this "body of knowledge" are then quite high. It even paves the way for us to dismiss or disregard what the body knows in favor of what the institution knows.

So then it is no accident that the idiom, *body of knowledge*, takes the metaphor of body—steals it *from* the body in order to *dis*embody education. But in the echoes of the idiom's erasure of the body, we can still hear that somehow what we know, or what we come to know is part of bodily expression and bodily composition. Most of us don't want to talk about our bodies, at least not in the brainy mind space of academic discourse, and especially when it comes to teaching and students. Part shame, part fear, part binary of body and mind, this hesitance can be particularly amplified for queer bodies, or bodies like mine.

* * *

I used to teach Tai Chi to elderly women from a church in the suburbs of Pittsburgh. After three years of teaching them, some refer to me as "he," some as "she." They don't seem to notice the disparity between their pronouns. I show Evelyn, a 76-year-old two-time cancer survivor, how to stand. I place my hands gently atop her shoulders and press down.

Her back and shoulders relax. I place my hand at the small of her back and push softly forward. Her knees bend as she falls into a stance known as "wu ji," the most balanced and relaxed a person can be. Perhaps another way to think about a body of knowledge.

In teaching Tai Chi, the physical relation is obvious, necessary. Even when I am not touching my students, they watch my physical movements intently, looking for when to step, when to circle their hands, and how to use their waists to lead the rest of their bodies. In the college classroom, the body's force is less obvious, or perhaps less admitted. In his essay from *The Teacher's Body,* Jonathan Alexander writes about the ways his "embodied queerness" had intense effects on his teaching and relationship with his students (163). He quotes Marjorie Garber's declaration that "It is [the] very potential for loving, and for falling 'in love,' that makes education possible" (324). Garber claims, he says, that "subconscious erotic interest underlies most student/teacher interactions—across genders" (Alexander 163). I read Alexander and Garber not as reducing teaching to seduction, not as easily dismissed Socratic romanticism, but as a theoretically and practically complex acknowledgment that bodies matter, that the relationships between bodies in a classroom are real and multi-faceted, contested relations. And these relations become particularly fraught with a gender-queer teacher, like myself. My body first, for most students and most people, watched for clues for what might be underneath my clothes, what body of knowledge my body conveys. What does it mean for my uncertain body to *teach* my students? What does it mean for my queer ambiguous hand to write words about my students' work? And do I also, in writing about their work, write about *their* bodies?

Bodies do matter. A body of knowledge has everything to do with bodies. And as a person whose scholarship draws most often on students and student writing, I have to contend with their bodies. I have to raise questions over and over again about how, if, and when to represent their bodies as part of their writing or their classroom presence. I have to make decisions about what representations are ethical or necessary. I have to consider my own fears about being a queer scholar who pays attention to bodies. *I am supposed to be one of those good queers, if I am to be a teacher, one who says appropriate things, unerotic, eunuch. I am supposed to desexualize and ignore my students' bodies.* Of course, the question arises, can I really do this when so many of my courses ask students to think about gender, sexuality, and embodiment, when I ask my students at times to write about themselves, their bodily experiences? Take, for example, the following passage, written by a student (whose permission I have to use her writing but not her name) in one of my first-year writing classes. I had asked students to spend the five days between two class meetings keeping a gender journal, one in which they were to take notice of anything they saw that they thought might be connected to gendered bodily expression. One student writes:

> When I am walking down the street alone, I rarely make eye contact with other people who are passing me. I never thought of this attribute as a female one. But I think maybe it might be. When I walked down the street, I tried to make eye contact with people I passed. I noticed it was much harder to make eye contact with other women than it was for me to make eye contact with men. I wonder if it's because women evaluate each other in secret. Like we look at each other's clothes and stomachs and stuff to see how we compare. With guys, who cares.

Does it help in trying to read her writing to know this student is a white body, an attractive traditionally gendered young woman, that she looks me in the eyes all the time, that she cried and slouched in my office two weeks earlier because she missed Australia, where she had spent the summer and had fallen in love with a man named Thomas? Do I tell you I put my hand on her shoulder? Do I tell you I spoke softly, and that when she asked me if I thought it was stupid for her to move back to Australia, I placed my hand on top of hers on the desk and said, "You do what you want to do." Do I tell you I am uncomfortable telling you that? Do I say she has a tattoo of the word "eternity" on her shoulder in Chinese, that she wears rings on every finger, that she closes her eyes when something is hard to think about in class, that she rolls her eyes whenever her classmate, Jennifer, speaks, that she crosses her legs always when she sits and has a habit of biting her nails. I learn, in her passage above, that I am easier for her to look at, that our bodies are not in competition, that she and I are not women to each other. This is her body of knowledge as I read it, as I am not supposed to be reading it. We know our students' bodies; we sometimes know the emotional terrain that is expressed through them. We are, by the very notion of an institutional "body of knowledge," encouraged to erase this embodied knowledge, to find it irrelevant to our classroom practices. To acknowledge the student's body would be, in part, to explode the myth of my own objectivity as her teacher, to admit there is more to my comments, more to my scholarship that cites her work, more to the grades I assign inside the institution, the grades that mark her position with respect to writing's ambiguous, shifting body of knowledge.

The truth is: this is what I am reading when I read this student's papers, when she raises her hand to speak in class—her body always part of my interpretation of her words. I can hear her voice in her response because I know the sound, because I recognize the sound, because I have watched and listened to the sound of her voice rising in her throat, because I even know the sound she makes the instant before she speaks—the quick taking of breath, the tight shift of the eyebrows. Reading student writing in a traditional non-digital classroom means always to read a body alongside or behind a text. Reading student papers is quite distinct from reading a novel, from reading a book of scholarship by someone whose body you have never seen, whose body you do not know. Reading student writing and representing that writing in our scholarship is always a representation of a body.

At the beginning of one of this student's essays, titled "A Journey to Womanhood," she writes:

> I was six or seven, and I was playing in the yard with all of my neighbors, all of whom happened to be boys. We were playing Star Wars and since I was the only girl I of course was Princess Leia. We set up the rules for the game and started to play. Only I wasn't running around with light sabers saving the galaxy. I was sitting in the tree house waiting to be rescued. Since I was the princess, I needed to be rescued.

In closing, she says:

> If I could go back and have a conversation with little [me], while she was waiting to be rescued by the boys, I would give her a few pointers. I would tell her that she should do what she wants. If she wanted to be Luke Skywalker, she should go be Luke Skywalker and if she wanted to be Princess Leia waiting for the boys to come rescue her then she should be Princess Leia. Either way, she rescues herself in the end by making a conscious choice. ("Journey")

Reading student writing is relational, and that relation is both the interpretative relation that occurs in any reading of any text and an embodied relation, in several ways. First, we might consider the ways I can understand and see her body in the text itself—my ability to imagine her younger self, how she might have sat waiting in the tree house, how she might have looked running with the light saber she did not get to wield, how she might have looked pre-tattoo, pre-silver rings, before she learns some of the woman lessons she knows—to cross her legs, and as she says, to keep her eyes away from the eyes of other women, the competition. Second, we might hear the echo of the moment I described earlier, her paper read in the context of my hand on top of hers, my telling her to "do what she wants"—her telling her young body the same, that "if she wanted to be Luke Skywalker, she should go be Luke Skywalker," as if her little girl frame might emerge from this tree house a new body, a Luke Skywalker body, a body of boy knowledge merged with a body of girl knowledge.

Composition, of course, as a field, has known for a long time that the idea of some official "body of knowledge" in our discipline is contradictory, even impossible. Consider how much time we spend reaching into other disciplines, blurring and contesting the boundaries of what counts *as* composition. Consider the ways we tell and re-tell histories of composition, knowing all along that the "body of knowledge" that counts as Composition is not a stable pre-determined body. Consider the work compositionists do in thinking about identity, knowing that this body of knowledge is *connected to* rather than *outside of* some notion of self. But what some recent turns in queer theory can tell us is that the idea of a "body of knowledge" is not only linked to identity as a concept, but also linked to actual bodies; that, in fact, identity is inextricably linked to actual material bodies. This is the pressure trans-theorists are putting on queer theory and a pressure I want to put on our practices of pedagogy and our writing about our students and their work. I want to bring the body back to knowledge, to acknowledge all the material realities of our classrooms— the student who shakes my hand firmly and introduces himself on the first day of class, the student whose hung over and vodka-seeping body slumps in the back row, me (their teacher) whose voice rings of her father's voice, whose broad shoulders curb her fears of no authority. There is no bodiless pedagogy, no disembodied scholarship to represent disembodied students and teaching. And I wonder, at times, what would happen if we stopped pretending there was, if we consider the meaning our bodies make, if we showed up (mortal, subjective, messy, and vulnerable as bodies are) to, as my student says, "rescue ourselves in the end."

WORKS CITED

Alexander, Jonathan. 2003. A 'Sisterly Camaraderie' and Other Queer Friendships: A Gay Teacher Interacting with Straight Students. In *The Teacher's Body: Embodiment, Authority, and Identity in the Academy*, ed. Diane P. Freedman and Martha Stoddard Holmes, 161–178. New York: SUNY Press. Print.

Butler, Judith. 2004. *Undoing Gender*. New York: Routledge. Print.

Garber, Marjorie. 2000. *Bisexuality and the Eroticism of Everyday Life*. New York: Routledge. Print.

Ritchie, Joy S., and David E. Wilson. 2000. *Teacher Narrative as Critical Inquiry: Rewriting the Script*. New York: Teachers College Press. Print.

Sperry, Armstrong. 1940. *Call It Courage*. New York: Macmillan. Print.

CHAPTER 13

Take a Left at the Valley of the Shadow of Death: Exploring the Queer Crossroads of Art, Religion, and Education Through Big Gay Church

Mindi Rhoades, Kimberly Cosier, James H. Sanders III, Courtnie Wolfgang, and Melanie Davenport

Five queer art educators intent on interrogating the intersections of religion, education, the arts, and LGBTIQ identities have engaged in an annual performance/session called "Big Gay Church" for the National Art Education Association's annual convention since 2009. In this chapter, we begin with

M. Rhoades (✉) • J.H. Sanders III
The Ohio State University, Columbus, OH, USA

K. Cosier
University of Wisconsin–Milwaukee, Milwaukee, WI, USA

C. Wolfgang
University of South Carolina, Columbia, SC, USA

M. Davenport
Georgia State University, Atlanta, GA, USA

© The Author(s) 2018
E. McNeil et al. (eds.), *Mapping Queer Space(s) of Praxis and Pedagogy*, Queer Studies and Education,
DOI 10.1007/978-3-319-64623-7_13

a script that is an amalgam across years of collaborative arts-based educational research. Following that, we explore what we have learned from this work in a more traditional scholarly format. We conclude by considering the impacts of the arts-based academic interventions in BGC on our group, and our congregation, with regard to imagining our paths forward, opening our hearts, and collaboratively building our hopes for the future.

Prologue

While "Big Gay Church" is the formal conference session title, its enactment is much queerer than the name might imply. We use *gay* deliberately in the title for audience familiarity and appeal and as an allusion to pop culture references such as the *South Park* episode "Big Gay Al's Big Gay Boat Ride" (Park and Stone). We use the word "gay," but our intent is to be inclusive of gay, lesbian, bisexual, transgender, intersex, two-spirit, and other marginalized gender and sexuality identities—as a palatable and playful stand-in for "queer" (Sanders).

The event itself, and its theoretical underpinning, aligns with queer theory and pedagogies. With BGC we are less concerned with "getting identities right" and using academically appropriate terms, and more concerned with exposing and refusing "the insufficiencies of identity" and the inequities these produce (Britzman, *Lost Subjects* 94). We want to create places and events "that encourage the proliferation of pleasures, desires, voices, interests, modes of individuation and democratization" (Seidman 106, qtd. in Sanders). Through a subversive use of the familiar term "gay" we not only intend to "queer" church, but to "queer" the conference itself. We strive to construct "a place to question, explore, and seek alternative explanations rather than a place where knowledge means 'certainty, authority and stability'" (Britzman, "Precocious Education" 51). We want to provide educators with tools and maps to "help create very real changes not only in our schools but in the larger world" (Zacko-Smith and Smith 8). To these ends, we deliberately collapse terms, queering the term "gay," and turning language back on itself.

Part I: Big Gay Church

Prelude

Lady Gaga's "Born This Way" unexpectedly fills a dim, cavernous, near-empty conference room early Sunday morning on the last day of the National Art Education Association's annual conference—a typical staid and sterile academic setting. The small troupe of inconspicuous academics enters the space, arms loaded with props and costumes. They simultaneously transform themselves. One member, Sister Sanders, taking inspiration from San Francisco's Sisters of Perpetual Indulgence, dons a nun's habit and masks his face in clown white makeup. His silvery beard is accentuated by the makeup, which is intended for campy, faux concealment. His wimple tenuously gripping his shaved head will provide comic relief throughout the morning as it slips and slides over his shiny dome.

Another member, Miss Jeanette, channels her childhood Sunday School teachers in a shapeless, barely-blue denim jumper, gray cat-eye glasses, a wig (possibly stolen from *The Golden Girls*), and her mostly hidden combat boots. Two other members become ushers and attendants, opening bottles of wine, left over from the previous evening's parties, and filling plastic cups for communion, offering them casually as people enter. Deacon Wolfgang tunes her ukulele, humming to warm her voice for the upcoming hymns. The Right Reverend Rhoades dons her black robe, places a Bible on the lectern, and prepares presentation technology as congregants file in and find their seats, not quite sure what to expect. BGC begins.

Welcome and Scripture Reading by Reverend Rhoades

The music fades and Reverend Rhoades smiles, raises her hands in a gesture of inclusiveness, and says: "Welcome to Big Gay Church! We begin, as always, with a moment for fellowship, please turn to your neighbors and welcome one and all. While you show each other some love, I'll share a passage of scripture from 1st Corinthians 13:4–8; 13:"

> *Love is patient, love is kind. It does not envy, it does not boast, it is not proud. It is not rude, it is not self-seeking, it is not easily angered; it keeps no record of wrongs. Love does not delight in evil but rejoices with the truth. It always protects, always trusts, always hopes, always perseveres. Love never fails. But where there are prophecies, they will cease; where there are tongues, they will be stilled; where there is knowledge, it will pass away.*
>
> *And these three remain: faith, hope and love. But the greatest of these is love.*

Opening Prayer: Projected and Recited by Reverend Rhoades

The Higher Principle of Love
Grant that the resources that we have will be used to do good—the great resources of education, the resources of wealth—and that we will be able to

move into this new world, a world in which people will live together lovingly. A world in which people no longer take necessities from the masses to give luxuries to the classes. A world in which we throw down the sword and live by the higher principle of love. At this time we shall be able to emerge from the bleak and desolate midnight of man's inhumanity to man into the bright and glittering daylight of freedom and justice. There will be a time we will be able to stand before the universe and celebrate this love with joy.
—Adapted from Reverend Dr. Martin Luther King, Jr.[1]

Hymn Led by Brother Love

Following our opening prayer, our roving minstrel songstress, Brother Love, stands, ukulele ready, and leads our first song. Lyrics are projected with a bouncing ball so congregants can participate at their comfort level.

All God's Children Got a Place in the Choir (Chorus)
All God's creatures got a place in the choir
Some sing low
Some sing higher
Some sing out on the telephone wire
Some clap their hands or paws or anything they've got now! (Staines)

The congregation makes a joyful noise, singing along and clapping. A look of slight embarrassment soon fades and is replaced with a one of delight and amusement. Our "congregants" have decided to play along with us.

Next, Sister Sanders takes the stage to deliver a Sunday School lesson like none before.

Adult Sunday School Lesson by Sister Sanders

Sister Sanders opens the lesson, entitled "A (Queer) Reading from the Old Testament of the Church, Art, and Art Education," with a video of his muses, the Sisters of Perpetual Indulgence, http://www.youtube.com/watch?v=7kv2PoetiQw:

> *[Why is] everyone so afraid of humor or laughter? This [performance] is a joke, I mean it's **not** mocking someone, but it's [aimed at] opening **you** up. It's the idea of the holy fool—that ancient idea that there's someone who stands, looking*

completely absurd, and gives you permission to say things that are completely true and honest without any misperception, or covering, or avoidance, or hypocrisy. (Sister Merry Peter [paraphrased])

Call and Response

I, Sister [*state name*], *as a member of the* Order of the Sisters of Perpetual Indulgence, *dedicate myself to public service, social activism, and spiritual enlightenment.—Pledge of the Sisters of Perpetual Indulgence*

Sister Sanders opens with the above video clip, then delivers the most traditional academic component of our session, complete with a PowerPoint presentation. He does it, however, as a nun caught in an awkward, constant, and doomed struggle to maintain her headgear against the laws of physics and friction. The impeccable slides offer the image-rich, theoretically dense, academic content common in conference circles as it queerly subverts their paradigms. Slide by slide, Sanders insistently recognizes queer artists and their contributions to religious art and cultural production; queers serving the Church, often closeted, as clergy and congregants; and queer theory as a valid framework for critically exploring the intersections of (visual) culture, religion, art, art history, and art education. Our sister proudly proclaims the presence, needs, and value of queer citizens. S/he demonstrates the subversive, activist potential of even corporate, controlled, and contained media and sites—playing with the master's tools to dismantle the master's house (Lorde).

Sister Sanders references historically successful queer acts of outrage as arts-based methods of political and social critique that create interventions, such as the Stonewall Riot (1968), the carnivalesque San Francisco Cockettes who were active in the late 1960s/early 1970s, the AIDS Coalition to Unleash Power (ACT-UP) in the early 1990s, as well as older traditions of drag king/queen performances and their campier updates, contemporary Pride Parades and significant arts and pop culture representation.

Children's Sunday School Lesson with Miss Jeanette

Miss Jeanette shuffles onto stage to a cascade of laughter from the congregation. Adjusting her glasses and wig, she begins her lesson, a digital take on the traditional Sunday School flannel board story. With a cartoon figure of an angel on the storyboard, she greets the congregation with a

Minnesota church lady voice saying, "Hellooo, do you know that angels don't just fly around in heaven? No siree, angels also walk among us!" Then Miss Jeanette sharply turns to follow Sister Sanders's subversive route. "Today we are going to learn about just such an angel. Her name is Rachel Maddow and she is a butch, lesbian, guardian angel! Can you say that with me?" The congregation burst into laughter once more, but dutifully responds in unison.

Miss Jeanette uses more cartoon characters of her own creation to tell the story of how Rachel Maddow exposed "The Family," a group of American politicians and so-called religious leaders who were revealed to be behind the "Kill the Gays" law in Uganda and many other hateful acts (Sharlet). Miss Jeanette declares The Family's members to be "false prophets" as they appear on the screen, Senator James Inhofe, Pastor Rick Warren, and anti-gay extremist Scott Lively and other men who have been charged by the leader of The Family to "learn how to rule the world" (Coe, qtd. in Sharlet 35). Miss Jeanette explains that The Family is really bad news, particularly for queer folk, and praises Rachel Maddow and Jeff Sharlet, the author whose undercover investigating first revealed the truth about The Family.[2]

Sermon by the Right Reverend Rhoades

As art educators grappling with issues of representation, interpretation, translation, and identity, this discrepancy between the thing itself and multiple contradictory or complicated interpretations and enactments of it may sound a familiar chord. Why—when we look for diverse interpretations and associations as a form of richness—in art-making, art criticism, and writing as and about art—do we continue to insist on singular interpretations of Biblical texts and a pure, unadulterated holy truth? Why would everyone interpret a text the same exact way? Don't we see the impossibility of complete consensus? Don't we recognize, when returning to texts—religious or otherwise—that they mean different things to us in each encounter or remembrance or enactment?

*Reverend King believed it is people like us who can make a difference. He insisted, "The question is not whether we will be extremists, but what kind of extremists we will be.... The nation and the world are in dire need of creative extremists." He adds, "Almost always, the creative dedicated minority has made the world better." Not only **can** we do this, he believes we **should** do this.*

This stands in such direct contradiction to many of the messages we receive socially and culturally about being LGBTIQ, particularly as people continue to vote for our rights as complete citizens—excerpts from iDo sermon (Rhoades, iDo)

The Right Reverend Rhoades wears a shiny black robe and carries her childhood Bible, mild-mannered preaching betraying multi-layered subversion. Her Southern Christian upbringing's conflict with her homosexuality and gender nonconformity catalyzed a personal crisis and rejection of organized religion. Ordained online, she circumvented the patriarchal, heterosexist system, avoiding years of seminary and official denominational affiliation. As a female minister, she disrupts fundamentalist religions' misogynistic gender hierarchy; as a fairly androgynous lesbian, she breaks traditional gender and sexuality church boundaries, too. She moves easily between Bible verses, religious texts, and popular culture. She reads, asking questions, seeking multiple possibilities, crafting productive tensions, and opening sacred and scholarly spaces for inclusion and love.

Testimony with Deacon Mel

Deacon Mel introduces a short video interview of a lesbian about growing up in, coming out, and being excommunicated by her church. Marie's story is emblematic of the longstanding conflict between Southern fundamentalist evangelical churches and LGBTIQ people. Deacon Mel frames an argument in light of Marie's story: Since most Americans are raised in families professing a religion, and because LGBTIQ people are born into families of all faiths (LeVay and Nonas), it is fair to assume that most LGBTIQ people in the USA "were raised in the context of some religion" (Schuck and Liddle 63–64). Religious families disowning their LGBTQ members, particularly parents disowning their children, present God as a very fickle, intolerant father-figure, not a loving protector. Mel says, "Big Gay Church aims to reclaim and refocus this story."

Twisted Offering

The BGC offering is as queer as a three-dollar bill. From our first service, we upended the flow of the traditional church offering. Instead of congregants giving a financial contribution to BGC, we offer gifts to our congregation. Miss Jeanette always distributes collectible Holy Cards that are connected to her lesson. The first was of Guardian Angel Rachel Maddow and others have recognized Saints Van Clyburn, Vito Russo, Elizabeth Taylor (who famously said to herself about the AIDS crisis, "Bitch, Do Something!"). Other offerings have ranged from small handcrafted artworks, to a pair of officially blessed and sanctioned "Loved" and "Forgiven" cards, to emblazoned kazoos for making a joyful noise.

Open Prayer and Meditation: Holding Us in the Light

Miss Jeanette opens our communal call to prayer. Explaining the Quaker tradition of prayer, she invites the congregation to name people they would like us to "hold up to the light." This seems the most precarious part, asking professional colleagues to participate wholeheartedly, becoming vulnerable by sharing personal concerns in such a public venue. Sister Sanders starts, requesting positive thoughts for a brother-in-law after transplant surgery. Other congregants follow, mentioning mostly family members and some friends for congregants' consideration. The most poignant request came from a prominent art education scholar who asked us to do this for another in the room, her best friend of many years who had an aneurysm that required brain surgery. Her request voiced something hidden silently in the shadows throughout the conference; she opened a space for an outpouring of genuine emotion and concern, a place for us to acknowledge our love and our fears—our connections—personally and professionally. BGC constructed a time and place to love, be loved, and emanate love out into the wider world.

Closing Hymn

Forever Love
Remember that we love you.
Remember that we care.
Remember that you're worthy;
For you we're always there.
For you, you are forgiven.
For you, grace from above.
For me, I am elated.
We are all forever loving;
We are all forever loved. (Rhoades, "forever")

Benediction

As so many prophets and poets urge us to do, we must learn to accept and love ourselves—and each other. We must listen for the repetition of the three most important Biblical beliefs: faith, hope, and love. We must remember, honor, and continue the longstanding ability and tradition of the LGBTIQ community to dance in the face of oppression, to sing over shouts of condemnation, to love regardless of hatred. Love each other and know that we love you. Forever.
Amen.

We close the service and invite the congregation to continue their fellowship in our Big Gay Sanctuary until the next session, as it transforms back into the nondescript, intentionally standardized traditional conference room. Our pews fade into seats locked in lines, our wine replaced by sweaty silver pitchers and half glasses for water. Our altar, a stage again. Our alter-egos disappear, pulled off and packed away in suitcases for travel home with the homos, to be stored and ready for our next service. We hug, shoving final items into our bags, saying our goodbyes, speaking of meetings for future plans. We walk out the church doors and into the convention center halls, out of the temple and into the marketplace.

PART II: A QUEER INTERSECTION: CONSERVATIVE CHRISTIANITY, EDUCATION, ARTS, + ACTIVISM

American Christianity and Queerness: The Fastest Route to Here from There

Aren't you beginning to at least get a glimpse of why God commands governments to put homosexuals to death (Lev. 20:13)? Or are you still foolishly closing your eyes, ears and hearts to the truth?—Society for the Practical Establishment and Perpetuation of the TEN COMMANDMENTS

In this section, we look at the struggle for LGBTIQ rights in relationship to efforts by conservative Christians to curtail them and condemn us. For that reason, throughout this section, we will use the term "queer" instead of LGBTIQ, given conservative Christianity's tendencies to conflate and condemn queerness. Great strides are being made in the USA regarding certain aspects of queer life. As the quote above suggests, however, a backlash in the name of God is also afoot. There is much to be learned through the study of this contradiction. Although there are many controversies and problems with the Bible and its translation across languages over millennia and around the globe, it remains a primary sacred text globally. Therefore, even though the concept of homosexuality did not exist in biblical times (Foucault), interpretations of what the Bible ostensibly *says* greatly influence the treatment of LGBTQ people in Judeo-Christian societies. Troublingly, these interpretations are based not in divine dictate, as so many believe to be true, but insinuated into Biblical translations during Europe's cultural shift against homosexuality. Consequently, early European colonists to the USA imported this punitive, condemnatory attitude toward homosexuals.

Many US fundamentalist and conservative Christian churches continue to adhere to anti-homosexual beliefs and practices. This contemporary crusade began in earnest in the late 1970s as conservative Christians entered the political arena with a vengeance. In 1978, religious leaders unsuccessfully supported California's Proposition 6 to legalize discrimination and force the firing of all homosexual teachers (Wolff and Himes). Jerry Falwell founded the Moral Majority in the late 1970s and declared HIV/AIDS to be "God's punishment for gays." The 1986 Helms Amendment, named for rabid homophobe Senator Jesse Helms of North Carolina, banned federal taxes for AIDS research and prevention efforts in schools. The Moral Majority supported 1986s California Proposition 64 to quarantine HIV-positive gay men as a threat to society (Wolff and Himes). Focus on the Family's Dr. James Dobson supported the Boy Scouts ban on gay scout leaders, calling gay men dangerous pedophiles (Wolff and Himes). In 2008, California's Proposition 8 to prevent (LGBTIQ) marriage equality was "primarily funded by Mormon, Catholic, and Evangelical churches" (Wolff and Himes; see also Cowan and Greenstreet). BGC asserts a different idea of God and faith, one that sees hateful acts against the moral minority as a grave sin.

Catholicism's anti-homosexual doctrine was formally codified in a 1975 official pronouncement that "incurable homosexuals should be treated kindly" but "homosexual behavior can never be justified" (qtd. in Lynch 387–388), what became colloquially "Love the sinner, hate the sin" (Callaghan 85). Cardinal Ratzinger (now Pope Benedict XVI) shifted this tone, condemning homosexuals as inherently evil, disordered people who provoke and deserve punishment with their wicked ways (Buchanan et al.; Callaghan), advocating discrimination against allowing homosexuals as foster/adoptive parents, teachers, coaches, or soldiers. In 2002, US Vatican spokesperson Joaquin Navarro-Vails attempted to blame gay priests for the exploding clerical child sexual abuse scandal (Lynch).

More recently, the Catholic Church is struggling to balance historically nurtured attitudes of disgust and condemnation with contemporary impulses toward respect, sensitivity, and love (Candreva). Pope Francis, who was called a "global spiritual rockstar" in *The Huffington Post*, rocked many with his simple yet powerful question "If someone is gay and he searches for the Lord and has good will, who am I to judge?" (Gehring). Even before this groundbreaking query, some American bishops sought to help parents/families of LGBTQ people negotiate the church directive to condemn homosexual behavior with the Biblical directive to love your children as gifts from God. Other more conservative bishops and Vatican officials countered, insisting Christian morality justifies religious condemnation and legalized discrimination against homosexuals (Lynch). Many US Protestant denominations have followed a similar trajectory. Some US denominations and congregations have made progress toward LGBTQ tolerance, others continue their crusade against queer people. Conservative Christianity still retains great cultural, political, and legal influence in the USA, perhaps most visibly in what H. L. Menken termed the "Bible Belt" of Southern States. Several fundamentalist Christian denominations, with large congregations and outsized influence—including Southern Baptists, Pentecostals, and newer denominations like Jehovah's Witnesses and Mormons—maintain very hardline positions against homosexuals, lobbying for continued legal oppression and penalization. In BGC, we seek to out contradictions and hypocrisy and expose them, without wholesale condemnation of other churches. We understand that faith is a complex fluid and mysterious thing. One might even call it queer.

You Are Here

Because [homosexuality] is such a great curse to humanity, the God who created humans says put homosexuals to death (Leviticus 20:13)! They ought not to be allowed to live!—Society for the Practical Establishment and Perpetuation of the TEN COMMANDMENTS

BGC operates against this complicated, conflicted backdrop of religions' relationships with queer people. More specifically, BGC's core members have extensive experience growing up and living in conservative and religious cities, small towns, and communities across the Bible Belt. As queer youth, and now as adults, we are sensitive to the power of Christian-influenced discourse around sexuality and morality in family and civic life.

Most Americans (including we queers) grew up in families subscribing to some religious faith (LeVay and Nonas; Schuck and Liddle). In many of these situations, queers face a "pervasive and potentially annihilating Christian discourse" (Schuck and Liddle 310) that precipitates near-constant fear of being outcast, harassed, or even physically injured. These fears can create or exacerbate self-loathing and general low self-esteem (Schwartz). Many queers express a desperate desire for congregational acceptance, to "go to church sometimes, and not be afraid of just being told what a horrible person you are" (Barton 466). It is an understanding of this desire that led us to create BGC.

Some queers from conservative faiths undertake a futile struggle to overcome or cure their non-normative sexual identity, and when this fails, they believe they have forfeited their "faith, God, their church, or their fellow believers" (Ganzevoort, van der Laan, and Olsman 218). In some cases, queers (and their congregations) believe that if they are unable to change their sexuality, accepting it comes at "the price of abandoning God," that "[a]postasy then may not be a choice, but an unavoidable conclusion" (220).

In BGC services, we confront Conservative Christianity's condemnation of queers and examine how their prevalence and power can create oppressive living conditions for queer people, undergirding homophobic laws, tolerating discrimination and harassment, and even promoting violence (Brooke; Cianciatto and Cahill; Dennis; Williams). We've shed light on the ways some conservative Christian congregations, pastoral leaders, and parents/guardians literally force queer minors into "conversion therapies" aimed at fixing a person's sexuality that more likely "result in psychological harm and are not effective" (Wolff and Himes 443; see also APA). Our congregants, many of whom are not queer themselves, learn of these damaging therapies as well as the hopeful message that California and New Jersey have outlawed the medically debunked practice and several others are following suit.

It is against the backdrop of this lingering conservative, religion-based persecution that members of the BGC troupe coalesced, bonding over mutual firsthand experiences in conservative churches and so-called God-fearing communities. We shared ways church still impacted our lives and how it shaped us as artists, educators, citizens, and activists. For us, every discussion of injustice eventually conjured the church, implicating it as the prime source of friction around sexuality in education. We acknowledge the chilling impact this has on teachers, students, and education.

We considered ways this chill creeps up in higher education—impacting our research, publication options, teaching, professional standing, job options, and tenure. While good Christian grandmothers from the Freewill Baptist Church haven't prowled the halls of academe, for some of us pervasive conservative values have dictated our marginalization and contributed to a resistance to queer ideas in our scholarship and teaching.

Each of us had experienced some shock to realize that the field of art education, which we had presumed to be more liberal, was every bit as apt to present challenges, from minor restriction and self-censoring, to penalizing unauthorized perspectives in higher education. Collectively, we wondered what our lives—and those of our students, colleagues, and community members—would be like if religion *didn't* demonize queer people. What if instead of rejecting all things queer, churches embraced and celebrated us in all our complicated, contradictory, and convoluted glory? What if we created our own alternative universe where queer people ran a church in which everyone was welcome and loved? We longed for a church that was fun and welcomed camp. BGC was born.

We began considering ways to productively and queerly explore these possibilities by asking how we could *queer* church (as a mis-service)? We wanted to exceed merely showing and discussing gay-friendly and welcoming examples, such as the Metropolitan Community Church and Unitarian Universalists and more tolerant congregations within larger denominations like the Dignity Roman Catholic congregations or the Baptist Peace Fellowship. We sought to create a religious community that explicitly embraces all sexualities, celebrates and theorizes transgression of gender binaries, and perhaps even embraces our own contradictions.

We wanted to disrupt the normative constraints around LGBTQ issues in art education by disrupting the conventional staid expectations for the standard conference presentations in terms of form and content. Instead of a symposium, we imagined a service; instead of a cathedral, we imagined transforming a conference room; instead of condemning, we imagined communing. We proposed inserting queers into religion to create a "gay church," inserting these queers with their "gay church" into academic contexts, and using this disruption to coalesce as a group, then question, challenge, and hopefully provoke change in participants' thinking, teaching, and daily lives.

Art + Activism = Artivism

At no point in American history have there been proper laws against the existence of gays. If any society foolishly allows them to live, they will gradually endeavor to shape society in such a fashion to legitimize their evil and extend to themselves the same rights that society should only extend to worthy citizens. If allowed to live, they will seek to be educated. If allowed to be educated, they will seek employment in key fields of society and positions of public trust so as to enable them to promote their evil and nasty agenda. They will become doctors, psychologists, scientists, senators, congressmen, judges, etc.—Society for the Practical Establishment and Perpetuation of the TEN COMMANDMENTS

Our troupe combines and deploys what youth development scholars Shawn Ginwright and Julio Cammarota call *critical civic praxis* and Chela Sandoval and Guisela Latorre call *artivism*. Such strategies provide productive ways for us to analyze, share, and apply arts-based educational research and pedagogies. For Ginwright and Cammarota, *critical civic praxis* (*CCP*) prompts marginalized populations to collective action. To create a strong roadmap for guiding collaborative learning and activist work, *CCP* combines recognizing current and potential political activism; awareness of socio-cultural inequities; a strong sense of community; collective action; transformation of learners to educators; and opportunities to imagine, design, and implement creative social justice-oriented responses/interventions (Ginwright, Cammarota, and Noguera).

Sandoval and Latorre's concept of *artivism* moves *CCP* into the world of arts and visual culture. Sandoval and Latorre define *artivism* as a hybridization of artistic production and activism that harnesses their symbiosis for transformational purposes. *Artivism* recognizes what Chicana artist, and out lesbian, Judy Baca stresses are "unprecedented means for young people to represent themselves outside of adult control," and for minorities to represent themselves outside of mainstream control (Chela and Latorre 86). Like *CCP*, *artivism* enacts pedagogy that recognizes the "persisting exclusions" of the arts and visual culture, yet builds on their "liberatory potential" and collective cultural capital, emphasizing ways "creativity can be channeled, augmented, and empowered" through "real-world and on-the-ground" arts-based strategies (Chela and Latorre 84). In a sense, *artivism* is creative *critical civic praxis*.

For BGC, *CCP* allows us to interrogate oppressive stereotypical institutional and interpersonal power dynamics; *artivism* allows us to present things differently through works of the imagination, to open negative aspects of the church to possibilities of change, and to help others transform from marginalized victims into agents (Ginwright and Cammarota; Rhoades "Video Artivism," Sandoval and Latorre). With BGC, we take an *artivist* approach on several fronts simultaneously. Since schools and education often derail non-heterosexual and/or gender queer identities and discourses, we make space for queer people and voices there. Since many churches make efforts to condemn, exclude, or "repair" queer folks, we find a way to turn our church into a place that recognizes the power of diverse sexualities and gender identities. Since these conservative, fundamentalist religious discourses impact public policy and the civil rights of queer people, we must find ways to use our pulpit to move queer people and allies to interrupt the status quo and work toward a more just world.

BGC and Performance Pedagogy/Studies

Once [gays] attain key positions, they will seek to remove all stigma against homosexuality and seek to redefine, reeducate (deceive) and reshape society to accept their depravity.—Society for the Practical Establishment and Perpetuation of the TEN COMMANDMENTS

BGC takes flight at the intersections of several fields in education including critical pedagogy, performance studies, and dramatic inquiry. In this way, BGC is both performance and pedagogy. During services, we become what McLaren calls the "researcher-as-performer," engaging fully in the political, kinetic, destructive, and transcendental aspects of presenting/ performing/creating. We interrupt the regularly scheduled program, using performance and its liminal spaces for encountering culture, politics, and education (Garoian and Gaudelius). We are queering and re-purposing the academy as a vital site for resistance and autonomy, a place for collective participatory action by critical citizens acting in concert. Through the performative, we hope to facilitate participants' connecting the personal and the pedagogical (Giroux). What can we learn from ourselves?

Embracing critical performance pedagogies as research, teaching, and learning paradigms emphasizes their potential educational, political, cultural, and societal benefits (Denzin, "Critical Performance"). For Dwight Conquergood, "Performance is a way of knowing, a way of showing, a way of interpreting and a method for building shared understanding. Performance is immediate, partial, always incomplete and always processual" (in Denzin, "Critical Performance" 29). For us, BGC requires research and teaching as we include rigorous academic content. It also requires us, as presenters/performers, to model "a communitarian dialogical ethic of care and responsibility" where everyone treats "persons and their cares and concerns with dignity and respect" (Denzin, "Politics" 133). We use these pedagogies to construct a "civic, participatory and collaborative project" where "members of the community, as cultural workers and co-performers in theatres of resistance, create empowering performance texts and performance events" (Denzin, "Critical Performance" 263). We want BGC to be an example of a

> radical democratic pedagogy [that] requires citizens and citizen-scholars committed to taking risks; persons willing to act in situations where the outcome cannot be predicted in advance.... [I]n these pedagogical spaces there are not leaders and followers; there are only co-participants, persons jointly working together to develop new lines of action, new stories, new narratives in a collaborative effort. (Bishop 207)

According to Conquergood, such critical, risk-taking citizen-scholars must also possess the "energy, imagination, courage, and commitment to create" new, more liberating texts and discourses (10). Critical performance pedagogies require criticism and action.

BGC, as Denzin advocates, uses performative pedagogies to embrace queer studies, transforming a traditional academic conference session into a "sacred aesthetic place" and time ("Critical Performance" 133). It provides "a way of acting on the world in order to change it" (Denzin, "Critical Performance" 267). BGC is a site of intervention, struggle, and "transgressive achievement" (Conquergood 32). It is a "concrete situation ... being transformed through acts of resistance" (Denzin, "Politics" 135). This resistance occurs simultaneously in multiple ways (in Brechtian theatre):

> The performance becomes the vehicle for moving **persons, subjects, performers** and **audience members**, into new, critical, political spaces. The performance gives the audience, and the performers, "equipment for [this] journey: empathy and intellect, passion and critique." (Denzin, "Critical Performance" 265)

BGC exists in a hyperactive, open-ended intersection of performance as imagination and action. As performers, we embody characters who may ordinarily represent a culture of exclusion and punishment of queer people. In our performance, we not only imagine what it might be like if these stereotypes were false, but we become these characters and enact this revision. The audience becomes a supportive congregation, co-participatory members in this performance (Denzin, "Politics" 133). We try to reclaim concepts like church, family, values, and Christianity from hate-based religious doctrines and practices. Where "the performative and the political intersect on the terrain of a praxis-based ethic," we use performance pedagogy to "embody love, hope, care, and compassion," attempting to use BGC "to change the world" (129).

Inclusion

BGC deliberately and specifically addresses a particular marginalized population within a particular set of contexts: queer people in art (and) education. However, in the spirit of greater inclusion, BGC conducts outreach to other interest groups and marginalized populations within art education, such as the Caucus on Spirituality, the Caucus on Multicultural Concerns, and the Disability Issues Caucus. In a service in Chicago, a visually impaired female Jewish cantor performed with us; in New York, an Indian colleague contributed a contemporary Hindu perspective on gender, sexuality, and arts. We hope to continue our own efforts toward greater inclusion, inviting others into our congregation, to journey with us.

On the Road

BGC stakes a territory within the academy, in art education, in our national organization and annual conference, and now in the scholarly record. We have also laid a claim to church and religion, challenging its overwhelming negative history with respect to queer people, forming our own flock. We seek to critically confront conservative Christian church doctrines, their positioning and treatment of LGBTIQ people, and the overwhelming influence their beliefs have on cultural beliefs, acceptable behavior, and public policy. We force a confrontation between our learned beliefs and identities, our occupations and our culture. We confront tough questions, asking how has church shaped us? How can we (re)shape it? How does/can recognizing, accepting, and supporting queer people, culture, values, presence, and contributions to the church change church? Change queer people? Change our political, educational, and socio-cultural climate? We interrogate the ways conservative Christian churches and queer people impact each other and aim to explore analyses and possible revisions to these relationships. We have the power to redraw the boundaries, make contact, build bridges, connect. BGC shows there are ways to hold such seeming contradictions in tension, to forgo resolution for exploration, rejection for consideration of possibilities, of what *was* and what *might be*.

NOTES

1. "Letter to Coretta."
2. See HRC, *Export of Hate*; HRC, *Scott Lively*.

WORKS CITED

Barton, Bernadette. 2010. Abomination—Life as a Bible Belt Gay. *Journal of Homosexuality* 57 (4): 465–484. Print.

Bishop, Russell. 1998. Freeing Ourselves from Neo-colonial Domination in Research: A Maori Approach to Creating Knowledge. *International Journal of Qualitative Studies in Education* 11: 199–219. Print.

Britzman, Deborah. 1998. *Lost Subjects, Contested Objects: Toward a Psychoanalytic Inquiry of Learning*. New York: SUNY. Print.

———. 2000. Precocious Education. In *Thinking Queer: Sexuality, Culture and Education*, ed. Susan Talburt and Shirley R. Steinberg, 33–60. New York: Peter Lang. Print.

Brooke, Heather L. 2005. Gays, Ex-gays, and Ex-ex-gays: Examining Key Religious, Ethical, and Diversity Issues: A Follow-up Interview with Douglas Haldeman, Ariel Shidlo, Warren Throckmorton, and Mark Yarhouse. *Journal of Psychology and Christianity* 24 (4): 343–351. Print.

Buchanan, Melinda, Kristina Dzelme, Dale Harris, and Lorna Hecker. 2001. Challenges of Being Simultaneously Gay or Lesbian and Spiritual and/or Religious: A Narrative Perspective. *The American Journal of Family Therapy* 29: 435–449. Print.

Callaghan, Tonya D. 2010. David Versus Goliath: Addressing Contradictory Catholic Doctrine Head On. *Journal of LGBT Youth* 7: 85–90. Print.

Candreva, Thomas D. 2006. A New Impediment: The Vatican's Document Regulating Admission to Seminaries and Ordination Revives an Almost Extinct Legal Device. *America*, 20–22, February 27, 2006. Print.

Cianciatto, Jason, and Sean Cahill. 2006. *Youth Caught in the Crosshairs: The Third Wave of Ex-Gay Activism*. New York: National Gay and Lesbian Task Force Policy Institute. Print.

Conquergood, Dwight. 1985. Performing as a Moral Act: Ethical Dimensions of the Ethnography of Performance. *Literature in Performance* 5 (1): 1–13. Print.

———. 1998. Beyond the Text: Toward a Performative Cultural Politics. In *The Future of Performance Studies: Visions and Revisions*, ed. Sheron J. Dailey, 25–36. Annandale: National Communication Association. Print.

Cowan, Reed, and Steven Greenstreet, dir. 2010. *8: The Mormon Proposition*. David v. Goliath Films. Film.

Dennis, Jeffery P. 2003. Lying with Man as with Woman: Rethinking the Impact of Religious Discourse on Gay Community Strength. *Journal of Homosexuality* 44 (1): 43–60. Print.

Denzin, Norman K. 2003. *Performance Ethnography*. Thousand Oaks: Sage. Print.
———. 2007. The Politics and Ethic of Performance Pedagogy: Toward a Pedagogy of Hope. In *Critical Pedagogy: Where Are We Now?* ed. Peter McLaren and Joe Kincheloe, 127–142. New York: Peter Lang Publishing. Print.
———. 2009. A Critical Performance Pedagogy that Matters. *Ethnography and Education* 4 (3): 255–270. Print.
Foucault, Michel. 1980. *The History of Sexuality, Volume I: An Introduction*. New York: Random House. Print.
Ganzevoort, R. Ruard, Mark van der Laan, and Erik Olsman. 2011. Growing Up Gay and Religious: Conflict, Dialogue, and Religious Identity Strategies. *Mental Health, Religion & Culture* 14 (3): 209–222. Print.
Garoian, Charles R., and Yvonne M. Gaudelius. 2008. *Spectacle Pedagogy: Art, Politics and Visual Culture*. Albany: SUNY Press. Print.
Gehring, John. 2013. The Year of Pope Francis, Top Ten Papal Quotes. *The Huffington Post*, December 23, 2013. Web. 22 Jan 2016.
Ginwright, Shawn, and Julio Cammarota. 2007. Youth Activism in the Urban Community: Learning Critical Civic Praxis Within Community Organizations. *International Journal of Qualitative Studies in Education* 20 (6): 693–710. Print.
Ginwright, Shawn, Julio Cammarota, and Pedro Noguera. 2005. Youth, Social Justice and Communities: Toward a Theory of Urban Change. *Social Justice* 32 (3): 24–40. Print.
Giroux, Henry A. 2000. *Impure Acts: The Practical Politics of Cultural Studies*. New York: Routledge. Print.
Human Rights Campaign (HRC). n.d. *Scott Lively Is One of America's Most Notorious Exporters of Hate*. Web. 22 Jan 2016.
———. n.d. *The Export of Hate*. Web. 22 Jan 2016.
King, Martin Luther, Jr. 2007. To Coretta Scott. In *The Papers of Martin Luther King, Jr. Volume VI: Advocate of the Social Gospel, September 1948–March 1963*, ed. Clayborne Carson, Susan Carson, Susan Englander, Troy Jackson, and Gerald L. Smith, 123–125. Stanford University, The Martin Luther King, Jr. Research and Education Institute. Berkeley and Los Angeles: University of California Press. Print.
Lady Gaga. Born This Way. *Born This Way*. Interscope Records, 2011. CD.
LeVay, Simon, and Elisabeth Nonas. 1995. *City of Friends: A Portrait of the Gay and Lesbian Community in America*. Cambridge, MA: The MIT Press. Print.
Lorde, Audre. 1983. The Master's Tools Will Never Dismantle the Master's House. In *This Bridge Called My Back: Writings by Radical Women of Color*, ed. Cherrie Moraga and Gloria Anzaldua, 94–101. New York: Kitchen Table Press. Print.
Lynch, John. 2005. Institution and Imprimatur: Institutional Rhetoric and the Failure of the Catholic Church's Pastoral Letter on Homosexuality. *Rhetoric & Public Affairs* 8 (3): 383–404. Print.

McLaren, Peter. 1999. *Schooling as a Ritual Performance: Toward a Political Economy of Educational Symbols and Gestures.* 3rd ed. Lanham: Rowman & Littlefield. Print.

Park, T., and M. Stone. *South Park* Episode "Big Gay Al's Big Gay Boat Ride," Season 1, Episode 4, originally aired 3 Sept 1997. Television.

Rhoades, Mindi. 2012a. *iDo.* Sermon presented at the annual conference of the National Art Education Association, New York.

———. 2012b. LGBTQ Youth + Video Artivism. *Studies in Art Education* 53 (4): 317–329. Print.

———. 2017. *Forever Love.* Unpublished hymn.

Sanders, James, III. 2007. Breathing Curiously: Queering the Curriculum Body. In *Curriculum and the Cultural Body,* ed. Stephanie Springgay and Debra Freedman, 217–234. New York: Lange. Print.

Sandoval, Chela, and Guisela Latorre. 2008. Chicana/o Artivism: Judy Baca's Digital Work with Youth of Color. In *Learning Race and Ethnicity: Youth and Digital Media,* ed. Anna Everett, 81–108. Cambridge, MA: The MIT Press. Print.

Schuck, Kelly D., and Becky J. Liddle. 2001. Religious Conflicts Experienced by Lesbian, Gay, and Bisexual Individuals. *Journal of Gay & Lesbian Psychotherapy* 5 (2): 63–82. Print.

Schwartz, Joseph. 2010. Investigating Differences in Public Support for Gay Rights Issues. *Journal of Homosexuality* 57 (6): 748–759. Print.

Seidman, Steven. 1993. Identity and Politics in a Postmodern Gay Culture. In *Fear of a Queer Planet,* ed. Michael Warner. Minneapolis: University of Minnesota Press. Print.

Sharlet, Jeff. 2009. *The Family: The Secret Fundamentalism at the Heart of American Power.* New York: HarperCollins. Print.

Society for the Practical Establishment and Perpetuation of the TEN COMMANDMENTS. 2004–11. Web. 1 May 2017.

Staines, Bill. 1979. A Place in the Choir. *Whistle of the Jay.* Mineral River Music, BMI.

Williams, Alex. 2005. Gay Teenager Stirs a Storm. *The New York Times,* July 17, 2005. Web. 23 Jan 2016.

Wolff, Joshua R., and Heather L. Himes. 2010. Purposeful Exclusion of Sexual Minority Youth in Christian Higher Education: The Implications of Discrimination. *Christian Higher Education* 9: 439–460. Print.

Zacko-Smith, Jeffrey D., and G. Pritchy Smith. 2010. Recognizing and Utilizing Queer Pedagogy. *Multicultural Education* 18 (1): 2–9. Print.

CHAPTER 14

Innovations in Sexual-Theological Activism: Queer Theology Meets Theatre of the Oppressed

Kerri A. Mesner

As I look through the photographic documentation of my master's thesis project, I'm struck once again by the power of Boal's "Image Theatre" to capture heightened moments of conflict, controversy, and challenge. The images are frozen moments in time—living photographs shaped by the participants' own bodies and created silently through touch, movement, and non-verbal communication.

In one particularly potent image, participants have shaped their bodies in response to my suggestion, "How you see the relationship between queerness and the Christian church." For these individuals, the responses are varied: one participant stands facing outward from the group, arms stretched wide, eyes open, indicating a stance of openness and receptivity. Another appears to be in a conversation mid-interrupted, with a lively, engaged facial expression. Two others show with powerful strength their definitive rejection of organized religion: one with arms closed, body turned away from the others, and the second with eyes shut, ears covered, and mouth firmly shut. Yet another participant

This article was first published as Mesner, Kerri A. "Innovations in Sexual-Theological Activism: Queer Theology Meets Theatre of the Oppressed." *Theology and Sexuality: The Journal of the Institute for the Study of Christianity and Sexuality*. 16:3. (2010) 285–303. Print.

K.A. Mesner (✉)
Arcadia University School of Education, Glenside, PA, USA

E. McNeil et al. (eds.), *Mapping Queer Space(s) of Praxis and Pedagogy*, Queer Studies and Education,
DOI 10.1007/978-3-319-64623-7_14

creates a stance with fist raised, mouth opened as though shouting and an unde-
niably angry facial expression—a stance that I read as aggressive, even violent.
I invite the actors to find their stance, to breath, and to hold their positions.
    Then I invite the surrounding group of observers to engage in "projec-
tions"—Boal's exercise where the remaining participants are invited to speak
aloud thoughts, feelings, or ideas sparked by this still image as they circle it from
all directions. Phrases are called out from the circle of people surrounding the
image, some words overlapping one another....
    "homophobic"
    "violent"
    "hopeful"
    "unnecessary"
    "useless"
    "part of my history"
    "longing"
    Finally, I invite the actors to relax and step out of their frozen image. The
entire group gathers in a circle to talk about what we've just seen and experi-
enced, and suddenly find ourselves in a deep and lively conversation about
whether it's possible to be a critically thoughtful queer student and a Christian.
The opinions are divided and varied.

This composite example[1] touches on my aim (and indeed my struggle), to interweave the varied and sometimes contradictory aspects of my work as a queer minister, a theologian, and an artist. In reflecting on my work as a queer minister, theologian, and arts-based researcher, several questions emerge. The language of such a "queer" self-naming, in and of itself, with the diverse range of debates, beliefs, scholarship, and activist stances that the word "queer" generates, could inform an entire article in and of itself. As a deliberately self-identified queer minister, theologian, and academic, I understand my queerness to include and extend beyond my sexuality, my genderqueerness, and into my framing of my Christian beliefs and praxis. Simultaneously, I recognize that academic framings (or disputing) of queer theory or theology are as diverse as they are multifarious.

My struggles bridge the theoretical and the contextual as well; as a minister, how do I navigate complex theological conversations with colleagues and professors in a predominantly mainstream seminary setting, where, for many students, the notion of "queer theology" is, at best, a new idea, and at worst, a direct confrontation with dearly held beliefs? As a scholar and activist, how do I navigate my conviction that "ministry"—and, indeed "church"—is perhaps most significantly what happens outside the church building on a Sunday morning, that ministry, for me, emerges evocatively within my academic scholarship ... and, moreover, that my understanding of ministerial calling compels me to confront the intersections of Christian theology and anti-LGBTQ violence? And as a theatre artist, how do I navigate my desire to keep my sexual body fully engaged in my scholarship ... to challenge what seems to be an oft-prevailing mind-body dualism in the academy?

This article outlines several years of theological/ministerial work that developed in response to these questions, interweaving the voices of queer theologian Marcella Althaus-Reid, and Augusto Boal, the originator of the Theatre of the Oppressed theories and methodologies. Boal and Althaus-Reid (who, sadly, died within a few months of each other in 2009) shared a prophetic approach to their work that not only valued but prioritized the marginal voice. I believe that their shared roots in Latin American political contexts and Freirean pedagogies positioned them particularly well to engage in this conversation between theology and praxis. At the same time, each brought an important contribution that complemented one another: Althaus-Reid, the critical analysis of religio-ecclesial oppressions through theological reflection; and Boal, the critical engagement of oppressive realities through theatrical praxis.

To explore the potentials in this theological-artistic partnership, we will look at Althaus-Reid's theologies as a response to the queer theological dialectic between mainstream acceptance and marginalization. From here, we will turn to Theatre of the Oppressed as a potential artistic partner to queer theology, culminating in an articulation of a beginning framework for a new queer ministry combining these two voices in theory and praxis.

QUEER THEOLOGY: CHALLENGING THE LURE OF THE MAINSTREAM

Althaus-Reid served as a primary inspiration in my work, both as a pastor in Edinburgh, where she sometimes joined us at Metropolitan Community Church, Edinburgh, for worship, and, later, in my work as a theological student in Canada. In my prior work as a pastor, and presently, as a theologian in academic settings, I also wrestled with occasional critiques of Althaus-Reid's scholarship in terms of its lack of (intellectual) accessibility. Some argued that her theological articulation often demonstrated a level of scholarly complexity that seemed to run counter to its commitment to grassroots communities. Conversely, however, when she preached at our congregation's LGBT Pride Service, her complex, nuanced, and theologically rigorous sermon was one of the most popular during my time in that pastorate. As I reflect on these differing views and experiences of Althaus-Reid's work, I recognize that, for me, the relationship between queer theological thought and on-the-ground practice was—and is—a complex dialectic.

I would suggest that in much queer theological scholarship, a noticeable gap has indeed emerged between queer theological thought and lived praxis. The historical rootedness of queer theologies within the contextual knowledge of the body makes this gap all the more troubling and pronounced. Queer theologies, uniquely positioned to challenge the historical academic and ecclesial mind-body split, run the risk of disconnecting from the embodied realities of the communities for whom they aim to speak. Put plainly, what does it mean if we are "doing" queer theology only from the head up? Further, how might praxis-based approaches help us to put queer theology's more radical statements into practice? Bringing Boal's Theatre of the Oppressed into conversation with Althaus-Reid's queer theology offers a unique bridge between queer theological thought and queer theological praxis.

Althaus-Reid offered a prophetic voice that advocated the deliberate "indecenting" of sexualized orthodoxy, theology, cultural normalization, and global economics (*Indecent Theology*). Althaus-Reid challenged scholars and ecclesial leaders to recognize the need for the "coming out of other discomforts and areas of tensions such as economics and racial structures of suppression of subjectivities, because heterosexual matrices not only provide us with the master narratives for bedtime, but economic epistemologies and social patterns of organisation" (*Indecent Theology* 83). Through this queering of multiple intersectional issues, as well as its epistemological rooting in the body's knowledge, queer theologies offer a prophetic challenge to the academy and the church.

The political terrorism of her Argentinean homeland informed Althaus-Reid's unique approach to queer theology, with its emphatic emphasis on the sexual and economic natures of theology. In *Indecent Theology*, Althaus-Reid critiqued mainstream theology as "a sexual ideology performed in a sacralising pattern." Traditional theology, she argued, is focused primarily on "a sexual divinised orthodoxy (right sexual dogma) and orthopraxy (right sexual behaviour)" (87). Althaus-Reid challenged what she refers to as "T-Theology"—that is, "theology as ideology ... a totalitarian construction of what is considered 'The One and Only Theology' which does not admit discussion or challenges from different perspectives, especially in the area of sexual identity and its close relationship with political and racial issues" (*Queer God* 172). She deliberately employed queer sexual hermeneutics within her theology, calling for a "critical bisexuality as a pre-requisite for being Christian..." and, further, for "a critical transgender, lesbian, gay, heterosexual-outside-the-closet, that is, full Queer presence, as a requirement for doing theology" (108–109).

These were not simply rhetorical semantics, however. Althaus-Reid's transgressive approach resisted the cultural institutionalization of the "decent" as "normal." Through this refusal of normalization, queer theologies resist "current practices of historical formation that make us forget the love which is different" (*Queer God* 50, 114). Here, we get to know Althaus-Reid's queer God of the margins, the God of that "love which is different," and her reminder of the keen difference between a God that *visits* the margins and a God that deliberately *resides* in the margins ("Divine Exodus" 33). As she frankly put it, "terrible is the fate of theologies from the margin when they want to be accepted by the centre!" ("Introduction" 3). These margins were—and are for queer people today—margins of sexual normativity. In explicitly choosing this sexual-theological edge, the queer theologian simultaneously reclaims sociopolitical agency in the theologian's own queer world-making.

One hears echoes of this power of the margins in constructive theologian Sallie McFague's notion of "wild space," the space where one does not fit into hegemonic strictures, and as a result, where "our 'failures' to fit the hegemonic image are our opportunities to criticize and revise it" (48–49). Theologian Anita Fast also echoes this in her call for a "hermeneutic of foolishness," and in her reminder that "by making the 'fool,' the 'queer,' the transgressive one a part of the mainstream social order, the transformative potential of those who reside on the margins is relinquished." When this happens, Fast notes, "liberal apologists can accurately announce that homosexuality is NOT a threat to society" (44).

And yet, it could be argued that the lure of the mainstream remains strong for many queer communities. Queer theorist David Halperin suggests that "there is something odd, suspiciously odd, about the rapidity with which queer theory—whose claim to radical politics derived from its anti-assimilationist posture, from its shocking embrace of the abnormal and the marginal—has been embraced by, canonized by, and absorbed into our (largely heterosexual) institutions of knowledge" (341). While Halperin's claim could certainly be debated within the academy (and even more so within the theological academy) I believe he nonetheless touches on a significant danger in terms of the potential co-optation of queer theory's more radical roots in the name of "acceptability." As a queer minister, I sense troubling hints of this co-optation outside the academy as well.

I would suggest that contemporary queer liberatory movements wrestle with the tension between utilizing a credible voice that can be heard by the mainstream and maintaining a prophetic stance that is willing to challenge those self-same centrist structures. This lure of the mainstream, often motivated by a legitimate desire for effective political agency and legal protections, has led to a troubling normalization of queer theological and political thought. I draw on my own denominational experience with marriage equality debates as one example.

As a pastor, I felt both honored and moved by the many opportunities I had to celebrate queer relationships ceremonially in our church contexts. I would in no way want to dismiss or minimize the liturgical and pastoral significance of these celebrations. And at the same time, I'm aware of my own growing unease with the constant focus on same-sex marriage battles within queer activist communities—and indeed within my own denominational tradition. Setting aside my concerns for the variety of relational configurations not recognized within current marriage equality debates (at the time of this writing), and indeed, setting aside my concerns around the (financial) prioritization of marriage over other urgent political issues, my concern within the context of this article is primarily a theological one. Simply put, while I recognize the strategic and socio-political value of foregrounding marriage equality as a flagship issue, I simultaneously wonder if this push is not partially—albeit perhaps unconsciously—fueled by a desire for mainstream acceptance. This lure toward the mainstream runs counter, I would suggest, to the subversively challenging potentialities of queer theologies like those Althaus-Reid put forward.

Queer theologies, with their critical analysis of multiple oppressions, as well as their unique appreciation of the particularities of embodied contributions to theological discourse, run the risk—when mainstreamed—of disconnecting from the socio-political praxes in which they were originally rooted. The increasing normalization and mainstreaming of many queer religious activist movements, while perhaps initially politically expedient, run the risk of losing their critical edge which had been formed in that unique nexus of the sexual, the political, and the spiritual. Only by moving to the sexual, theological, and political margins can a queer theological voice and praxis remain true to its potential for socio-political transformation and the creation of queer life worlds.

Boal's work offered praxis-based methodologies to explore, debate, and challenge these issues within specific communities working toward this kind of socio-political transformation. Intriguingly, Althaus-Reid also worked as a Freirean community educator in Buenos Aires and later in Scotland ("Education for Liberation"). Althaus-Reid herself alluded to connections with Boal's work; in her article discussing the concrete ramifications of a sexualized global economic order, Althaus-Reid draws on Boal's Theatre of the Oppressed in her description of "lunchtime crucifixions"—performative acts reminiscent of street theatre, where Argentineans voluntarily tied themselves to crosses in a public park to protest the crucifying violence of external debts ("Lunchtime Crucifixions" 66). Indeed, in my own conversations with Althaus-Reid, she seemed intrigued by the potentialities of the conversation between queer theology and Boal's work. In 2006, Althaus-Reid invited me to present a Theatre of the Oppressed workshop at the British Irish Society of Feminist Theologians' Conference in Scotland, where we used theatre to explore the links between bodies, theologies, and our own understandings of erotic power (Mesner). As we move more deeply, then, into this notion of queer theological praxis, we turn now to an overview of Boal's methods as they relate to this dialogue.

THEATRE OF THE OPPRESSED: PRAXIS-BASED RESPONSES IN BRIDGING THE GAP

How do we bridge the gap between queer theological thought and theologically rooted queer praxis, between normative and transformative socio-political discourses? Theatre offers one such bridge. However, we look here not to traditional theatre (with a performance in front of a passive audience), the primary goal of which is to stimulate empathetic audience responses to a problematic situation without any ensuing action (Boal, *Theatre*). Rather, we seek theatre that carries the potential to bridge the gap between reflection and action, theatre that serves as what theatre activist Daniel O'Donnell identifies as a form of "social acupuncture" to explore, articulate, and provoke different aspects of the social body. O'Donnell draws metaphorically on acupuncture's ability to stimulate the physical body's energetic flows to encourage greater holistic health. Similarly, O'Donnell suggests that provocative theatre can be used to stimulate the *social body*, suggesting that social blockages created by classism, racism and sexism can all be read this way.... [S]ocial acupuncture offers the opportunity to directly engage with social flows, applying the same principles as real acupuncture, only the terrain is the social body instead of the physical body.... [This] will usually generate discomfort, the social equivalent of confusion, a necessary part of any learning process. (47, 49–50)

As we will see, this embrace of productive discomfort is integral to Boal's practices as well.

Augusto Boal, a Brazilian actor, playwright, director, and activist, offered one such form of theatrical social acupuncture. Theatre of the Oppressed, developed by Boal from the early 1970s until his death in 2009, was inspired by Paulo Freire's *Pedagogy of the Oppressed*. Boal, like Freire, sought to find explicit ways to activate subjective awareness and capacity for change in the journey toward liberation. Like Freire, Boal developed his theories and methodologies within the context of Brazilian political dictatorship, and both men were eventually exiled for their revolutionary work. These shared historical and philosophical roots emerge clearly within Boal's theatrical methodologies. Boal developed a rich and varied set of theatrical methodologies designed not only to break down the separation between actor and audience, but also to bridge the gap between art and activism.

In Theatre of the Oppressed (hereafter, T.O.), the audience is challenged to explore multiple possibilities within a given oppressive situation, and to actively engage in the theatrical process to attempt to overcome that oppression (Boal, *Games* 262). This process is not simply limited to verbal or intellectual analysis—action is required as response. Boal shared Freire's belief that without radical transformation, education has not taken place. As Boal writes in his seminal *Theatre of the Oppressed*, the focus is

on the action itself: the spectator delegates no power to the character (or actor) either to act or to think in his place; on the contrary, he himself assumes the protagonic role, changes the dramatic action, tries out solutions, discusses plans for change—in short, trains himself for real action. In this case, perhaps the theatre is not revolutionary in itself, but it is surely a rehearsal for the revolution. The liberated spectator, as a whole person, launches into action. No matter that the action is fiction; what matters is that it is action! (122)

Like Freire, Boal challenged coercive models of education, suggesting that educators should start with strategies arising from the experiences of the participants themselves (127). The use of images was central to Boal's work; he chose to deliberately subvert a traditional reliance on verbal expression, challenging actors instead to find non-verbal means of communication and expression. Paralleling Freire, *intervention* is also critical: through onstage interventions, *spectactors* (Boal's term replacing traditionally passive audience spectators) are challenged to actively test out potential responses to oppressive situations rather than simply watching passively as professional actors intervene on their behalf. In *Theatre of the Oppressed*, the *Joker* plays the critical role of facilitator, *problematizer*, *difficultator* (again, terms coined within Boal's practice), and intermediary between the actors and the *spectactors*, challenging both groups to create a community of critical dialogue, reflection, and action.

While Boal initially developed T.O. to address systemic oppression within the context of political dictatorships in Brazil and other parts of Latin America, he discovered, particularly during his subsequent exiles in other countries, that its relevance extended to other cultures and contexts. As his work traversed into Western Europe and North America, he also developed additional methodologies that explored internalized oppressions at individual levels, and, over the years, increasingly sophisticated combinations of the various techniques that bridged both individuals and systems, both the personal and the political. Boal's *arsenal*[2] of techniques includes *Forum Theater* (where a short play is presented and audience members have opportunities to intervene on stage to try to combat the oppression presented), *Image Theater* (a series of exercises utilizing frozen and then activated images to explore and unpack the many layers of analysis and meaning within a particular non-verbal image), and *Rainbow of Desires* (a complex series of strategies designed to make explicit the internalized oppressions experienced at individual and collective levels) (*Theatre* 126; see also *Games; Rainbow*). More recently, Boal also developed *Legislative Theater*, whereby T.O. methods are used to explore and effect political change in local governments; he used these methods successfully to effect legislative change during his tenure as a Councilman in Brazil.

Boal's work has been contextualized internationally in a variety of cultures, communities, and issue foci; its applications are diverse, flexible, and innovative, reflecting the practitioners and communities where those applications are rooted. There is also a growing body of scholarship analyzing T.O. praxis and theory. Several scholars and practitioners have looked at T.O.'s efficacy as a tool to analyze and address a range of societal issues. Hsia Hsiao-Chuan, for example, used T.O. as praxis-oriented research in literacy work with Southeast Asian "foreign brides" brought into Taiwan.

Paul Heritage outlines a T.O.-based project aimed to explore human rights issues with inmates and prison staff in prisons across Brazil. In addition to a wide range of projects using T.O. to address issues of inequity, discrimination, and violence, its use as a qualitative research strategy has been documented, among others, in Barbara Dennis's exploration of cross-cultural anti-bullying research, and Shauna Butterwick's exploration of feminist organizing ("Acting Up"; "Your Story"). As the academic T.O. field develops, theoretical and praxis-oriented debates are also opened up. Paul Dwyer, for example, has problematized the *Jokering* methodologies through his analysis of the ideological influence of T.O. facilitators' practices in a Vancouver-based project addressing sexual harassment on a college campus. In exploring the praxis-based approaches instigated in these varying contexts, we can see the potential for Boal's methodologies to offer an approach that can make Althaus-Reid's complex theologies more accessible.

Intriguingly, I have also noted (anecdotally, over the years, in my work as a T.O. *Joker*), a tension within T.O. practitioner communities around the desire to document and theorize this methodological framework. My sense is that some practitioners fear that the move toward formal T.O. scholarship, while perhaps fueled by a desire for wider legitimacy and recognition, may in fact run counter to the grassroots origin of Boal's own work. Indeed, we could argue that this desire for mainstream legitimization is similar to the one we explored earlier within queer theological movements. These two potentially competing tensions—between the desire to keep T.O. as a radical community-fueled movement, and the need for clear analytical and evaluative tools within T.O. praxis and scholarship, are not easily reconciled, and will likely continue to form a central debate in T.O. communities in years to come. Just as I am suggesting utilizing participatory theatre to evoke praxis-based shift in academic theological thought, I suspect we need to find equally radical means of documentation and theorization of this work. For example, while taking a doctoral course on Community Service Learning, I undertook a service-learning placement in an applied arts company that utilizes T.O. methodologies. For me, this was an opportunity to work toward finding a bridge between the theoretical abstraction of my university context and the on-the-ground realities of this radical activist theatre company. The conversations that ensued—both within the weeklong placement and afterwards—in my written analyses, were provocatively generative. I sense that this kind of interweaving of praxis and analysis may prove essential to academically oriented T.O. work. Further, as this debate continues to unfold, I suspect that a key measure of academic approaches to T.O. will be found in their ability to remain in active dialogue with their researched communities.

As we focus in on Boal's approach, we move to the heart of a key principle in Boal's work—as well as the source of key critiques of his philosophy by many T.O. scholars: the oppressed-oppressor dichotomy. For both Freire and Boal, careful analysis of the dialectic relationship between oppressor and oppressed is essential: oppressor and oppressed cannot exist without one another. Given this foundational assumption, Freirean and Boalian approaches aim to find explicit ways to activate subjective awareness and capacity for change in the journey toward *conscientization* (Freire 35). For Boal, such transformative processes happen through theatre; the wall between audience and actor is dissolved, and communities use Boal's interactive theatre methods to explore and articulate their own responses to oppressive situations within their politically situated realities.

At the heart of Boal's approach is the belief that T.O. must be focused on the protagonic character or characters experiencing oppression. Interventions (where audience members can replace a protagonic character in a scene), should therefore, in Boal's view, be focused explicitly on means of overcoming that character's particular oppression. Such an approach (and indeed, even the very title of Boal's book and methodological umbrella) relies on the clearly defined category of "oppressed," and by implication, of that person's "oppressor" (Boal, *Theatre*). While some T.O. practitioners view this approach as "pure T.O.," others see it as a reliance "on outmoded and restrictive binary oppositions between 'oppressor' and 'oppressed,' between 'antagonist' and 'protagonist'" (Dwyer 160).

Vancouver theatre director David Diamond, for instance, challenges the utility of the oppressor-oppressed paradigm. Diamond has developed his own extrapolation of T.O. called "Theatre for Living," integrating systems theory analysis into T.O. practices. Diamond's model understands the community as a living system that needs ways of telling and exploring its stories to maintain or return to greater communal health. He strives to look for connections between theatre and systems theory, and to challenge mechanistic/dualistic models—even, for example, in the traditional T.O. oppressor-oppressed dichotomy. Within his model, Diamond sees both oppressor and oppressed as part of the living community system, and as such, believes that the needs of both protagonist and antagonist need to be addressed. He further notes the connections of systems theory to Freire's work on cyclical nature of oppression, and points to the need to change those systemic patterns to avoid recreating oppressions (Diamond 46–47). Similarly, T.O. practitioner and scholar Mady Schutzman brings a postmodern perspective in her exploration of the oppressed-oppressor relationship within the context of North American cultures. Schutzman notes that the word oppressor may be a less obviously definable term when politics of identities further complicate the issues of the oppressed-oppressor dichotomy; she problematizes, for instance, who the oppressor actually is when multiple identities/issues overlap (138–141).

On the other hand, T.O. Practitioner Ann Armstrong brings a feminist critique to her argument for retaining the simplified oppressor/oppressed relational model first set out by Boal. Armstrong states that "Boal's techniques have frequently been criticized for the oversimplification of relationships between the oppressor and the oppressed. However, Armstrong argues that 'the oppressed-oppressor distinction is crucial (even if it must be made provisionally) in order to fully understand the embodied experiences of a particular group'" (178). Armstrong suggests that this clear demarcation allows for authentic theatrical explorations of particularized experiences of oppression.

Alberta T.O. and disability arts practitioner Michele Decottignies challenges the move toward eliminating dichotomous language in discussing oppression. Clearly situating her company's work within anti-oppression theoretical frameworks, Decottignies notes that

> T.O. jokers who have told us that they don't use the "oppressed/oppressor" lingo anymore are in a position of privilege to do so: affluent, well educated, white, heterosexual, Christian, able-bodied men. We're not saying that they or their choice around language is wrong, but that they have to carefully consider the consequences of their choice on a community to which they do not belong. (39)

I share some of Decottingnies's unease with this theoretical move, and I suspect that T.O. practitioners and scholars have yet to plumb the depths of the oppressed-oppressor debate.

I wonder, too, if some of the drive within T.O. communities to exorcise the oppressed-oppressor dichotomy isn't rooted in what Kevin Kumashiro refers to as "detached rationalism," as he notes that "what many people consider to be detached rationalism is really the perspective of groups in society whose identities and experiences are considered the mythical norm" ("Against Repetition" 5). I agree with Kumashiro's belief that "what is problematic is when educators continue to privilege rationality without questioning ways that it can perpetuate oppressive social relations" (5). Perhaps this debate within T.O. theory and praxis might pick up on Kumashiro's poststructural approach to anti-oppressive education, and particularly, his call for an embrace of paradox, uncertainty, and nonbinary third parties. Wherever a T.O. practitioner lands in this debate, I would suggest that Althaus-Reid's theoretical nuances can offer a critically important counterbalance to what is sometimes argued as the overly simplistic dichotomous thinking inherent in Boal's frameworks.

Indeed, the integral importance of contradiction, ambiguity, and third spaces resonates both with Althaus-Reid's call to theological instability, as well as the potential for deliberate theatrical discomfort within Boalian methodologies. Here, we are inviting the productively destabilizing elements of participatory theatre to engage with the theological uncertainties within queer theology to articulate new approaches to applied theological praxis. In interweaving Althaus-Reid and Boal's voices in conversation, a theologically rooted praxis—or, indeed, a practically applied theology— begins to emerge. To better understand what such a praxis might *look* like, we turn now to some concrete examples of this work.

QUEER THEOLOGY AND THEATRE OF THE OPPRESSED: THEOLOGY AND PRAXIS IN CONVERSATION

Over the last several years, I began to explore the theoretical and praxis-based implications of this approach, both as a pastor in the UK, (where I also had opportunities to work collegially with Althaus-Reid, and to study T.O. with Boal), and later, as an integrated part of my masters' thesis research in Canada (Mesner, "Jokering"). The emergent possibilities were intriguingly varied. For example, in a Lenten workshop series with a local Canadian church, we used T.O. to explore congregant responses to the recent (and possibly homophobic/anti-religious) vandalism of their gay-friendly church sign. We then took our findings into an interactive theatrical conversation with the congregation within the body of a sermon during their Sunday worship. As I preached the sermon, we paused for the workshop actors to enact their still images portraying both their responses to the current issues, as well as the issues' connections to scripture. We then invited the congregation to leave their seats and to physically interact with the images, and to call out their own verbal responses to what they were seeing. In terms of my own ministry, this was a challenging opportunity for me to re-envision my own homiletical praxis. For many years, I'd intuited that theatre and preaching were very close bedfellows—here was an opportunity to begin to experiment with that relationship! Perhaps more importantly, the congregation's courageous willingness to engage in this way challenged my own assumptions about their ability to embrace these unusual liturgical-theatrical approaches.

In another context, I devised a short dramatic scene with some classmates from my (secular) university classroom, to explore the issue of transgender/queer-related harassment in public bathrooms. We then took our scene into the classroom and I invited the larger class to engage in Forum Theatre exercises to explore the issue of harassment, as well as practical responses for the various individuals involved. The exercise was motivated by my own experiences of similar harassment, and the classroom conversations and theatrical interventions that emerged from this deceptively simple exercise were fascinating for me—both personally and academically. I was intrigued, for instance, by the very practical ambiguities that arose—both in terms of attempted theatrical solutions to bathroom harassment, and, moreover, in terms of the complex and layered debates that emerged as a result.

In a very different context, at my denomination's international conference in Mexico, I worked with a small group of clerical and lay leaders from around the world to create and rehearse short scenes based on our own experiences of religiously motivated anti-queer violence. We then shared these scenes with a larger workshop audience. As a larger group, we engaged in a forum theatre-based exploration of these complex issues, and began to try to name our hopes and visions for different possibilities. Not surprisingly, the limited time of the workshop allowed us to only begin to touch the surface of these difficult issues—particularly within such a multicultural context.

In these and many other examples of this nascent ministry development, I attempted to challenge the historic dualistic split between theology and praxis—and, indeed, between theological scholarship and active ministry. Drawing on Althaus-Reid and Isherwood's notion of queer theology as an "I theology," (while simultaneously recognizing the inherent instability of a definitive "I" identity), I sought to bring my own embodied experiences to the work of ministry (308). Indeed, learning how to more explicitly integrate my own lived experiences into this work was challenging for me, and proved an area of personal growth in my own ministerial praxis. My hope, in learning to bring the "I" into my own theological praxis, was to encourage other participants to do the same. In so doing, we hoped to engage in "a disclosure of experiences which have been traditionally silenced in theology" (308). This included both sexual disclosures ("coming out" in varied forms), and theological disclosures around ecclesial practices and beliefs historically excluded from mainstream and queer theologies.

Drawing on O'Donnell, I hoped to engage in "social acupuncture" within the corporate bodies of the church and the academy, challenging both, albeit in small ways, "to start engaging with unease and discomfort" (23). Through the deliberately provocative use of embodied theatrical strategies, I endeavored to expose and challenge the historic ecclesial and academic mind-body split. Whether through the use of Image Theatre or Forum Theatre within the body of a sermon, through the invitation to congregants to move out of their pews and into a theatrical conversation, or through the actual content of the theatrical work that addresses issues of the physical, the sexual, and the erotic as they relate to our lives in the church, the goal was, quite simply, to bring the sexual body back into the church.

Such a goal brought with it productive discomfort and a lack of familiar ecclesial/theological ground. O'Donnell's reflections on the theatrical process apply equally well to *Jokering* within theological/ecclesial contexts. He notes that "the social awkwardness and tension it [social acupuncture] generates can feel stupid, the projects seeming to constantly teeter on the brink of embarrassment and failure. As any system experiences a shift into higher complexity, there will be a time when it feels like there has been a drop in understanding, dexterity or control" (O'Donnell 50). Like Kumashiro, I aimed to both instigate and embrace this discomfort as a sign that learning, and, indeed transformation may well be at work (Kumashiro, "Teaching and Learning").

As a scholar and minister, I also became aware of the limitations and constraints of this emerging ministerial praxis. A particular challenge surfaced around criteria for the evaluation and measurement of this work. For example, while I utilized the (arguably traditional) measurement tools of pre- and post-project questionnaires within my master's theatre project, I simultaneously struggled with the limitations of these tools in addressing the less-easily defined outcomes and findings of the project, as well as what I experienced as modernist constraints of formal written questionnaires. Group "interviews"—through participatory theatrical conversations—offered one strategy to begin to address this challenge, allowing opportunities for more informal participant findings to emerge. I found, for example, that I elicited much more robust and generative feedback from workshop participants when I asked them to create, and then discuss, a still (theatrical) image encapsulating their experience of the workshop, than from the more formal written feedback generated by the traditional pre- and post-workshop questionnaires. Evaluative measurement is clearly one area for future development for this work. A challenge will be to find a means of rigorous evaluative processes that simultaneously cohere with this approach's commitment to praxis-oriented approaches, as well as its appreciation for the ambiguity of less-easily defined outcomes. Perhaps this is also a reflection of the ongoing dialectical challenge between queer theology's complex theorizing and Theatre of the Oppressed's practical application.

In/Conclusions: Celebrating Ambiguity in Theology and Praxis

The issues of theological ambiguity and emergent practice continue to be core strengths and challenges in this work. Certainly, Boal recognized that the dialogical nature of his processes often generated more questions than it answered—and in my own experience training with him, he not only celebrated this, but tried to provoke it in his own Jokering praxis. Queer theologies, in turn, recognize such uncertainties as theological gifts, challenging the theologian's own reflexive processes as well. Althaus-Reid reminded us that "claiming our right to limbo means to claim our right to Queer holy lives and innocence and by doing that we end up destabilising many powers and principalities by simply refusing to acknowledge their authority in our lives…. [A]s such, Queer saints are a menace and a subversive force by the sheer act of living in integrity and defiance" (*Queer God* 166). Through the application of a queer theological hermeneutic to Freire's *conscientization* cycle of action—reflection—and new action that emerges, a queer theologian/practitioner continually queers the processes of self-reflection, activist praxis, and ensuing reflexive evaluation. Such queer reflexivity engages the practitioner's embodied experience, while simultaneously recognizing and embracing the ambiguities inherent in reflexive evaluation. Indeed, such queer reflexivity might draw on Althaus-Reid's exploration of the instability of a Bi/Christology, helping "us to discover Christ in our processes of growth, the eventual transformation through unstable categories to be, more than anything else, a Christ of surprises" (*Indecent Theology* 120).

This is an area of scholarship and ministry that values theological fluidity and instability—affirming, as Althaus-Reid did, that it is "a sense of discontinuity which is most valuable" and recognizing that queer theology will likely have a distinctly different face a few years from now, as will queer theology's ministerial applications (4). Queer theology is more than a simple integration of the sexual and the spiritual. It requires us to engage in "indecenting" as a verb—that is, to actively transgress theological, political, and cultural structures. It involves a deliberate choice to move to the margins of Christian decency, making explicit the interwoven nature of theology, sexuality, politics, and globalization. Boal's strategies, in turn, draw on participatory theatrical strategies to wrestle with these complex questions in dialogical communities of actors and *spectactors*.

A determinedly queer theological approach to Theatre of the Oppressed therefore needs to remain deliberately marginal and provocative. By raising the "ceiling of decency" on sexually scripted orthodoxies, theologies, trends toward normalization, and global economics, Althaus-Reid offered such a voice (167). As we weave Boal's praxis into this conversation, a distinctly queer theological trajectory begins to emerge, one that requires a deep integration of the sexual, the political, the theological, and the economic. This makes of theology, as Althaus-Reid puts it, "something worth the effort" (148).

In conclusion—or perhaps more accurately, *inconclusively*—this article has aimed to outline the scope and possibilities for a new ministry model. This ministry recognizes, simultaneously, the profound value of a queer embrace of the changeability and instability of its theological roots and its praxis-oriented applications. In the spirit of Marcella Althaus-Reid and Augusto Boal, this model is offered as a beginning question—to open up further interventions, *queeries*, instabilities, and discoveries inspired by that very "Christ of surprises!"

Notes

1. To protect the confidentiality of workshop participants and processes, the examples are composites from a wide range of my experiences as a T.O. facilitator.
2. Boal uses the term *arsenal* to refer to his own wide range of theatrical strategies, perhaps as a response to the politically violent context within which they originally were formulated.

Works Cited

Althaus-Reid, Marcella. 2001. The Divine Exodus of God: Involuntarily Marginalized, Taking an Option for the Margins, or Truly Marginal? In *God: Experience and Mystery*, ed. Werner G. Jeanrond and Christoph Theobald, 27–33. London: SCM P. Print.

———. 2002. *Indecent Theology: Theological Perversions in Sex, Gender and Politics*. New York: Routledge. Print.

———. 2003. *The Queer God*. New York: Routledge. Print.

———. 2004. Introduction: Queering Theology. In *The Sexual Theologian*, ed. Lisa Isherwood and Marcella Althaus-Reid, 1–15. London: T & T Clark. Print.

———. 2006. Education for Liberation. *Studies in World Christianity* 12 (1): 1–4. Print.

———. 2008. Lunchtime Crucifixions: Theological Reflections on Economic Violence and Redemption. In *Weep Not for Your Children: Essays on Religion and Violence*, ed. Lisa Isherwood and Rosemary Radford Ruether, 65–76. Oakville: Equinox. Print.

Boal, Augusto. 1985. *Theatre of the Oppressed*. New York: Theatre Communications Group. Print.

———. 1995. *The Rainbow of Desire: The Boal Method of Theatre and Therapy*. Trans. Jackson, Adrian. New York: Routledge. Print.

———. 1998. *Legislative Theatre: Using Performance to Make Politics*. New York: Routledge. Print.

———. 2002. *Games for Actors and Non-Actors*. New York: Routledge. Print.

Butterwick, Shauna. 2002. Your Story/My Story/Our Story: Performing Interpretation in Participatory Theatre. *Alberta Journal of Educational Research* 48 (3): 240–253. Print.

Decottignies, Michele. 2010. Applied Arts '10: Introductory Information for Our Workshop Together. In *Stage Left*. ed. Productions. Canmore: Stage Left Productions. Print.

Dennis, Barbara. 2009. Acting Up: Theater of the Oppressed as Critical Ethnography. *International Journal of Qualitative Methods* 8 (2): 65–96. Print.

Diamond, David. 2007. *Theatre for Living: The Art and Science of Community-Based Dialogue*. Victoria: Trafford. Print.

Dwyer, Paul. 2004. Augusto Boal and the Woman in Lima: A Poetic Encounter. *New Theatre Quarterly* 20 (2): 155–163. Print.

Fast, Anita. 1999. *Called to Be Queer: Towards a Theological (Re)Vision for the People of God*, Master's Thesis. Vancouver School of Theology.

Freire, Paulo. 2007. *Pedagogy of the Oppressed*. 7th ed. New York: Continuum. Print.

Halperin, David M. 2003. The Normalization of Queer Theory. *Journal of Homosexuality* 45 (2-4): 339–343. Print.

Heritage, Paul. 2006. Staging Human Rights: Securing the Boundaries? *Hispanic Research Journal* 7 (4): 353–363. Print.

Hsiao-Chuan, Hsia. 2006. Empowering 'Foreign Brides' and Community through Praxis-Oriented Research. *Societies Without Borders* 1 (1): 93–111. Print.

Kumashiro, Kevin K. 2000. Teaching and Learning through Desire, Crisis, and Difference: Perverted Reflections on Anti-Oppressive Education. *Radical Teacher* 58 (Fall): 6–11. Print.

———. 2002. Against Repetition: Addressing Resistance to Anti-Oppressive Change in the Practices of Learning, Teaching, Supervising, and Researching. *Harvard Educational Review* 72 (1): 67. Print.

McFague, Sallie. 2001. *Life Abundant: Rethinking Theology and Economy for a Planet in Peril*. Minneapolis: Augsburg Fortress. Print.

Mesner, Kerri. 2010. *Jokering as Queer Ministry: Queer Theology Meets Theatre of the Oppressed*, Master's Thesis. Vancouver School of Theology.

O'Donnell, Daniel. 2006. *Social Acupuncture: A Guide to Suicide, Performance and Utopia*. Toronto: Coach House Books. Print.

Schutzman, Mady. 1994. Brechtian Shamanism: The Political Therapy of Augusto Boal. In *Playing Boal: Theatre, Therapy, Activism*, ed. Mady Schutzman and Jan Cohen-Cruz, 137–156. New York: Routledge. Print.

CHAPTER 15

Queer Homes in a Non-Queer World

Katie Goldstein

I am a queer femme, a housing organizer in New York City, and a founder of a queer home in Brooklyn. My identity, work influence, and experience with queer homes have led me to want to explore the political implications and opportunities of the queer home, queer space, and queer place within the context of a predominantly non-queer landscape.

Home can be a fraught place for many queers, a place where we are not seen and where we are marginalized for who we are and who we love. The act of creating queer homes redefines what home is and can be, and it challenges the invisibilization and marginalization of queer community. Creating queer homes puts a queer mark on a non-queer landscape and, through that act, demands that queerness be recognized as an identity that must be seen.

A white queer with economic privilege, I explore queer homes that are made up of mostly white folks in Brooklyn. My interest in this topic is both self-focused, as someone who loves this city and wants to continue to live here, and concentrated on a society, as someone who believes that queers should be working hard for the communities in which they live, both with other queers and beyond the queer community.

K. Goldstein (✉)
Brooklyn, NY, USA

© The Author(s) 2018
E. McNeil et al. (eds.), *Mapping Queer Space(s) of Praxis and Pedagogy*, Queer Studies and Education,
DOI 10.1007/978-3-319-64623-7_15

In Brooklyn, the physical landscape is filled with the tensions of gentrification. Gentrification is the process by which lower-income folks are displaced by higher-income folks. The gentrification process is facilitated by real estate developers and urban policy. It is impossible to have a conversation about Brooklyn without discussing the implications of the changing racial and economic landscape of the borough. Heralded as the creative capital of the USA, the gentrification of Brooklyn is the result of the effects of neo-liberal capitalism on space. Though there is important anti-gentrification organizing happening at the grassroots level, the effects of gentrification have been and will continue to be a scourge on neighborhoods throughout Brooklyn (see "Anti-Gentrification Resources" at end of chapter). The borough will undoubtedly be a very different in ten years.

New York City has always been home for queers. George Chauncey, in *Gay New York*, argues that New York has been the gay capital of the nation for a century. In this era of hyper-gentrification, the space and place of queer home raise the important question about where queers can live safely and affordably. Queer folks have both been pushed out of different neighborhoods due to gentrification and have contributed to gentrification because being queer is a multi-class and multi-racial identity.

A prominent story of the gentrification debate is that queers bring gentrification and embody a flawed relationship between the physical space in which they inhabit. In that story, the experience of urban, and/or working class, and/or queers of color is invisibilized. Young white queers moving to urban areas have had the effect of raising rents and increasing displacement pressures. Both stories are true and must be held together.

We are in a unique historical moment in New York City for queer-identified folks. Gay marriage passed in the New York State Legislature in 2011 to the joy of the mainstream lesbian and gay movement and to indifference and some annoyance by many queer-identified folks. It is within this context that queer homes have proliferated throughout the borough where queer folks are not being represented politically by the mainstream lesbian and gay movement. Queer homes are a part of the tensions of the global phenomenon of gentrification and can be a challenge to it. Collective housing is an important tool to combat gentrification. However, a queer space located in a gentrifying neighborhood can help to contribute to the gentrifying forces within a neighborhood. This can happen if the home is not as racially or economically diverse in the community in which the space is located. This can also happen if the queer house and space is not politically engaged in the struggle against the displacement of low and moderate-income folks often associated with gentrification.

In the gentrification narrative, the central theme is about home. Who is from a place? Who deserves to make a home in a place? Whose presence makes it difficult for long-time community residents to remain in that place? Where can I be safe with my community and my loved ones?

These are questions that queers are always asking, wondering where we can be our full selves in where we live. We must ask the question of where is it safe to be out and queer? Where can I be in public with my partner/lover? Where is a place I can be where I am not discriminated against because of my gender presentation and sexuality, whether in the workplace or simply walking down the street? Thus, the importance of queer space: a place to be where people can fully practice their gender and sexual identity. In the city, there is creation of queer space through a queer community that can be made up of folks from the city and not from the city, but who share having found the city as a place where we have made our home. The active creation of queer space contributes to queer safety.

The threats of gentrification are clear throughout the city, and if there isn't a significant shift, the future of this city for low-income, working-class, and middle-class folks will be extremely dire. In the eight years I have lived in Brooklyn, I have seen businesses fail, tenants I work with get displaced, and a divide grow between a working-class and upper-class Brooklyn. Community members tell me that common effects of gentrification (besides being concerned that they will not be able to pay their rent) is that communities are breaking up, people don't say hi to each other on the street, and common courtesy with transient neighbors that existed in more stable neighborhoods and communities has diminished. This is a powerful critique of how the political effects of gentrification change the culture of a neighborhood.

This is true as well for what makes a strong queer community; folks need to be connected. Queers create alternatives to straight spaces, and work together to support and care for one another in our projects.

THE POLITICS OF QUEER HOMES

I define a queer home as a queer space created by queer residents who can be but are not necessarily transgendered/gender non-conforming. It can be collective in nature, but it is primarily a space for queer folks to celebrate and be recognized for their identity. Queers create home with one another because too often a common queer experience is the displacement from communities and spaces due to having a marginalized sexuality and/or gender presentation. In queer homes, there is space for variant and gender-non-conforming folks to be seen fully for their gender identity within the created queer space. Some queers have both experienced a physical displacement and a cultural displacement where their sexuality and gender identity is not represented or celebrated by mainstream culture.

In my queer home, we process with each other constantly, and through that processing we make our thoughts, feelings, desires, and identities seen and heard. We see each other as complete people with complicated sexualities, genders, and identities.

Queer homes are important in that they resist this displacement and create a new narrative. They provide an alternative to an expectation that one lives by oneself until it is time to be partnered and re-create the nuclear family. Queers have always created alternative family structures, and the queer home can be a part of those alternative systems of support.

Queer homes in a predominantly non-queer world are inherently political. For both myself and other queers, being queer can be an all-encompassing term that articulates a political identity alongside a sexual identity. Queer homes are important politically as a space for advancing conversations about how we want to live together, about diversity and community, and in regard to challenging patriarchal values of the nuclear family. In our queer home, we provide a space for folks to not be judged, tokenized, or invisibilized because of their gender or sexuality. And I believe this is, in and of itself, a political act.

In a response to a question about the definition of queer space, Yana Walton, an economic justice organizer and a lay historian of queer homes and lesbian lands, responded with:

> For me, a queer space necessarily comes along with values that not only deal with understanding our gender and sexual orientation (and those of others) as social/historical constructs, and thus trying to undo all the homophobia, transphobia, cissexism, heterosexism, sexism, patriarchal values, gender roles, biological "limitations," etc. that we've all learned. But I think it also is actively trying to detach and self-define and deconstruct the way those assumptions have built our society. A queer space is never finished, but it is an active process created by the shifting identities inside and around it to undo racist, sexist, classist, capitalist, cissexist, colonialist and essentialist notions of who we are and how we should be treating each other. Who the fuck is queer? It's all a designation we give, and I think that this designation should come along with this active un-learning and re-creating process. At least that's what I hope. And really, I think I've been in a lot of spaces that were queer as fuck and didn't sound a thing like what I just wrote.

This definition illuminates how I'd like to engage with queerness: in its anti-oppressive engagement, it's self-naming, and that "queer" is an active process of definition and creation.

Throughout the country, queers have organized themselves in different living situations, urban and rural, collective homes, nuclear families, and by themselves. Walton explains their interest in queer homes in this way:

> I've been interested in queer homes as a contemporary continuation/extension of spaces set up by radical lesbian feminist separatists that created womyn's lands in previous generations. I've started thinking about contemporary queer homes in urban areas as today's manifestation of the impetus that radical folks have to create intentional environments around shared values and identification primarily around sexuality and gender—but also very much as our response to wanting to create bubbles that try to unravel the capitalism, classism, and racism that permeates our daily lives in such ubiquitous ways.

As illuminated by Walton's point, the gay rights movement is not giving folks who are queer all that we need, and folks are thinking about how to strengthen queer community and build an anti-oppressive queer culture, and queer homes have been a manifestation of that work.

Collective living has been prominent for decades, where folks have chosen to live in spaces where their identity becomes the norm rather than the aberration. In New York City, the population is mostly renters and the housing stock has meant that it's mostly unaffordable for folks to be able to buy full homes. Within affordable homes and apartments, queers have mostly rented homes that they have developed as a communal queer space. Communal living is a way to live relatively cheaply in the city.

For decades, there has been a continued migration into the city of queers who want to be close to queer history, culture, and people. Many queers are in it for the parties, the spaces, and the opportunity to meet multiple lovers. Queers are creating and manifesting their world in the city—creating new norms and practicing different ways of taking their values into the way they live. Walton said about queer homes,

> I think queer homes are these gorgeous little factories/production sites of culture that in ways get branded and mythologized as mini radical queer justice centers in some ways. Because many have organization-like functions, and folks engage in lots of organizing that goes far beyond homes within them. For many folks, they are the "LGBT Community Pride Center" that none of us visited. The cultural capital they hold within a larger

queer community or scene means there's a constant proliferation of queer homes as younger queers make their great gay migration to places like Oakland & Brooklyn, and I think just like there are Land Dyke conferences every few years, residents of queer homes getting together and engaging in community organizing and visibility can really be the new frontier in a queer politic that addresses the shit that marriage and hate crimes legislation simply cannot.

Queer homes are a physical manifestation and celebration of us in the urban landscape. We look inside our homes as our nest and our space of protection and safety. In a city that is under attack for public space to become privatized, there is a need for more and not fewer spaces that are accessed by queers. There is a need for queers to make an imprint on the New York City landscape in a way that is not a part of a corporate culture in a responsible way. I care deeply about how queer values manifest politically.

The explicitly political nature of a queer home can be de-emphasized to become more social and cultural space, which can become disconnected from a broader political struggle. We need to challenge this tendency and re-center the political potentialities of queer homes.

QUORUM: QUEERS ORGANIZING FOR RADICAL UNITY AND MOBILIZATION

Since I have lived in Brooklyn, there have been new parties that have been created, new houses, and new groups. One of the more exciting organizations that has been created is QUORUM: Queers Organizing for Radical Unity and Mobilization. QUORUM organized Queer House Field Days and QUORUM FORUMS with workshops, skill-shares, and a big final party. Participating in QUORUM were 15 houses, mostly but not exclusively queer collective houses, who hosted workshops on a variety of topics such as queers and gentrification, queers and *The Hunger Games*, and yoga and breathing exercises. The workshops got folks to open their homes and teach, learn, and have discussions together that led to the development of strong relationships between houses and individuals. QUORUM gave voice to folks who were disconnected from one another while living in queer homes, and it helped to facilitate a sense of broader queer community.

Katie Blouse, one of the founders of QUORUM, spoke with me about the founding of the organization. She said that, at the beginning, QUORUM tried to create an alternative to the queer parties that she felt, as someone who was new to NYC and searching for queer community, were exclusive spaces. QUORUM started as an idea of bringing together queer collective houses to provide mutual aid for one another and supporting queer collective housing being created. She saw "untapped potential for folks to work together and strengthen our community through mutual aid." She was surprised by the level of interest that the initial Queer House Field Day elicited and that QUORUM so obviously filled a deep need as shown just by the sheer numbers of participants. It was extremely clear to her that folks wanted alternatives to the party scene and hungered for spaces in which to share and organize with each other.

Blouse is also critical of QUORUM. To her, QUORUM is a prototype. One flaw of the initial grouping is that participants were from majority white social groups. QUORUM quickly became the assumed voice of the queer community, resulting in the invisibilization of voices of queer communities of color and movements/organizations from those communities. She said:

> As QUORUM became less about being a queer collective housing organization and more of a queer organization, there was a sense of QUORUM speaking for or being a symbol for the New York City queer community and QUORUM was and is incredibly white. It became problematic to become a behemoth queer organization where it was perceived to be the voice of the queers where it was all these white kids in Brooklyn. That became a problem.

She spoke poignantly about the internal tension among the QUORUM organizers about whether QUORUM was more of social space or a political space. This is currently and has been a live question for the queer community. As one of the political actions that QUORUM folks took on, a group went to the New York City Annual Pride Parade and passed out materials about the corporate sponsorship of Pride. To illuminate her point about the tension within QUORUM, she said that only ten folks came to the political action, whereas hundreds of folks came through the final party.

Katie is no longer a part of the core organizing team with QUORUM, but they are in the midst of re-organizing, and she is supportive as they re-group themselves. She repeated throughout the interview that the process QUORUM went through of being created and then falling apart and then being re-created is part of the natural ebb and flow of queer activism in the city. In QUORUM, the political potential of queer houses was explored through activities folks worked on together.

These types of projects build queer community in a context where there are many different queer communities and ways to be in a queer community. In 2010, I hosted a workshop in my house during QUORUM about queers and gentrification. In that workshop, we discussed queerness as a multi-racial and multi-class identity, as both being folks who end up being the ones who perpetuate gentrification and those who are casualties of the process. In discussing and celebrating the queer effect on an urban space through QUORUM, we were able in this workshop to hold both of those effects simultaneously while seeing the importance and political potential of unification of queer collective homes.

Queer houses are very important, but they are not always created with deep consciousness in which their political importance can be celebrated. My hope is that, through this subject, I can explore a vision for creating a responsible, conscious, and powerful queer landscape of queer homes in Brooklyn.

Self-determination is an important political goal, where we can make choices over our homes and communities. For us to realize this political goal, we need to question what the relationship is between queer homes and their broader geographic and political communities. How can a community that is both transient and permanent make a responsible mark on an urban landscape?

Where Do We Go from Here?

Being queer is a work in progress. Queers constantly create and recreate our communities and our norms. I believe that queer houses are a tool for protection of queer community and an opportunity for shared political learning. As we see the landscape changing in many fundamental ways as gentrification ravages the city, the queer landscape will change and queers will respond to the changes. I want to be a part of the movement of a queer home translating into a network of queer homes and toward creating a new consciousness about queer home and inclusive and celebratory queer space. I want to see queer homes becoming politically permanent, and to see them create alternative cultures and change what safety and home can mean to a queer community, while at the same time challenging gentrification.

Queers fighting against gentrification can't just mean one thing. It has to mean queers defending neighborhoods in which they have lived, organizing against police brutality for queers and folks who are gender non-conforming, and ensuring that the queer youth of color can stay on the piers as multimillion dollar condos are built, sold, and occupied (see

"Anti-Gentrification Resources"). It also has to mean queer collective homes developing a model for responsible urban living. Queers (and everyone else) need to unite to build an anti-gentrification movement. I hope to see the increase of communal queer homes. Queer homes can be an antidote to the psychological effects of marginalization and gentrification, where communities are split a part. My hope is that the queer community comes out steadfastly against gentrification and seeks to unite to combat gentrification everywhere, in our health care, our bars, and most importantly, our homes. We need a political movement: for queers to be able to come and enjoy queer space and proliferate and create more.

I want to add to the gentrification narrative where we both want long-term residents to be able to stay and new residents to be able to come so folks can create the city together. If the world remains unsafe for queers outside of the city except in small pockets and with few tolerant people, then we need both to organize to change that and to continue to create affordable homes for queers just moving to the city, for unemployed queers, and for queers making their way between dreams and partners.

I want to participate in both expanding and narrowing the debate by exploring the following questions: Who does gentrification serve? Who are the winners and who are the losers? What do queer homes have to offer broad struggles for justice, both as a concept and as a model? How do queer homes need to be transformed to make this possible? How must broader political struggles be transformed to make this possible?

We are in a key political moment to challenge the system of gentrification by presenting another model through responsible queer homes. Queer homes must be an accountable and political mark on the urban landscape. Let's make this choice of how to proceed as queers, together.

WORKS CITED

Blouse, Katie. 2013. Personal interview. January 24, 2013.
Chauncey, George. 1994. *Gay New York: Gender, Urban Culture, and the Making of the Gay Male World*. New York: BasicBooks. Print.
Walton, Yana. 2013. E-mail interview. February 1, 2013.

ANTI-GENTRIFICATION RESOURCES

Audre Lorde Project. http://alp.org/.
FIERCE. http://www.fiercenyc.org/.
Right to the City. http://www.righttothecity.org.

CHAPTER 16

Teaching Desire in Third Space: A Queer Prison Pedagogy for the Unknowing Spirit

Elizabeth McNeil and Joshua O. Lunn

The USA has the highest rate of incarceration in the world (Walmsley). With more than 2.2 million people in American jails and prisons (International Centre for Prison Studies), our country houses nearly 25% of the world's 10.2 million inmates, though the USA makes up less than 5% of the global population (American Civil Liberties Union). According to the US Bureau of Justice Statistics, "1 in every 35 adults in the United States, or 2.9% of adult residents, was on probation or parole or incarcerated in prison or jail" in 2012 (Glaze and Herberman).[1] As startlingly commonplace as incarceration is, and as familiar as it is in our news and creative media, we do not often engage, through academic or other social discourse, what it means to be institutionalized by legal confinement, or how one might break free of the constructs that define prison, have led to one's imprisonment, and define a former inmate after release.

E. McNeil (✉)
Languages and Cultures, College of Integrative Sciences and Arts,
Arizona State University, Phoenix, AZ, USA

J.O. Lunn
Snowflake, AZ, USA

© The Author(s) 2018
E. McNeil et al. (eds.), *Mapping Queer Space(s) of Praxis and Pedagogy*, Queer Studies and Education,
DOI 10.1007/978-3-319-64623-7_16

279

Those who have not experienced incarceration perhaps cannot imagine what it means to live for a while or for the rest of one's lifetime held by others in a highly controlled space, with one's desires—in fact, oneself—denied. The constant presence and acts of waiting. Life crammed into overcrowded, dirty spaces. Repressed desires for sex, nature, belonging, relationship, learning, growth, purpose, aliveness, agency. The hyperpresence of violence, and the systemic incompetence, corruption, and intimidation that feeds it. Those who have lived or taught in prisons know, as bell hooks puts it, that inmates, like any other learners, "do want an education that is healing to the uninformed, unknowing spirit. They do want knowledge that is meaningful …[,] addressing the connection between what they are learning and their overall life experiences" (19). To those who control the incarcerated, however, prisoners' intellectual acumen is an obvious threat, while kindness, affection, desire, and basic humanity all seem to be regarded as criminal in the prison environment.

As a place of so many profoundly delimited aspects of human being, prison is, by definition, abnormal, ill, obsessive—and, as such, can also be a "third space" of concentrated queer possibility for transformation. "Third space" is a fractious and creative space of hybridity and synergy, a space of thoughtful disruption of received and perceived norms.[2] Queer as third space is radical space for the deconstruction of conventional binary genders, sexualities, and general ways of thinking, and an even more radical space for the reconstruction—or acknowledgment—of the fluidity of gender identities, sexual identities, and patterns of thought and behavior. In his work on queer studies in education, David V. Ruffolo defines "queer" not as a state of being but as an action, a process:

> [Q]ueer is in many ways a third space outside binary categorizations where the existence of queer does not depend on a definitive Other.... [Q]ueer theory offers a body that is less fixed and stable and more mobile and fluid: the body is an open materiality that is always shifting. In doing so, queer becomes less of a noun and more of a verb: a radical process of disruption committed to challenging fixed subjectivities embedded in normative practices. There are therefore no normal bodies but bodies that become normalized over time through (hetero)normative discourses. (290)

Prison, an abnormal/queer space and process that itself has morphed over time—physically, ideologically/culturally, socioeconomically, politically, and so on—is both a manifestation of and, increasingly, the origin of key cultural (white hetero patriarchal) norms and values. Though it inculcates and spreads repressive, dangerous norms throughout our society, prison is also a real meeting place for all constituents involved in this drama, a queer third space of radical possibility at the blurred margins of our shared humanity.

Through the lens of queer theory, Josh and I wanted to write together to explore our personal and intellectual transformation as teachers of queer thought—Josh incarcerated and teaching other inmates, formally and informally, and me teaching undergraduates at a state university, as well as older learners in the community and, occasionally, inmates. As a couple whose relationship began under the literal as well as emotional strictures of incarceration, we also wanted to ponder how desire has played out queerly within and between us, and what that has meant in our teaching. Informed by Judith Butler and others, we examine how the space of prison condemns desire and the self—all that is natural and queerly unique about being alive and human—and how we found ways to find ourselves and each other despite this space, and due to it.

Trying to recognize, access, and help ourselves live through that transformative possibility, all the while dealing with the rules and corruptions common to incarceration, Josh and I found that we, individually and together, had to become queer third space, arousing and occupying a transformative dimension that considers layers and levels of being—and a fluidity of being—disallowed by our society. In our desires and our interactions, we have had to transform the way that our physical-emotional-intellectual desire can be expressed and fulfilled. To express this queer process in writing, we wanted to compose together, a feminist collaborative process that itself still occupies a third space in academia and in much of our society that prizes individualism and hierarchy. We wanted, instead, intellectual intimacy and joy in this composition process. So through his pages smuggled in and passed to me in visitation, and my research, cutting, crafting, and discovering our story and its form, that's what we did.[3]

* * *

Josh and I met in a poetry workshop I taught in 2007. I had long wanted to teach inmates, to offer something to this population who, as I saw it, were probably most in need of what writing and intellectual engagement could offer. After collecting and delivering books to Arizona prisons for several years, I gained the opportunity to provide a six-month poetry workshop to a select group of inmates at a private prison in Florence, Arizona, run by the GEO Corporation. Much later, Josh told me that "nothing good like that" had happened in the six years he had been in prison to that point, and that "nothing that good" had been offered there since.

This facility was designed to warehouse men in large dorms where the lights are on 24/7 and there is absolutely no privacy at any time for any reason. This place is also without a single bush, tree, or blade of grass. One of the stories my workshop participants told me bespeaks the general GEO mindset. After a large indented area in the recreation yard had filled with water from one of Arizona's rare torrential rains, tiny toads began squirming up through the mud, awakened from their long, dry slumber. Naturally, in a place ordinarily so devoid of life, the inmates were entranced by these tiny creatures. One day soon after, a guard walked out onto the yard and tossed bleach tablets into the remaining pool, to kill the toads. And the life of no-life returned to order.

After the success of the poetry workshop, I had been going to offer another class there, but only a few men signed up, so my department chair and I concluded it just wasn't worth the time and expense. I'd thought that it was the inmates who hadn't been interested, which seemed odd, since our workshop had been one of the most powerful experiences of my teaching career, and the librarian had told me the participants had expressed the same feeling, continued, in fact, to talk about it. I learned later that at least 40 qualified inmates had applied for the reading group, and, for no apparent reason, the administrators had admitted only six.

Two years after the workshop, Josh wrote to ask if I would be willing to do more study with him through correspondence. He had been one of the most engaged learners I had ever taught, and was also a highly skilled writer, so I said yes. We did that for two years. His analytical and creative prose in my ecofeminist literature course was astoundingly good. I'd never had an undergraduate learner incorporate and respond to theory with such depth and apparent ease. He told me later that the pieces—memoir and analysis— were extremely difficult for him to write. I couldn't tell. Then I got on his visitor list so that we could discuss his studies in person, too, since I knew that would make the learning even more productive and enjoyable.

Several visits in, we sat in the plastic chairs at a plastic table in the visitation room, playing Scrabble. Suddenly and rather ironically, since this place teems with such anxiety and despair, a rush of self-acceptance and peace filled me, like I'd known only once or twice before. I knew Josh was looking at me, but I kept my head down, pretending to concentrate on the game. Staring at the Scrabble board, I realized what had just hit me: I cared for this person. I had not planned on that.

* * *

It began, with a poetry workshop that Elizabeth headed and in which I and a dozen or so others participated. I don't recall why I chose to be one of these, other than the fact that I like poetry and it was novel. I would never have thought of such an activity in prison, and I found myself amused by the cross-section of prisoners who chose to join, homosexuals and homophobes, Christians, Muslims, Jews, and atheists, black, brown, and white racists, old and young, myself, and Elizabeth. I had for years recessed into a pattern of violence and callousness, yet here I was. She sat there, surrounded by us all, in a dress, her hair tied into a ponytail—ardent, sincere, and unapologetic. I couldn't help thinking, Why are you here?

Six months after it began, the class ended, and I realized a chafing absence of light, a gross sinking from the creative, active, and transformative process of workshopping simple turns of language to the daily trudge of carceral life. What was more was the removal of Elizabeth's presence. I realized then how subdued the incarcerated become, how rarely we notice, even in those people who choose to visit us, the qualities of passion and love, and subtleties of difference within them. That's when my trouble began, with actually taking the time to see others. Not that it mattered, I remember thinking at the time. The only person I believed could help me understand this problem left at the end of the workshop, and it would be years until I would pluck up the nerve to write her.

But eventually I did.

* * *

Sitting in the visitation hall, I shook my head that she actually sat across the table from me as we played Scrabble. We had written each other for some time, and she had even taken the time to help educate me in her areas of study. I had spent a longer-than-needed period undertaking an ecofeminist literature class she had put together, and was having difficulty receiving the freaks studies materials she kept sending, each time receiving contraband slips for one image or another because they were deemed pornographic (which is funny, because if I wanted porn I could get it from one of the guards).[4]

It was my study of the material in the ecofem course that helped me to become open to the freaks material, and similarly it was the ecofem and freaks material that prepped me for the introduction to queer theorists.

My mind was not always so open, and, fully immersed in this prison culture, it was a long, troubling road. As a white male, I have historically fit in with my forebears. Whether I was aware of it or not, I subscribed to the order of differences that made me superior and everything and everyone else an inferior subsequent variation. Females were certainly different in ways I failed to grasp, and people of different cultures and skin tones were even more so. And queer was a wholly different sort of different.

It seems odd to me now that my preoccupation with all of these differences had never inspired me to ask questions regarding why any of it should be a cause for concern.

* * *

On my way to visitation, I travel along a concrete walkway, alongside squat gray buildings and loess-dusted galvanized chain-link fence laced by coils of razor wire. I approach yet another brick-shaped building, push the button to announce myself, and wait for the guard to arrive, pat search me, and allow me into the visitation hall proper. I check in with the visitation hall floor officer, display my identification, declare any jewelry or religious medallions, then I am free to visit with those people cleared to enter this space by way of the outside world.

I turn away from the visitation officer and go outside to meet Elizabeth, who looks up from where she sits, playing solitaire with a beat-up deck of dark cards, and stands to greet me. We take a moment to look directly at one another, then hug and kiss in a brief manner, so as to remain within the rules of the Arizona Department of Corrections Code of Conduct for visitors, and begin to talk, all the while both attempting to exist in this space and transcend this place that imposes such a conservative hegemony as to surpass the hyperbolized, a queer pairing if ever there was one.

We walk around the graveled pen and occasionally glimpse other couples who sneak a kiss or wrap an arm about a waist for a moment, turning a normally innocent gesture into something sordid and criminal, before eyeing the guards and resuming a chaste hand-holding. The absurdity occurs to me of instilling within the prison populous a need to be criminal to feel fully human and present. Of all the possible violations that a prisoner may commit, I am astounded by the way one's natural being is most damaged by this pedagogy and the praxis of retribution employed by the prison system. I can understand the reasoning behind policy stating that inmates shall not do violence to any person, or those policies deterring harmful criminal behavior. Sell, purchase, or use drugs, destroy state property, incite a riot, extort, steal, rape or kill, escape, intimidate, and ye shall tempt the fates—I get it. But to restrict a person from the simple physical comfort of a two-minute hug seems a bit absurd.

Not that long ago, an amendment to the rules added "no hand-holding" by prisoners. Not that I've seen a lot of that going on in here. Certainly, not so much that it should be deemed a pandemic issue requiring its own rule for the state prisons. As Elizabeth and I began to discuss this during one visit, I began to experience an utterly paranoid sensation, a need to revolt against what this prison space drowns its captives in: the conservative white heteronormative ideal. I remember looking up at a comically large "Rules of Visitation" sign at the facility and reading rule number 4: "No male or same-sex kissing." I thought how odd it was that they would post such a rule, for in the 12 years of my incarceration to that point, I had seen a lot of wild stuff, yet I had never seen two men kiss, anywhere, let alone within visitation, which I find odd because I've known gay and bisexual people within these walls, but have never noticed them showing affection. That, in itself, struck me a resounding blow, as I pride myself on my observational skills, or, I should say, in my situational awareness. I can tell you by the way someone walks whether he has a shank, or by the way a guard hunches that she/he has no intention of being personable, despite their typical behavior. I can tell by the way cliques move that something serious is going down, but for the life of me, I couldn't tell you the last time I saw a prison queer act naturally or show affection that was not an intentional performance meant to mock the other prisoners who routinely call him "faggot."

I felt like cold water had just been splashed across my face as I realized what corrections means.

* * *

Several years after Elizabeth began sharing texts with me, I introduced a fellow inmate named Red, a white supremacist, to feminist and queer theory scholars. I understood his shattered reaction to their texts. I have not been exempt from Red's conflict. In fact, Elizabeth has induced such a state within me on more occasions that I would care to count, first, with feminist and multiculturalist reasoning that began in the poetry workshop, then with the freak studies and intersex introductions, and finally with queer theorists. With each of these, moments of panic hit.

I remember the first time I was called to the property window to pick up some of the books she had sent me without warning: the odd looks from the officers as they brought the materials, the confusion as I wondered where the books could have come from, and the cautious glances the other prisoners shot my way as they noted the titles. At each new delivery, ever more curious looks confronted me, seeking some defensive jerk or an admittance of something they feared to know.

Meeting none of this, but, instead, a wholly new method of argumentation, left people unsettled. As I began to discuss issues of perceived difference between inmates of different color, culture, sexuality, and proffered gender, occasional irrational protestations erupted, but rarely evolved into much more than a moment of panic, as they had to come to terms with the idea of my actual being. As one of the dominant males on the yard, a certain philosophical skew was expected, and when the first time I queried why someone else's sexuality bugged them, many felt a sort of betrayal, as if gravity or some other aspect of reality might cease to hold true. Admittedly, I felt similarly toward Elizabeth on several occasions as she introduced me to queer thinking, and I had to reorient my view of the world to maintain equilibrium—or revolt. But since I knew she was moved toward learning and not lies, this became increasingly easier for me to do.

Soon, I began to understand how I had used education for the past decade to escape prison in a metaphysical sense and had pushed others to do the same, with great effect. I had provoked hundreds of students to follow my lead and example, yet it had never occurred to me to investigate why escape was necessary, how it was achieved most effectively, or from what I was truly seeking to escape. I have come to an understanding of this, thanks to Elizabeth, an education employing compassion, and feminist and queer studies scholars.

* * *

The previously mentioned material may seem irrelevant to the concept of desire, but the connection exists in that prisoners don't typically use words like *desire, yearning*, and *erotic* in ways that don't involve sex, if they use them at all. Because to give voice to these is to acknowledge a loss and a source of self-consciousness that bespeaks an underlying reason for their behavior beyond that of which they are aware or are willing to face. And so, in my education with you, Elizabeth, I have evolved from merely one of these. I have transformed from the cold, violent, intransigent convict the others have known into a prisoner who speaks of desire, of yearning, of love and the erotic in contexts outside of the expected, in open company, creating waves of reactions ranging from understanding and admiration to fear, confusion, and ridicule.

Our dynamic has changed dramatically since we first met. Obviously. But, what is important to this discussion is not that it has, but how it has, and in this regard desire comes into play. When you and I interacted in the poetry workshop, we were at a distance. In that temporal frame, I existed in the state of escapism, yet desire played within me. My desire to write poetry, and, indeed, to write better poetry, is a clear representation of this "presuppositional" desire, as Butler puts it, that "obscuring of the existential and psychological difficulties at work" in the "metaphysical finesse" I unconsciously obeyed ("Desire" 52). Poetry represents a beauty and frankness I had denied myself in prison, and in much of my life preceding prison. As we created a dialogue in the workshop, I was still uncertain of what my desires were, on a grander scale, and it took much of your openness for me to see that someone could be unsure and still be respected. The day it was clear that the workshop had come to an end was a signifier that my desire would be denied. And, in my struggle to combat that denial, I began to realize my symptom.

I was combatting my own pursuit of desire as a way of reinforcing the drive toward imperviousness. Impenetrability is a well-played-out theme among the incarcerated, and I am no different in this respect. As is at least clear to me, to own and give voice to one's desires is eventually to share that voice with another, and sharing that desire, any desire, with another, no matter how meager, is to give that other a power over oneself. In prison, power relations are tantamount to existence, so most refuse to relinquish theirs, often creating entire fantastic versions of themselves to share with others so that no part of themselves is ever truly known, which eliminates the possibility of loss of power and, thusly, their very existence.

Continuing along this line of thought, I recall moments when I revolted against this relinquishment of power by admitting to myself that I did indeed desire. I was indeed self-conscious, and so there was indeed a loss or lacking. I remember reading that quote from Nicholas Evans's *The Horse Whisperer*, in which the main character says, "'Sometimes what feels like surrender isn't surrender at all. It's about what's going on in our hearts. About seeing clearly the way life is and accepting it and being true to it, whatever the pain, because the pain of not being true to it is far, far greater'" (417). These lines reverberated within me, and still do, and eventually led to why I write.

It was in that surrender that I began to allow myself to desire, to admit that truth to myself. The specificity of the desire was still not clear, but I was aware of its presence, and that was something.

By the time we began to write regularly, and I began studying the materials for your ecofeminist class, I was already operating on the concept of desire—that desire manifesting as a wish to be compassionate within a space that typically misreads such demonstrations as weakness. But there was space for this desire within myself and within the classroom, as I had awareness that I was not weak, and so was not self-conscious, and if any area should incorporate compassion, it should be in the act of helping others to learn. So I began to adapt my more regimental methodology to one of guiding, and to guide a student/prisoner, trust is an issue, as one can imagine. A student in prison needs to know that he is safe with the instructor, that the person who's helping him is not doing so as a trick, to later belittle him for needing that help or use that knowledge to oppress him. As a means of defense, most students in the prison classroom become obnoxious and attempt intimidating feats to thwart the confrontation that comes about when one combats the drive to desire. What struck my students most about my methodological inversion was the demand to own oneself. Whereas once I made a point of silencing desire and, indeed, the self, as a means of rigid training—a sacrifice of the subjective self, to pursue the objectivity that the act of learning may require—I now created a space in which progressive movement in education was a tacit practice of desire. They, knowing my will and refusal to suffer the humiliation often created by one's vulnerability, were shocked to hear me state my fears, my yearnings, and the sort of affection I realized I have for every person who honors me by allowing me in enough to help them learn. I imagine that this could be a form of transference, but I'll call it an association that I developed from my learnings with you, Elizabeth.

And so, a sort of desire-education reverberation sprung from our connecting. We began to have amazing conversations through the mail and then in person, and as we began to close the gap between each other and within ourselves, our interactions with others benefitted, too.

Shortly after you sent me the queer studies books, I read Butler's "Desire, Rhetoric, and Recognition in Hegel's *Phenomenology of Spirit*," and while I have little familiarity with Georg Hegel's work, I still found much of Butler's discussion shockingly apropos to the carceral condition. In one section, she explains:

The substance that is known, and which the subject *is*, is thus an all-encompassing web of interrelations, the dynamism of life itself, and, consequently, the principle that all specific determinations are not what they appear to be. And yet, as beings who must be cultivated to the absolute standpoint, we begin with the determinate, the particular, and the immediate, and treat it as if it were absolute, and then learn through that misplaced certainty that the Absolute is broader and more internally complicated tha[n] we originally thought. The history of these deceptions is a progressive one inasmuch as we understand how these deceptions imply each other as necessary consequences, and that together they reveal that the *insufficiency* of any given relationship to the Absolute is the basis of its *interdependence* on other relationships, so that the history of deception is, finally, the unity of internal relations which is the Absolute. ("Desire" 53)

As soon as I read this I knew I had to share it with my students. I wrote the passage on the white board in the middle of class, without explanation, and waited. It took days, but eventually students began to ask questions, each of them making a comment, then adding to or arguing for or against what another had proposed, until the whole class was involved, eventually drawing out the Department of Corrections educator who demanded to know what all the ruckus was about.

All I contributed to the discussion was to say, "This is the trap that holds us back from fully embodying ourselves."

Moments later, I erased the whole board and wrote, again from Butler, "As a being of metaphysical desires, the human subject is prone to fiction, to tell himself the lies that he needs to live" (53).

The next day, I began a whole new list of vocabulary words that began *pedagogy, hegemony, catachresis, queer,* and the ball was rolling.

As this dynamic developed in the classroom, a similar excitement rippled between us as we talked about the texts and ideas and began to express ourselves as closer friends, and then as we surrendered to each other and ourselves.

* * *

The resonance of Butler's words in respect to desire bespeaks the tendency of the prisoner to deny that aspect of the self. In Butler's critique of the Absolute, the point most notable in the carceral conversation is the determination of how the pressure of this—"the determinate, the particular, and the immediate"—existence becomes the absolute (53), in turn creating within the imprisoned mind the dialogue in which desire as a fiction becomes manifest, yet desire as a function of the self, as a real (as opposed to theoretical) tendency of being. This negative construction of the world (prison) and ourselves in that world perpetuates a form of self-hating corrections epitomized by the American prison industry. As I have travelled along this path, progressing with the march of years, I have seen one pattern in the recurring criminal: a reinforced belief that who and what he is, is unacceptable.

But, instead of treating the symptom—the denial of desire—the system hauls hundreds of thousands of people back to prison where it is hoped their individuality will be annihilated, that the prisoner will become institutionalized, relying on the system for direction. This seems like a rather grand and condemning assertion, yet one has but to exist within this space, and revolt against that programming long enough, to see it as I have. Are there opportunities for education and job training? Yes, but those opportunities are predicated by a requisite knuckling-under by the hopeful and often drowning prisoner. Step out of line, even in the most obscure of ways, and these advantages will be revoked. Thus, most prisoners fail even to attempt to take advantage of a program, for the fear of owning a desire, only to have it stripped away on the whim of the prison staff. To have an awareness of such a dynamic pervading one's world does not mean one experiences that dynamic any less, but forces the prisoner to choose between one of two possible futures: criminality or annihilation.

As Butler offers:

> The role of externalization and alterity in the determination of something as true is made clear partially through the introduction of the notion of Force.... Force is essential to the transition from consciousness to self-consciousness because it posits the externality of the world of sensuous and perpetual reality as one that is essentially related to consciousness itself; in effect, Force posits externalization as a necessary moment of thought. (55–56)

Force, in this sense, is the policy of normative behavior within the prison construct. The externality is the desire of recreating oneself through education and, in general, gaining enough distance from the prison construct to perceive alterity in the first place. For while Force may be "essential for the transition from consciousness to self-consciousness," because it reminds one of the "sensuous reality" of the world, the destination establishes a desire for violent validation of that consciousness, or a psychic suicide.

One goal of the criminal within prison is to exist amidst that Force and deny the destination, thereby remaining fervently as oneself. Sometimes the violence of this validation is made real, physical, a manifestation of psychic turmoil that lacks an alternate means of expression. Other times, that violence equates to disobedience, whether civil or a refusal to engage the system or its agents at all, all the while maintaining agency and initiative, states not often experienced, and experienced only more rarely as the years fade away. How then do prisoners transcend the confines of their incarceration and reach any form of rehabilitation while enduring the constant barrage of dehumanization and indoctrination of normativity? The battle of attrition seems always to favor the construct of prison and not those imprisoned.

Prison should be a place where those of us who have committed crimes can go to commune with ourselves and better understand who we are and what motivates us—a chrysalis or cocoon whereby those who transgressed the law can rehabilitate themselves and redefine success by their standards, not by someone else's. But this is not the system we have. The system we have is bent on stamping out one type of human: one that will not ask questions, one that will not stand up for him/herself or anyone else—one that will not, in other words, buck the system or disrupt their ideals. For people to heal and change, they must be allowed to be themselves, and prison doesn't do that. As naturalist and former inmate Ken Lamberton states, prison "scours you down to essences—shelter, food, and hope.... Prison has the power of a lapidary with his rock tumbler. It can produce polished gems or worthless sand, depending on the time, depending on the rock" (137). Those few whose being is not turned to dust and who are positively transformed—by becoming comfortable with their queerness or some other facet of their being—do so as a form of revolt against the system, a political act bucking the stricture of policy. Those who find themselves do so despite the DOC, and they are few, less than 1 percent by my observations, and that is a poor investment.

* * *

You and I, Elizabeth, have completely different perspectives and methods regarding prison, experiencing desire, and how we approach science and education. Whereas I am imprisoned, the object of my desire remains primarily outside of this construct. Even my intentional and bloody-minded struggle for education and to educate others within this space is a manifestation or projection of my desire to be free, to experience the liberty of choice. To learn what I like, love who I feel I must, in effect, own my freedom—the Ultimate Other as defined by my desire.

My desire for you, Elizabeth, is a cognitive denial of the imprisonment of liberty, friendship and compassion, eros and logos, a space in which I can exist in which I am not in-prison-ed. And the development of our desire of and for one another, for me, has meant, equally, a commitment to creating a place within myself for education and for investigating internal relations, that, as Butler points out, "are … what desire seeks to articulate, render explicit, so that desire is a tacit pursuit of metaphysical knowledge, the human way that such knowledge 'speaks'" ("Desire" 55). In my becoming aware of this, I combat my own imprisoned mind's tendency to reject desire and embrace the death drive, as Lee Edelman describes the Lacanian conceptualization in this respect. The realization of this continually spurs me to encourage the prisoners around me to resist the Forces of the prison construct and retain agency for themselves. Not to suggest that my audience is always so receptive, yet neither my desire nor the drive I experience to fulfill my desire is reliant on that. To the contrary, I understand that limited or diminished receptivity as proof of the pervasiveness of the Force that the prison construct infuses and with which it confuses most of the population, both in and outside of prison.

* * *

In Butler's "Bodily Inscriptions, Performative Subversions," she writes that "In *Discipline and Punish*, Foucault challenges the language of internalization as it operates in the service of the disciplinary regime of the subjection and subjectivation of criminals" (109). I know so little of Michel Foucault; even so, I would suppose a constitutive understanding by dint of my carceral habitation. As Butler relates, Foucault asserts that, in relation to the incarcerated:

> the strategy has been not to enforce a repression of their desires, but to compel their bodies to signify the prohibitive law as their very essence, style, and necessity. That law is not literally internalized, but incorporated, with the consequence that bodies are produced which signify that law on and through the body; there the law is manifest as the essence of their selves, the meaning of their soul, their conscience, the law of desire. ("Bodily Inscriptions" 109)

This idea is well understood by the inmate on a cellular level, but from the receiving end. Whether queer, criminal, criminal-queer, or just some unlucky civilian caught in the machinations of the system and imprisoned, that deep inscription of the repressive, prohibitive law has the feeling of obliteration.

The (temporary) obliteration of the ability to desire, resulting from incarceration, also speaks to a more universally experienced conflict in the impossible balancing between the desire for self and for that which is outside the self. Butler writes:

> Insofar as we desire, we desire in two mutually exclusive ways; in desiring something else, we lose ourselves, and in desiring ourselves, we lose the world. At this stage in the dramatization of desire, unacceptable impoverishment seems to be its consequence; either as narcissism or as enthrallment with an object, desire is at odds with itself, contradictory and dissatisfied. ("Desire" 63)

Every time I read this passage, I am reminded of the criminal career of denial of desire and how that plays into learning, how that denial of desire transfers into a denial of education. For to surrender to the desire of education is to relinquish a part of the already-diminished self, that diminishment a direct result of incarceration and the humiliation of needing, per the social standard, to be corrected.

Few enterprises are available or more capable of restoring to a prisoner a sense of accomplishment, self, or *jouissance* than is education. In my early correspondences with you, Elizabeth, the sheer scale of my restoration was little different than having several bones broken then reset at once, such was the shock and relief. Moved to offer others that very same restoration, the past several years have continued to afford me respite within this place. I feel a type of reverberation. Elizabeth, you are moved toward a radical styling of human learning and appreciation, an understanding that incorporates one's being, and your bringing that style of teaching to me created a wave or surge that I then used to help those I taught and continue to teach, which spread out into the prison, and eventually prisons, as those students moved to other facilities. Similarly, ideas on queer theory were transferred, and the return message was embrace.

Recently, another inmate, Jeffrey, questioned me about what I was up to. I explained the above passages from Butler, then my own perception of how heteronormative attributes were inscribed upon us, and met one of the most enthusiastic audiences I have ever encountered. Most rewarding was not that he agreed with me, but that he wanted to understand more of what I was discussing—the words themselves, the ideas. His understanding of my sharing what I had with him was that I wanted his thoughts on it, not simply to have him absorb mine. That's the greatest aspect of teaching and of owning desire: the communication, the exchange.

* * *

I have found the actual process of learning within prison to be one of the most exhausting pursuits an inmate can undertake. I say this both as a student and as a teacher in prison. The prisoner endures a constant barrage of stimuli over the course of any given day, particularly in high custody levels where ever more violent and disruptive prisoners are generally held. So, for the prisoner pursuing education, any time spent giving such an amount of focus to learning does not receive a respite from having to maintain focus on the potential dangers of carceral life; instead, he or she must invest even more energy and attention to both. This may at first appear contrary to my earlier writing, in that I have relayed how I used the learning process to escape the pressures of prison. My meaning, I should clarify, is that in maintaining such disciplined focus on personal safety and on learning, I had less time to consider myself; I became almost consumed by study. I analyzed the prison, the prisoners, the guards, and the subjects found in books. I toed chinks in walls, and rust-rotting fences, weak points in the prison perimeters and the prisoners' posturing, and all this objective thinking shielded me from the subject of myself until I was strong enough to do that.

In considering myself with regard to prison, I came to a point in which I could appreciate the emotional difficulty I, as a prisoner, experience every waking moment within these walls, and how closed off from myself I was (and still am in many ways). I found that my coping method in prison is the same as what I had before prison, only several orders of magnitude more severe, that method being to repress every emotional twitch I feel into something unrecognizable; to metabolize all emotion into focus and energy I use to perform a task, much of this energy expended in workouts and study sessions.

I cannot speak on the inner workings of any other; I do not know, often enough, what pushes or holds another prisoner back. But I have tried to give other prisoners the benefit of my help in their educational pursuits and at times have seen the same emotional turmoil boiling within them: so much of it fear and sadness, in my opinion, the largest contributors to the negativity in prisons and the motivating force that fuels a person's, for lack of a better term, paralysis of hope, that negative of self that leads to inaction, violence, drug use, lying, and the perpetuation of the prison construct. What I find inspiring in all of these are those who refuse to submit to that paralysis and struggle and muddle on, sometimes for years, learning to read, to pass the state-mandated literacy test, to earn their GED, and to take their first college courses by correspondence. I cannot adequately describe the sort of pride or enthusiasm in such moments when a student of mine receives the results of a test he has recently taken, a test by which he had been beaten so many times before, that he can't even look at the report, bringing me the envelope in the hope that I'll skip the "You failed again" and get right to the "Okay, we need to work on...," only to see me smiling and handing the paper back to him with a "Well done." That moment of disbelief and triumphant joy is one of the most incredulous and validating moments many of my students have begun with. Having seen students squirm in the classroom beneath the stress of having to admit the weakness of ignorance, illiteracy, or some other issue like having the desire for more education and fearing losing face among peers because of that desire, I am repeatedly reminded of the power education affords people. To see one of these people evolve, in my presence, into a man who can more fully represent himself, is nothing short of an honor, rare though it is.

I always think of Gerald Wayne when I think of this. As a 40-year-old man, he entered the prison system completely incapable of reading even his own name. I could not believe that at first. I could not believe that to such a degree. I called him a fake, a fraud, a lazy no-good wannabe gangster, and we fought right there in the middle of the classroom. Afterwards, I asked him, "You really can't read?"

And he said, "I told you no, motherfucker. Keep fuckin' with me. We can fight every day, honky."

He could not read. And we did fight, three times more over the next seven years. He got his ass kicked every time, but he never backed down or even hesitated once. You might question why I would put up with a student who was so eager to fight his teacher. But it wasn't about the violence: it was his presence that moved me. He wanted to learn; he just didn't have anyone who would or could brave his terrors.

At first I only aimed to make sure he could read enough to pass the state literacy test so he could earn his sentence's 85 percent mark and get out early. Our second fight began when he told me he was done, that he was too old, too stupid, and too stubborn to learn "all this bullshit." The head teacher, who had become used to our arguments, grabbed his pack of cigarettes and called the rest of the class for a smoke break, mumbling, "Just clean up the blood," on his way out. After we had turned the classroom into a crime scene, and re-set it all, he asked me why I gave a damn. I told him I didn't—lying—and asked that he take the test one last time before quitting. He agreed.

Gerald passed with a tenth-grade average. He accused me of cheating for him, and we fought again. But not once after that did he ever again threaten to quit.

On the day he graduated, he told me two things. He had written a letter to his son, and I was the only person to give him anything for free.

I couldn't help asking what I'd given him. "What do you mean, Gerald?"

"We bled together, Lunn. You've sat so many hours beating that stuff into my head. I wanted to kill you, man. I wouldn'ta ever done any of this if you wouldn'ta been here. You gave me this, man. I get out five years early because of you. I'm starting college because of you."

"All I did was point the way," I said. "You did the rest."

"Yeah. Well, thanks."

That was the last time Gerald and I spoke, though we remained on the same yard. We had no reason to avoid one another, but without our mutual movement toward his education, we were back to being two people with nothing in common but history, which isn't much in prison. He did begin referring people to me, though—friends who dared to hear his story and who dared to intimate the same whispered desire to think beyond what they believed was closed off to them.

Not all of my students in and out of the classroom dove so deeply as did Gerald, nor pushed me to reach as far into myself to find the right path for them on which to learn, but all my students have shared a common trait: the nerve to resist the past and rise up with a full heart against the learned despair of incarceration; to say to themselves that there lies more in the world and within themselves.

* * *

In the classroom, interpersonal landscapes collide with the anxiety of coming out, of wanting skills and knowledge, the coming out always a combination of desires, conscious and unconscious. And as can be imagined in any classroom, the interplay of those personal upwellings develops the classroom dynamic. Inside the prison classroom, where fear and power subsume all other currents of consciousness, prisoners regularly revolve through cycles of desire, expectation, despair, doubt, fear, and relief as new learning affirms their desire. I remember the first time I realized how queer the whole process was. The idea made so much sense in prison, where no one presents one's full self, and the conflict within eats away at one's self-image, undermining the liberation that education provides.

Finding oneself in a prison classroom chock full of competing personalities, with some shutting down, creates a demand to remove the students from the usual defensive condition and create an atmosphere of acceptance and appreciation where difference and intelligence measure along alternate lines, affording the students opportunity to contribute as in colloquy rather than the normal soliloquy of lecture. I have always found the interactive approach effective for classroom learning, often reducing my influence to initial guidelines, a goal, and support, allowing conversation between the students to develop, arguments to flare, and ideas to form naturally. While this is the slow road, it creates a third space in which more aggressive personalities must cooperate with other, more introverted ones, where queerness is experienced as students come to recognize their strengths and weaknesses together, help one another, and come to new understandings.

I keep thinking of chemistry and our world, and what thrills me the most in all of this: the idea of our being naught more than atoms and those atoms composed of electrons, protons, and neutrons that are made up of quarks, and those, strings. And all that matter a relationship between energy and vibration, which leads to the theory that the universe is nothing more than this and those pockets of sentience commuting and communicating with each other. And, as each of us rises to the challenge of learning about our world, and about our yearnings, we add our voices, our vibration to the collective of the universe.

In the classroom, as I combat the difficulties prison itself creates, in the way prisons generally and systematically encourage psychological repression, I must find a way to eliminate that effect upon myself and the rest of my class. In so many ways, each person is different, and insecure and full of desires, which they have learned not to communicate, and my best method for dispelling this indoctrinated psychic lethargy is to discuss chemistry. Chemistry is unusual to teach in a prison classroom, because most students enter into the experience without the ability to properly navigate the periodic table or basic mathematics, but for this I skip the numbers and only focus on the relationship of matter/energy and posit that, regardless of your view, we are matter, and our particles interact and mingle with each other. We are all connected, whether we are different in origin or spin, and we need that difference to further the dialogue, to achieve greater knowledge and wisdom about ourselves/our universe. With that said, the type of learning you choose is not so important as that you learn and lift your voice in the chorus of minds all desiring, all yearning to express themselves in this universe, in this space, contributing to our progress, to finding out who we are, because, in the end, we, each of us, feel that we matter.

We are matter, and we all matter.

* * *

It's a point of pride that I can so easily state that I study queer theory. I recall, not that long ago, I would have to clear my throat beforehand. And now I confront others in this space with a praxis and pedagogy that queers us both simultaneously in that confrontation.

Sometimes, I find myself shaking my head, still, at this queerness I have imposed upon myself in this place, among the dangers the other captives represent by dint of their suppressed fears and unpredictable reactions. Even so, I cannot deny the power such an approach lends to this situation. For, it is queer to me that I, a straight-identified, white, educated male with a history of violence and a background of normative leanings, should be so intrigued by the issues queer theorists interrogate that I should want to separate myself from the familiar and safe mantle of heteronormativity to better interrogate the construct of who I am within the construct of prison to better understand others and to better understand the hegemonic underpinning of prisons as a whole.

In years past, I would have dodged such alienation, content to keep silent about my observations and questions. Throughout my youth and into adulthood, I held back from vocalizing arguments, because they felt moot. And, as a criminal, I fully appreciated that questions could create problems. Yet now my view is different. I feel I must challenge ideas, ideals, and ideations, if only to better understand our interpersonal fluctuations. This is typically misconstrued as my acting the devil's advocate, but no one gave me such worried stares before I met you, Elizabeth.

* * *

Prisoners wait. Their loved ones wait. We and so many others wait, holding on to desire while bracing against the careers of the systemically death driven. In all this waiting there is the recognition of despair, despair resulting from a system of "domination and enslavement," as Butler might well describe the prison system, and "what Kierkegaard termed the despair of not being able to die" (Butler, "Desire" 80).[5] Despair against the struggle of desire for identity/subjectivity, creativity, autonomy, "the desire to become the whole of life … always an implicit struggle against the easier routes of death; … contradictions, that keep one from wanting life enough" (81). As Butler conveys regarding the Hegelian concepts in "Lord and Bondsman," "In the case of the bondsman, the desire to live, specified as the desire to create the goods to live, cannot be integrated with the desire to be free until he relinquishes his shackles through disobedience and the attendant fear of death" (81). Our desire then is positioned in a time and space in which it can be expressed only through disobedience, since, to be whole (one of our desires), we must subvert the mores of this prison, and deny the implicit paths of our lives.

* * *

To begin writing this piece in which we witness to our desires and bracing, and embracing, Josh and I asked ourselves what had become beautiful in us as a result of our thinking queerly. What was more poignant or human that was not before? What dimensions of our existence had opened—what revealed and exorcised of that which Toni Morrison calls the "unspeakable things unspoken" ("Unspeakable")?

You and I, Josh, have both been closed and broken open by the unspeakable, both becoming fuller human beings through our confiding our nightmares, crimes, and griefs, and our recognition of our desire for self-realization. Through compassionate education, we have found meaningful knowledge that serves as a healing balm for our fragmented "uninformed, unknowing spirit[s]," where learning has meaningfully connected us to our lives (hooks 19).

As you have entered the last two years of your incarceration, the stressors of confinement have split you, and us, apart, but "The point," you reminded me in your last letter, "is the effect our being together had on the other and others. The point is our love for living and education." Indeed, it is.

In *Beloved*, Morrison asserts that the past's horrors can be recognized and integrated into a certain beauty essential for us to fulfill "the desire to become the whole of life" (Butler, "Desire" 81). Josh, you, and I have struggled against despair, but in that fractious, queer third space we have also seen ourselves as wholly human, desiring the quantum exchange of love, and at the center of that love realizing our own being.

As the poet Jack Gilbert urges, "We should insist while there is still time." And we are.

Notes

1. The ACLU cites 1 in 31.
2. Though the concept of liminality, interstices, etc. is not new, Homi Bhabha's "third space," from *The Location of Culture* (1994), is that specifically post-colonial meeting place of cultural clash, hybridity, and synergy.
3. At least eight of Josh's letters sent to me over a three-month span, letters that contained many pages toward our essay, disappeared while he was housed on a yard well known for its lack of accountability in regard to mail delivery. Many of my letters to him during this period likewise vanished. We had to resort to his bringing pages into visitation (a clear violation of DOC policy), or I could not have completed the conference presentation that predated this essay, or the essay itself.
4. In spring 2011, Josh was sent to "the hole" (solitary confinement in a 6' × 8' cell) for a week or so for a book I had sent him for the ecofeminism class, science historian Londa Schiebinger's *Nature's Body: Gender in the Making of Modern Science*. On the cover is the painting "Nature" (1791), by Hubert-Francois Gravelot, which, as was iconic for the period, depicts Nature as a woman with breasts bared. The property people kept it for a while, as possible contraband, then determined, after numerous tries on his part to explain the text to them, that it was not sexually explicit material and so let him have it. Later, in a routine search of his personal property, the book was confiscated as pornography and Josh was issued a ticket. He appealed, following the usual tiresome process up through all the levels, but was ultimately sent to the hole. Later, the book was approved again and returned to him. The ticket was not removed, however, and certainly no one apologized. More recently, they confiscated as sexually explicit an issue of *The New Yorker*.
5. Butler is referring to Søren Kierkegaard's *Sickness Unto Death* 18.

WORKS CITED

American Civil Liberties Union (ACLU). n.d. *Prison Crisis*. American Civil Liberties Union and the ACLU Foundation. Web. 25 June 2014.

Bhabha, Homi. 1994. *The Location of Culture*. Abingdon/New York: Routledge. Print.

Butler, Judith. Desire, Rhetoric, and Recognition in Hegel's *Phenomenology of Spirit* (1987). In Salih and Butler, 39–89. Print.

———. Bodily Inscriptions, Performative Subversions (1990). In Salih and Butler, 90–118. Print.

Edelman, Lee. 2004. *No Future: Queer Theory and the Death Drive*. Durham: Duke University Press. Print.

Evans, Nicholas. 1995. *The Horse Whisperer*. New York: Dell. Print.

Gilbert, Jack. 2001. Tear It Down. In *The Great Fires: Poems 1982–1992*. New York: Knopf. Print.

Glaze, Lauren E., and Erinn J. Herberman. 2013. *Correctional Populations in the United States, 2012* (NCJ 243936). Bureau of Justice Statistics, Office of Justice Programs, US Department of Justice, December 19, 2013. Web. 18 July 2014.

hooks, bell. 1994. *Teaching to Transgress: Education as the Practice of Freedom*. New York: Routledge. Print.

International Centre for Prison Studies. n.d. *World Prison Brief*. ICPS. Web. 18 July 2014.

Kierkegaard, Søren. 1983. *The Sickness Unto Death: A Christian Psychological Exposition for Upbuilding and Awakening*. 1849. Ed. and trans. Howard V. Hong and Edna H. Hong. Princeton: Princeton University Press. Print.

Lamberton, Ken. 2007. *Time of Grace: Thoughts on Nature, Family, and the Politics of Crime and Punishment*. Tucson: The University of Arizona Press. Print.

Morrison, Toni. 1987. *Beloved*. New York: Knopf. Print.

———. 1988. *Unspeakable Things Unspoken: The Afro-American Presence in American Literature*. Ann Arbor: The University of Michigan, 7 October 1988. The Tanner Lectures on Human Values. Rpt. in *The Tanner Lectures on Human Values, XI*, ed. Grethe B. Peterson, 123–163. Salt Lake City: University of Utah Press, 1990. Print.

Ruffolo, David V. 2012. Educating-Bodies: Dialogism, Speech Genres, and Utterances *as* the Body. In *Queer Masculinities: A Critical Reader in Education*, ed. John Landreau and Nelson Rodriguez, 289–306. Dordrecht/Heidelberg/London/New York: Springer Science+Business Media B.V. Print.

Salih, Sara, ed., with Judith Butler. 2004. *The Judith Butler Reader*. Malden/Oxford/Victoria: Blackwell. Print.

Schiebinger, Londa. 2004. *Nature's Body: Gender in the Making of Modern Science.* 1993. Piscataway: Rutgers University Press. Print.

Walmsley, Roy. 2013. *World Prison Population List.* 10th ed. London: International Centre for Prison Studies and University of Essex. November 21, 2013. Web. 18 Aug 2014. PDF file.

AnimalQueer

CHAPTER 17

The Bestiary of Friends

Margot Young

My queer landscape is haunted by beasts. They spectrally inhabit pastoral "scenes," for agriculturalism represents a form of humanization as normalization which has literally resurfaced the earth, and in doing so has marginalized, extirpated, and confined those other beasts with whom we once co-habited. Thus "the human," like all beasts, is inextricably bound to the history of agro-colonial claims upon territory once shared.

The notion of the bestial was used by colonialists in construals of Native peoples as "brutes" (Brickman 24), "primitives" (Roberts 56–57), and sexual deviants (Gaard 126–127), and the bestialization of indigenous peoples has also been closely associated in agro-colonizing discourse with the demonization of the lupine (Marshall 16). The charge of rapaciousness leveled at the wolf was also used to characterize Native peoples and represented a form of moral condemnation that justified violences against them both. The bestial was construed as synonymous with *in-humanity,* the lack of qualities proper to the civilized human, and I will argue that it comprised those *intractable deviants* who could not be incorporated because they resisted agro-colonial normalizations. The wolf, the archetypal deviant beast, resists the territorial normalizations of the land, and as Jacques

M. Young (✉)
Site for Contemporary Psychoanalysis,
Church Hill, Lydbrook, UK

E. McNeil et al. (eds.), *Mapping Queer Space(s) of Praxis and Pedagogy*, Queer Studies and Education,
DOI 10.1007/978-3-319-64623-7_17

Derrida notes, the exclusion of the wolf instates borders that delineate human societies under the law (*Beast* 1–31). The figure of the queer, who, like the wolf, has been subject to demonization and bestialization, also patrols the borders of normative humanity in resisting incorporation to heteronormalized human identities. The bestial was equated with madness and sexual nonconformity during the "Great Confinement," prior to these states becoming classified in psycho-medical discourse as deviant, abnormal, and yet specifically "human" conditions that could be subject to diagnostic and treatment regimens (Foucault, *History of Madness* 148–149).

The cultural and ecological effects of wolf hunting have not yet been fully acknowledged, and the history of their extirpation cannot be separated from the persecution and marginalization of indigenous peoples. Wolves and Native peoples were simultaneously driven from territories they had shared for thousands of years in Europe, Asia, and the Americas. Settler colonialists equated wolves with Native people by describing both as bestial and as deviant. A narrative that attributed a quality of "lupine savagery" to Native people was employed in justification of genocidal and ecocidal violence. The joint demonization of wolves and Native people is tellingly illustrated by their becoming the subjects of joint bounties offering double payment for the killing of both an Indian and a wolf (Marshall 16). I will suggest that this joint bestialization continues to characterize settler-colonial attitudes toward wolves and Native peoples, particularly where Tribes have defended wolves against the resumption of wolf hunting as sport or for "population management."

Wolves, Native peoples, and queers represent resistance to the moral incorporations and physical confinements that have constructed agro-colonial subjectivities. This piece seeks to recuperate the bestial in a queer reversal of the assimilation of treatable and tractable deviance to the category of the human, in other words, the *re-bestialization of* the human. In relation to agro-colonialism, queering the landscape represents nothing less than human decolonial withdrawal, an aim that is already being pursued by Native peoples and some queer and two-spirit activists (Morgensen).

The deviant has been deployed both as a signifier of the bestial nonhuman and as a figure of the "abnormal" within the *specifically* human. The deviant and the beast have been deployed to define what counts as inclusive to, and what, *or who*, is excluded from the properly human. The instability of the category of the human is revealed through a study of the shifting positions of deviance, which has been located on opposite sides of the human/animal divide, depending on the specific historical time periods and/or geo-political context in which the category of the deviant has been constructed. This essay will propose that the identity of "being human" is itself intrinsically normalizing, and that both psychological and agro-colonial discourses work together to instate and re-iterate normalized identities as specifically human. I will also argue that queer theoretical work on identity, including some "queer ecological" writing, due to its reliance on psychoanalytically derived accounts of the psychic constitution of the human subject, has yet to address psychology's conflation of human exceptionalism with heteronormative subjectivity.

QUEERING SUBJECTIVITY *Is* QUEERING THE LAND

Rather than conceiving of themselves as only one animal being among a multiplicity of eco-systemically connected others, settler-colonial humans have assumed a subjectivity that is *ecologically separative*. This has arisen, according to Tim Morton, as a consequence of humans becoming agricultural and assuming that Others of all kinds are always available for exploitation, not only as a source of production, but also for *reproduction* ("Oedipal Logic"). For Morton, the presumption that nonhuman beings constitute an endless supply of "natural resources" is a disavowal of eco-systemic reality ("Oedipal Logic" 10–12). Agriculturalism produces "the human" as a category of being that is "exceptional," separatively singled out from nonhuman beings, while animals and plants are collectively Othered as "nature" or as "the environment" (Morton, *Ecology Without Nature*). Yaqui animal rights activist Rod Coronado makes a similar point when he describes the settler-colonial position as one that views animals, people, and land as resources "to be exploited and dominated.... [, which] is the foundation for the invasion of planet earth" (NAALPO). He connects animal liberation and decolonial activism by pointing out that, "long before there was an animal rights movement, there were indigenous peoples defending the earth and her animals with their lives. And they still are!" (NAALPO).

The hunting of wolves *en masse* was part of human agro-colonial appropriation of land that established the borders of agriculturalized human settlements, whose social organization also brought forth agriculturalized human *subjects*. Those who would not, or could not, become domesticates; those deemed to be unassimilable to agricultural, and later, to agro-industrial resource exploitation, came to represent the deviant beast who was both opposed to, and excluded from, the world of human domestic organization where agriculturalism is the norm.

When settler-colonial humans projected their own rapaciousness onto bestialized others, Native people and wolves were particular targets, partly because as hunters, they were rivals for agricultural territory. But this projection also staked out the psychic territory of settler-colonial subjecthood in opposition to the *intolerable bestial other* who threatened the norm of exploitative colonial agriculture. Queering the land means dismantling normalized territories, both physical and psychic, that act to Other the "world." This includes commonplace notions of "the wild" and "the environment." Denuded of the bestial, "the wild" has become a set of geo-political bordered zones, including areas such as national parks or territory at an ever-decreasing margin of land yet to be unexploited. The entire surface of the earth is now designated as land subject to human control.

The Instability of "The Animal"

Human separation from, and control of, populations of nonhumans signifies, as Derrida argues, a "radical discontinuity" between the animal and the human, including the presumption that certain specific psychological capacities, including the capacity to mourn, delineate humans from animals. For Derrida, even when we name "the animals" collectively, as an Othered heterogeneous group, we practice a form of violence against them (Derrida, *The Animal* 134–135). This "scapegoating" of the nonhuman legitimizes the "industrial mechanical chemical hormonal and genetic violence to which man has been submitting animal life for the past two centuries" (26). Animals inhabit spaces beyond the horizon of imaginary human landscapes of interiority. Viewed from the interior of the human psyche, nonhumans are fantasmic psycho-bio-political objects. This fantasy legitimates their mass consumption not only literally as food, clothing, and medicine, but also as visual objects of the human gaze, of anthropomorphic projections, and as the scopic objects of environmental consumerism (Mortimer-Sandilands).

Morton has proposed a queered ecology that will abandon the "disastrous" term "animal" that erroneously presumes a clear boundary between what is and isn't life. Rather than determining where life forms begin and end, he describes this border as "thick," and filled with "paradoxical entities" ("Queer Ecology" 276). Ecology, he argues, "humiliates" the human and spawns "politicized intimacy with other beings ... an intimacy well described by queer theory when it argues that sexuality has never been a case of norm versus its pathological variants" (278).

The deconstruction of the human/not-human divide means invoking boundary crossings that query the divisions derived from the notion of "species," as Donna Haraway has proposed, in favor of co-habiting bodies and the multiplicity of beings who share mortal commonality. While the agricultural "domestication" of the nonhuman has existed for several thousand years (Diamond), the intensification of human exploitation of nonhuman beings and objects over the past 300 years, into the global-scale organized exploitation of Others as resource, is significant for the development of ecologically separative human subjectivity, because of the presumption that there always *is* an Other available for exploitation.

THE INSTABILITY OF "THE HUMAN"

As Cary Wolfe has noted, there is a difficulty with contemporary rights discourse due to the assumption that the violence inherent to "dehuman-ization" also means that degradation is intrinsic to the state of "animaliza-tion" (21), as is shown by the negative construal of humans being "treated like animals." Liberal rights discourse presumes that a less violent, or a more "civilized," humanity is needed to counter "inhuman" treatment. Haraway makes the point that "humanity" is, by virtue of its distinction from nonhuman Others, predicated on violences inherent to the human having become set apart. She notes that only a human can be murdered; it is seen as a moral outrage to degrade the human to the level of the "kill-able"; we call this "genocide" and conceive of it as a loss of our "humanity." But, for Haraway, humanity itself is being constructed through the exclu-sion of suffering animal others (78–79).

The identity of "being human" will always, by virtue of its intrinsic constitution through Otherings, be the cause of inhuman(e) violences. The insistence that we become more "humane" runs the danger of entrenching further the separative and delusional position that generated the ecocidal and genocidal imperatives underpinning the agro-colonization of the planet, and which has resulted in the global ecological predicament of the *Anthropocene*.

If civilized humanity enacts violences, including the violences of nor-malization, upon others of all kinds, including other "peoples," then an eco-queer critique of human/nonhuman relations suggests a reading of "de-humanization" that, rather than propelling us to become *more human,* urges that we should become *less human,* or as Lee Edelman suggests, queerly "inhuman" (109).

The ejection of the bestial from the human and the projection of bestial animality onto Native peoples act together to instate "the human" as ecologically separative. However, shifting parameters in relation to what counts as human reveal the instability of the category of "the human" itself. Forms of bestialization vary according to the normalizing requirements of a given biopolitical context. What counts as properly human morphs across different historical periods and cultures, and can either incorporate or exclude Others when defining and redefining what constitutes the human. In relation to the signification of deviance, two seemingly opposite trajectories can be identified: one in which the deviant is de-bestialized and *assimilated* to a medico-judicial category of humanity, and the other where the deviant is bestialized and entirely *excluded* from the category of humanity.

Whether producing animalized or humanized deviants, or bestialized nonhumans, "humanization" functions as disciplinary normativity. The discursive productions of human/beast dualisms have justified colonial and medico-legal violences and confinements, and the ecological destructions that have led to the global agro-industrialization of the planet have culminated in the irreversible alteration by humans of the biosphere.

THE DE-BESTIALIZATION OF DEVIANCE

Hidden in Michel Foucault's *History of Madness* is a history of the relation of the bestial to modern (Western) subjectivity. During the Great Confinement, the mad, who actually consisted of undesirables of all kinds, including the sexually depraved, as well as "the poor, the lame, the old and the lunatic" (Porter, "Foucault's Great" 47), were deemed to be "unnatural" and equated with beasts (Foucault, *History of Madness* 149). The emergence of psychological and medical discourses brought about a shift in the conception of bestial madness whereby it became differentiated into classifiable and/or treatable human sicknesses and abnormalities. When medical discourse divorced madness from bestiality, those formerly considered inhuman beasts became seen as abnormal variants of the human and were categorized as mentally or physically ill, or as in the case of many forms of disability, as mentally or physically defective. Enforced confinement was once again frequently the consequence in the nineteenth and twentieth centuries (Brignell, "When the Disabled").

As medicine and psychology were recuperating treatable or tractable deviance to the category of the human, the bestial also became differentiated from the "animal," in the sense that the term "animals" increasingly referred to nonhuman beings who were subject to control or confinement, for example, in zoological or agricultural contexts. In Foucauldian terms, animal bodies became docile. Although the term "docile" was originally applied by Foucault to human prison regimes (*Discipline and Punish*), it has since been extended by Foucault scholars from the field of animal studies to include all bodies, human and not-human, that are subject to human control within normalized physical spaces, such as prisons, zoos, slaughterhouses, and farms (Thierman).

Now "animals" became associated with "harmonious" nature (Foucault, *History of Madness* 373), and even pastoral idyll, in the Western cultural imaginary, while real nonhumans were subject to mass scale confinements, productions, and consumptions. Beasts, on the other hand—that is, those who were neither domesticated nor docile, such as wolves—were subject to intensified persecution. The marginalization of the latter was intrinsic to both the spatial delineation of agro-industrialization territory and the institution of modern agriculturalized *subjectivities*.

The Colonized Beast

While European medical discourse was expanding its classification of abnormality and incorporating deviance to the category of the human, European settler-colonialists were specifically associating sexual deviance with the bestial, in a move that excluded Native peoples from the category of the human. Respect for non-heterosexual subjectivities is common to many indigenous cultures across continents (Neill). Those identified by setter-colonialists as non-heteronormative were specific targets, and the esteem in which "two-spirit" persons were held in some Native cultures was viewed as evidence of primitivity. As Katz notes, "the colonial appropriation of the continent by white, Western 'civilization' included the attempt by the conquerors to eliminate various traditional forms of Indian homosexuality—as part of their attempt to destroy that Native culture which might fuel resistance'" (Katz, quoted in Gaard 126).

Even as European models of human deviance were incorporated into their own social structures, colonialists justified policies of genocide and marginalization by associating Native people with wolves (Roberts 47–56). Both lupine and indigenous bodies were viewed as irredeemable to "civilized" humanity, producing an unspeakable and uncanny paradox in which the so-called ravening wolf (Marvin 45) and "savage" native (Byrd 27) were subject to extirpational violences that exactly mirrored the qualities that "civilized" colonialists projected onto them.

The Psychoanalytic Beast

Psychology's de-bestialization of the human culminated in the psychoanalytic instatement of a specifically human sexuality, defined in terms of the repression of Oedipal sexual desires. This construed interiorized human psychicality as arising from the conflictual context of the heteronormative human family. Ironically, wolves were the source of this interpretive strategy. The trajectory that led Freud to construct the Oedipal "primal scene" as a site of forbidden incestuous longings was derived from Freud's interpretation that his most famous patient, the "Wolf-Man," had, aged 18 months, witnessed his parents engaged in sexual activity "in the manner of beasts" (*Infantile Neurosis* 41). This scene, never actually recounted by the patient, was retrospectively constructed by Freud from a dream the Wolf-Man reported having had at age four.

In the dream, several white wolves gazed in from a walnut tree outside the Wolf-Man's bedroom windows (29). Through a series of highly inventive interpretive maneuvers, these wolves' physical features—and the Wolf-Man's uncanny fairytale associations—were systematically denuded of their beastly characteristics in favor of significations relating to the traumatic repression of human incestuous longings (30–38). Freud "humanizes" the Wolf-Man's desires and fears by overlaying his experience of the bestial Other with specifically human sexual meanings. This effectively deletes the wolves as real presences in his patient's life and forecloses other possible meanings relating to real wolves, whom the young Wolf-Man had witnessed being hunted (Genosko 613–16).

In the nineteenth-century rural Russian context of the Wolf-Man's upbringing, multiple symbolic meanings were attributed to wolves, including being signifiers of mourning and arbiters of morality (Kelly). For Freud, however, the wolves as real beings had already been deleted, emptied of meaning, foreclosed by his own unwitting assumption of modern agriculturalized subjectivity. This disallows the possibility for significations that relate to real human-wolf relations, such as the unacknowledged effects of wolf hunting practices in Russia, which had been graphically detailed by Leo Tolstoy in *War and Peace* several decades earlier (580–592). Freud renders transparent his own duplicitous vision in relation to the imaginary divide between beast and human, because *he* is the one who envisions his patient's parents' sexual actions as *bestial*, prior to overlaying the scene as Oedipal *and* specifically human. Thus, he simultaneously inscribes human subjectivity as heteronormative and as exclusive of non-human others.

Freud repeats this strategy in *The Uncanny*, where experiences of the strange, monstrous, or fearsome are also linked to forbidden sexual desires and castration anxieties. It is hardly surprising that Gilles Deleuze and Felix Guattari, in their account of Freud's "Wolf-Man" case, deride Freud as having a talent for brushing up against the "uncanny truth" and passing it by. They argue that Freud's obsession with establishing the law of the castrating Oedipal father prevents him from developing a "truly zoological vision" in which there is a recognition of nonhuman multiplicities (Deleuze and Guattari 43).

THE DE-HUMANIZATION OF QUEER THEORY

Queer theory has relied heavily on psychoanalytic discourse, albeit in a subverted Butlerian form, for its account of the construction of hetero-normalized subjectivity. As I have discussed elsewhere, psychoanalytically derived "queer ecologies" also run the risk of re-iterating the human-animal divide when they uncritically apply theories that accept the central-ity of the human psyche (Young, "Queer Mad Animals"). If queer theory does not account for the exclusion of the bestial from the psychologized human subject, then opportunities for connecting the hetero-norm with the human-norm are missed.

Queer ecology has applied queer theory to normative conceptions of environment and ecology, through the application of Judith Butler's the-ory that subjectivity is characterized by melancholy due to the foreclosure of homosexual attachment, to propose that human subjectivity is also characterized by the foreclosure of human interrelatedness with the non-human, resulting in "environmental melancholy" (Morton, *Ecology*). While I am indebted to the contribution this analysis has made to my understanding of *ecological separativity*, I consider the reliance on psycho-analytic notions of repression and foreclosure problematic, as these con-cepts have not yet been queered in relation to their anthropocentrism, which matters for queer theory, as the ejection of the bestial is bound to the heteronormativity at the heart of the Freudian Oedipal primal scene. The use of the dream wolves as an interpretive foil for human sexualized subjectivity means that queer theory's reliance on Freudianism cannot be sustained unless the idea of the interiorized and separative psychological human subject is questioned. Butler suggests that identity is itself both an inevitable outcome of heteronormative Oedipalization and endlessly open to subversion (*Gender Trouble*). The question here is whether human identity, in the sense that Butler conceives of it, is merely a historically transient formation linked to the fantasmic notion of human exceptionalism. The construction of the psychologically symptomatic and interiorized "human" requires the deletion of the bestial other, binding psychoanalytically derived queer theory to the discourse of the specifically human, and to the agricultural presumption of nonhumans as exploitable resource.

Edelman, like Butler, draws on Lacanian psychoanalytic theory, and although he does not deconstruct Freudian anthropocentrism either, he comes closer to a queer critique of "the human" itself, with his proposal that queers identify as *inhuman*. Edelman suggests that the reach of the "inhuman" should be expanded, and argues for the impossibility of Butler's proposal for a radically antinormative human, as it is always predicated on a "liberal humanist future" (106). For Edelman, the "cult of the Child" as a signifier of normative futurity represents what it means to be human (30). In his well-known polemic that queers should oppose this by allying themselves with the death drive, he argues that we must turn our face from "everything 'human'" (Edelman 109). While I believe that this provocative exhortation has been misunderstood in relation to Edelman's Lacanian construal of the death drive, what is interesting for this piece is that he appears (perhaps inadvertently) to propose what amounts to an eco-queer critical praxis through his opposition to progressivity as a specifically *human* ideal. In this context, Edelman does not need to be read, as he so often is, as nihilistic, as from a queer ecological perspective he places queers in opposition to the normative and progressive humanization of the planet.

MANY BESTIAL RETURNS

While relations of enmity to wolves, as territorial and predatory nonhumans, arose within the ecological context of settler-colonial and agricultural land use, their demonization relates not only to their status as rival predator but to their signifying nonagricultural, or pre-agricultural, life. In this context, the bestial can be seen as a depository for the disavowed normalizations, losses, and violences inherent to the separative category of the agriculturalized human.

The marginalization of the bestial took a mere moment in the context of the history of the humanization of the biosphere. But the bestial is making a comeback. The tracks of beasts linger, not only because they are not long gone, but because humans appear to harbor not-so-secret desires for their return, and they are now, paradoxically, being "re-called to life"; "recovered" and "re-introduced" into what humans call the "wild." These recalled beasts inspire love and desire, provoke hate, evoke loss. But when we bring them back, do we know what we do? What do these wolves bring with them? How do they trouble us now?

Significant changes in the perception of wolves followed the initiation of wolf recovery programs in response to the listing of wolves in the US under the Endangered Species Act (Wyedeven et al.). Wolves were subsequently delisted in 2012, as their "recovery" was deemed "successful." Legal battles over the status of wolves have been fought since 2009, when the Obama administration upheld a decision to delist wolves made in the last days of the George W. Bush presidency (Earth Justice).

Following their re-introduction into Yellowstone National Park in 1993, wolves have become a source of fascination that has seen a reversal of their image in the popular imagination, from that of demonized beast to wilderness icon. This interest is not only evident in environmental politics, but in cultural productions that range from wildlife documentaries to a plethora of filmic and literary representations of wolves and wolf-human hybrids (van Horn). It seems that aspects of wolves' uncanniness formerly attributed to their fearsome characteristics have been increasingly supplemented, and even replaced, by their having become objects of desire and, arguably, markers of the lack intrinsic to identification as separatively human. It seems the bestial Other can become the beloved Other. What implications ensue for "the human" as psychic and biopolitical category if its bestial and deviant twin is recuperated, subject to a reversal whereby its beastly characteristics are replaced with desirable ones? Or, as is the case in many contemporary cultural productions of werewolves and vampires, the beastly characteristics *become* desirable ones? One unintended effect of wolf recovery is the re-kindling of human desires for the not-human bestial Other.

In this context, the de-listing, and consequent hunting, or "harvesting" of formerly protected wolves has been very controversial. Now subject to widespread "population control," between 2012 and 2016 over 4200 wolves were killed (Predator Defense). Collared Yellowstone wolves, unaware of the geo-political territorial borders that humans had drawn around their permitted zone of habitation, were also killed when they strayed across park boundaries (Maughan, "All Yellowstone"). Pro-hunting groups have achieved a series of state legislative moves that have relaxed regulations governing the killing of wolves in numerous states (e.g., Idaho Fish and Game). Wolves are, to the dismay of many, now viewed as an exciting new "big game" opportunity (e.g., Sportsmen's Alliance). Concerns have also been raised by the methods used to kill wolves, which include trapping, poisoning, and hunting with hounds (Howling for Justice; Wolf Patrol).

For the Nez Perce, responsibility for wolf recovery in Idaho brought opportunities to honor ancient relationships that enabled their culture to be "re-born." However, they were placed in an invidious position by the state wildlife service, who, after de-listing, told the Nez Perce to kill wolves themselves or have state helicopters carry out the killing. After the Nez Perce decided that it was better to kill the wolves themselves, the state undertook helicopter killings the following season without consultation (Marvin 179–180). For the Ojibwe, placing limits on wolf numbers, in accordance with population management aims, does not take wolf recovery nearly far enough, and they have banned wolf killing on tribal lands (White Earth Reservation). Some conservationists also want to extend wolf protections on the basis that the evidence gathered in Yellowstone demonstrates that wolf recovery rapidly led to eco-systemic benefits, in terms of vegetative regeneration and biodiversity (Anderson and Rooney 207–208).

As Foucault maintained, all discourses proliferate and have points of resistance within them (*History of Sexuality* 100). In relation to agro-colonialism and normative environmentalism, difficulties in sustaining the discourses of population and territory upon which they are predicated have produced resistances and shifts both in subjectivities and in activist alliances. If human exceptionalism is specific to the historical global context of agro-colonial domination of the land and the living, perhaps it might be un-done through recuperative ecologies that re-figure human relations to land. While wolf recovery in the USA has ostensibly been part of mainstream environmental discourse, it has also opened up political questions about rights in relation to land use, including public land, where wolf hunting is increasingly permitted. The traces of agro-colonial histories have not been erased and are manifesting in the context of activism that seeks to apply indigenous knowledge and law to the use of land formerly populated by wolves and Native people (e.g., Indigenous Environmental Network).

Wolf Patrol is a wolf protection and hunt-monitoring movement that believes there is no "right" to hunt wolves on public land. In a statement on their website, they "formally recognize that every indigenous nation in the Great Lakes region opposes the slaughter of wolves" (Wolf Patrol). Tribal assertions of the importance of ancient bonds with wolves, and of their wish to see wolves repopulate territories that they once both occupied prior to agro-colonization, show how decolonial praxis has been given impetus by wolf recovery. Wolf Patrol promotes "biocentricity and indigenous cultural preservation," and emphasizes the importance of the gray wolf as both biologically necessary and as "a sacred component of the ecosystem in which they belong" (Wolf Patrol).

Unsurprisingly, agro-colonial subjectivities remain insistent and imbued with anti-wolf sentiment. In the face of Native people defending wolves, some have responded with a colonial narrative of racialized bestialization of wolves and Native peoples identical to that of earlier settler-colonialists. For example, a news article about the Ojibwe campaign to defend their "brother" wolves, whom they consider to be allies and sacred companions in their joint journey upon the earth, attracted the following commentary: "In calling themselves the brothers of wolves, they demean themselves. May they one day be set free to realize that they are not the brothers of beasts" (Johnson, "On the Eve").

THE BESTIARY OF FRIENDS

Wolf recovery is a particularly uncanny reversal on the part of humans, whereby those who were demonized, and whose deletion was nearly complete, have been returned, and they have become, both ecologically and culturally, "re-animated." Yet agro-colonialist identities that normalize the hunting of wolves for pleasure or sport, or wish to see them eradicated once again as a territorial enemy, have also been reasserted.

This begs the question of what human relations to wolves might signify, when we can re-call them to life only to reinvent them as "big game." Are new lupine ghosts now being raised? The heavy tread of "the human" unwittingly leaves behind visible tracks of what went before, and now, on the contested terrain of wolf recovery, older specters are becoming more visible. Decades and centuries of extirpations past have not erased the cultural memories of those whose histories are interwoven with the histories of wolves. Wolves uncover a human desire to become-not-so-human and provoke resistances to discourses that have sought to confine all of life in forms of exploitation and "population management." The contested terrain of wolf recovery may yet become the territory upon which an assembly of the disavowed can form decolonizing, ecological, and queer recuperative alliances. Affinities between the marginalized, the deviant, and the bestial emerge from their co-subjections to, and joint exclusions from, colonizing agriculturalism. Their shared positioning on the borderlands of the humanized realm, where questions concerning which beings count as human, which as beast, and who will be made to live and who to die, are determined. This reclamation of the bestial represents a proposal for de-humanization whereby, rather than our problem being construed as our not being *human enough,* it is that we are *too human by far.* Those deemed not-human, not fully human, and not normatively human share the bond of subjective mortal commonality which que(e)ries the boundaries of agro-colonial humanization and opens a window onto a landscape of the bestial and the re-bestialized where the colonial and ecologically separative identities of "humanity" become un-done.

Works Cited

Brickman, Celia. 2003. *Aboriginal Populations in the Mind: Primitivity in Psychoanalysis.* New York: Columbia University Press. Print.

Brignall, Victoria. 2010. When the Disabled Were Segregated. *New Statesman,* December 15, 2010. Web. 10 Apr 2017.

Butler, Judith. 1997. *The Psychic Life of Power: Theories in Subjection.* Stanford: Stanford University Press. Print.

———. 1999. *Gender Trouble.* New York: Routledge. Print.

Byrd, Jodi A. 2011. *The Transit of Empire: Indigenous Critiques of Colonialism.* Minneapolis: University of Minnesota Press. Print.

David, Peter. 2009. Ma'iingan and the Ojibwe. In *Recovery of Gray Wolves in the Great Lakes Region of the United States,* ed. Adrian P. Wydeven et al., 267–278. New York: Springer. Print.

Deleuze, Gilles, and Felix Guattari. 1987. *A Thousand Plateaus: Capitalism and Schizophrenia.* Trans. Brian Massumi. Minneapolis: University of Minnesota Press. Print.

Derrida, Jacques. 2008. *The Animal that Therefore I Am.* Ed. Marie-Louise Mallet and Trans. David Wills. New York: Fordham University Press. Print.

———. 2009. *The Beast and the Sovereign.* Vol. I. Trans. Geoffrey Bennington. Chicago: University of Chicago Press. Print.

Diamond, Jared. 1998. *Guns, Germs, and Steel.* London: Vintage. Print.

Earth Justice. 2017. *Wolves in Danger.* Earth Justice. Web. 6 Apr 2017.

Edelman, Lee. 2004. *No Future: Queer Theory and the Death Drive.* Durham: Duke University Press. Print.

Foucault, Michel. 1977. *Discipline and Punish: The Birth of the Prison.* Trans. Alan Sheridan. New York: Random House. Print.

———. 1978. *The History of Sexuality, Volume 1: An Introduction.* Trans. Robert Hurley. London: Random House. Print.

———. 2006. *History of Madness.* Ed. Jean Khalfer and Trans. Jonathan Murphy and Jean Khalfer. Abingdon: Routledge. Print.

Freud, Sigmund. 1918. *From the History of an Infantile Neurosis.* Standard Edition XVII. London: Hogarth Press. Print.

———. 1919. The 'Uncanny.' In *The Standard Edition of the Complete Psychological Works of Sigmund Freud, Volume XVII (1917–1919): An Infantile Neurosis and Other Works*, 217–256. London: Hogarth Press. Print.

Gaard, Greta. 1997. Towards a Queer Ecofeminism. *Hypatia* 12 (1): 137–156. Print.

Genosko, Gary. 1993. Freud's Bestiary: How Does Psychoanalysis Treat Animals? *Psychoanalytic Review* 80 (4): 603–632. Print.

Haraway, Donna. 2007. *When Species Meet.* Minneapolis: University of Minnesota Press. Print.

Howling for Justice: Blogging for the Gray Wolf. 2017. Wordpress. Web. 7 Apr 2017.

Idaho Fish and Game. 2016. Idaho Department of Fish and Game. Web. 30 Jan 2013.

Indigenous Environmental Network. 2017. Web. 5 Apr 2017.

Jiang, Rong. 2008. *Wolf Totem.* London: Penguin. Print.

Johnson, Bob. 2013. On the Eve of Michigan's First Wolf Hunt. *Mlive*, November 15, 2013. Web. 9 Apr 2017.

Kelly, Catriona. 2007. *A Wolf in the Nursery: Freud, Ethnography, and the History of Russian Childhood.* Российский государственный гуманитарный университет (Russian State Humanities University). Web. 15 Mar 2013.

Marshall, Joseph. 1995. *III. On Behalf of the Wolves and the First Peoples.* Santa Fe: Museum of New Mexico Press. Print.

Marvin, Garry. 2012. *Wolf.* London: Reaktion Books. Print.

Maughan, Ralph. 2012a. All Yellowstone Park Wolf GPS Collared Wolves Were Killed in the Wolf Hunt. *The Wildlife News*, December 12, 2012. Web. 23 Jan 2016.

———. 2012b. As Expected, U.S. Gov't Delists the Wolves of Wyoming. *The Wildlife News*, August 31, 2012. Web. 23 Jan 2016.

Morgensen, Scott Lauria. 2011. *Spaces Between Us: Queer Settler Colonialism and Indigenous Decolonization.* Minneapolis: University of Minnesota Press. Print.

Mortimer-Sandilands, Catriona. 2010. Melancholy Natures, Queer Ecologies. In *Queer Ecologies: Sex, Nature, Politics, Desire*, ed. Catriona Mortimer-Sandilands and Bruce Erikson, 331–358. Bloomington: Indiana University Press. Print.

Morton, Timothy. 2007. *Ecology Without Nature: Rethinking Environmental Aesthetics*. Cambridge, MA: Harvard University Press. Print.

———. 2010. Queer Ecology. *PMLA* 125 (2): 1–19. Print.

———. 2012. The Oedipal Logic of Ecological Awareness. *Environmental Humanities* 1: 7–21. Print.

Neill, James. 2009. *The Origins and Role of Same-Sex Relations in Human Societies*. Jefferson: McFarland. Print.

North American Animal Liberation Press Office (NAALPO). 2014. *Interview with Rod Coronado on Indigenous Resistance and Animal Liberation—Still Defending Wildlife*. NAALPO. February 26, 2014. Web. 7 Apr 2017.

Porter, Roy. 1990. Foucault's Great Confinement. *History of the Human Sciences* 3 (1): 47–54. Print.

Predator Defense. 2017. Web. 6 Apr 2017.

Roberts, Mark S. 2008. *The Mark of the Beast: Animality and Human Oppression*. West Lafayette: Purdue University Press. Print.

Rooney, Thomas P., and Dean P. Anderson. 2009. Are Wolf-Mediated Trophic Cascades Boosting Biodiversity in the Great Lakes Region? In *Recovery of Gray Wolves in the Great Lakes Region of the United States*, ed. Adrian P. Wydeven et al., 205–216. New York: Springer. Print.

Sportsmen's Alliance. 2012. *Judge Stops Part of Wisconsin Wolf Hunt*. Sportsmen's Alliance, September 12, 2012. Web. 23 Jan 2016.

Thierman, Stephen. 2010. Apparatuses of Animality: Foucault Goes to a Slaughterhouse. *Foucault Studies 9*, September 2010: 89–110. Print.

Tolstoy, Leo. 1957. *War and Peace*. Trans. Rosemary Edmonds. Harmondsworth: Penguin. Print.

Van Horn, Gavin. 2012. The Making of a Wilderness Icon: Green Fire, Charismatic Species, and the Changing Status of Wolves in the United States. In *Animals and the Human Imagination*, ed. Aaron Gross and Anne Vallely, 203–237. New York: Columbia University Press. Print.

White Earth Reservation. 2012. *White Earth Wolf Proclamation*. PDF file. maiingan.org/pdfs/White_Earth_Wolf_Proclamation_2012.pdf.

Williams, Walter A., and Toby Johnson. 2006. *Two Spirits: A Story of Life with the Navajo*. Maple Shade: Lethe Press. Print.

Wolf Patrol. 2017. Web. 7 Apr 2017.

Wolfe, Cary. 2013. *Before the Law: Humans and Other Animals in a Biopolitical Frame*. London/Chicago: Chicago University Press. Print.

Wydeven, Adrian P., Timothy R. van Deelan, and Edward Heske, eds. 2009. *Recovery of Gray Wolves in the Great Lakes Region of the United States*. New York: Springer. Print.

Young, Margot. 2012. Queer Mad Animals: Foucault, Eco-psychology and the De-humanised Subject. *European Journal of Ecopsychology* 3: 5–32. Print.

CHAPTER 18

Animalqueer/Queeranimal: Scatterings

Aneil Rallin

1. In "For Memory," Adrienne Rich writes:

> Freedom. It isn't once, to walk out
> under the Milky Way, feeling the rivers
> of light, the fields of dark—
> freedom is daily, prose-bound, routine
> remembering. Putting together, inch by inch
> the starry world. From all the lost collections. (22)

2. We are discussing a passage in Alice Walker's remarkable novel *Meridian*.

> "Truman," Meridian said, when she lay back, exhausted, on the floor. "Do you remember what happened the last time we went out? Remember how that woman attacked me and then slammed the door in our faces?"
> He remembered.
> "I never explained to you why she did that. She did it because I know something about her life that she told me, but now wishes I didn't know it because she's afraid of what people will think about her if

A. Rallin (✉)
Soka University of America, Aliso Viejo, CA, USA

© The Author(s) 2018
E. McNeil et al. (eds.), *Mapping Queer Space(s) of Praxis and Pedagogy*, Queer Studies and Education,
DOI 10.1007/978-3-319-64623-7_18

they know. That woman left her husband because he was infatuated with his dog."
Truman laughed.
"No, no, I mean it. He was in love with a dog. He bought the best of everything for the dog to eat. He brushed its coat a dozen times a day. He talked to it constantly, ignoring his children and his wife. He let it sleep on the best bed in the guest room. Some night he would stay with it. When his wife finally screamed and asked him why, he explained that the dog had better qualities than she had." (239–240)

Several writers in the class find it inconceivable that a man would prefer a dog over his wife. Sachiko Orui insists quietly, maybe the dog had better qualities than his wife, and asks: Why is this inconceivable? What comes in your way of imagining a rich and complex relationship between the man and the dog?

3. Roy Choi, inventor of the kogi taco, a Mexican Korean fusion taco that galvanizes the food trucks craze and food culture in Los Angeles, blogs:

[What does] profitability [mean] when our whole existence is at stake?
Fuck you.
I stopped eating meat this week. That's why I'm thinking about leaving cooking.
… I will no longer eat meat….
Animals be talking to me. They told me … stop. Stop, Roy. Please.

4. "The production of sexual identity, through which unpredictable constellations of desire, knowledge, and practice become concretized into limited models of sexual identity, is bound up," Meg Wesling suggests, "in the way capital produces subjects accommodated to its own needs" (107).

5. If queer is about the capacity of finding pleasure in strange ways and unexpected places, what comes in the way of imagining that nonhuman animals may also have the capacity to find pleasure in unexpected ways and strange places?

6. How does the "othering" of nonhuman animals, the constitution of nonhuman animals as animal, limit our imaginaries? And how do our particular co-constitutions of humans and nonhumans matter for who lives and dies in this world, and how?

7. "Arrogance is arrogance," Terry Tempest Williams writes in *Finding Beauty in a Broken World*, "and cruelty committed to a person or animal is cruelty" (90).

8. Apropos of nothing, they say in class, the whales are dying. They ask: Are the whales committing mass suicide? Do you think dying collectively is their way of saying to us they are finding it impossible to live in a world that has been made so inhospitable to their existence? Do you think they are saying something to us and we are not listening because we don't know how to listen or don't want to listen? Or if we say the whales are committing suicide is that our way of possibly getting off the hook for killing them? And if we say the whales are committing suicide are we anthropomorphizing the whales?

9. What is erased and produced in the constitution of nonhuman animals as animals—and of humans as humans? Susan McHugh notes:

> human ways of being [which in any case are always themselves unstable and varied] ... when used as a measure of social agency ... set precise limits to what can be known about "the" animal, even the so-called autobiographical or anthropomorphizing one.... Hence, the need for other models of agency at the bleeding edges of queer studies and animal studies. (155)

10. A writer in the class declares having read that Aristotle wrote about whale strandings more than 2000 years ago, so it doesn't appear this is a recent phenomenon or produced by human impact.

11. News arrives of another gay teen suicide and I get caught up in the frenzy over adolescent suicides.

12. Haunted by the suicides of adolescents, Eve Sedgwick writes, "the knowledge is indelible, but not astonishing, to anyone with a reason to be attuned to the profligate way this culture has of denying and despoiling queer energies and lives" (1).

13. Another writer in the class proclaims: I don't trust Aristotle. Didn't Aristotle argue that some people are naturally slaves and some are naturally master? In any case, maybe Aristotle didn't know how to read what the whales were saying?

I don't know what to say.

14. New Jersey Governor Chris Christie reportedly calls the 2010 suicide of Rutgers University student Tyler Clementi an "unspeakable tragedy" and is apparently unable to "imagine how the two students accused of secretly filming Clementi can sleep at night 'knowing that they contributed to driving that young man' to suicide" ("NJ Gov.").

15. *The Huffington Post* reports "Conservation staff in New Zealand have put down 33 stranded whales.... As well as the 33 whales that were shot, 36 had died naturally" ("New Zealand"). *Naturally?*

16. *Squid Ink: You know, one would hope that animals would talk to more chefs, if not literally, then metaphorically. You want people to have a responsibility to what they're cooking, especially in this era of whole-animal cuisine.*

Roy Choi: Right now, we're buying thousands of pounds of meat, between all the [restaurant] outlets. And if I continue to grow the business, that'll become tens of thousands of pounds of meat. The business is predicated upon giving the best quality for the cheapest price, so then if the businesses continue to grow at the pace they're growing, then I'm only going to be forced to make commodity decisions, which means I'll be forced in a way to give in to mass slaughter.... I was reading some of the things ... [Gonjasufi] was saying about breaking patterns that no longer serve you. (Scattergood)

17. Dan Savage launches the *It Gets Better* campaign in response to Clementi's and other gay teen suicides. Everybody, including President Obama, gets in the act and records an "it gets better" video. Jasbir Puar observes:

Savage's IGB video is a mandate to fold into urban, neoliberal gay enclaves, a form of liberal handholding and upward-mobility that echoes the now discredited "pull yourself up from the bootstraps" immigrant motto. Savage embodies the spirit of a coming-of-age success story. He is able-bodied, monied, confident, well-travelled, suitably partnered and betrays no trace of abjection or shame. His message translates to: Come out, move to the city, travel to Paris, adopt a kid, pay your taxes, demand representation. But how useful is it to imagine troubled gay youth might master their injury and turn blame and guilt into transgression, triumph, and all-American success?

18. Amid the voices clamoring for Dharun Ravi to be punished with a significant prison sentence, Eric Marcus compares their own father's suicide with Clementi's and affirms, "We've turned Tyler Clementi into

a two-dimensional symbol of anti-gay bullying and Dharun Ravi into a scapegoat.... This ... case ... screams out for compassion and understanding."

19. Adrienne Rich urges, "We need to know the writing of the past, and know it differently than we have ever known it; not to pass on a tradition but to break its hold over us" (*On Lies* 35).

20. What makes for a grievable life? The suicides of certain gay adolescents here and now, but not third-world teenagers or nonhuman animals, some of whom may be queer, dying of US and other imperialisms, the dropping of bombs and drone strikes, capitalist greed.

21. Bombs drown "Fallujah, Basra, Beirut, Gaza" (Rallin).

22. What kinds of understandings and compassion are possible within dominant structures and frameworks? In the wake of the 2012 ballot initiative banning same-sex marriage in North Carolina, I, too, get wrapped up in the fervor for gay marriage, even though I believe that rather than focusing our energies on legalizing gay marriage we should be working to dismantle marriage for everyone. How does the current obsessive focus on gay marriage normalize gay, banish perverse, and domesticate and despoil queer energies and lives? Tony Kushner asks, "Is there a relationship between homosexual liberation and socialism? That's an unfashionable utopian question, but I pose it because it's entirely conceivable that we will one day live miserably in a thoroughly ravaged world in which lesbians and gay men can marry and serve openly in the Army and that's it" (9).

23. Ferguson, Cleveland, Staten Island, Sanford, Berkeley, Baltimore, Los Angeles.

24. Cary Wolfe, drawing on Cora Diamond and Stanley Cavell, reminds us that "philosophy can ... no longer be seen as mastery, as a kind of clutching or grasping via analytical categories and concepts that seemed for Heidegger, 'a kind of sublimized violence'.... Rather, the duty of thinking is not to 'deflect' but to suffer ... our 'exposure' to the world" (71). L. Michael Sacacas suggests that Wolfe, like "Diamond[,] begins to ground our response to nonhuman animals in a shared sense of frailty, vulnerability, and ability to suffer," but "wants to go further still."

25. To suffer ..., grieving perhaps for the energies (queer? perverse?) disciplined in the constitution of the modern subject promoted and subsumed by capitalism ..., haunted by the lives lost in the constitution of

nonhuman animal/human animal as distinct …, distraught about the conditions of life produced by late capitalism that are antithetical to the flourishing of animal/queer … and, rhetoric?

26. "The difference between poetry and rhetoric / is being / ready to kill / yourself / instead of your children"—Audre Lorde's famous words.

27. "Falling back on old equations of non/human and non/heteronormative identity forms," McHugh asserts, "compounds the problems with understanding the significance of queerness and animality alike, by restricting our receptivity to the complex social operations embodied in and across species forms" (167). Disruptive queer theoretical spectrums are needed to investigate new understandings of social creatures.

28. My former colleague J. C. Ross advises students as they work on their papers to spend time at local animal shelters reading aloud their works in progress to the dogs at the shelter.

29. Elizabeth Costello: "Calm down, I tell myself, you are making a mountain out of a molehill. This is life. Everyone comes to terms with it, why can't you? *Why can't you?*" (Coetzee 69).

30. Maybe the suicides of adolescents are not just the result of ostracism, but a resistance to socialization into dominant gender? Is the fear motivating the suicides not a fear of not fitting in, but the fear of being forced to fit in? Or is it the fear of acceptance, the horror of acceptance? Can we read the suicides as moments of queer resistance? Are queer teenagers killing themselves because they are perverse and find pleasure in strangeness, because they are terrified of the gay and gender normalizations that are being thrust on them and because they feel they are being coerced into gay and gender normalizations? Is it gender and gay hegemonies that are killing their queer energies and queer lives? Are the suicides of adolescents a mark of their unwillingness to live in a world that denies and deprives them of imaginative ways of being? Do their suicides thwart what has come to be the only realizable goal of gay—normalcy?

31. As for the whales, could it be that not only are we are killing the whales, but that the whales, like the Buddhist monks who immolate themselves, are killing themselves in radical political protest, as witness? Could we read their collective dyings over a span of centuries as the whales fighting back, acting up?

32. Since (heteronormative) Western rhetoric appears to be failing us, is it time (again) to listen to nonhuman animals? "Animals have been talking to me," Choi says, "and any shaman will say that that's not that weird. So they've been telling me to stop. One of my best friends told me: **If animals are talking to you, you better fucking listen, dude**" (Scattergood). Although Choi's listening to animals and rejection of profitability seem to be fleeting, perhaps Choi's momentarily opening himself up to listening in ways we are not expected to listen can be constituted as a queer listening, a moment of queer human animal/nonhuman animal kinship predicated on queer propensities for unpredictable sites/styles of alliance and pleasure. Perhaps Choi's perverse (queer?), albeit ephemeral, imagination can serve as invitation to us rhetoricians in the here-now: If we could listen without the burdens of 2000 years of so-called Western rhetoric, what would we hear and (how) might listening queerly provoke us not into reclaiming, but into imaginatively "Putting together, inch by inch / the starry world. From all the lost collections"?

Acknowledgment I am indebted to Ian Barnard, my research assistants Alexander Scott and Nana Yamada, and the writers in my seminars.

WORKS CITED

Choi, Roy. 2012. *Riding Shotgun*. April 30, 2012. Web. 13 Mar 2013.

Coetzee, J.M. 2001. *The Lives of Animals*. Princeton: Princeton University Press. Print.

Kushner, Tony. 1994. A Socialism of the Skin. *The Nation*, July 4, 1994: 8–13. Print.

Lorde, Audre. 1978. Power. In *The Black Unicorn*. New York: Norton. Print.

Marcus, Eric. 2012. Dharun Ravi Wrongly Blamed for Tyler Clementi's Suicide. *NJ Star-Ledger*, March 30, 2012. Web. 5 Jan 2013.

McHugh, Susan. 2009. Queer (and) Animal Theories. *GLQ* 15 (1): 153–169. Print.

New Zealand Stranded Whales Shot After Failed Rescue Attempts on Farewell Spit. *The Huffington Post*, January 25, 2012. Web. 5 Jan 2013.

NJ Gov. Wonders How Rutgers 'Spies' Can Sleep at Night After Tyler Clementi Suicide. *ABC News*, September 30, 2010. Web. 5 Jan 2013.

Orui, Sachiko. 2010. Soka University of America, Aliso Viejo. Fall 2010. Class Discussion.

Puar, Jasbir. 2010. In the Wake of It Gets Better. *The Guardian*, November 16, 2010. Web. 5 Jan 2013.

Rallin, Aneil. 2007. Dreads and Open Mouths: On Writing/Teaching. *Text* 11 (2). Web. 11 Oct 2014.

Rich, Adrienne. 1981. For Memory. In *A Wild Patience Has Taken Me This Far: Poems 1978–1981*. New York: Norton. Print.

———. 1979. *On Lies, Secrets, and Silence: Selected Prose 1966–1978*. New York: Norton. Print.

Ross, J. C. 2010. Phone conversation.

Sacacas, L. Michael. 2010. Cary Wolfe, *What Is Posthumanism? Rhizomes* 20 (Summer). Web. 11 Oct 2014.

Scattergood, Amy. 2012. Q & A with Roy Choi: Slinging Tacos at Midnight, Calling Out Jamie Oliver + Choi's Vegetable Moment. *LA Weekly Blog*, May 16, 2012. Web. 5 Jan 2013.

Sedgwick, Eve Kosofsky. 1993. *Tendencies*. Durham: Duke University Press. Print.

Walker, Alice. 1976. *Meridian*. New York: HBJ. Print.

Wesling, Meg. 2012. Queer Value. *GLQ* 18 (1): 107–125. Print.

Williams, Terry Tempest. 2009. *Finding Beauty in a Broken World*. New York: Vintage. Print.

Wolfe, Cary. 2010. *What Is Posthumanism?* Minneapolis: University of Minnesota Press. Print.

Index[1]

A

The Academic Family Tree, 21, 22, 27
Academic kinship, 4, 22, 29, 30, 33, 36
Agro-colonial, 13, 305–307, 316–318
Agro-colonialism, 13
Ahmed, Sara, 5, 22, 27, 28, 61, 68
Allison, Dorothy, 129, 135
Althaus-Reid, Marcella, 11, 251–255,
    258, 261, 262, 264, 265
The American Jeremiad, 118
Animal studies, 14, 311, 323
Animalqueer, 13, 321–327
Anti-gentrification, 270
Art education, 232, 233, 241, 245
Artivism, 242–243
Asegi, 39, 40
*Asegi Stories: Cherokee Queer and
    Two-Spirit Memory*, 49
Athique, Adrian, 185, 194

B

Bercovitch, Sacvan, 118
Bestial, 13, 305, 306, 308, 310–318
Bestialization, 305, 306, 310, 317
Bestialized, 13
Bestiary, 13, 317, 318
Bhabha, Homi, 12, 300n2
Big Gay Church (BGC),
    11, 229–245
Binary, 12, 41, 54n4, 64, 76, 81,
    85, 88, 93–96, 108, 222, 259,
    261, 280
Binary gender, 10
Boal, Augusto, 11, 249–252,
    255–261, 264, 265, 265n2
Bodies That Matter, 9, 145, 159
Body of knowledge, 222–226
Bornstein, Kate, 204, 213n3
Britzman, Deborah, 6, 62–64, 230

---

[1] Note: Page numbers followed by "n" refers to note.

© The Author(s) 2018
E. McNeil et al. (eds.), *Mapping Queer Space(s) of Praxis
and Pedagogy*, Queer Studies and Education,
DOI 10.1007/978-3-319-64623-7

The manufacturer's authorised representative in the EU is Springer
Nature Customer Service Centre GmbH, Europaplatz 3, 69115 Heidelberg,
Germany. If you have any concerns regarding our products, please
contact ProductSafety@springernature.com

Printed and bound by CPI Group (UK) Ltd, Croydon, CR0 4YY
24/04/2026
02096336-0003